FEARLESS FARM FINANCES

Farm Financial Management Demystified
2nd Edition

By Jody Padgham, Craig Chase, and Paul Dietmann

Published by Midwest Organic & Sustainable Education Service (MOSES)

With funding from the USDA National Institute of Food and Agriculture
Beginning Farmer and Rancher Development Program

 United States Department of Agriculture   National Institute of Food and Agriculture

Visit the companion website: mosesorganic.org/farming/farm-finances

MARTIN COUNTY LIBRARY

Fearless Farm Finances
Farm Financial Management Demystified 2nd Edition
Copyright 2017
By Midwest Organic and Sustainable Education Service (MOSES) mosesorganic.org

Thanks to all who have contributed to this book, including the numerous farmer contributors.

Project manager and editor: Jody Padgham
Cover Design: Audrey Alwell and Gemma Ryan
Illustration: John Goodrich, Goodrich Graphics LLC
Design and layout: Audrey Alwell and Jody Padgham

Contributors:
Sharon Astyk, "Armchair Farming"
Rachel Armstrong, Farm Commons, Chapter 23: "Business Structure Decisions"
Badgerland Financial, "Simple Farm Cash Flow Projection"
Chris Blanchard, for original content
Dairy Grazing Apprenticeship "Building a Dairy From an Impossible Dream"
Tom Kriegel, University of Wisconsin Center for Dairy Profitability "Managing through Difficult Times: What is Your Level of Profitability and Survivability?"
Oklahoma State University Ag Econ Extension, "Farm and Ranch Account Book"
Sauk County Wisconsin Extension, "Sauk County Livestock Budget"
University of Iowa Extension, "2016 Iowa Farm Custom Rate Survey"
University of Minnesota Center for Farm Financial Management, "FINPACK" software
University of Vermont Extension, "Farm Financial Scorecard"

Thanks to members of the American Pastured Poultry Producers Association (apppa.org) for their contributions.

All rights reserved. No part of this book may be reproduced, stored in a retrieval system or transmitted in any form by any means – electronic, mechanical, photocopying or other – without written permission from Midwest Organic and Sustainable Education Service.

The information in this book is presented by independent authors and believed by them to be true and complete. All recommendations are made without guarantee on the part of MOSES. The editor and publisher disclaim any liability in connection with the use of this information.

Photos have been contributed by those pictured.

Any questions may be directed to MOSES, PO box 339, Spring Valley, WI 54767
715-778-5775, mosesorganic.org info@mosesorganic.org
Discounts are available for bulk orders of books used for educational purposes.

Printed in the United States
Library of Congress Cataloging-in Publication Data
Includes Index
ISBN 978-0-692-80188-8

This book has been supported by the USDA National Institute of Food and Agriculture Beginning Farmer and Rancher Development Program

CONTENTS

Farmer Profiles 4
Introduction 6

Section One — Starting With Financial Management 7
Chapter 1 — What is Gained from Farm Financial Management? 8
Chapter 2 — Getting a Grasp on Farm Startup Finances 13
Chapter 3 — Planning for the Farm you Want 21

Section Two — Farm Data Collection and Organization 31
Chapter 4 — Getting Organized: Bookkeeping Tools and Basics 32
Chapter 5 — Setting Up Your Financial Records 38
Chapter 6 — A Computer Bookkeeping Program That Works for You 45
Chapter 7 — Entering Data into Your Computer System 56
Chapter 8 — Learning Though Non-Financial Data 64

Section Three — The Big Picture: Organizing Basic Financial Information . . . 69
Chapter 9 — Owning and Owing: The Balance Sheet 70
Chapter 10 — Are You Making a Profit?: The Income Statement 82
Chapter 11 — When is the Money Moving? Assessing Cash Flow 91

Section Four — Analysis and Decision-Making Using Your Numbers . . . 101
Chapter 12 — Comparisons Tell a Story: Ratios 102
Chapter 13 — Factors that Improve Profits 122
Chapter 14 — Should You Buy That Tractor? Farm Investment Analysis . . 129
Chapter 15 — Getting the Most from Your Lender Experience 139

Section Five — Analyzing Specific Elements of Your Farm 147
Chapter 16 — Enterprise Budgets: Where are You Making Money? 148
Chapter 17 — A Tool for Comparisons: Partial Budgets 160
Chapter 18 — What is Your Best Market? Comparing Marketing Costs . . 167
Chapter 19 — Making Assessments About Pricing 176

Section Six — Thinking About the Future 183
Chapter 20 — Annual Cash Flow Planning 184
Chapter 21 — Plans vs Reality: Monitoring and Control 196

Section Seven — Other Factors That Affect Your Financial Situation . . . 201
Chapter 22 — Who Does the Work on Your Farm? 202
Chapter 23 — Business Structure Decisions 208
Chapter 24 — Exiting the Farm: Transfer and Sale 212

Conclusion 224
Appendices Index 227
Resources 256
Glossary 261
Index 264
About MOSES 268

The Authors

MOSES assembled a diversified team of authors to address the many sides of farm financial management.

Jody Padgham, the project manager and editor, is the finance director of the Midwest Organic and Sustainable Education Service. She has owned and managed a 60-acre grass-based sheep and organic poultry farm in north central Wisconsin since 2001.

Paul Dietmann is Emerging Markets Specialist with Badgerland Financial, part of the Farm Credit System. Paul spent 11 years as a county agriculture agent with the University of Wisconsin-Extension, and five as director of the Wisconsin Farm Center. He has worked closely with hundreds of farmers, helping them assess their farm financial situations.

Dr. Craig Chase works for Iowa State University helping producers with business planning, financial analysis and decision-making, risk management, and sustainable agriculture. Since 2011, he has been the Marketing Food Systems Initiative Program Manager for the Leopold Center for Sustainable Agriculture and the State Coordinator for the Local Food and Farm Initiative.

FARMER PROFILES

Throughout the book, you will see comments and tips titled "From the Farmers." We conducted interviews with a diversity of farmers to collect tips they'd like to pass on about financial management systems. The farms range from full-time third generation operations to new enterprises generating only a portion of the family's income. Look for these comments sprinkled throughout the text to highlight the concepts we are explaining.

Hans Breitenmoser
Breitenmoser Farm
Lincoln County, Wis.

Hans owns and manages a 435-cow, second-generation dairy. The cows are housed in an airy free stall barn, and the dry cows and heifers rotationally grazed. The family farms about 1,350 acres of owned and rented land, raising corn, alfalfa, grasses and some soybeans as a cash crop.

Carmen Fernholz
A-Frame Farm
Madison, Minn.

Carmen has been farming for over 45 years on a 450-acre certified organic operation in western Minnesota. Carmen and his family raise a diverse rotation of organic row crops, including corn, soy, wheat, oats, barley, flax, dried field peas and alfalfa. Although they used to raise hogs, they no longer have any livestock on the farm. All but the small flax crop is marketed through wholesale markets.

Laura Frerichs
Loon Organics
Hutchinson, Minn.

Laura and her husband, Adam Cullip, own a 40-acre farm, Loon Organics. Laura and Adam bought their farm in 2008, after a several-year learning and planning process, and run a diversified vegetable operation whose products they market though a CSA. www.loonorganics.com

Andrea Gunner,
Rosebank Farms,
Armstrong, British Columbia

Andrea and her husband, Stephen, farm on almost nine acres in the dry southern interior of British Columbia. They started farming in 1994 and raise pastured roasting chickens and turkeys. They partner with other farms to produce birds using their specifications for their market. Andrea is also is a consulting agricultural economist. www.rosebankfarms.ca

Jackie Hoch
Hoch Orchard
& Gardens
LaCrescent, Minn.

Jackie and Harry Hoch raise certified organic apples, grapes, strawberries, plums, cherries, apricots, raspberries and vegetables on a farm started by Harry's family in the 1940s. With over 8,000 trees on 25 acres, they produce, pick, process, market, sell and distribute everything themselves, with the help of three year-round employees and seasonal interns. They sell primarily wholesale and at a few farmers' markets. www.hochorchard.com

Sharon Hoerichs
Little Sioux Orchard
Milford, Iowa

Sharon, her husband, Chris and four teenage children farm 160 acres in Northwest Iowa. Starting their diversified farm in 1998, in 2011 they decided to follow a dream and planted 1,000 fruit trees. The orchard opened for u-pick in summer 2016. littlesiouxorchard.com

Brad Igl
Igl Farms LLC
Antigo, Wis.

Igl Farms LLC has been in the Igl family since 1934. Father, Tom and sons, Brad and Brian, currently farm about 185 certified organic acres. The main crop is organic potatoes, which they market both direct and wholesale, but they also grow oats, other small grains, and hay as part of their rotation and have a small herd of beef cattle.

Kay Jensen
JenEhr Family Farm
Sun Prairie, Wis.

A northwestern Wisconsin born and bred native who grew up on the family's dairy farm, Kay is a proud product of the UW system with an MBA from Edgewood College. After ten years of ag industry employment and marriage to life and farm partner Paul Ehrhardt, they moved to a 110-acre organic produce and chicken farm; raising their family, actively participating in the community and growing food for farmers' markets, CSA and wholesale accounts.

Lauren and Caleb Langworthy
Blue Ox Organics
Wheeler, Wis.

After spending years researching, participating in farm training programs, working on diversified farms and renting farm land, the Langworthys bought their 153-acre farm in western Wisconsin in 2013. They now produce organic vegetables and lamb, which they market through farmers' markets, a winter CSA and wholesale accounts. blueoxorganics.com

Matt O'Hayer
Vital Farms
Austin, Texas

Vital Farms is a collection of over 90 independent, small family farms that jointly produce and market organic eggs from hens that have been raised on pasture as well as grass-fed butter. Matt O'Hayer started Vital Farms in 2007, but has been in the egg business for many years. Vital Farms eggs and butter are marketed throughout the nation through a diversity of retail markets. vitalfarms.com

Jody Padgham
Wild Crescent Farm
Boyd, Wis.

Jody purchased a 60-acre grass farm in 2001. She raises between 100 and 200 pastured organic broilers each season, and has also raised organic turkeys. She manages a small flock of sheep and rents out most of her pasture to a neighbor for a cow-calf operation. Jody is the project manager and editor of this book.

David Perkins
Vermont Valley Community Farm
Blue Mounds, Wis.

Founded in 1994 by Barb and David Perkins, Vermont Valley Community Farm packs 900 CSA boxes each week during a five-month regular season, with special add-on spring and fall seasons. Three adult children also work on the certified organic farm, along with a full-time, year-round crew. vermontvalley.com

Erin Pilgrim
Pilgrim Family Farm
Boyd, Wis.

Mike Pilgrim took over his third-generation dairy farm in 2007 after working with his father on the farm his entire life. Now milking about 70 cows, and producing feed on 200 acres, Mike and Erin share chores while raising their four young children.

Bob Scharlau
S&S Grains (retired)
Arcadia, Wis.

Bob, a lifetime beef and grain farmer, as well as co-owner of S&S Grains, LLP, recently transferred his fourth generation family farm. Bob and Connie spent seven years looking for non-related farmers to take over their 200 acres of certified organic crop land.

INTRODUCTION

Whether you are a new farmer or have years of experience, you've probably heard how important it is to manage your farm finances. While every farmer collects numbers well enough to file annual Schedule F federal tax forms, there is a lot more that you can gain by maintaining detailed financial records.

Knowing what is happening financially is necessary to assess profitability, to set prices, and to enable decisions about products, purchases and the development of the business, among other things.

We offer straight-forward techniques and strategies for successfully setting up and monitoring your farm's financial system. We include numerous examples for how farmers, using financial information, solved problems on their farms. We point you to tools and resources available to set up functioning systems unique to your operation.

It is our goal to demystify farm financial information so you will be able to comfortably collect data, get familiar with "crunching numbers," assess your farm's financial situation, and make good farm management decisions.

Hearing about this book in its planning stages, a hopeful beginning farmer exclaimed, *"Great, I have been looking for a book on how to make money farming!"* That would be a very popular book, wouldn't it?!

Unfortunately for this farmer, this book is *not* about how to make money farming. It is about *how to know* if you are making money farming; how to figure out what part of your farm business is making, or not making money; how to assess if the potential impact of changes you are considering will leave your farm more or less profitable; and what you might do to address any problems.

This book is also *not* about how to manage your farm for the lowest tax liability. Although the methods we share with you will be very helpful in generating numbers for your tax reporting, our focus is on helping you create sustainable farm management strategies, not tax management strategies. Your tax advisors can help you with those options.

Background on *Fearless Farm Finances*

The idea for this book began in early 2009, when the board of directors of the Midwest Organic and Sustainable Education Service (MOSES) identified lack of understanding of farm financial management as one of the biggest stumbling blocks to the success of sustainable farmers, particularly those just starting.

Led by the mission of "MOSES educates, inspires and empowers farmers to thrive in a sustainable, organic system of agriculture," the team (with the help of contributor Chris Blanchard) undertook this book to helping sustainable farmers succeed. The first edition was published by MOSES in 2012.

As we gave presentations using the contents of this book, we noticed a few things we had missed, and a few tweaks that would help with understanding. So, we have made a few adjustments.

While a lot is the same—we had a base of good, solid content—here's what's new:
- Non-computer users requested more details about recordkeeping on paper. You can now first explore the concepts, and then see how to execute them on paper (Chapters 4 and 5) or computer (Chapters 6 and 7).
- An updated chapter on farm business structures (Chapter 23)
- A new chapter on farm transitions (Chapter 24)
- New "From the Farmer" profiles
- Updated Resources and Appendices

Tips on Using this Book

We recommend you read this book cover to cover, and use the index to refer back to sections as you work on your finances. We have included examples from working farms, which, obviously, have a particular production focus. Read these examples with the view of how the overall concepts might pertain to your own farm. An example quoting figures for computing the break-even price of green beans sold at the farmers' market should give you enough of a picture that you'll be able to figure out if you are charging the right price for your ground beef in your farm store.

The appendix contains sample reports and ratio calculations. Our accompanying website at mosesorganic.org/farming/farm-finances has links to numerous online resources developed by University Extension services and others that will be helpful once you are ready to get into your own analyses.

The book has been designed to simplify complex concepts and point you to useful resources in hopes you can fearlessly manage the financial aspects of your farm. Enjoy!

SECTION ONE
STARTING WITH FINANCIAL MANAGEMENT

There are many reasons people go into or persist in farming. Generally, a desire to spend a lot of time with numbers is not one of them. Farm financial management often doesn't get the attention it deserves.

Those of you who have been farming for a while may not be keeping very close track of what is happening financially on your farms. Or, you may be collecting information, but don't know how to effectively analyze it.

If you are new to farming, your learning has perhaps focused on maintaining animal health, or designing good crop rotations, or proper post-harvest handling techniques, but not what is going on with your numbers.

Equally important to the design, understanding, and refinement of your production methods is the collection and analyses of a diversity of numbers to help you understand analytically what is happening in your operation. Properly collected and interpreted numbers can tell you many things, for instance if you are making money, if you are being efficient, or if you are charging the correct prices.

Those just starting in farming want to know the answer to the question "How much does it cost to start farming?" Although farming is too diverse an occupation for us to offer a simple numerical answer to this question, we do offer several suggestions, tips, and guidance as to how the rest of this book can help each new farmer answer this question for themselves.

A strong farm starts with a strong plan. Knowing what you want when you start, and the on-farm implications of those desires is key. Ongoing planning allows you to set goals and figure out ways to reach them. Your financial record keeping helps you determine if you succeeded in accomplishing the goals you set. We offer many things to consider as you plan, set up, or refine your farming systems.

CHAPTER 1
What is Gained from Farm Financial Management?

Key questions addressed in this chapter:

What will good financial management bring to you?

Why is farm financial management so challenging?

How can you overcome the things that make it difficult?

Ongoing farm financial management is critical to the development and maintenance of a sustainable farming system. Creating good systems allows you to know where you are at financially, and reduces the tension caused by having to guess. Financial knowledge allows you the comfort of making solid decisions based in reality and on a long-term plan. This will improve your quality of life and allow you more time away from worrying about the farm in the short term.

Key Reasons to Keep Financial Records:

Assess Profit. The income statement will help you determine how your farm is performing (at a profit or loss). The balance sheet will determine your farm's financial condition by comparing your assets (what you have) to your liabilities (what you owe).

Assess Cash Flow. The statement of cash flow will help you determine how your farm is meeting its cash requirements. For example, the statement will show if you are receiving enough cash at the right times to pay your bills on time. The statement of cash flow is critical to your ability to manage your money flow, particularly if your cash and expenses are seasonal in nature.

Determine Profitability. Financial analysis allows you to determine how profitable and financially sound your farm is. If you keep the necessary records, you can arrange your numbers into different comparative ratios and "benchmark," or compare your farm to other operations similar to yours. Or you can benchmark against your own operation over time (trend analysis). The use of ratios and benchmarking allow you to find out where the strengths and/or weaknesses are in your farming operation.

Manage Cash Flow. Good records help you predict and prepare for variations in cash flow. Fluctuations between high and low income and expense periods can be managed through saving, pre-paying, and short-term borrowing based on good record keeping. Some farmers will be able to provide relief through changes in the timing of their farm activities once they can predict cash flow tight spots.

Analyze Investments. Each farm operation at some point purchases land, a significant piece of equipment, or crop or livestock inventory. Good financial records can help predict whether a new investment would increase the overall profitability of the farm.

Obtain Loans. Accurate records increase the likelihood you will be able to get a loan to either operate or expand your farm enterprise. Lenders are generally risk-averse. If you don't have good records, lenders will often make conservative guesses and assume a poorer financial condition and performance for your farm. Poorer assumptions often lead to higher interest rates and more loan limitations.

Measure Enterprise Performance. Financial records help you measure performance of individual production lines. Assessing financial performance at the enterprise level allows you to determine which parts of your farm operation are contributing to the overall profit or loss. If you know how each enterprise is doing financially you can make better decisions, including eliminating or fixing those enterprises that are losing money.

File Taxes. A good set of records will allow you to identify deductions, exemptions, taxable income, and income tax liability.

Throughout this book we introduce you to tools and systems to help you accomplish each of these activities.

Things that Make it Challenging

It is common for farmers to spend a lot less time managing farm finances than is needed.

There are a lot of reasons you might avoid crunching the numbers to see if you are running a financially sustainable operation. Perhaps you've never been very good with numbers. Perhaps all those numbers collected together look too confusing. Perhaps it feels more comfortable to "hope for the best" and not really know the details. Perhaps it seems to make more sense to "trust the experts" and let your accountant tell you once a year if you are doing a good job. Perhaps you have money to buy holiday presents for your loved ones at the end of each year, and that feels like success enough.

All these are solid reasons to talk yourself out of financially managing your farm. But, if you ignore this work, you are cheating yourself out of a complete understanding of your farm business. You will not be aware of the full potential your farm business holds. You will not be prepared to make well informed, timely decisions and to take maximum advantage of opportunities that come your way.

It is very likely you will not be able to fully achieve the goals you have established for your farm and your life unless you spend at least a minimum amount of time managing your farm's finances. And, you may be putting your family's wellbeing and your farm career at risk in a down year if you are not financially prepared.

Those who advise farmers often hear that analysis takes too much time. Though very real, this reflects a question about priorities. Is it more important that the oil in the tractor gets changed, or that you know you have enough money to make the payments on the tractor for the next three months? One decision to spend time seems more immediate than the other (especially if the tractor is blowing black smoke), but each are equally important

Emotional Barriers

Many of the reasons we've listed for avoiding farm financial management can be distilled down to two common underlying causes: a fear of numbers and a fear of money. This is an emotional and volatile combination.

Although we all use numbers and money every day, for many of us both concepts bring up old fears (struggles with algebra in sixth grade math class) or tension (arguments over saving and spending priorities). Perhaps you are telling yourself, *"I shouldn't have to do this,"* or *"I can't do this,"* or *"I don't want to do this."* Recognizing and overcoming these sometimes old emotional hurdles is a good first step to opening the door to setting up successful financial management processes.

Shame over what the numbers tell us can be another powerful underlying inhibition. There can be embarrassment on the part of the farm bookkeeper if the numbers aren't showing success. This can lead to avoidance of the work (*"What you don't know can't hurt you"*), and difficulties between spouses or other farm partners.

Many of us are taught as youngsters not to talk about money, not to ask others about money, and to keep our money situations quiet. Emotional reactions give money great power. Once recognized, the emotional aspects of both money and numbers have the potential to be defused, so that an objective, detached approach to the information can be made.

and must be treated as such as you are prioritizing your daily or weekly activities. If the tractor gets repossessed, it won't matter how well you cared for it.

Not knowing, or understanding, what is going on with your farm at a deep financial level creates stress. It can also feed bad decision-making that could threaten your financial well-being, or even your farm.

Succeeding at Farm Financial Management

Making a commitment to yourself to take on the responsibility for financial management is important. Understanding and trying out different parts of financial record keeping and analysis in small increments can help to overcome the fears and challenges. Setting up data collection systems that actually fit into your life is essential. There is no greater waste than a great set of financial systems that are rarely used.

You have to set aside specific time for financial management each week, even more at the beginning as you are learning and setting up your systems. As with anything new, it will take time to understand how to do good financial management. If you have an accountant or bookkeeper entering your financial data you still need to know how your accounting system is set up, and how to use and understand the financial numbers that he or she generates for you.

We have included a wide range of financial management tools and suggestions in this book. You don't have to (and probably won't) start using everything we suggest right away. Filing annual tax forms will lead you to create data collection and basic bookkeeping systems. The balance sheet and income statement are needed for taxes, too. Those are the natural places to start.

As you read upcoming chapters, we recommend that you take note of additional concepts that sound interesting or doable, and add those to your financial management as your comfort grows.

It won't necessarily be easy, but if you take it slow, follow the suggestions we offer in this book, and trust that you can do a good job, you will very likely succeed at becoming competent at managing the financial aspects of your farm.

Summary

Although farm financial management is not easy, there are many long and short-term benefits to setting up a system that works for you and your operation. Time spent at the desk will be rewarded with better informed decisions and reduced stress. Understanding some of the resistance and challenges to good farm financial management can make it easier to overcome them. We hope the information and tools presented in this book allow you to fearlessly approach your farm's financial management.

Use the Numbers

As financial advisor to the successful Dairy Grazing Apprenticeship, Tom Cadwallader has helped a lot of farmers with their financial information. He offers this wisdom:

"Where I see the greatest failing is that farmers collect and look at the numbers, but then don't use them to make their decisions. Farmers can be stubborn, and fall in love with a particular idea, piece of land or farm, etc. and make decisions that aren't supported by what the numbers say. If you don't use the numbers to help make your business decisions, it won't be worth a lot of time to collect them."

Armchair Farming

By Sharon Astyk

Phil-the-Housemate asked me recently for advice on getting his dissertation done. The sum total of my advice to him went pretty much like this "Phil, there's no substitute for the ass in the chair." And this, I think is probably the nitty gritty of getting things like this done. You sit at the computer with your behind on the chair and do the work. That means that at some point you have to give up on getting it perfect, you have to accept that the time for new research, going to hear that important talk, etc. is over. It means saying "no" to almost everything fun, and many things that seem like they'd improve life.

This is pretty obvious stuff. What is probably less obvious, however, is that there's a considerable and deeply important ass-in-the-chair component to farming. This is something that it took me a long time to learn—perhaps because, as an author, all my other work was so devoutly rear-down. I felt that farm work, real farm work, was done with muscles and involved being up and moving, or down on your knees in a field full of weeds. It didn't count, I thought, if I was sitting at the dining room table writing things down—this was not agriculture.

Because of that, I tended to relegate the administrative details of agriculture—the recordkeeping, the billing of customers, the calculation of budgets, breeding plans, and organizing—to two periods, late winter, when there wasn't much else to do, and very late in the day after we were all too tired to do anything else.

I have a fairly good memory for many things, and at first it was easy enough to keep track of what varieties I liked and how much grain a month we were feeding and where the hay I liked came from last year. The problem is that year over year over year, I lost track. A friend just asked me about milk production from one of our does, and I confidently reported a number. Then I realized...oops, that number applied several years ago. The reality is that I can't hold it all in my head anymore.

The problems with this emerged pretty quickly. It is not feasible to do all the paperwork and recordkeeping for a functioning small farm during the winter. One can get ahead, set up the system and do much advance planning, but the realities of a cold climate agriculture where much of the on-the-ground work happens between April and November means that one needs to record things, tally accounts, track inputs and outputs, calculate costs, etc., while things are happening.

But again, because I did not think that keeping records was "real" farm work in the same sense that scything or digging or weeding or harvesting were, I tended to leave it to the end of the day—that was when I was justified in sitting down with my accounts or my plans. Once the kids were in bed, the chores done, the dishes washed, the lights low and Eric and I were settled down on the couch to relax, well, now we could discuss how to handle the breeding season or whether to manure the main garden or the pasture.

Continued on next page

From the Farmers

Financial Records are Valuable Tools

Jackie Hoch, Hoch Orchards & Gardens

Jackie stresses how valuable her records—both financial and non-financial—are to decision-making on the farm. The Hochs use their data to plan future crop expansions, and to plan expected sales volumes for an upcoming year, among other things. Jackie tracks data on the exact amount of each crop sold to each customer, in what packing form (bulk or bagged, for instance).

She also tracks the total dollar value of each product each store purchased per year. She is currently using QuickBooks computer record keeping system, and uses the Vendor section to track each store customer, and Items to track each specific product the farm offers.

The data is also very useful for the stores' decision-making processes. Jackie exports data showing each store's buying history from QuickBooks to Excel, does a little sorting and adding, and sends the reports to the produce managers and buyers once a year after the heavy season ends. She then sets up meetings with each store in the spring to discuss their buying trends, how things are going on the farm, and any anticipated product changes, from both the store and farm aspects.

After these meetings, she can sit down and plan the farm season in great detail. "The stores really appreciate getting this data, and meeting with us to talk about their trends and needs," Jackie says.

Armchair Farming ... continued

You can probably imagine how successful this was. I'm good for about 20 minutes of intense staring at a piece of paper before I start falling asleep after a day that included hours of farm work, child rearing, and household chores. And what we found is that a lot of things were going undone—we weren't keeping good records. We weren't taking the time to plan and strategize. Marketing materials needed making, costs calculating, sources researching—but since that didn't count as farming, I wasn't doing those things—and we started to fall behind. After a while we didn't know how much we were making (or not) on individual crops, or how much grain the goats were eating. Moreover, during the CSA years, I eventually realized that several customers hadn't paid us in full—while I'd sent out bills, I hadn't kept close track of who actually paid.

And that's when the blindingly obvious struck me – when I finally got frustrated with the state of things. It isn't only in writing and academia in which there is no substitute for the ass in the chair. It seems strange to think that I would become a better farmer by doing less farmwork, but in a measure, it was true – I needed to take a few hours every single week and sit down and take care of the paperwork, the administration, the sourcing, the research, the materials.

Of course, in weeks with too few hours in them, the only way for this to work was to have the time pay off—that is, I had to save time by sitting down and figuring things out. And we did. We stopped running to town so often for that feed we were almost out of, or to pick up that thing from the hardware store, because we planned better. Money began to come in a bit more smoothly during our CSA years, because I was sending out reminders on time.

Figuring out the books more carefully gave me some ideas for time and money savings. Spending more time on marketing meant more customers and more revenue.

It was obvious in retrospect, and maybe I don't even need to say it to all of you, but there's no substitute in agriculture for putting your ass in a chair sometimes. It is certainly possible to spend too much time there—to over design, to obsess as you research, to feel that you can't go forward on your garden or your farm until you know everything. But there is also a balance that needs to be struck between simply going at things as hard as you can, and thinking, planning, tracking, and researching. Keeping records is as essential as haying on time.

I mention this because I know particularly that young farmers of the sort I once was tend to go at this with all their energies and passion. I recommend that you bring those things, but also make sure that you are allotting some time to use those energies for those administrative details that are as essential as laying good fence, planting good seed, or weeding. In the end, no matter what you are doing, there's a place for putting your ass in the chair.

Sharon Astyk is a science writer, teacher, environmental activist, and small farmer.

Reprinted with permission.

CHAPTER 2
Getting a Grasp on Farm Startup Finances

Those of you in the beginning planning stages of farming—not yet on the land doing the work—likely have many questions related to the big one: How much money does it take to get started farming?

Farming operations can be started for $100 or for $500,000. They can begin in an urban backyard or on 1,000 acres of inherited bottom land. There is no standard answer to the question: How much does it cost to start a farm? This is the primary reason we've decided to not include financial examples for farm startups in this book, even though this is highly sought information.

Each farm startup is unique and must be planned individually. One farmer may rent land, another buy, a third inherit family land. One will do a workshare to earn cows, another will take out a loan. One will plan to sell to one big nearby market, another to three small markets, including internet sales and a third to a feed co-op or commodity market.

In order to thoroughly assess your unique situation, you must learn and use the concepts of financial management outlined in this book to estimate what your specific expenses, incomes, and cash flows will be in the years you are setting up your farm business. You must then utilize those skills to continue assessing your operation to maintain sustainability.

Another challenge to generalization is that real startup numbers change over time. Fluctuations in costs and prices can easily lead to false assumptions about what it actually costs to get set up. Expenses to put up a loafing shed in 2017 will not be the same as in 2020. People who base cost estimates on old information in books can be led into personal and business disaster by the assumptions they made from the examples presented. We don't want to tempt anyone into this difficulty. There is no shortcut to doing your own good work to plan a new farm business.

Given what we won't tell you, what advice will we share for farm startups? There is plenty. Read on.

Key questions addressed in this chapter:

How much does it cost to start a farm?

What should you do to get started?

What are some tips for farm startup success?

From the Farmers

Planning Your Farm

Lauren & Caleb Langworthy, Blue Ox Organics

Holistic Management (holisticmanagement.org) helped Lauren and Caleb Langworthy plan their new farming operation, and continues to be useful as Blue Ox Organics develops. "Holistic Management really helped us think through the scale we needed to set up," Lauren says.

Caleb adds: "In HM, we began by developing long-term and broad goals for our life and the farm business. Ours include obvious goals such as 'To be fiscally stable now, with a plan to improve the future farm business.' However, they also include much larger goals such as 'To develop sustainable farming practices conducive to our long term health.' Yes, they're big goals. No, we won't achieve them this year. However, it's the guiding intentions that are so valuable."

Lauren has also found free holistic management worksheets to be especially useful for several different types of ongoing record keeping. holisticmanagement.org/free-downloads

Decide What You Want

You may have started your farming career at the age of three, on your dad's knee on the tractor. Or, perhaps you are starting in later years, with a satisfying nest egg and a long-planned vision. Many of you are choosing farming as your career, but based on little experience, early in your peak activity years.

However you come into farming, you must clearly identify what your goals are, what you will produce where and, in general, what your farming operation will look like. A minimum of one to three years of research and experience is recommended before embarking on your own farming operation.

Field days, farm conferences, workshops, beginner farmer trainings, farm visits, internet resources including webinars and podcasts, as well as books are invaluable in giving you the background information you'll need to decide what kind of farm will fit for you, as well as exposing you to key elements of successful farming. The Resources section lists numerous opportunities to explore. There is no end to learning the techniques of successful sustainable farming; you will benefit by cultivating an attitude of life-long learning.

Those who participate in hands-on learning experiences, such as internships or work as hired hands on farms, gain immensely from real-life knowledge. Farming is generally very time intensive, hard physical work and will not be for everyone—experiencing one season (or many) will help you explore the reality of farming's fit for you.

Those intending to farm with spouses or other family members must carefully involve them in planning, experiences, and decision making. A spouse who has grown up in the city may be caught unaware of the time commitment, financial sacrifices, and lifestyle changes he or she may be agreeing to in following your passion. Stress from unequal expectations can be challenging for relationships. Clear knowledge of what to expect can help smooth the way.

In the next chapter on goal setting and planning we walk you through the process of deciding how much money you will need to maintain the lifestyle you desire. This is a key exercise from which you will work backwards to plan your start-up costs and financial needs.

How do You Feel About Risk?

Dependent on the whims of the weather, farming is inherently a management intensive, risky business. It is also a business that involves a vast amount of decision making, much of it utilizing large quantities of resources. Should you cut the over-ripe hay today, even though there is a twenty percent chance of rain? Should the veterinarian be called, or will the $1,800 heifer come around with home treatment? Should the harvest crew be sent home, or pick into the dark because there is threat of hail?

Crop insurance is a tool that has helped many farmers moderate price and production risks, but there are still multiple risks involved in farming. Even highly experienced farmers experience variations in productivity and prices, leading to variability in income and expenses, and thus profitability.

As a new farmer you want to assess how comfortable you are with risk, and how much financial stability you need to feel in your operation. Are you okay owing the bank a lot of money, or utilizing a line of credit, or do you prefer a large nest egg for emergencies? How much debt, or how much in cash reserves, will allow you to still sleep comfortably at night?

These are assessments only you can make for yourself. The answers are very important in guiding your startup planning. Risk assessment tools listed in the Resources section will help you understand your own risk comfort.

Develop a Business Plan

Business plans have reputations much like tax forms—complicated, murky documents that are a necessary evil. If you are planning to take out loans, your lender will most likely require one. A farm is a business, and as complicated to start and run as any other business is. Although you may be able to start a farm without a business plan, the experience of going through business planning exercises will be extremely useful in identifying what you expect to happen.

Business planning forces you to make realistic estimates, and to think through your plans from many angles. Who will you sell to, what quantity, and for what price? Who will do the work, what will they get paid? What resources—land, equipment, livestock, etc.—will you need to accomplish your goals?

Even if there aren't external reasons to do a business plan, we recommend you explore some of the business planning resources listed in the Resources section and undertake some of the exercises. Thinking about your planned farm in this holistic way will contribute significantly to your success.

Planning Cash Flow

Are you the older new farmer with a healthy financial reserve, or the young college grad that has discovered a true passion for farming but doesn't have much equity to invest at start-up? Are you planning to farm full-time right from the start, or are you going to slowly increase your investment of labor into the farm as you ease out of your full-time, off-farm job? Are you going to have to take out large loans to get going, or are you able to work into a situation that doesn't require a lot of borrowing? Each of these scenarios will have drastically different cash flow situations in the startup years. You must carefully identify your startup situation to understand the many elements you must plan for and manage.

A month-by-month projection of cash flow for the first year or two is a very important exercise as you contemplate starting your farm operation. You'll want to know where your farm's cash inflow is likely to come from each month, how it is likely to be spent, and how much will be left in the farm checking account at the end of the month.

You may find that you will need to save up a bit more cash before starting the farm, or may need to keep your off-farm job a little longer than you hoped you would. Doing upfront cash flow planning allows you to anticipate and develop a strategy for cash shortages rather than reacting on the fly when the farm checking account is empty and you still have a stack of bills to pay. We'll give you information on how to do a pro-forma cash flow in Chapter 20.

Crowdfunding

The innovative world of Crowdfunding has hit the sustainable farming world. A diversity of platforms, including Kickstarter, Indiegogo, Barnraiser and GoFundMe, allow anyone to seek funding from backers by posting online profiles of their projects. While crowdfunding has long been used by writers, filmmakers and other artists, farmers are now turning to it for support of sustainable ag projects.

As a rule in crowdfunding, project proposals, featuring written pleas and lively videos are posted online and shared with their creator's community. Some kind of small reward must be promised, perhaps a T-shirt, a pound of beef or a farm tour. The community pledges support, and if the project meets or exceeds funding goals within the posted deadline, then all pledger's credit cards are charged. If the project falls short of its goal by the deadline, then no one is charged and the project does not receive any funding.

Barnraiser, (www.barnraiser.us) a newer site specific for sustainable ag producers and food entrepreneurs, reports that the average sum raised on the platform is $12,000, and that about 65% of projects meet their funding goals. While that isn't a lot of money, it's enough to make a serious difference for many farmers. Barnraiser sets the minimum for any project at $2,000. Successful campaigns pay a percentage of their total take (between two and nine percent) to

Continued on next page

Crowdfunding ... continued

the platform. Competition is intense, especially on some of the larger crowdfunding sites. For instance, less than 30% of all projects get funded on Kickstarter.

Crowdfunding has its advantages and disadvantages. Do your homework. Speak with your accountant about tax implications of donations, and ask a lawyer how to protect yourself against unforeseen circumstances. You're also responsible for getting the rewards to your donors.

But, for a few hours of video production and creative thinking, a crowdfunding campaign may well be a worthwhile endeavor. Thousands of success stories show that this kind of fundraising works!

Tips for crowdfunding success:
- It takes months to build a crowd – sometimes up to a year or more. Expect about 5% of your crowd to donate at an average donation of $10. To bring in $10,000, you have to reach 20,000 people!
- You will need to share your project budget with your potential donors. Remember to include the cost of the rewards!
- Videos don't have to be professional, they just need to tell the story and make your audience know, like and trust you.
- Odds are that if you aren't at 1/3 of your target goal within two weeks of kicking off your campaign, the campaign will not be successful.

Most businesses will take three to five years of management before they make a profit, farms are no different, or perhaps even a little slower, depending on the type of farming enterprise. You must plan how your farm will be established, develop, and grow for five or more years without bringing a lot of extra cash back into your pocket. Preparing for how to accomplish this takes very careful planning.

Non-Purchase Startup Options

In times of high land prices, many new farmers have found their success more possible and debt load more feasible by considering non-purchase asset options. These options include renting land, going though a farm transfer with an older farmer, equipment sharing, or doing a share agreement to earn equity in land, livestock, or equipment. The value in these options is they don't tie up vast amounts of available assets in the early years while you are investing in developing your farm business. We talk about how you can assess these options in more detail in upcoming chapters.

Using Financial Tools

Throughout this book we introduce you to various financial tools that should be instrumental in your farm startup planning process.

As you develop your business you will be setting up a bookkeeping system. Section Two: Farm Data Collection and Organization will help guide you in doing so.

By developing an understanding of income statements, balance sheets, and cash flows you will learn what numbers need to be tracked, and how the numbers relate to each other in your farm business. For example, if you are planning a dairy operation, you must project for at least the first five years how much each input will cost; how many cattle of various ages and stages of production you expect to manage; how they will be housed; where you will get feed, where it will be stored and how much it will cost; what milk yields you can expect and what price you expect to be paid; what infrastructure you will need; and what debt you expect to incur. Putting these numbers into projected financial statements will allow you to realistically assess the feasibility of your ideas.

Information in the farm investment analysis chapter (Chapter 14) will help you compare the financial implications of different asset options—does it make more sense to rent or buy a piece of large equipment or a 40-acre pasture parcel? The exercises in this chapter will help you look at the financial implications of each.

As you begin farming, enterprise budgets and partial budgets can be used to assess what on your farm is making money, and will help you compare one enterprise to another. You may start out thinking that you will specialize in raising farrow-to-finish hogs, but after a few years recognize that buying feeder pigs will better fit your needs. Enterprise analyses and partial budgets will help you to more clearly see the financial implications of these decisions.

If you plan to market direct to customers you must determine proper prices for your goods and compare different marketing options. Information in Chapters 18 and 19 will help you in these exercises.

As a new farmer you will want to develop good cash flow projections. Your projected financial statements, developed through business planning, will help you assess the feasibility of your various enterprises, and the timing of incomes and expenses. Continuing these projections as your farm develops will allow you the benefit of projections and advanced planning.

Comparing what actually happens to your projections through monitoring not only allows you to make adjustments, but gives you feedback on how realistic you are being in your estimations of what will happen. The learning that comes with this awareness is an invaluable tool for improving your operation.

Choices about who does the work on your farm has legal and financial implications that you must consider. As you start your business you will make decisions on how to legally structure your business. We offer some basic guidance on the choices available. And, even as you make decisions while setting up your business, how the business might eventually end or transfer to new hands will be impacted by today's decisions.

Tips for Start-up Success

- Attend as many educational programs as you can such as workshops, conferences, and field days. You will benefit not only from the information shared at these events, but from the informal interaction with other participants.

- Utilize resources available for new farmers. See the Resources section to find them.

- Intern or work on one or more farms before you plan your own farm. Decide if you like the work. Work on operations of different scales to decide what best fits your tastes.

- Save as much cash as possible before you start. Don't invest all of it in the farm right away; hold some cash back for emergency purposes.

- Seek out mentors that can teach you the fine details and answer your specific questions.

- Consider non-purchase land options for the first few years of production. Explore renting, share cropping, and farm transition programs. Lower risk production scenarios allow you to experiment to find out what you are best at, to make mistakes, and get feedback.

- Consider flexible lease arrangements that keep your rent affordable in average years but gives your landlord a premium when you have a particularly good year.

- Carefully plan before purchasing equipment or other capital assets. Explore renting or sharing options.

- Explore markets very carefully before investing in any production activity. Be careful about marketing assumptions. Explore competition and opportunity in the markets you expect to utilize.

- Determine your risk comfort level.

- Make a list of as many potential risks you can think of that you might face in the early years, and develop contingency plans in case things don't go as well as expected.

Rent Responsibly

Farmers who intend to lease buildings, land, or equipment need to exercise caution in developing operating agreements. Your agreement should be in writing and should cover all important details such as who is responsible for maintenance and repair expenses, who is responsible for paying utility bills, when the rent is due, and how disagreements between the parties will be handled. Even if you get along very well with your prospective landlord, you need to be planning for the days when you may not see eye to eye on some issues. There is great information on rental contracts from Farm Commons at Farmland Leases Built to Last: Content and Legal Context (webinar at: farm-commons.org/farmland-leases-built-last-content-and-legal-context-1)

From the Farmers

Starting With Little Overhead

Laura Frerichs & Adam Cullip, Loon Organics

Laura says that being able to start slowly, learning without taking on debt has led to a successful farm startup for her and her husband, Adam. Although neither planned to be farmers, they both fell in love with the occupation while working at Gardens of Eagan (GOE) near Minneapolis in 2003. They each had worked on other farms before coming to GOE, experiences that they say were instrumental in their success.

In 2005, the owners of GOE, Martin and Atina Diffley, offered to rent land to Laura and Adam, allowing them to start up Loon Organics and to plan, grow, and market their own crops with very low overhead and risk. Rent was $200 per acre, less than the market rate, and the new farmers were able to borrow the equipment they needed from GOE. The two sets of farmers signed a detailed rental agreement each year, stipulating each group's responsibilities and expectations of the other. Laura and Adam wrote a business plan in 2005, which evolved into a production plan that is now updated annually.

Laura says that their time at GOE was critical, as they were able to farm without financial risk, "make mistakes, get feedback, and refine our production practices." They were also able to develop a strong market for their produce, sold through a CSA, and supplemented by purchases from GOE fields.

Laura and Adam stayed at GOE through the 2008 growing season, when they were able to buy their own 40-acre farm

Continued on next page

- Set up good record keeping systems to track activity.

- Take on debt very carefully. Consider off-farm income to support the farm until it is self-sufficient.

- Cultivate a strong working relationship with your lender. Keep the lender apprised of new developments on your farm, good or bad. Avoiding contact with your lender or other creditors when you are experiencing financial trouble will only make the situation worse. They will be much more willing to work out a resolution if you communicate openly and honestly with them before a major financial challenge hits.

- Consider developing an advisory team of professionals who can meet with you every few months to help you work through significant challenges. The team might include your county Extension agent, your banker, crop consultant, veterinarian, or other professionals who have a strong interest in helping you succeed.

- Develop your business slowly to ensure consistent product quality and understand your land, resources, capability, and market.

- Plan for growth.

- Do annual enterprise budgets and cash flow projections to understand where your profit centers are. These will develop from inexperienced guesses to well-reasoned assessments over time. Compare your actual activity to your budgets on a monthly or quarterly basis to see how you are doing. Make adjustments in income or expenses throughout the year if needed.

- Get in the habit of updating your farm balance sheet every year on January 1. With an annual balance sheet and the Schedule F (Profit or Loss From Farming) from your federal tax return, you can do a comprehensive analysis of your farm's financial performance

- Explore and take advantage of traditional farm support programs, such as Farm Service Agency and other USDA programs, local university, college, and Extension resources.

Summary

Each farm startup will be unique, and so generalizations on what it costs to get started will be misleading. Those in the startup phase must do significant research and planning to set up a farm business. The later lessons in this book will be key in creating financial systems and assessments valuable from the early planning years on. We offer several tips to help focus your early thoughts and activities.

Building a Dairy from an Impossible Dream
By Raylene Nickel

Andrew (Drew) Votis grew up in the city, but learned just enough about farming to know that he wanted grass-based dairying to be his career and way of life.

After graduating from UW-Green Bay, he began searching for ways to gain experience in grass-based dairying. His search soon led to the Dairy Grazing Apprenticeship (DGA). The fully accredited, national two-year program gives beginners the chance to gain experience while working as paid employees for established grass-based dairy producers—Master Dairy Graziers—who mentor the development of managerial skills in Dairy Grazing Apprentices.

Drew was soon matched with Master Dairy Graziers Jim and Tammy Schreiner, Athens, Wisconsin. Two years later, on Dec. 31, 2013, Drew completed his DGA Apprenticeship with the Schreiners.

By midsummer 2015 the grass-based dairy farm of 26-year-old Drew and his wife, Ashley, was in full swing. Renting a farm just seven miles down the road from the Schreiners, the young couple now own a herd of 43 cows and rent the farm's milking facilities and pasture.

While observing how knowledge and experience feed the process of making strategic, whole-farm management decisions, Drew learned subtle but critical lessons. "I tried to help him understand my reasoning behind day-to-day decisions," says Jim Schreiner.

"A lack of experience is the biggest risk facing beginning farmers; you could inherit a million dollars, and without management skill and experience you could still lose the farm," says grazing-based dairy farmer Joe Tomandl, III co-founder and executive director of DGA.

Building an Efficient Production System

Drew and Ashley follow these guiding practices as they build a whole-farm production system they intend to be both practical and profitable over the long term:

Invest wisely and manage debt. "We're trying to figure out how to make good investments," says Drew. "We are tending to invest in things that gain value over

Continued on next page

From the Farmers...continued

about 70 miles away, within the same marketing area as GOE. Moving onto their own farm, they increased their production acreage from two acres to six, and expanded both the size of their CSA and their gross income. They slowly made investments in infrastructure and equipment, and by 2010 had invested almost $86,000 in capital assets, including the $15,000 down payment on the farm. They invested only personal savings and farm income until they took out a $250,000 Farm Services Agency loan in 2008 to buy their farm. They did not pay themselves for their own farm labor throughout the first four years of their development period, instead investing all farm proceeds back into their farm development fund.

Laura says that it took them until 2010, Loon Organics' sixth year, to feel that they were out of the "extreme growth stage," the period of high capital investment. It also took these six years before they both could afford to farm full time. One or both of them worked full time off the farm between 2005 and 2009.

Laura is an exceptional financial manager and record keeper, especially so after participating in the Minn. State College and Universities Farm Business Management Program, which has helped their success. Well established farmers now, they have successfully managed a 200-member CSA for over 10 years. In 2015, Loon Organics Farm was chosen as the McLeod County Farm Family of the Year!

Building a Dairy from an Impossible Dream ... continued

time. We have invested in cows, and we hope to eventually invest in land."

They presently rent a farmstead with 40 acres of pasture and a swing-six parlor, a loose-housing barn and an outdoor, cement-surfaced feeding strip. The young couple bought a home in a nearby town after Ashley got a job as an elementary teacher. Drew commutes the seven miles to their dairy.

During Drew's Apprenticeship he had the opportunity to buy every third heifer calf born, with the purchase price deducted from his wages. He paid a dollar a day per head for the feed costs. By the time Drew and Ashley started their dairy, they had purchased 14 heifers from the Schreiners.

After finding a farm to rent, the Votises purchased 18 dairy cows from a nearby retiring producer to expand the herd to a more economically viable scale of production. They also bought a small line of equipment including tractors and haying equipment.

To finance the relatively modest purchases of cattle and equipment, Drew applied for and received a low-interest beginning farmer loan from the USDA Farm Service Agency. The equity the young couple had already built in cattle helped them qualify for the loan.

Provide cost-effective feed for cattle. To operate efficiently, Drew models Jim's practice of feeding cows high-quality feeds as affordably as possible. Forage is the cornerstone of the ration. "The key is to feed highly nutritious feeds cheaply," says Drew. "Grazing is a big part of that because pasture is reasonably priced." Drew plans for his grazing season to extend from early May through early November.

Manage for a healthful level of production. By feeding primarily high-quality forages, Drew maintains excellent cow health, a critical and cost-effective goal. He manages so the cows produce well but not so much that their metabolic systems are stressed, and hopes to avoid costly metabolic disorders like milk fever and ketosis.

Maintain low-cost overwintering facilities. Overwintering cows in a loose-housing barn lets Drew keep investment in housing to a minimum while increasing cow comfort and soil organic matter levels on his farm.

"We couldn't have done this by ourselves," says Drew. "To get started in dairying you have to have a lot of good help and a lot of good advice. You have to pay attention and don't think you know everything. Learn as much as you can so that you're prepared when it's time for you to make your own decisions."

Drew and Ashley Votis deeply appreciate lessons learned from Jim and Tammy Schreiner. The learning has opened doors to the life they hoped they'd find on a grass-based dairy farm.

Summarized from an original profile from Dairy Grazing Apprenticeship.

Printed with permission. www.dga-national.org/Home

CHAPTER 3
Planning for the Farm You Want

When it comes to long-term planning, owning a farming operation is different than owning most other businesses. Most people choose to go into farming, or to stay with a current farming operation, for reasons relating to lifestyle choices: to work on the land, to enjoy a certain type of daily life, or to continue a family tradition. In most kinds of farming, you are working with a physically constrained resource base. You can't just pick up your soil and move it to another location. This makes the occupation unique and enduring, but also creates limitations.

Whether you are starting out in agriculture or are already deep into your farming operation, planning far into your future isn't easy. Nobody can tell what will happen to the economy, the weather, technology, market, or food trends in the next ten years. Add to this the fact that your own expectations and circumstances, and those of your family, are also likely to change significantly over any given ten year period, and it becomes clear that to avoid leaving the future of your farming enterprise, and your life, to chance, you need to structure your business for economic resilience and stability.

What does economic resilience and stability require? Fundamentally, you need to know the answer to the questions: "What do you need and want?" and, "What will it take to support that?"

What Do You Need?

A good long-term plan goes beyond a traditional business plan, although a business plan wouldn't hurt as part of the planning process for your farming enterprise. In our experience in training young farmers, we've found that beginning farmers especially struggle with how to come up with a business plan as they get started, because they don't know anything about the financial costs and the time requirements of doing the business of farming. One way to start is to plan your life needs and goals, moving into the specifics of your farm business from there. A good life plan will help you determine what you need from your business, as well as what it will need from you.

Key questions addressed in this chapter:

How can you plan your farm so that it gives the financial support you need?

How do you balance the need for economy and also plan for growth?

What kind of planning should you do?

PLANNING YOUR FARM

Change

Needs and wants often change dramatically as time goes on. The simple life can look appealing at the outset, but become disillusioning to one or more partners in a farming operation over time. The long hours that were easy without kids can become grueling with youngsters, and impossible when those same children grow into teenagers needing transportation home from soccer practice after school. The falling-down farmhouse that seemed like a steal can turn into a loadstone around your neck when the roof starts leaking and you don't have the time or the money to make the needed repairs.

Marriages and business partnerships can fall apart over disagreements about priorities, business direction, stress, or inattention to maintaining the relationship.

Add to this the potential for weather-related disasters, changing markets, and a shifting regulatory landscape, and you've got a recipe for change.

How Much Profit?

The first question to ask is, How much money do you want to make? This isn't just how many dollars of product you want to sell, but how many dollars profit you want your farm to provide on an annual basis. A farm is a business just like any other small, owner-run business. For your investment of time, energy, and money, you should expect a reasonable return not just on the labor you put into running and managing the farm, but on the investment you've made and the risks you take by being in business for yourself.

As you plan your profit you must take into account the fact that your financial needs will change over time. Aging tends to bring on added complexities and demands for increased financial resources.

You are the only one that can say what an ideal profit will be, and you can't really know what this number will be ten years from today, so it may seem impossible to plan for. Regardless of the difficulty of pinning this number down, the investment and operational decisions you make this year will determine your ability to meet your profit goals—whether you've made them clear or not—years down the road. Making investments in land, buildings, fence, livestock, and machinery that fit your farming operation's future, as well as its present, helps to secure a greater likelihood of overall success over the long haul.

If the farm is not profitable, (even if it is providing enough cash flow for you to live comfortably), you will never be able to sell it to the next generation at market value and have them make a decent living from it. If one of your goals is to pass the farm on to your children, you owe it to them to maintain a profitable operation.

How Much for Yourself?

If you haven't started farming yet, one good place to start to figure out how much money you'll need is to begin writing down every penny that you currently spend. After a short time, you'll be able to figure out how much money you are accustomed to spending. If you categorize your expenditures into "essential for existence" and "non-essential" you'll be able to evaluate how your expenses would change if you were self-employed (maybe you wouldn't need a suit and a tie, or need to pay for commuting expenses), and what might change when you're living on a farm.

You'll also want to develop an awareness of the benefits you might lose if you leave your current job to become self-employed, because losing them will come at a real cost. If you want or need health insurance, or a retirement plan, you will need to plan for those as part of the returns you receive from your farm operation. Those of you with debt, or planning to take on debt, will have to also factor debt payments into your plan.

OTTO'S TIP: *Those who like to utilize technology can easily track your expenses by consistently using a debit card for purchases, and using an online management service with smart phone applications like mint.com*

How Much Production?

Once you've determined how much cash flow—or "take home pay"—you want your farming operation to provide, you can determine how much production you'll need to achieve that income. Because production values vary widely depending on land, breeds, production strategy, scale, and markets, this is definitely back-of-the-envelope planning. However, it provides a starting point for understanding the scale of farming operation that will support the lifestyle you imagine having.

For example, if you decide that your market vegetable farm should provide a total salary of $60,000 for two adult partners on the farm, you can look in the literature about market farming and find average net income figures of 30 percent to 40 percent of gross sales income. This varies largely due to the relative percentage of labor provided by the farmers. (See the sidebar on page 24.) If you use a middle figure of 35 percent, divide your $60,000 net cash income goal by 0.35. This will lead you to the need for a gross income of just under $171,500 per year. ($60,000 / 0.35 = $171,428.57).

OTTO'S TIP: *"Gross Income" is the total amount of money you take in, before you subtract anything for cost of production or expenses. "Net Income" is the amount you have left over after you take out the expenses.*

We will assume average gross sales per acre of around $14,000 for a market vegetable farm. This means you would need to produce a little more than twelve acres of vegetables to achieve the net income that you decided you needed. ($171,500 gross income / $14,000 per acre = 12.25 acres)

This kind of figuring not only tells you how much land you'll need for your market farm, or how many stalls you'll need in your freestall barn, it also provides information to determine, for example, the labor structure you'll need. Here's how: if you plan to gross $170,000 on a southern Minnesota market farm, where the harvest season runs for about 25 weeks from June to October, you need to sell about $6,800 of produce each week.

Staying again with our back-of-the-envelope methodology, let's say that an average unit of produce, such as a bunch of swiss chard, sells for $2 at the farmers' market. That means that you'll need to harvest the monetary equivalent of 3,400 bunches of swiss chard each week. The price of produce in the local market place is largely based on how much labor goes into it. Even at a good rate of harvesting 45 bunches of chard each hour, to make $6,800 you'd need 66 hours each week of harvest alone, not to mention the time to seed, weed, wash, pack, and sell the produce.

A quick assessment like this doesn't give you exact figures to work with, as you might decide to sell wholesale to stores and restaurants instead of top-dollar at farmers' markets, and you probably won't harvest the same amount of produce each week for 25 weeks. However, it does tell you that, unless you figure out a way to increase your financial productivity per unit of production, you'll need a lot more than a few acres to make this kind of living for two people, and you'll almost certainly need to hire some help.

From the Farmers

What size to aim for?

David Perkins, Vermont Valley Community Farm

When David and Barb Perkins started Vermont Valley Community Farm they first talked about what income would make it worthwhile. David thought a goal of the same level of income as their average customer would be respectful of them as farmers. "We chose CSA because the Community Supported Agriculture (CSA) model turns commodity agriculture on its head," he claims. "The farmer sets the price, decides on the products, determines the season, and the farmer receives all of the revenue. With urban populations wanting to support farmers, this model allows them to make that choice."

The Perkins' set a goal of 500 annual CSA shares within five years to reach the scale they wanted. "That gave us a rough income goal to aim for at the beginning," David says. "I hadn't started vegetable farming yet, and so didn't know exactly what it would cost, but I had to assume that 2/3 to 3/4 of gross income would go toward costs of production."

With good jobs, David and Barb were able to each reduce to 50% time as they started the farm. Keeping nearby city jobs part time, Barb for 2 years and David for 3, allowed them the option to return to the city if the farm didn't work out, and provided the equity needed for a loan on 40 acres. "Taking on a farm is a big financial risk," David explains. "We didn't make any money for the first two years." He points out that you should never plan to make money for the first few years in any small business.

Take Care When Developing Your Farm Projections

Whatever data you use to develop your farm projections—acres, head of livestock, labor hours—you should be aware that published numbers draw from widely-variable production values and systems. When you are looking at dollars per unit-of-anything, those numbers can vary widely based on the intensity of production, value of the final product, organizational structure, income tax strategies, and market where the product is sold.

Be careful with published economic performance data because it often doesn't tell you what's included or not included in those figures. For example, some farms might include health insurance for the owners, or owner provided labor as expenses when they figure net income. Depreciation expense may be accelerated to take advantage of tax laws, as opposed to basing depreciation on the useful life of assets. The farm house and personal vehicles may or may not be included as farm assets. Farms that rent land and/or lease equipment instead of owning it will show land and equipment rent as expenses, where a farm that owns its land and equipment will show interest paid on farm debt as an expense, but principal on farm debt is paid out of net farm income. Per-acre performance on a market farm might not include the land in cover crops and field access roads, which can add up quickly. Be certain you know what's included in the data you are using to compare your farm to so that you are comparing apples to apples.

In addition to telling you what sort of physical capacity you'll need to run your operation, these quick numbers tell you the sort of skills capacity you'll need to manage your farm. If you don't know how to drive a tractor, you'll probably want to learn, because this farm will need more than a rototiller to run it. You'll want to look at ways to build your capacity for labor management—maybe read a book or take a class if you don't have experience. You'll want to make certain you've got an understanding of farm finances, since you'll be handling a lot more than pocket change in this operation.

The swiss chard example above didn't take into account a couple of important considerations. First, most assets on a farm have a tendency to rust, rot, or otherwise depreciate. The blades on the rototiller eventually wear out, farm trucks need to be replaced, cows need to be culled out of the herd, and trees fall on fences. Your farming operation has to generate enough money to not only pay your wages, but also to cover the investments you need to make to replace worn out equipment, implement new systems, adjust to changing markets, and facilitate your own continued involvement as you grow older.

Capacity and Flexibility

To do long-term planning successfully you must balance capacity with flexibility. Capacity describes the ability to perform or produce. A laborer has the capacity to harvest a certain quantity of broccoli, a milking parlor has the capacity to milk a certain number of cows per hour, and a tractor and its attached implement have the capacity to prepare a certain number of acres for planting in a day. Capacity creates production flexibility, but it takes away financial flexibility. Managing capacity presents a fundamental challenge to any business. You need to have enough capacity to do the work that needs to be done when it needs to be done, but you don't want to have wasted capacity that ties up capital or operating funds. So, how do you find a balance?

Unfortunately for your finances, capacity always comes at a cost. A larger crew of laborers to harvest your broccoli costs more than one laborer, and two milking stalls cost more than one. Managing capacity so that you have enough of it to do the work that needs to be done in a timely fashion, but also so that you don't waste money by not having enough production or performance to use all that capacity is challenge enough. Add to that the seasonal variability of farming, where a wet spring may mean you have only two days instead of the normal week to prepare the soil and plant your corn, and you've got a complicated formula to work with.

Extra capacity entails extra expense, not only for initial capital outlay, but also for upkeep and maintenance. If you are driving a delivery van that can hold eight pallets of produce, but only delivering two pallets of produce, you're paying for six pallets of extra space in ownership cost, insurance, maintenance, and fuel. In addition, if you only use that truck thirty-two weeks of the year, you still have to pay for owning the truck during the twenty weeks of the year that it sits idle. United Parcel Service (UPS) makes money because they run their trucks every week of the year, and every day of every week. A market farmer who only drives her truck to market twice a week faces an uphill battle in overcoming the ownership cost of a delivery vehicle.

Balancing Capacity and Growth

A growing operation needs to balance capacity for expansion with current output, plus the likely obsolescence of current equipment and infrastructure. If you plan to graze cattle on 500 acres when your business reaches its final size, but only have the ability to graze 40 acres due to your current skills, markets, and capital, you've got a quandary. How do you get into business in a way that allows you to grow at an appropriate pace, but doesn't hamper you down the road?

Keep Your Overhead Low

If you can find ways to get the work done without having to invest capital in additional equipment or infrastructure, you'll be ahead of the game right from the start. Custom-hiring farm work done, whether it's tillage or haymaking, means you only pay for the acres covered or the bales made, instead of the interest on the equipment loan and the right to say "I own that equipment" the 360 days it sits in the shed—it can even save you the cost of building a shed to keep it in! Custom-hiring field work may mean that you don't get everything done at exactly the right time—a neighbor on a tight tillage schedule isn't likely to prioritize your three-acre market garden—but that's a small price to pay for not having to pay for upkeep and idle time on a large tractor and tillage equipment. (See Appendix A for a sample of custom hire rates.)

Renting land instead of buying it means you can rent just as much as you need, and don't have to carry the ownership cost of additional acres for later expansion. As a bonus, renting land can put you in the right neighborhood to find the perfect piece of land to buy when it is financially feasible.

Use Labor Instead of Capital

Hiring labor comes with its own set of challenges, but it can provide more flexibility in both growth and day-to-day operations than an investment in machinery does. A mechanical brussels sprout cutter might do a really great job of cutting brussels sprouts off of the stalks, but that's all it can do. A person can cut brussels sprouts one day, and sell them at farmers' market the next, and probably not be paid for the days that they aren't helping you farm. Mechanization also tends to require best-possible scenarios. With a hoe, straight rows don't make a huge difference, but when you mount weed-control tools on a tractor, straight rows are almost required. And while people can harvest vegetables in a weedy field, weeds can make mechanical harvesters impossible to use.

The scale of the operation you are running will dictate the practicality of each of these options, but the question is always worth asking: Would this job be better and more cost effectively done by a person or a machine?

Flexible Infrastructure

While your farm enterprise may require an investment in infrastructure to make it viable—for example, a walk-in cooler for a produce farm, or fence for a grazing operation—you should look at ways to make that infrastructure as flexible as possible.

Farming is a Business

OTTO'S TIP:

When you think about your farming business, you might be tempted to say, "But farming is different than other businesses." Try not to think that way.

Instead, ask yourself, "In what way is my farm business similar to other businesses?" That way, you'll find yourself constantly exposed to new examples and solutions to the challenges you face, especially in the realms of employees, marketing, and business system development.

PLANNING YOUR FARM

From the Farmers

Planning is More than Numbers

**Jackie Hoch,
Hoch Orchard
& Gardens**

"Planning is about more than the numbers—you have to make choices that fit your philosophies and the kind of life you want to lead," says Jackie Hoch, of Hoch Orchard and Gardens.

Jackie and her husband, Harry, have truly incorporated planning into the kind of life they want to lead. For the several years of their union Jackie was working full-time off the farm. But, knowing that they wanted to get her on the land, the Hochs started going out for a "working breakfast" every Sunday.

Jackie thinks that her transition onto the farm would have been a lot slower without these focused meetings. "We talk about immediate goals and philosophies. Whether to add a product, how we might change planting, what our business and life goals are," she says.

It has been important that they leave the farm with all its activity, and talk things through during this dedicated time. They bring a notebook and make lists. "If we forget the notebook, then we talk about different things," Jackie laughs. "I thought that I was pretty on top of what was going on with the farm, but these

Continued on next page

In particular, while your operation is growing, consider temporary solutions to infrastructure problems. Besides growing vegetables, hoophouses can provide livestock shelter and machine shed space, and you can remove or relocate them relatively easily. Temporary electric fence can be used to establish a grazing operation while you build the capital to install permanent fencing. When building a new freestall barn, perhaps think of your retirement days, and put in big enough doors so that motor homes can be driven in. A little retrofitting after the cows are sold will leave you with a profitable winter storage business for recreational vehicles.

Be certain that what you put in place can accommodate future needs. If your farm requires a significant amount of materials handling, make certain that doors are sized for standard pallets, and that ceilings are high enough for a forklift. Machinery shed doors should be built for larger equipment than your present scale of operation requires.

If you bury electrical line or water pipe to a building, consider dropping additional lines in the trench, or burying non-perforated drain tile so that additional wires can be pulled through later to accommodate new technology or communication needs, or expanded electrical capacity. Surface mounting utilities in buildings also facilitates future expansion and repurposing.

Plan for Expansion

If the future scale of your business will require something more than you can afford to install or maintain right now, you should consider how you will transition into a new space when the time comes, especially if a new structure will occupy the same physical space as the interim solution.

Construction, whether new building or remodeling, takes a significant amount of time. If you are installing new infrastructure at the same time you are using your current facilities, you may put yourself into a real bind for current operations. If you know that you will need a new building to accommodate your plans for business expansion, you may want to decide where that new building will eventually go, and put your current building someplace else.

Including the Catastrophic Situation

Nobody likes thinking about all the things that can go wrong with your farming operation, let alone the worst thing that can happen. But that is exactly what you need to do in order to keep your farm business operating. For example, if you have a livestock operation, have you calculated what would happen if you incurred a significant health problem? What would you do if your market prices fell drastically below your cost of production and marketing? How would you pay your bills or meet your debt obligations? Do you have enough cash laid aside or capacity in an existing line of credit to meet your short-term obligations or would you need to go talk to your lender? If you need to get additional money from your lender, is he or she on-board with the additional loan? Or would you need to liquidate some assets just to make your payments on time?

In order to answer all these questions, you will need to prepare yourself for when things don't go as planned. First, consider putting together a group of advisors or management team to help with quick response. Second, prepare several catastrophic scenarios to determine how badly different situations will impact your financial situation. Share these with your team as a reality check and share with your lender to determine how much the lender is willing to work with you. If your lender does not appear to want to work with you under catastrophic conditions, look for another lender.

Third, put together a response to each catastrophic condition and determine how much additional money will need to be borrowed, how much of your savings will be needed, etc. In other words, determine the path your farming operation needs to take to stay in business. It is much easier to respond to a catastrophic condition if you are prepared and have a plan.

The Planning Process

Although observing and assessing your production successes and failures will be an everyday part of your farming experience, in order to capture the long-term trends and affects you will want to institute a regular, formal time for reflection and planning.

At a minimum you will want to plan annually. Sit down with your balance sheet, your income statement, your statement of cash flows, your budget-to-actual report, and review how your farm fared in the previous year. (We'll show you how to create and read these reports in upcoming chapters.) Did your income assumptions play out? Were your expenses under control? Have you planned appropriately for borrowed money?

Stepping back a little further, you'll want to ask deeper questions: Were equipment replacements made on time? Have you been able to take enough for family living expenses? Have you had the time you needed to do your management properly? Have you been able to take the vacation time away from the farm that you'd hoped for?

From the Farmers...continued

meetings have really deepened my understanding, made me a lot more fully a part of the management team."

Jackie says that a lot of people questioned the wisdom of her quitting her full time, well-paying job with health benefits to join Harry on the farm. But, she says, "Though we may not be better off financially, we are better off as a business, and as a couple, with me on the farm."

Jackie cautions: "It can be hard for other people to know all the details of why we are making the decisions we are." She explains that honoring your own thoughts, doing your research, and knowing very clearly why you want to do something are also critical in effective decision making.

OTTO'S TIP: *Have each family member privately write out their goals for the farm. Come back together to discuss each member's ideas. We promise you will have a very interesting (and hopefully fruitful) discussion.*

Take a moment (or an hour, or a day, or a week), to think about what you'd like to change on your farm. Write it down. Do some of the calculations we'll suggest in upcoming chapters to assess the financial impact of any changes.

In assessing everything from the details to the big picture, you can evaluate if your farm operation is allowing you to meet your personal, family, and business goals. Doing this once a year is essential, but checking in on these questions more frequently—as often as quarterly or monthly—will keep the issues more present in your mind and allow you to make changes more quickly.

Including the entire family or farm team in at least part of the planning process will not only bring new ideas to the table, it will also help everyone to feel involved and well informed on key farm issues. Your farm will certainly be more sustainable if everyone is part of the goal setting and large-scale decision making process. You may want to bring

From the Farmers

Change as Needed

Sharon Hoerichs, Little Sioux Orchard

Sharon Hoerichs of Little Sioux Orchard started her farming operation with a significant focus on raising pastured chickens - both broilers and egg layers. At the peak her family of four was doing chores for 200+ laying hens and 750 broilers per year.

While each operation was running a profit, and the products were in high demand, a few years ago the family decided to quit raising any commercial poultry.

"No one else in the family liked the work, I was finding myself doing all of the chores, or dealing with grouchy workers. The egg layers also kept us on the farm every day." When Sharon did a comparison of profit vs headache, the net didn't compensate for the stress. "Moving away from chickens took a huge load off my shoulders. I was able to make this lifestyle choice, as I had an exact understanding of the dollars I'd be sacrificing."

in a neutral, outside person to facilitate the discussion, and help keep the discussion open and respectful. This could be an Extension agent, a college farm management instructor, or other trusted advisor.

A planning process can end with a series of lists, which will then be referred to as you make an annual budget or cash flow projection. These may include one-year and five-year "improvement wish lists" which will lead you to doing your investment analyses we'll discuss in Chapter 14. Or, it may result in a more complex document that reflects your vision, your annual and long-term goals in more wordy phrases and paragraphs. Many farmers have enjoyed turning to the planning model of Holistic Resource Management™ There are many good planning models available, for more information see the Resources section.

Getting Help From an Advisory Team

It is extremely difficult, if not impossible, to know everything about all aspects of your business. So who do you seek advice from for what type of question or concern? Many farmers have found success in setting up a group of voluntary advisors that they can call on for help when planning or making decisions. Some even go so far as to have regular meetings with an advisory group to discuss the farm's operations and get advice on any questions or concerns.

An advisory team can be thought of as somewhat like a board of directors; each member has different specific knowledge and experience where they can offer advice on various aspects of your farming business. The advisory team should not make the farm decisions for you. Instead, you ask them questions so they can use their specific expertise to provide recommendations to you. It is your choice whether to accept or reject each recommendation.

For example if you are a livestock producer, who might help you make the nutrition, health, and other farm management decisions related to your livestock enterprise? Do you have a veterinarian, feed, or production specialist (or all three) that you might ask to be on your advisory team? If you are growing crops, who might help you make the nutrient and weed management decisions? Who could help you make the marketing, financial, legal, and tax decisions? Do you have a tax accountant, lender, and/or lawyer that would be willing to be on your advisory team? Generally there will be people in your community that you can ask to help build or support your operation.

The more experienced and complete the advisory team, the more comfortable lenders and other business partners will be regarding your ability to grow or raise your farm's products profitably. The more specialized the knowledge and experience of each advisory team member, the easier it is to determine which member needs to be contacted regarding a particular question or concern. This is particularly important if your farming operation includes multiple family members and/or employees and it is their responsibility to contact the appropriate advisory team member.

Developing a Business Plan

If you are thinking of getting into farming, are considering a major production or capital change, or are planning to go to a lender for a loan, it is time to consider creating a

From the Farmers

Planning and Responding

Andrea Gunner, Rosebank Farm

Andrea Gunner runs end-of-the-year financial reports for her farm each December. She and her husband, Stephen, sit down to talk about the previous year and plan any adjustments for the upcoming season. In March they come back to their discussion to see if anything has changed. They talk about any problems, changes they want to make, and then they update their Three Year Production Plan, a key piece of their overall business plan.

The Three Year Production Plan is summarized into a list of major acquisitions, major tasks, or key changes that they hope to accomplish at Rosebank Farms. They pay for the plan's items with previous (accumulated) and current profits each year. Included in a recent four-year list were: new tractor, 220V power for the processor, reallocate production to new paddock, ice machine, perimeter fencing of compost pasture, and rainwater catchment system.

The key to the plan's success, though, is perhaps not what is on it, but where they can find it. This list, with its six bullet points, is stuck on the family refrigerator with a couple of magnets. Along with estimated completion dates, the current plan boasts handwritten notes and check marks, indicating new thoughts, modifications, or progress on the plan.

Andrea says that putting the plan on the fridge keeps the plan a part of the farm life and that it helps with their commitment and sense of progress.

Rosebank Farms

Production & Processing Plan

- increase chicken production to 3,000 [4,000] birds/year by 2015, *lease land from Bev + Nick*
- continue to renovate and reseed pens but improve use of pasture
- increase turkey production to 100 birds/year by 2012 ✓
- add nut trees to provide both income and shelter
- address water quantity constraints through the installation of a rainwater catchment system using metal roofs from the workshop, 2 existing barns and house
- install pasture and nut tree irrigation system

Planned Acquisitions

What	Why	How Much	When
Tractor (35-40HP) with loader & forks	Materials Handling	New $20,000-25,000 Used $12-15,000	2011
Rainwater catchment system	Potable water for processing, irrigation water	$20,000	2011
220 V power	Docking site for on-farm processing, workshop use	$5,000	2011
~~Production quota~~ *Permit to 2000 birds/yr* ✓	Legality at our economically viable production volume	300 birds @ $57/bird ($17,100)	2011 ✓
Walk-in Freezer/Cooler	Improve inventory management, reduce energy costs	$5,000 – 10,000	2012
Ice machine		$3,000- 4,000	~~2011~~ 2012
2-4 spit Rotisserie		$2,000 – 5,000 (used->new)	2012
Perimeter fencing *Compost pasture*	Reduce predator access	$800 + gate (incl).	2011
Moveable day range electric net fencing	Reduce predation, save labour		2012
Nut trees (walnuts, hazelnuts)	Shelter & income		2012
Refrigerated delivery van		$15,000	2013
Production quota	Legality at our desired production volume	300 birds @ $57/bird ($17,100)	2015 *Rain*

From the Farmers

Utilizing an Advisor Team

Hans Breitenmoser, Breitenmoser Farm

Hans Breitenmoser has found that the best way to manage the vast amount of knowledge needed to manage his 400-cow dairy is to surround himself with very smart advisors. "In getting a good support team together, I don't have to be an expert in every realm. I only have to be smart enough to ask halfway intelligent questions," Hans said.

Every three months he meets on his farm with his group of advisors: his veterinarian, his nutritionist, the cow breeder. They review the Breitenmoser data and discuss milk production, breeding, and any other issues that are timely for the farm.

Hans appreciates that these professionals are visiting hundreds of other farms, and can help him compare his operation to the others they have seen. "It is really fun for me to see my advisor's interest in our operation. I don't feel so alone, knowing that I have their support. They really want the farm to succeed—it's a feather in their cap too!"

business plan. A business plan is a multi-dimensional document, involving both numbers and word descriptions, explaining on paper what you are planning over a period of time (usually in increments of one, three, five and perhaps ten years). Business plans generally include a market survey, projected income and expense statements, budgets and balance sheets for three and five years, and a complete rationalization of what you plan to do. There are many sample business plans and business planning tools available. For more information, see the Resources section.

Summary

When planning for your farm, whether as you are starting up or on an annual basis, you will want to first assess what you hope to get out of the farming operation. It is important to match your goals with a reality that is based on feasible estimates of production potential and sales volume. The potentials for income must be tied to your family needs and the costs of maintaining your farm infrastructure.

Farming as a whole is an occupation that involves much that is not in your control. It is impossible to plan for all that could happen. Instead, it is best to plan for flexibility and resiliency so that you are well positioned to respond to whatever weather, price fluctuations, or other variables come up. A balance must be maintained when considering capacity and growth.

A planning process can be annual or more frequent, but should be intentional, informed, and focused. Many farmers have found that talking about their farm goals and bigger issues more than annually helps them stay more focused and on track. Developing a business plan is extremely valuable when planning a major change in product line or infrastructure, and critical when approaching a lender for funding this kind of project.

How do you plan for change? By trying to build more flexibility into your system wherever possible, whether it's the way you lay out your infrastructure, the amount of debt you take on, or the ways you document the critical systems on your farm.

SECTION TWO
FARM DATA COLLECTION AND ORGANIZATION

We will now switch from the big picture and goal setting to the details of collecting and organizing your financial information. Setting up your procedures and systems is the next big step in successful financial management.

Good financial management is only as good as the background data that informs it. There is generally a lot of money coming and going through a farm—products being sold, seeds, supplies, and equipment being bought, bills being paid, and checks being deposited. The careful tracking of all of this activity is what adds up to your data collection, or bookkeeping system. Every farm needs to have one, but the way it is set up and run will dictate how accurate and useful the information is.

The information that you collect in these systems is what you will use to prepare the standardized reports and do the analysis we will describe in upcoming sections. You also use your data to prepare your Schedule F tax form, and so it is useful to set up your bookkeeping to make it easy to do tax reporting.

In this section we will introduce you to successful and simple methods for organizing your record keeping system, from the files and folders to the bookkeeping system, either paper or computer-based. We will give you suggestions on how to organize your data within your systems. We'll also share a few tips on efficient data entry procedures.

In the first edition of this book we emphasized utilizing computers to record financial information, as they allow the most comprehensive analysis. However, we received feedback that many farmers using paper-based systems wanted information on record keeping and analysis as well. So, in this updated version we have reorganized, introducing general concepts first. We then explain paper system record keeping, with a separate chapter for computerized systems.

Although we are focusing this book on financial record keeping, there are non-financial records that are also key in understanding your financial performance. We will give you suggestions of several kinds of non-financial data you may find useful (or essential!) to track.

CHAPTER 4
Getting Organized: Bookkeeping Tools and Basics

Key questions addressed in this chapter:

What tools do you need to make capturing financial information as easy as possible?

Should you do bookkeeping yourself, or hire it out?

One of the first things to do for successful farm financial management is to create a series of systems to collect and organize your financial data. You will do this by setting up your farm bookkeeping system. Before you set up your system, however, you will want to choose your tools and organize your workspace.

The majority of the information in this book pertains to any kind of bookkeeping system—paper or computer based. The basic concepts hold true, the difference comes with the actual input of the data into the system.

Farmers have been doing a good job of tracking financial activity for generations without the use of computers. Computers are not essential to good record keeping. In fact, some farmers know that with a good paper trail, they may be able to find a number quicker than it takes to turn on a computer.

However, we do recommend that you use a computerized record keeping system if possible. If you have now, or are planning anything but the most basic farming operation we suggest that you buy a good basic computer and financial bookkeeping software package. Basic computers continue to become less expensive and offer more features.

If you are committed to using a paper system, you can certainly succeed with it. Paper-based systems don't take a lot of money to set up, and are straight forward to understand and use. However, without a lot of extra work, they will only generate the simplest of data.

We will give details in the next chapter about tools and the basic structure of a bookkeeping system, with paper-based examples, and then detail computerized entry in the following chapter.

The information presented here and in upcoming chapters on how to collect and organize your data, how to do various analyses with it, and how to use the numbers you generate to understand what is going on financially on your farm will be relevant if you are using a computer or not.

Setting Up Your Bookkeeping Area

Regardless if you use a computer or a paper bookkeeping system, you'll need to find a comfortable and secure place to do your work. If you have the room it is ideal to have a dedicated farm finances desk. If not, at least a file cabinet or storage box for keeping papers isolated and secure from family wear and tear is crucial. Those using the kitchen table for bookwork will want to keep ledgers and other equipment in a storage box that can be pulled out and contents spread out to make the work efficient and as easy as possible.

The tools you select for bookkeeping should be chosen with the same care as you would choose your shop or field tools—maybe more, since you probably already have some resistance to sitting down to the task. Those using a computer will need a relatively up-to-date machine that will run the bookkeeping program you have selected. A good sized monitor will allow you to see a lot of numbers without scrolling the screen. Be sure your keyboard has a number pad on the side—if it doesn't, you can buy an add-on ten key number pad.

Have a dedicated file cabinet to hold all of your records, and both colored and manila file folders to go in it. You may want a stand-up folder rack for the top of your desk. A calculator with a large number pad will come in handy for doing any figuring. You may want one that prints if you have to do a lot of adding up of checks and other figures. If you wish to print checks using your computer you'll have to order pre-printed checks that fit your printer. A copier or scanner can make duplicates of papers that come in.

Setting up for Data Entry

In preparation for the actual data entry you will gather all of the paper and electronic records of your financial activity and enter the information into your bookkeeping system. You will also pay bills, record any income, and generate invoices as needed.

Most farmers find that weekly entering of data provides a good balance between the effort it takes to find the time needed to do the work, the set up time required, and the amount and timeliness of the data to be entered. Doing bookkeeping every seven days also gives you time to pay an invoice that comes in with a ten-day due date.

Gathering Your Financial Information

Every farm has financial information coming in through numerous paths. Bills, invoices, bank and credit card statements come in the mail, cash receipts are collected as you go out in the community and make purchases. Some of you buy and sell items online, others do online banking, generating computer receipts and reports. Sales income comes in via in-person transactions such as on-farm sales, at a farmers' market, or from a delivery route. Cash payments may be received via checks in the mail. Electronic payments can also come in through websites and online services such as PayPal.

However your financial information comes, a system must be developed to ensure that records of daily transactions are physically collected in one place so they can be entered into your bookkeeping system. Key features of a collection system are that it is easy to use and secure, yet obvious enough that it will act as a reminder that items sitting there

---

Bookkeeping vs Accounting

Bookkeeping describes the act of recording the day-to-day transactions of a business. For example, a business needs to pay its bills, so it needs to keep a record of the bills that come in and ensure that the correct amounts get paid at the correct times—that's the work of the bookkeeper.

Accounting describes the work of building on and interpreting the information that is put together through bookkeeping. Accounting activities include compiling reports, adjusting accounts at the end of the year, putting together tax returns, analyzing financial performance, and budgeting. This section deals primarily with the bookkeeping aspect of farm finances. The rest of the book has much more to do with the accounting aspects of farm finances.

From the Farmers

Record Keeping

Caleb Langworthy, Blue Ox Organics

The last few years on New Year's Eve, I've made a habit of emptying out of my wallet any lingering farm store receipts and adding them to the farm's "Inbox." From there, we enter a detailed description of the purchase into an antiquated farm finance software developed in Iowa a long time ago.

We're able to run reports on the volume and cost of each bolt or average fuel prices for the year. We keep track of receipts and lay out how we spent our money in the past year. Record keeping not only makes the tax man happy, it allows for Lauren and I to make informed assessments of our farm enterprises.

---

need further processing. You may have to experiment with a few different organizational methods before you find one that works for everyone responsible for financial transactions in the business.

Think about what ways your financial information does or will come in and plan a way to capture it so that it is safe and accessible for your weekly data entry. You may use a couple of different collection points, such as a manila envelope in the truck to collect "gone to town" receipts, and a box in the milk house or packing shed to temporarily store "came to the farm" receipts for later collection and merging into a box in your office or house where the mailed pieces are already waiting. This "inbox" (at least 9 x 12 inches to collect full size sheets of paper), should be set in a place that is out of daily traffic flow but easy to get to.

Some may prefer a file folder or wire basket to a box for collecting daily financial transactions. Whatever you try, be sure to change systems if you find you aren't using what you've set up.

Make sure that papers that are waiting in your folder or box have enough information so you'll know how to enter the data into your system. We all have one or two vendors in our community who still give out old-fashioned cash register receipts showing only lines of numbers and a total, possibly not even the store name. Develop the habit of writing what was purchased, who was paid, and the check number or credit card used on the slip if it isn't otherwise clear. The detail of what aspect of the farm the purchase relates to will also help, especially if whoever is buying isn't also doing the data entry. For example, noting that "mineral" was purchased is necessary, but "mineral-chickens" or "mineral-sheep" is that much more valuable, and critical for any of you who want to later do an enterprise analysis, as we'll explain in Chapter 16.

It is a good idea to open all of your bills the same day that they come. This allows you to quickly scan for due dates that may be sooner than you expected if something got held up in the mail. Paperclipping or stapling the bill with the payment envelope will assure they stay together.

If you have a lot of information to manage, you may want to take an intermediate step of filing your inbox materials into a series of file folders until you need to do something further with them. One way to organize these files is to group receipts, bills, and other paper by the cash account that it relates to. For instance, most incoming financial information can be grouped as payments received, credit card receipts, check receipts, cash receipts, or bills that need to be entered. Organizing them this way groups them efficiently for later data entry.

Now that you have your receipts and other paper representing financial transactions in one place, you've set the stage for entering the data into your bookkeeping system in a simple, linear process. If your papers are still in a box, it will be most efficient if you collect like things together—any receipts for things you paid for with cash together, check and debit receipts into a group, all of the credit card receipts into a group, all of the income together, all of the bills together and any miscellaneous things, such as bank statements, into a group. You can then stack the groups on top of each other and put them back in your box or folder to keep them organized as you work. Those who have previously sorted incoming papers into file folders should be all ready to start.

Managing Bills

Every business person knows the importance of paying bills on time. However, intent and action don't always match up. Setting up a system to help with bill management will help assure they get paid on time. You have several options of ways to set up bill reminders.

Many small business people use some version of a tickler system to keep track of when bills are due, or when they want to pay their bills. A common tickler system is to use 43 labeled file folders—numbers 1 through 31 for the days of the month, and January through December (shown in Figure 4.1). The daily files are kept in front, beginning with the file for tomorrow's date (if today is March 14, the first file in line is 15) The rest of the numbered files represent the rest of the days of the month (16 through 31), and the beginning of the next month (1 through 14). Behind the daily files are the month files, starting with April, followed by the rest of the year (May through December) and the beginning of the next year (January through March).

Figure 4.1 Tickler File System

Paper copies of bills are filed either by the date you want to pay them or by the date they are due. A bill due within the next month is put in the appropriate daily file. A bill due more than one month out is put into the appropriately named monthly file.

During your weekly bookkeeping tasks, the files for all the days of the upcoming week are emptied and paid. Once empty, the files representing the days that have been processed are moved to the back of the sequence. Look through the upcoming monthly file and move bills into the daily date files as appropriate.

OTTO'S TIP: *Those using a computer bookkeeping program can choose to circumvent this filing system by using the "Bill Pay" feature, which allows you to enter bills as they come in, with a pay-by date and automated reminders.*

As you work, marking receipts with a red pen confirms that they've been processed into your bookkeeping program. After you've finished entering the data, your receipts are ready to be filed into an archive. You may decide to postpone the work by putting the completed receipts in a temporary To Be Filed file for later filing. Or, you can create a Current Month file and then, at the end of the month, just transfer all of the receipts into an appropriately labeled archive file for the month. We'll talk about filing options in a bit.

In the upcoming chapters we will talk about how you enter the data into your paper or computer bookkeeping system.

Tracking Amounts Due

If you invoice your customers, delivering items prior to receiving payment, you'll need a reliable mechanism for tracking which invoices have been paid. It is bad customer service to come back to a customer six months after an invoice was issued and ask for payment. A computerized invoicing system will track which invoices have been paid, as long as you are careful to use the Receive Payments function when payments come in. If you write invoices by hand, you'll want to track them by customer in a spreadsheet or on paper, marking off invoices when they are paid. Filing copies of all of your invoices in numerical order or by vendor will make it easy to find and copy one if necessary. With a computerized version, you can view or print a copy of an invoice whenever you need one.

You will want to review your accounts receivable (who owes you money) on a monthly basis to look for anything you might need to follow up on. Often, a lack of payment is from a simple mistake, so initial letters or calls should take as friendly a tone as possible.

Filing Your Receipts and Other Bookkeeping Papers

You want to file your receipts and any other information after you've processed it in a way that the amount of effort you put in to organizing your archives correlates to the frequency and urgency with which you might need to later access the information.

There are four generally used archival filing systems. In one, you file your paper records according to the vendor that was involved. In this system you might have files with names like "Eau Claire Energy," "Equity Livestock Sales," "Fleet Farm," and "Direct Chicken Customers." In the second, you file records according to the account they relate to. In this system you may have files labeled "Electric and Propane," "Live Animal Sales," "Misc Farm Supplies," and "Broiler Income."

In a third system you create files for each letter of the alphabet (or multiple letters, such as A-C, D-F etc.), and file receipts alphabetically by vendor name.

In each of these filing systems you will have to clean out the old files or create new files when they get full, probably annually. The older files can be moved to storage.

Many farmers just starting choose to file records by month. In this system, each receipt or invoice is put into a file with the title of the month in which the transaction occurred. Your files will have names like August 2017, September 2017, and March 2017. As they age the files can be archived as-is, and new ones created. This is the easiest of the systems, and takes the least time to set up and manage. If you rarely need to look at your paper records, this is a good one to use.

Besides receipts and invoices, you'll have other papers, such as bank statements and loan documents. Create folders for each of those, too, so they are readily accessible.

At the beginning of each year, make a new file for tax documents for the year, where you can keep things like receipts for donations that your accountant will want to see. This also becomes the place to put any income documentation, such as IRS 1099 forms, that come early in the new year for the previous year's activities.

From the Farmers

Pocket Folders

Erin Pilgrim, Pilgrim Family Farm

Erin Pilgrim uses common pocket folders to store monthly receipts. Using a folder for each month, the pocket on one side holds income receipts, the other side is for expense receipts.

When she goes to enter the detail into an Excel spreadsheet, the monthly data is well organized. When the year is over, the files are archived in order with the month and year written on the outside.

Signed Invoices

OTTO'S TIP:

Even if you have a strong trusting relationship with your customer, it will avoid any possible controversy to have them sign the invoice at delivery. Consider printing two copies and putting carbon paper between the copies when they sign, so you each will have a signed copy.

Setting up a comfortable and functional system for both the style and the naming of individual files will be unique for everyone. You may want to create a combined system, in which vendors you do a lot of business with have their own file, but everything else is filed by alphabet or account name.

You must find a system that works well enough so that you get papers filed in a timely way, and that you can find something when the occasion comes up. A filing system must be used to be functional. If you don't expect to retrieve paper documents often, a very simple system may be the most time effective.

Hiring Out Your Bookkeeping?

In the next two chapters we will discuss how to set up a bookkeeping system specific to your farm. You have the option of doing this yourself, or hiring someone else to do your bookkeeping. Although there are many benefits to having the work done by someone intimately involved in the operation, if for some reason that is not possible or feasible, there are people who can help.

There are advantages of doing the work in-house. A strong familiarity with the operation can lead to more accurate categorization of individual incomes and expenses, and regular in-house record keeping can mean more timely updates on problems or areas of concern. However, if the work isn't getting done, then these advantages disappear. Bookkeeping is a fairly standardized process. If you have limited labor time on your farm, you may decide that the key farmers' management time is better served doing farm production management rather than the regular tasks of bookkeeping. In this case, you may decide that hiring a bookkeeper is worth your while.

You may find someone willing to come to your farm to do bookkeeping, or you can take your records to a bookkeeper's office. A good bookkeeper may only cost $100 to $200 or so per month, depending on the going rates in your area and the complexity and size of your operation. To find a bookkeeper, ask your tax accountant or lender for recommendations. You will want someone organized who has experience with farm finanicals. Ask for references of other farmers a prospective bookkeeper works with. Be sure that you feel comfortable communicating with your bookkeeper, and that you can understand his or her explanations.

Whoever you hire, you must develop a good relationship with that person, and work closely with him or her to set up your initial record keeping system so that it accurately reflects your operation and the information that you need and want to track. Plan to spend time on a monthly basis so that you can review reports and fully utilize the information collected to make any management adjustments.

Summary

Setting yourself up with the tools you need in a comfortable work environment will make your bookkeeping more efficient and accurate. We recommend various systems for collecting and organizing the sources of information that you will need to use in whatever bookkeeping system you choose.

CHAPTER 5
Setting Up Your Financial Records

Key questions addressed in this chapter:

What goes into setting up a good record keeping system?

How do you organize your data so it produces the most useful information?

How do you enter data into a paper bookkeeping system?

Now that you have your tools collected, and a good place to work, you can start thinking about how to organize the data in your bookkeeping system. At its most fundamental level, bookkeeping consists of keeping track of all your money-based transactions so that you can access, summarize, and interpret your financial data. Whether you use computer software or a paper-based system, your bookkeeping "program" comes down to making records of where your money came from—selling a case of potatoes—or where it went, such as to purchase a bag of chicken feed.

When you start tracking financial information in your life, either personally or in your farming operation or other business, you probably begin with a checkbook ledger. This is a simple structure which lists when you bought something, who you bought it from, how much you paid and what the tracking (check) number is.

You will also list where income came from, how much it was, and when you deposited it, so that you can keep a rough idea of how much money you have. Entries can be checked against your bank statement. In the world of credit and debit cards and online transactions, these simple lists may also be online. A checkbook ledger such as this is the most rudimentary type of financial tracking, and while it is where most people start, it will not capture everything that happens in your business.

A step up from managing by checkbook balance is to take the information from your checkbook, cash receipts, credit card and online purchases and deposits and transfer it into a paper bookkeeping ledger. A step beyond this is to use an electronic spreadsheet program, which will automate the math and allow for quick sorting of information. A full computer bookkeeping system will allow you to set up complex entry and reporting that allows deeper analysis.

As you move from a simple checkbook system to something more complex, the first thing you will do is decide what categories you want to track your financial information in. We recommend you base these categories on those needed for annual IRS Schedule F tax reporting.

As you set up a basic tracking system, you can itemize your incomes and expenses within these categories. As you do this, you are setting up a "chart of accounts." The chart of accounts is the cornerstone of your bookkeeping system. Every financial transaction you make in your operation will use accounts in one way or another.

Entries made using the chart of accounts will be used to build select reports, which we'll describe in upcoming chapters. For instance, an income statement will show how much you have spent in each of your income and expense accounts, such as feed expenses or heifer sales. A balance sheet, which we'll talk about in Chapter 9, will show how much

Double- vs Single-Entry Accounting

When people really begin to feel their heads swirl with bookkeeping, it usually has to do with the concept of "double-entry accounting." In double-entry accounting, every purchase changes at least two accounts, and sometimes more.

The term "bookkeeping" comes from the fact that financial information started with pen and ink in ledger books; each ledger, or journal book represented an account, and each transaction was recorded twice, with each transaction having a "debit" and a "credit."

Computer bookkeeping systems have been programmed to make debits and credits in the appropriate accounts with a single entry, such as writing a check or making a deposit.

Most small-business people and individuals who chose to use paper-based systems opt for "single-entry accounting," in which the primary means of record keeping is similar to a check register, allocating the amount of check, cash or credit card purchases and incoming payments to different expense or income accounts. People who do this generally will also keep a check register, so they know how much is in their checking account.

The methods we suggest in this book will be based on single-entry paper-based bookkeeping or computer bookkeeping programs.

Table 5.1 Single-entry Accounting

Farmer State Bank Checking Account					Incomes		Expenses			
No.	Date	Description	Income	Expense	Farm Market Sales	Restaurant Sales	Fertilizer	Fuel	Labor	Seed
	1-Sep	Balance forward	11,486	5,639	5,635	5,851	600	300	4,253	486
	3-Sep	Big City Market	700		700					
1356	3-Sep	Jane Smith - Market help		50					50	
1357	5-Sep	Little Creek Farm – garlic seed		300						300
1358	9-Sep	Fuel for market van		60				63		
		TOTALS	12,186	6,049	6,335	5,851	600	363	4,303	786

Basic Categories Needed for the Schedule F
(Recommended for Your Chart of Accounts)

Income:
Sale of livestock bought for resale
Cost of livestock bought for resale
Sale of livestock, produce, grains, etc. raised
Co-op distributions
Ag payments
Commodity Credit Corp. loans
Crop insurance proceeds
Custom hire income
Other income

Expenses:
Car and truck expense
Chemicals
Conservation expenses
Custom hire expense
Depreciation
Employee benefits
Feed purchased
Fertilizers and lime
Freight and trucking
Gasoline, fuel and oil
Insurance (other than health)
Interest- mortgage
Interest- other
Labor hired
Pension and profit sharing
Rent or lease vehicles, machinery, equipment
Rent of lease-other (land, animals, etc.)
Repairs and maintenance
Seeds and plants purchased
Storage and warehousing
Supplies purchased
Taxes
Utilities
Veterinary, breeding and medicine
Other expenses

---

money you have in your various bank and other asset accounts, and how much you owe in your liability accounts, but it won't show the detail of how much you spent on an individual category of expenses, such as fertilizer or fuel.

Your chart of accounts will also be used to build your cash flow budgets, which we will also describe in upcoming chapters.

Setting Up Your Chart of Accounts

While most charts of accounts are set up using the basic categories needed for tax reporting, you have the flexibility to set up accounts that track information in the ways that are most useful to you in making management decisions. You can make your chart of accounts as simple or as complex as you desire.

If you are just starting out with your farm financial management we recommend that you start with relevant accounts from the standardized Schedule F chart of accounts. Pre-printed paper spreadsheets are set up using these categories. As you go about the business of data entry, and money flows in and out of your business, you will be able to tell if this basic chart fits your needs.

If you find yourself confused about what account a given entry should be assigned to, you will probably be led to adding to or modifying your chart of accounts. "Where does land rent income go?" or "I want to track calf sales separate from cull sales" are thoughts that should drive you to creating the new income accounts of Land Rent, Calf Sales, and Cull Sales.

You can create an unlimited number of accounts. The limit or deciding factors will be how useful itemization will be, how easy it is to split information into reportable units, or perhaps how many accounts will fit on a report page. This last may sound trivial, but if you have a simple operation and are looking at reports on a regular basis, being able to see everything on a few pages makes it a lot easier than going through page after page of detail.

Be practical in your decisions about your accounts. For instance, in our sample chart several accounts have two or more items listed, for example "Seeds and Plants Purchased." If you think you will need to know how much was spent on seed and how much on bedding plants, then certainly split them. But it is possible that you only need to know how much was spent on your total plant propagation items, and can keep them together. You can create new accounts later if you want them.

In a paper system you will choose the items for your chart of accounts and list the accounts across the top of sheets in your account book, with the dates of individual transactions listed on the left side. To make any changes in a paper system you will need to start over with a fresh account register.

We will explain the detail of creating a computer-based chart of accounts in the next chapter.

Asset, Liability, and Equity Accounts

Standard account types include more than just income and expenses. You'll also need accounts for assets, liabilities, and equity. Asset accounts are used to track the value of significant items owned by the farm that have a useful life of more than one year. Examples include land, buildings, breeding animals, equipment, etc.

In Chapter 9 we'll bring up the topic of intermediate assets, with a life of two to ten years. You will probably want to set up an account for those. Accountants have different recommendations on what counts as a long-term or fixed asset, and how they would like to see that information tracked, so you'll want to consult your tax professional to decide how to organize your asset accounts. Asset accounts also include bank accounts, such as checking, savings, and cash.

On the liabilities side, you'll potentially have credit card and loan accounts. You may want to distinguish between short- (due within a year), intermediate- (one to ten years), and long-term liabilities. Loan accounts are generally set up to track only the principal on the money you owe, with the interest portion of the payments allocated to an expense account.

Equity accounts track the money invested in, or taken out of the business by owners and shareholders. If your farm is a sole proprietorship, the money you take out for personal expenses comes out of an equity account often called Owner Draw.

In a paper system, each of these types of accounts will have a portion of a page or a separate page in your recording system. Assets (beyond your checking and cash accounts used in your primary spreadsheet) will be listed with beginning of year and end of year balances. Credit card and loan balances will be listed in a liabilities section, once a year or as often as you wish to update them. The values in these asset and liability accounts are important when creating the financial statements we'll discuss in upcoming chapters.

Computerized bookkeeping programs will guide you through how to set up each of your relevant accounts.

Entering Data into a Paper System

Those moving forward with a paper system are now ready to set that up. Those using computer spreadsheets such as Excel can also follow along, as the setup will be similar, although will utilize electronic calculations rather than hand adding. Those using computer bookkeeping programs can move onto the next chapter.

Setting up Your Spreadsheet

We have included sample record keeping forms from the Oklahoma Farm and Ranch Account Book in Appendix B. These forms show the types of records that must be kept.

Outside the Shoebox

Accountants laugh (in a sad kind of way) when they talk about the high number of farmers that show up once a year with a shoe box full of receipts and ask the accountant to fill out their Federal tax form.

The accountant will take all of the receipts and enter them into a system that categorizes incomes and expenses according to the lines on the Schedule F.

Your setting up a system to track this on your farm first will not only bring a smile to your accountant's face, but allow you to potentially use the information in other ways to make management decisions.

FINANCIAL RECORDS

Income Detail

Income related to your production must be tracked with enough detail about what you've sold to help your future decision making.

In each market, you may decide to track different levels of income detail. For example, if you sell at a farmers' market, you might only want to track total income per market. In this case, volumes of individual products sold may be best tracked outside of your bookkeeping system, perhaps through notes on a printed spreadsheet at the packing shed, for instance. This allows you to relax in keeping track of exactly how many dollars you make on carrots versus tomatoes in the cash-frenzied market environment.

On the other hand, if you are selling to a commodity market, restaurants, stores, or institutions, you will almost certainly need to track quantities of individual items sold using an invoicing system or a cash sales receipt.

You have a few options on how to set up your paper forms.
- Make copies on 8 1/2 x 11" paper of the forms we share in Appendix B
- Take the information show on the sample forms and transfer it to an 11 x 7" or 8 ½ x 14" ledger book. If you find what you create works well for you, you may want to take unfilled pages to a copy shop to make your own customized set of templates that you can reuse each year.
- Contact your local Extension office and ask if they have blank farm record keeping books.
- Go to your library or a neighbor's and use a computer to find the Oklahoma Farm and Ranch Account Book, which prints on legal size paper (8 ½ x 14"). The book is 82 print pages, and will print on 41 sheets of paper. The web address is agecon.okstate.edu/farmbook.

Entering Income

Money will come into your farm operation a diversity of ways, and receipts or incomes should be listed as they come in. Sales of livestock or crops can be tracked by individual marketplace (for instance, wholesale or farm stand, farmers' market or CSA). You can decide what categories of tracking will be most useful to you, that will become more clear as you go through this book.

The date, where the income came from, what you sold, and the amount of income must be recorded. Totals for each account can be done monthly, on one page or several months to a page with subtotals, depending on the amount of activity in your operation. Table 5.2 hows what a reciept (income) ledger looks like.

Entering Expenses

As you pay for activities on your farm you will save receipts, as we explained in the last chapter. Your next step will be to enter the information into your spreadsheet. Each transaction, whether it is an electric bill you paid or a check you wrote to the feed store or to your neighbor for renting land, must be entered into your spreadsheet. You will probably want to mix check payments with any cash payments, as they will need to be put together for your overall expense accounting.

Credit card receipts should be kept separate, with the entries into your account book made when the credit card bill is paid, whether through check or electronic payment.

For each transaction you will enter the date, the number (check number), how much you paid, who was paid, and then the amount in each of your accounts. For instance,

Table 5.2 Detail from a Farm Receipt Ledger

Month _Jan_ Year _200X_   **RECEIPTS**

Line	Date	Amount Received		From Whom Received	Item, Units, Weight, Price, etc.	Sale of Livestock & Other Items Bought For Resale		Raised Market Livestock & Livestock Products (calves) Hogs	
1	2	10,500	00	Farmer's Supply	Wheat 3000 bu. @ 3.50				
2	5	8,530	50	Co. Grain & Feed	Soybeans 1410 bu. @ 6.05				
3	9	33,670	25	ABC Packers, Inc.	42 steers 1075# @ 75.25	33,670	25	(reported net of selling expenses)	
4	10	1,012	10	Deep Rock Energy	Gas Royalty				
5	15	620	05	XYZ Lvst. Auction	1 cull cow (raised)				

Source: Oklahoma Farm and Ranch Account Book, OSU Ag Exrension http://agecon.okstate.edu/

if you went to your local farm store and bought chicken feed and cover crop seed, you would record $50 in the "Feed" column and $120 in the "Seeds and Plants" column. Table 5.3 hows what an expense ledger looks like.

Continue entering each of your expenses for a month. Most farms will use a separate record page for each month, unless you have very few transactions, and then you can put a few months on each page, with sub totals separating each month. Add up the totals for each account for each month.

If you wish to track expenses from specific parts of your farm independently, such as the cattle operation separate from cash crop production, or greenhouse activity independent from chicken production, you can keep separate account pages for each enterprise. This will get cumbersome, as each record page has many accounts, but if you are setting up your own paper system you can include only the accounts relevant to each specific enterprise. For instance, the chicken operation won't have seed costs and may not need hired labor, but will need feed and supplies. You can include just those accounts you will use.

When tracking enterprises you will at some point have to merge the information into whole-farm totals per account for tax reporting and use in the reports we will be explaining in upcoming chapters. Monthly whole-farm totals should be summed in a cash flow statement to track the cash inflows and outflows as the year progresses.

Family living and personal expenses are kept on a separate page, as these will be recorded independently in your tax forms and other totals.

Summary

To have successful financial management, your financial data must be organized in ways that give you back the information you need to manage and make decisions. Setting up a chart of accounts is the first step in organizing your bookkeeping system. Thinking through what information you want to track will lead you to various options for setting up the names and order of your account categories, which may change over time as your needs change. Those using paper systems will set up an account ledger to track incomes and expenses month-by-month.

Table 5.3 Detail from a Farm Expense Ledger

Month: Jan   Year: 200X   **EXPENSES**

Line	Date	Check Number	Amount Paid		Items, Units, Weight, Price, Etc.	From Whom Purchased	Cost of Livestock & Other Items Bought For Resale		Car & Truck Expenses	Chemicals: Herbicide & Insecticide	Conservation	Custom Hire		Employee Benefits
1	2	1615	110	20	Hot Wire REA	Dec. Bill								
2	3	1617	10,786	00	Farm Credit	Annual Pymt on S ½ Sec. 10								
3	9	1623	22,504	40	F&M Nat'l Bank	Payoff Cattle Note								
4	10	1624	1,280	00	F&M Nat'l Bank	Labor - Fed. Empl. Tax Deposit								
5	11	1627	2,410	66	Farmer's Supply	Fert; Feed; Fuel; Seed; Supplies								67
6	11	1628	2,449	75	OK Co. Treas.	Farm 2060.10, House 389.65								
7	15	1632	800	00	Sam Smith	80 A. Grass Rent SSN 333-22-4444								
8	18	1637	22	00	Ag News & Mkt	Quarterly Subscription								
9	18	1638	1,500	00	OSU Bull Sale	14 Mo. Old Bull								
10	21	1641	1,054	50	Sam Smith	Combining Milo						1,054	50	
11	22	1644	28,477	52	OK Lvst. Inc.	61 Steers 525# @ 88.92	28,477	52						
12	31	1655	1,205	01	Handy Andy	Gross = 1,500; FICA = 114.75; FWT = 151; SWT = 29.24								

Source: Oklahoma Farm and Ranch Account Book, OSU Ag Exrension http://agecon.okstate.edu/

NOTES

CHAPTER 6
A Computer Bookkeeping Program That Works for You

Key questions addressed in this chapter:

Will a computer bookkeeping program add value to your operation?

What decisions must be made in setting up a bookkeeping program?

How can you manipulate the chart of accounts, classes and jobs to give you the most useful information?

To Computerize, or Not?

As we've said in previous chapters, we recommend using a computerized bookkeeping system for your financial management if at all feasible.

A computer system can do things that a paper system can't. Most of these relate to the analysis part of your record keeping, which is especially critical to keep on top of in running a profitable farm. Once your data has been correctly entered into a computer system, at the push of a button you will be able to see your income and expenses, to compare to your budget, to compare to previous years, or to easily collect data that can be used to analyze through ratios.

And, perhaps most important, you don't have to wait until you have time to create the standardized reports we'll look at in upcoming chapters, or the accountant fills in your tax form, to get a rough idea of your farm's financial position.

Those unfamiliar with computers or computerized record keeping systems will have to take some time to learn how to use the systems. But, once past the initial learning period, most will find a computerized system will be as easy, or easier to use, than a paper-based system.

Classes on computer basics and bookkeeping software are available at your local library or technical college. These classes are set up to help you gain comfort and understand the basics of the system, and can save you time and frustration in learning these complex systems on your own.

A computerized bookkeeping program can be used at the most basic level—more or less like a checkbook register—or can be expanded with built in features such as check writing, invoice creation, bank deposit preparing and payroll. You can start simply and bring in more complexity as you get comfortable with the system, or you can hire someone that understands the program to set it up and manage it for you, or you can learn all the complexities and set up a comprehensive bookkeeping system from the beginning. Any of these will work and bring advantages over the limitations of a paper reporting system.

Computer Bookkeeping Programs

Once you have decided to use a computer bookkeeping program, the next choice is which program to use. The relatively user-friendly computer bookkeeping software available today makes entering data and running reports a simple undertaking, with large amounts of flexibility. One of the most commonly used affordable accounting software programs is QuickBooks, developed and sold by Intuit. We'll refer to that program as we go through this section, but other programs will be very similar in how they function.

While you'll want to update your computer program every several years to the most recent version, you generally don't need to do this every year. However, if you are using your program for payroll, you will need to purchase regular updates to keep your tax tables up to date.

Computer Spreadsheets

University Extension departments are especially fond of setting up templates that use Excel spreadsheets for farm record keeping. You certainly can do a good job of tracking your financial information using Excel or another spreadsheet program. You will set up a template using the format explained in the previous chapter, or look in the Resources section to find an online template that works for you. Many farmers find spreadsheets are a great complement to more complicated bookkeeping programs, as they are simpler, and offer a lot of flexibility as well as transparency.

Cloud-Based Systems

In the last few years online programs have been developed as alternatives to purchasing software that you load on your computer. Programs, both custom-designed and standard ones such as QuickBooks are offered as a "cloud" version, in which you enter data into a system that exists in a remote location only.

Cloud-based systems have the advantage of not relying on software installed on your computer, and are generally accessed through a web browser, such as Google Chrome or Microsoft Internet Explorer. This means you can enter data from your phone or other electronic device as well as from your computer, increasing flexibility and the possibility of a more user-friendly option to access your data.

The difference between cloud-based and traditional software is that when you access the cloud, your desktop, laptop, or mobile device isn't the thing doing the actual computing. The computing happens in a large datacenter outside your organization, and you simply see the results of it on your own screen.

Several entrepreneurs have looked at the needs of farmers and created customized systems designed to serve very specific functions. Those interested in cutting-edge record keeping can explore several dynamic programs.

From the Farmers
The Balance of Information

A neighbor recently told the story of a computer crash, and the loss of a year's worth of data plus all the hard-to-prioritize time his wife put into getting it into the computer. "If we would have stuck with my old paper system, we'd have nothing lost," he exclaimed.

But, they are now still entering data into a computerized Excel spreadsheet, as they do see advantage in being able to easily sort and modify entries. However, they now make regular backups to not lose what they have entered.

Other Computer Programs

In this book we give detail on bookkeeping using QuickBooks, as it is the most common program used by farmers for financial record keeping. However, there are several other programs available that you can also consider. Most will have very similar features to QuickBooks, but offer slightly different entry and reporting methods.

Some programs will allow you to export or move reports and data into Microsoft Excel, which can be a great advantage in doing further analyses. It will be important to track down a user manual for any program you choose to help you understand its specific operation.

On the down side, cloud-based systems require regular and steady internet access, and some people fear the security of having their data online. There are new cloud-based options appearing all the time, as developers create customized systems. Finding one that fits your needs, and trusting that it will still be around in a few years, offer additional challenges and limitations.

While some worry about having their financial data online, in today's climate of sophisticated hacking, trusting the security provided by professionals vs. trying to keep a secure system at home may be the safer option.

Those with simple farming systems may choose to use a straight forward spreadsheet program, such as Excel, to track financial information. A spreadsheet is basically a computerized version of a paper and pencil ledger, with the advantage that the data can be easily changed or sorted, and various mathematical calculations can be performed.

Setting up your Farm Business with Computerized Bookkeeping

Whether you purchase software or use a cloud-based system, you will begin by creating a "company" and setting up company preferences. This is where you decide on a few rules, such as if you are recording using a cash or accrual system, and if you will be doing payroll. Most programs will offer a step-by-step setup, allowing you to answer questions to make your choices.

We recommend that you start with a cash-based system, meaning that income and expenses will be assigned when they are deposited or paid, rather than when they are obligated, or "accrued."

As we introduced in Chapter 5, a key task will be to set up your chart of accounts. Most computer bookkeeping programs will have a standardized chart of accounts you can choose. Some, such as QuickBooks, even have the option of choosing a list titled "Agriculture, Ranching, or Farming." It is easy to start with a standardized account list and make modifications that fit your business. Because the computer program can track more complexity and detail than a paper system, you will set up a larger number of accounts. The system will tie accounts to each other in appropriate ways, and a single transaction entry will make relevant adjustments to the appropriate accounts.

The chart will group accounts by type. Accounts grouped as "banks" will track the balances and activities in your checking, savings, and other money accounts. "Income" accounts are where you record money that comes in as you sell your products, or take in other income on your farm, such as interest or property rental. "Expense" accounts track money that is outgoing for farm activities, such as payments for feed or seed or electricity.

OTTO'S TIP:

The bookkeeping program Quicken uses the term Categories instead of Accounts to generate what is basically a chart of accounts. Quicken uses Accounts to refer only to banking or other money accounts. Explore your bookkeeping program to find the exact terminology used to identify the basic system of grouping your transactions.

What Can a Computer Bookkeeping Program do?

Different computer programs offer different services, but most computer bookkeeping programs will help you:

- Record transactions for and reconcile various bank accounts
- Enter bank deposit detail
- Write and print checks, or enter the details from hand-written checks
- Maintain a check register
- Record cash, electronic transfer, and credit card transactions
- Maintain vendor and customer lists
- Maintain item lists for inventory management
- Enter bills, and then allow you to pay them when due
- Create invoices and receive payments
- Create yearly budgets
- Track asset values and investments
- Manage loans
- Create reports, such as balance sheets, profit and loss (income statements), etc.
- Track and report transactions by group or enterprise, such as class, project, or job
- Manage payroll (this feature is often optional and may include added expense)

Online Resources

For an overview of hundreds of online record keeping systems: go to:

www.capterra.com/farm-management-software

A few of the options include:
farmbrite.com
agsquared.com
easyfarm.com

COMPUTER PROGRAMS

From the Farmers On Computer Bookkeeping Programs

Simple Spread Sheets

Andrea Gunner of Rosebank Farms is convinced that Excel spreadsheets offer the best tracking system to simply and quickly assess how her business is doing. She doesn't use any kind of financial software program, and tracks all of her expense and income figures on spreadsheets. "I like the flexibility—I can get a lot of information by just looking at the numbers in different ways—it is simple and clear."

Quicken

Carmen Fernholz of A-Frame Farm recommends keeping track of farm numbers using any of the good computer software financial tracking programs available. He appreciates how easily these programs allow you to know where every dollar is going, and where income is coming from. He has used the program Quicken by Intuit (quicken.intuit.com) to track his diversified organic row crop operation for many years. He likes Quicken for its simplicity and ability to perform all the functions he needs. Carmen tracks expenses using his checkbook, and once a week or so transfers the data from his checkbook to the computer program.

QuickBooks vs Peachtree

Jackie Hoch of Hoch Orchard and Gardens used the bookkeeping program Peachtree (www.peachtree.com) for years. However, she switched to QuickBooks so that she can better transfer files to her accountant, a QuickBooks user. "I liked Peachtree, as it did what I needed and I was familiar with it," Jackie says. "It seems that QuickBooks is easier to navigate, but has fewer options for the number of levels that things can be broken down to."

Moneydance

Sharon Hoerichs of Little Sioux Orchard started out using the program Moneydance (moneydance.com), for her diversified operation. "I liked Moneydance because it is cheap, runs well, is adaptable, and the company had great support when I had problems." However, a few years ago she changed to QuickBooks to better meet her accountant's needs. "I can just upload my whole QB file to my accountant, we're both very happy with the change." Sharon still recommends Moneydance for those who want a program for home use. The company offers a reasonable purchase price (still $49.99 in 2017), with a 90-day money back guarantee. Sharon supports her QuickBooks numbers with various Excel spreadsheets, a combination that gives her confidence that she knows what is going on financially on her farm.

Just Do It!

Matt O'Hayer of Vital Farms says that it doesn't really matter what software you use, just that you need to keep good track of your financials. "Get Quicken or QuickBooks, or one of the other programs. Or, if you or a family member can't regularly produce reliable numbers, then you need to go to an outside service to do it for you." Hiring someone will cost about $100 per month, but the information is too key not to have, he says.

OTTO'S TIP:

As you sit down to do your weekly data entry, you'll want to start your program before you do anything else. Bookkeeping systems are generally large programs and take a while to boot up. You may want to set up a second company file during the learning phase, so that you can make mistakes and try things out.

48

Your chart also lists "assets," or property that you own, and "liabilities," or amounts that are owed to you. "Equity" is the amount that various entities "own" of your operation. Once you set up your chart you will use the accounts to do your daily farm business, such as record income and expenses. Your computer system can also help you create invoices, receive payments, pay bills, and other financial transactions. Your program will make modifications to the balances of accounts automatically as you perform these various activities.

Your bookkeeping program can generate reports that will automatically choose which accounts are relevant to your request. In computerized financial reports, the various accounts are listed down the left side of the page, with periods of time or other groupings (we'll talk about classes in a bit) across the top.

OTTO'S TIP:

Although it can be fun to create your own customized names for accounts (perhaps "Blue Bessy" instead of "Farm Truck"), this can drive your accountant or tax helpers wild. The more closely you stick with standardized account names the happier you will be when it comes time to fill out tax forms.

Refining Your Chart of Accounts

Computers give you the ability to add deeper function to your chart of accounts by grouping your individual accounts together using subaccounts. You can nest accounts to two or three levels. This detail may be useful in making cash flow projections, monitoring, and making decisions. Reports can provide single subaccount detail, as well as summaries at the category heading level, which can be used for quick assessments or general comparisons. As you get used to your operation's financial reporting needs you can determine the need for subaccounts and how they might be organized.

For example, you could choose to set up subaccounts for each major piece of machinery, as shown in Table 6.1.

The organization shown in Table 6.1 allows you to run reports on the fuel, insurance, and maintenance expenses for the tractor, the truck, and implements. It would also give you a summary total for the fuel, insurance, and repairs you spent for all your equipment.

You could choose to organize your accounts differently, such as with each piece of equipment

Table 6.1 Chart of Accounts Subaccounts

Fuel		Expense
	Tractor	Expense
	Farm Truck	Expense
	Implements	Expense
Insurance		Expense
	Tractor	Expense
	Farm Truck	Expense
	Implements	Expense
Repairs and Maintenance		Expense
	Tractor	Expense
	Farm Truck	Expense
	Implements	Expense

From the Farmers

Moving Bookkeeping to a Computer

Hans Breitenmoser, Breitenmoser Farm

Hans Breitenmoser is not a computer kind of guy. But several years ago, when he was looking at getting a new Milk Volume Production (equity expansion) loan, he knew that he needed to do better record keeping, and set up with QuickBooks. He's never looked back.

"I didn't want to deal with all the complication of computer bookkeeping, but now I wouldn't live without it," Hans says. "My wife, my financial advisor, my accountant – they all recommended I use QuickBooks." He adds that as long as he puts good data in, he can get good information back out. "Now I can get reams of information," he says.

He is obligated by his bank to produce a monthly profit and loss, and can do so in "about 30 seconds," Hans says. He and the banker both look at these and see if anything doesn't look quite right. If he sees something, he clicks through in QuickBooks to the entries involved to see if he can spot the problem.

"Using a computer program allows me to let my curiosity run wild," Hans says. "One question leads to another and another—I can easily answer 'How much did this cost in comparison to last year?'" Hans concludes that, because QuickBooks allows him to be more efficient, he has more time to be curious and to access more useful information.

Table 6.2 Another option for Subaccounts

Farm Truck		Expense
	Fuel	Expense
	Insurance	Expense
	Repairs and Maintenance	Expense
Tractor		Expense
	Fuel	Expense
	Insurance	Expense
	Repairs and Maintenance	Expense

Table 6.3 Grouped Expense Accounts

Account	
Infrastructure and Land	
	Rent Expense
	Utilities
Machinery and Equipment	
	Repairs and Maintenance
	Small Tools and Equipment
Operations	
	Seeds and Plants Purchased
	Fertilizers and Lime
	Control Products Purchased
	Fuel Used on the Farm
	Storage and Warehousing
	Freight and Trucking
	Truck Expenses
Overhead	
	Car Expenses
	Depreciation Expense
	Professional Fees
	Bank Service Charges
	Office Supplies
	Interest Expense
	Computer and Internet Expenses
	Insurance Expense
Sales and Marketing	
	Telephone Expense

as a major category, and the itemized expense accounts listed under each. With this organization (shown in Table 6.2) summary reports will total all of the expenses of operating the tractor or truck. However, this organization will not make it easy for you to see the total amount that you spent on all fuel, insurance, or repairs, as Table 6.1 would. As you get familiar with your farming operation you will begin to see ways to group data that gives you the information that is most useful. Each operation will have its own particular needs.

Overall Organization of Income and Expense Accounts

You can group various incomes and expenses into much broader categories that allow you to see how you receive or spend money in summarized form. These broad categories should reflect the various activities going on in the financial part of your operation. You can move the accounts out of the alphabetical sequence that your bookkeeping program started them in, and group them within your new headings of broader categories.

For instance, you might choose to set up major expense categories such as Infrastructure and Land, Labor, Machinery and Equipment, Operations, (for direct production related expenses), Sales and Promotion, and Overhead (for general expenses). Your bookkeeping program can create reports on a "collapsed" or "total" view, allowing you to quickly see all of your machinery and equipment costs for the year to date, or compare your overall sales and marketing costs from period to period.

Table 6.3 shows an example of a way to organize expense accounts. You could further divide these accounts to provide more detail, if desired. For example, Utilities could have additional subaccounts such as Propane and Electricity.

The way you set this up will depend on the information you want to get back out. In this simplified example, you could easily assess whether most of your expenses were going to growing the crops in Operations or to the Overhead needed to run the farm.

If you are running a labor-intensive farm, you will want to add a major level category for Labor, with subaccounts that could look like those in Table 6.4.

Organizing your chart of accounts logically can provide important perspective on what different activities actually cost. In Table 6.4, rather than putting worker's compensation insurance in Overhead: Insurance Expense, you are allocating it to the larger category it really affects, which is the cost of labor on the farm.

You may also use all of the above tools to organize your income accounts. For example, you may decide you want to organize your income to distinguish between what you make on your crops and what you bring in from government support payments and other income, as shown in Table 6.5.

You can move, add or merge accounts in your bookkeeping program at any time. However, there are some things to keep in mind before you do. If you add accounts, when you compare to previous periods the new accounts won't be represented. You can merge accounts if it seems that you have too much detail, but in doing so all previous transactions using either account will be converted to the new account. Names of accounts are also easy to change. (See the sidebar on page 52). Because of the complexity of comparing to previous records, it is best to make these kind of changes at the end of a fiscal year.

Other Ways to Categorize Your Information

Once you have your chart of accounts set up, your computer program allows additional ways to further classify financial information. In QuickBooks, the most commonly used method is called Classes. Classes turn the one-dimensional chart of accounts into a two dimensional grid, making it possible to organize any transaction in two ways instead of just one.

Classes were designed to facilitate things such as reporting by division or department, or by location. Think of this as a way to "classify" the financial activities on your farm. Classes allow you to categorize each income and expense entry into groups or categories of whatever definition makes sense for your operation.

Here are some examples of how you might use classes:
Separate expenses and incomes for different types of production or various enterprises. For instance, you may want to know how much you have coming in and out for either livestock or vegetable production on your farm. To track this, you might set up classes named something like Beef, Hogs, or Vegetables.

Distinguish expenses and incomes for different ways that you market your products. If you market your meat directly to consumers, to retail stores, and to a wholesale distributor, you might want to separate your income and expenses into classes named Direct, Retail, and Wholesale.

Track expenses and incomes for two different production locations. An example would be classes named Home Farm and North Farm.

Just like all lists in most computer bookkeeping programs you can set up the class list in a hierarchical structure, using class and subclasses to group different classifications to facilitate analysis. This helps if you want more detail on a specific class, but occasionally want to group it with other like classes. An example might be the class Farmers Markets, with subclasses St Joes Market, Raleigh Market, and South St Market.

When setting up classes it is important to choose parallel categories. For instance, if you had classes named Beef, Vegetables and Farmers' Market, you wouldn't be able to choose where to put the $100 you made selling steaks at the Saturday market, as the income

Table 6.4 Sample Labor Subaccounts

Labor		
	Payroll	
		Wages
		Payroll taxes
	Casual Labor	
	Contract Labor	
	Perks for Employees	
	Payroll Processing	
	Workers Compensation Insurance	

Table 6.5 Sample Income Subaccounts

Farming Income- production
Crop Sales
Farming Income- other
Fuel Tax Credits and Other Inc.
Cooperative Distributions
Crop Insurance Proceeds
Commodity Credit Loans
Agricultural Program Payments

Nested Accounts

To set up nested accounts in QuickBooks, first create the major categories in your account list. As you create subaccounts, you will have the option of selecting another account that it is a subaccount of.

If you have already set up accounts, you can reorganize them at any time by going into Lists>Chart of Accounts, selecting the account you'd like to change and clicking on the Account tab below. Select Edit Account, where you'll be given the option of making the account a subaccount.

Changing Account Names

Most computer bookkeeping programs will let you change the names and groupings of your accounts whenever you want to. Take advantage of this if you feel that how you initially set things up isn't quite right. Renaming or reassigning an existing account will change the name of all the transactions that you have used the account for.

If you would like to merge two accounts, most bookkeeping programs will allow you to rename the second the same as the first and then choose "yes" when asked if you'd like to merge the data.

You never want to delete or de-activate an account that you have used for any transactions, as it might not show those transactions when you run reports. If you decide you no longer want to use an account that you have entered transactions for, first go back to each of those transactions and assign them to a different account. (You can find these by running a profit and loss report and clicking on the total amount for the account you want to work on to see a display of each individual transaction. Click on each transaction, which you can then change.)

Once the account is empty you can make it "inactive" and it will be hidden from view. To do this in QuickBooks, go to Lists>Chart of Accounts, click on the account you want to make inactive. Go down to the tab named Account, click on Edit Account and then mark the Account is Inactive box.

QuickBooks won't let you name two accounts exactly the same, even if one is inactive, so if you change your mind, you will have to go back into Lists>Chart of Accounts, select the Accounts tab and click on Show Inactive Accounts. You can then click on the desired account and re-activate it. Or, you can create a new account with a slightly different name and go forward from there.

would belong in both the Beef and the Farmers' market classes. You can only identify one class for each unique entry. Though, of course, if you brought $300 home from the Saturday market, $100 could be for Beef and $200 could be for Vegetables, these could be entered on different lines of your sales receipt or deposit slip.

Sorting Your Data on a Third Plane

QuickBooks, and other bookkeeping programs, offers a third way to categorize your financial numbers. In QuickBooks this is called the Job function. Jobs allow you another way to sort your piles, and can be used much the way the Class function is used. If your operation is fairly simple, you may not use jobs (or even classes, for that matter), but some more complex operations may benefit from this deeper splitting system.

Let's look at an example. Say you happen to be farming in two locations – one the home farm, and one a rental property two miles down the road, which you call "Joe's Farm." Your main crops are grains and forages from a row crop rotation. You decide that you want to track both income and expenses from each piece of property. You also would like to track things by the type of crop or product. Using both the Class and the Job functions allows you to track both streams of information.

You have some corn and soybeans on both farms, but all of the hay is on the home farm. You may decide to set your classes up like those shown in Table 6.9.

But, if you decide you'd like to see what is going on at each farmstead, you can also set up job categories like those in Table 6.10.

We show here the total amount spent in each account for a given period. You can see that you have spent the same total dollars in each expense account, but they have been divided into different "piles." Setting up classes and jobs this way allows you to see how much you spent overall on seed by looking at the expense account line item total for Seed. You can see how much you spent on producing corn by running a class report and looking at the total for the class Corn. And you can see how much was spent at Joe's Farm by running a jobs report and looking at the column for Joe's Farm.

Table 6.9 Smith Farm Class List

Class Account	Corn	Soybeans	Hay	Total
Seed & Plants	950	520	0	1,470
Fertility & Lime	1,180	280	90	1,550
Labor	420	380	1,440	2,240
Total expenses	**2,550**	**1,180**	**1,530**	**5,260**

Each of these totals may be useful to you in your budgeting and decision making, such as how to allocate your time and labor resources. When you enter each income and expense transaction (a deposit from a sale, or a purchase or payment) into your bookkeeping program, you will enter each as an account item, and then choose a class and a job. You can decide to ignore either classes or jobs (or both), but if there are reasons to track things in two or three dimensions in your operation, jobs and classes make both possible.

A transaction, such as writing a check, would look like Figure 6.1 to capture your classes and jobs in QuickBooks.

As you enter the check you must choose what account each part of the transaction is assigned to (in this case you spent some on seeds and some on fertilizer), and then also choose a job and a class for each piece of the transaction. In this QuickBooks example, you can also leave the job and class blank if you don't use them.

Unfortunately, in QuickBooks you cannot generate a report that gives you both the job and the class—you will only be able to see the totals of one or the other at a time.

Summary

Anyone with the capacity to do so will benefit from setting up a computerized bookkeeping system. This can be as simple as a spreadsheet, which allows you to move data around and sort easily, or as complex as a number of bookkeeping programs. As you set up your bookkeeping program there are several decisions that must be made. The first will be the chart of accounts, which can be manipulated with account groupings for easier reporting. The use of classes and jobs helps to further sort data to help management. Most systems can and will change over time as you become more familiar with what you need.

Table 6.10 Smith Farm Job List

Job Account	Home Farm	Joe's Farm	Total
Seed & Plants	500	970	**1,470**
Fertility & Lime	530	1,020	**1,550**
Labor	1,640	600	**2,240**
Total expenses	**2,670**	**2,920**	**5,260**

OTTO'S TIP:

Turning on the Class Function
You may need to turn on the Class function in your bookkeeping program. To do this in QuickBooks, click on Edit at the top of your screen, then choose Preferences. When the preferences screen opens, click on Accounting, then the Company Preferences tab. Click on Use Class Tracking.

Figure 6.1 Smith Farm Check Entry

OTTO'S TIP:

Setting up Jobs in QuickBooks
To set up the individual jobs in your QuickBooks program you can go through the Customer Center and click on New Customer, and Job tab and then Add Job. Or, you can create new jobs as you are doing your data entry. Click on <add new> in the prompt window that will appear as you enter the Jobs field when you are writing a check, creating an invoice, or doing another kind of transaction.

From the Farmers

Help with Setting up your Computer Program

Kay Jensen, JenEhr Family Farm

"I love QuickBooks," says Kay Jensen of JenEhr Family Farm, "it is easy to use, and very intuitive." However, she recommends that you pay $500-800 to have an experienced bookkeeper or accountant set your system up.

"We're not accountants, and while we'll decide to set something up that makes sense to us, in two or three years we'll find that we can't get the numbers that we need." Someone with experience can set the program up in a standardized way. "The accountant will ask you questions that you haven't even thought of to set your system up right."

Kay points out an added bonus: if your system is standardized, it will be much easier to turn the work over to someone else if you ever decide to not do your own bookkeeping.

Class Options

You might not get your classes set up exactly the right way on the first try. As things change on your farm, your needs to track information change, too. Our farmer Sue started raising poultry, and was happy to track the sales at different markets using the classes Broilers and Turkeys. But then she started raising beef. She added the class for beef, but it got cumbersome for her to track all of the sales in her different markets. She realized that she really wanted to know how much she sold at each market, and so she changed her classes to reflect each of those. Table 6.8 shows what she ended up with, which worked well.

Table 6.6 Sue's First Accounts

Class / Account	Broilers	Turkeys	Total
Poultry Sales			
Poultry- farmers market	450	2,000	2,450
Poultry - co-op	600	4,000	4,600
Poultry - wholesale	1,200	2,400	3,600
Total Poultry Sales	***2,250***	***8,400***	***10,650***

Table 6.7 Sue's Sales Diversification

Class / Account	Broilers	Turkeys	Beef	Total
Meat Sales				
Poultry Sales				
Poultry- farmers market	450	2,000		2,450
Poultry - co-op	600	4,000		4,600
Poultry - wholesale	1,200	2,400		3,600
Total Poultry Sales	***2,250***	***8,400***		***10,650***
Beef Sales				
Ground beef			1,490	1,490
Roasts			1,650	1,650
Total Beef Sales			***3,140***	***3,140***
Total Meat Sold	2,250	8,400	3,140	13,790

Table 6.8 Sue's New Accounts

Class / Account	Farmers Market	Co-op	Wholesale	Total
Meat Sales				
Poultry Sales				
Broilers	450	600	1,200	2,250
Turkeys	2,000	4,000	2,400	8,400
Total Poultry Sales	***2,450***	***4,600***	***3,600***	***10,650***
Beef Sales				
Ground beef	450	365	675	1,490
Roasts	650	800	200	1,650
Total Beef Sales	***1,100***	***1,165***	***875***	***3,140***
Total Meat Sold	3,550	5,765	4,475	13,790

NOTES

DATA ENTRY

CHAPTER 7
Entering Data into Your Computer System

Key questions addressed in this chapter:

How do you enter specific types of data into your computer program?

How do you pay bills?

What are the best ways to track income?

What reports will be useful?

Getting Your Data into Your System

Now that you have the basic structure of your computer program set up, you can start entering data. Take the box or files of papers you created following our suggestions in Chapter 4 and one by one enter the data into your bookkeeping program. This will be easiest if you have a clear workspace in front of you. You will use several features of your computer program. In QuickBooks these will be Write Checks, Enter Credit Card Charges, Pay Bills, Issue Invoices, Receive Payments, Make Deposits, Reconcile Statements, and Create Reports.

Entering Receipt Data

If you have spent cash, used a debit card, or hand written checks out in the community for products or services, you will have a pile of receipts. To enter these into your computer program, open Write Checks and duplicate the information from your receipts or your handwritten check register onto the check screen. Choose the appropriate Bank account (including Cash on Hand) and the expense accounts for each transaction (there can be more than one expense account per check) and assign classes and jobs if appropriate. If the transaction has a meaningful number attached to it, such as a check or invoice number, enter that appropriately. The transaction date should be the date on the receipt, not the date you are doing the entry. Your bookkeeping program requires you to Write Checks whether you plan to print them or not—the check is your record of a cash payment transaction.

OTTO'S TIP: *In QuickBooks or Quicken you use the Tab key to move through the various fields on a screen in logical order. Hitting the Enter key will save the current transaction and create a new one.*

For instance, a $625 receipt for a check number 3252 written to the feed store will be recorded on a check, with the appropriate vendor listed as the check payee, and the check detail: $100 listed as Feed (account) and Horses (class), $320 as Feed (account) and Chickens (class), $200 as Bedding (account) and Chickens (class), and $5.00 for a bag of candy bars (including the tax) as Owner's Draw, class Household. This is shown in Figure 7.1. Since this was a hand-written check, the To be Printed box is not checked.

In QuickBooks or Quicken you can enter payments directly into your account Register by going to Banking and selecting Use Register and then selecting the appropriate banking account. However, if you simply fill data into the register screen you will not be able to split the transaction between different accounts or assign classes or jobs. In QuickBooks, if you double click on a transaction in the Register, it will open to the Write Checks field where you can then enter the detail. In Quicken this feature is found by clicking on the down arrow found next to the category field and selecting Split.

Debit card purchases are treated the same as a check, only without a check number. If you use one or more credit cards, you can enter those charges through the Enter Credit Card Charges function in the QuickBooks Banking Tab.

Paying Bills

If you pay bills directly from invoices and bills that come in the mail, you will either print checks through the computer or by handwriting and then recording in the program's check registry, as shown in Figure 7.1. If you want to use pre-printed computer checks you will have to order them from your bank or another vendor. We recommend that you get checks with at least one stub, so that you can staple that to an invoice once a bill is paid.

After you've written or printed the correct checks for your invoices, be sure to sign the checks, mark the invoices as "paid," remove any payment stubs and include those in the envelope with your check. The bill statements can then be filed in your To Be Filed or Current Month file.

Figure 7.1 Sample QuickBooks Check Entry

From the Farmers

Excel Spreadsheet Data Entry

Erin Pilgrim, Pilgrim Family Farm

Erin Pilgrim finds an Excel spreadsheet works well to do the basic bookkeeping needed for their dairy operation. She tries to always write checks for their farm purchases, and organize their system based on the needs for their annual Schedule F tax form reporting.

The spreadsheet is setup to track the same information as the paper forms that Mike learned to use from his mom, with checks numbers, dates and vendors listed down the first column, and expense categories across the top of the form. Erin enters data from the check ledger, with back up from her filed receipts to prepare for going to the accountant for annual tax prep.

Personal Expenses

OTTO'S TIP:

In the example here, since the candy bars are a personal expense and not part of the farm business (unless you want to categorize them as "Fuel"??!!), they are listed under Owner Draw, as they are a financial benefit back to the owner.

Paying Bills in QuickBooks

In QuickBooks you can use either of two methods to pay bills. You can either write checks directly, or enter the invoice information using the Pay Bills feature. If you wish to directly write checks in response to an invoice received, use the Write Checks feature shown in Figure 7.1, checking the To Be Printed box if you are using computer printed checks. QuickBooks will auto-fill a check number, be sure that it matches the next check in your stack of checks. Put your blank checks in the printer, and from the Print column choose Print Batch. After your checks print, cross check with your check Register to be sure the right numbers are assigned. (This is important for reconciliation. You can change check numbers in the Register if they come out wrong). Remember to take any unused checks out of the printer.

If you wish to pay bills by first entering invoices and then writing checks, in QuickBooks you will use the Vendors>Enter Bills screen. (In Quicken, go to Business>Create Bills.) Enter the vendor, the date of the bill, a reference or invoice number, the amount due, and the due date. You also use this screen to allocate the expense among various accounts. After you have entered the bills into your system, you can file the papers into a Bill Payments folder, so you can later come back and get payment stubs and any payment envelopes.

Later, using the Pay Bills function, you can see all of the bills you need to pay. Select the bills you want to pay, select the payment date (this is what will print on your checks), and select the appropriate money account. QuickBooks can accommodate paying bills either with a credit card or a check. If you use computer printed checks, QuickBooks will print them from the Pay Bills feature in alphabetical order. Don't forget to sign them before mailing!

If you accidentally print something else onto one of your check forms (very easy to do), be sure to enter that ruined check into your bookkeeping system. Enter the check information, and then go to Edit and click Void Check. Voiding damaged checks is important for bank statement reconciliations.

Most bookkeeping programs have some kind of Pay Bills feature. Although it may involve a little extra work, this can be useful for those with more complex operations or a need to manage tight cash flow. In using the Bills feature you enter bills into the computer as they come in, and then just press a few buttons after a reminder pops up at the appropriate time when your payments are due.

This feature puts the majority of your data entry at the front end of your process instead of the back end, providing insurance against unforeseeable events that may keep you from the thinking-work of data entry. It also provides a valuable way to manage your available cash on hand, allowing you to compare short term outflows of cash to expected inflows. (See the Sidebar about how to use this feature in QuickBooks).

It can save some time to sit down once a week and write post-dated checks for upcoming bills, waiting to put them in the mail until the day you've designated. Write the mailing date on the stamp spot, or use your tickler or reminder system to track when to mail them.

Tracking Income

QuickBooks, and most other computer bookkeeping programs, has three primary ways of accounting for money flowing in: by using the deposit function to list income ready for deposit, by receiving payments of cash sales and creating cash receipts, and through creating invoices and receiving payments on those invoices.

The simplest of these is to account for income directly by making a deposit. While this doesn't let you account for individual items you've sold within a transaction, it does allow you to account for who you received payment from, the check number, and how you want to allocate that income. Direct deposits like this work well for non-production income, such as land rent and government payments received. Figure 7.2 shows a QuickBooks Make Deposits screen.

You may prefer to use sales receipts and invoicing functions, which allow you to allocate a single payment to more than one account, and itemize what you have sold. If you have more than a couple of different items that you sell, the itemized sales information these methods can provide will be useful for tracking and production decision making.

You can use the Enter Sales Receipts function when you get money at the time you sell your product. This can be used, for example,

OTTO'S TIP: *Window envelopes come in two sixes—"Check" and "Invoice." Check-sized envelopes fit computerized checks, which are slightly smaller than a regular piece of paper folded into thirds. Invoice-sized envelopes—also called #10 or standard business-sized envelopes—fit a piece of paper folded into thirds. Buying the right kind of envelopes is important, as the address of a check's recipient won't line up correctly on a #10 envelope, and the amount of a check can often be seen through the window.*

From the Farmers

Items Preserve a Lot of Information

Brad Igl, Igl Farms

Potato sales at Igl Farms are tracked using invoices created in QuickBooks with separate items and categories (potato variety, package type and size, potato size, and grade), for everything sold. From this Brad Igl can see at the end of the month, or end of the season, how much they have sold to each customer, and how much of each variety and pack size has been sold.

He uses this information for ordering supplies such as potato bags and cartons, and for planning on how many acres of potatoes to plant for the next season.

The Igls use the information from customer sales to plan how much of each variety they will plant for the coming season. Some varieties get a better premium than others, so they try to make sure to plant enough to meet what their sales expectations may be, but not too much so they don't have to lower the price to sell excess.

for income received at a farmers' market, or for a commodity payment that comes in the mail. You simply create a sales receipt for any products sold, detailing items sold, prices, and quantities. For environments such as a farmers' market, where you make dozens or hundreds of small transactions in a given sales event, you could choose to account for each of those sales with a separate sales receipt, but most growers choose to lump all of the sales for a given market on a given day into a single transaction.

For example, in Figure 7.3 on page 61 the customer on a receipt is Farmers Market Customers, and the item is Farmers Market Sales with a single entry of the entire $628 brought in on that day at that market.

The Invoicing function is used when you deliver an item before you receive payment for it, such as selling produce or meat to a retail store or wholesale distributor. You enter the same information as you do for a sales receipt, with the addition of a field for Terms that tells a customer when you expect payment (see Figure 7.4). These invoices can be printed and given to the customer and will be stored electronically.

Paper copies of invoices should be filed in a folder labeled Due, which is helpful for collections tracking. Most farmers write invoices when orders are packed and ready for delivery instead of as part of a weekly bookkeeping regime, although some find it easier to hand write the invoices and enter information from a copy into their computer program later.

Figure 7.2 QuickBooks Make Deposit Screen

Deposit To	rs Credit Union	Date	01/14/2020	Memo	Deposit			
Click Payments to select customer payments that you have received. List any other amounts to deposit below.								
RECEIVED FROM	FROM ACCOUNT		MEMO		C...	PMT M...	CLASS	AMOUNT
Neighbor Rusty	44200 · Rent Income		annual pasture rent			Check	General Farm	600.00
U.S. Government	41200 · Agricultural Program Payments		DCP			Check	General Farm	283.00

DATA ENTRY

Speeding up Data Entry

Your bookkeeping program will offer a number of ways to speed up data entry. The following are some QuickBooks examples.

You can set up Memorized Transactions for frequently recurring items. If it's always exactly the same—the way a local phone bill might be—you can set the memorized transaction to automatically enter the information on a given day of the month. If you have a monthly bill that automatically comes out of your checking account or gets charged to your credit card, you can set up that transaction to happen every month and simply forget about it. (In QuickBooks create a transaction as you would like it to be memorized—you have the option of leaving parts blank to fill in each time. Then go to Edit>Memorize Transaction. A screen will open in which you can set the frequency and level of automation.)

You can set QuickBooks to use the most recent past transaction for a vendor to auto-fill fields for the current transaction. This way, even though your electric bill varies from month to month, when you enter the name of the electric company on a bill or a check, the right account and class automatically fill in. You will have to modify the amount each month before you save the current transaction. (Go to Edit>Preferences>General>My Preferences and click "Automatically recall information"). This feature will affect all of your transactions, so if you have more things that change than stay the same, you may be better off to not use this option.

You might decide that the name of the vendor doesn't even matter for some transactions, and use instead a shortcut for a certain type of always-the-same transaction. For example, if you don't need to track the name of the station where you buy gas for your truck, you could create a vendor "tGas" (for Truck Gas) that auto-fills the correct account name and classification.

If you use the Invoicing feature in your computer program, you'll want to process payments you receive on a weekly basis, just like you do checks and credit card charges. Using the Receive Payments function, you enter the customer, the amount of the payment, the date of the payment, the payment method, and any check number. QuickBooks will generate a list of the outstanding invoices for that customer, and you can select which invoices to apply the payment to.

QuickBooks allows you to customize an invoice template, including things like your logo and website. They can be printed from the Create Invoice screen and mailed or given to your customer at delivery.

You will be able to print a list of outstanding invoices to help with collections. Run the "A/R" (Accounts Receivable) report once a week to track who owes you money and if they are due for a reminder. Computer programs allow you to reprint invoices, making sending a new copy easy. Remember that a non-payment may be from a lost invoice or a simple mistake, a phone call or email with a cordial tone is the best approach in maintaining good customer relations when tracking overdue payments.

Setting up Your Item List

If you want to track the individual items you sell you'll need to set up an Item List which is used to generate invoices and sales receipts. Your item list will be a list of all of the things that you sell, in the various units they are offered, each associated with one of your accounts, and prices attached (if desired).

You have the option of editing the item price when you enter the information for a particular transaction. Items also have a particular Type associated with them. If you are providing goods (such as carrots, hamburger, or cows) and don't use your bookkeeping program to track inventory, you'll want to set up your items as Non-inventory Parts.

In QuickBooks you set up items by clicking on Item List in the Customer tab. Each item can have a standard price associated with it, or the price can be left blank if it varies. It can also be changed as needed when used in transactions.

You can run reports using dates of your choice that will tell you the number and dollar value of all of the items you have sold. This is very useful for planning, inventory tracking and profitability analysis, which we'll talk about in upcoming chapters. Knowing this, you can make your item list as complicated or as simple as you want. For example, you could simply have one item for Beef and another for Lamb. Or, you could have items named Beef—Halves, and Beef—Quarters, or you could create items for each cut of meat you sell.

Likewise, you could track farmers' market sales down to the individual items sold—pounds of tomatoes, or bags of salad greens—or you could lump them all together into an item called simply Farmers' Market Sales.

In organizing your item list you may want to nest your items to make it easy to find the items later, and to create groupings and subtotals in reports. You will need to think about how you'll want to extract information later when you put together your nested list of items. In Figure 7.1, we see two choices on how a list could be set up. The first group is organized into Bulk Herbs and Bunched Herbs. The items are named for quick data entry B30Dill (30 bunches) or 1Dill (1 bulk unit). Organized this way, you can get total numbers sold and income of bunched herbs or of bulk herbs. In the second grouping, reports would tell you how much dill or parsley you'd sold in a particular period of time. Since you also have the option of assigning each purchase to a class, you have a lot of options for tracking your sales data.

Back up Your Data

Any computer technician will tell you: all hard drives will fail, it's just a matter of when. Because of the importance of financial records and the huge mess that can result from losing even a day's work, you can't afford not to back up your financial files. You should back up your data in a way that gets it off of your hard drive, and ideally out of your computer. It is very easy to transfer a copy of your files to a memory key/thumb drive/stick on a regular basis,

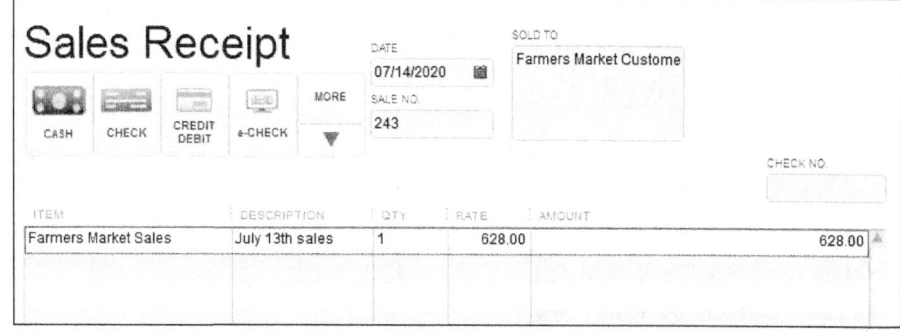

Figure 7.3 QuickBooks Sales Reciept

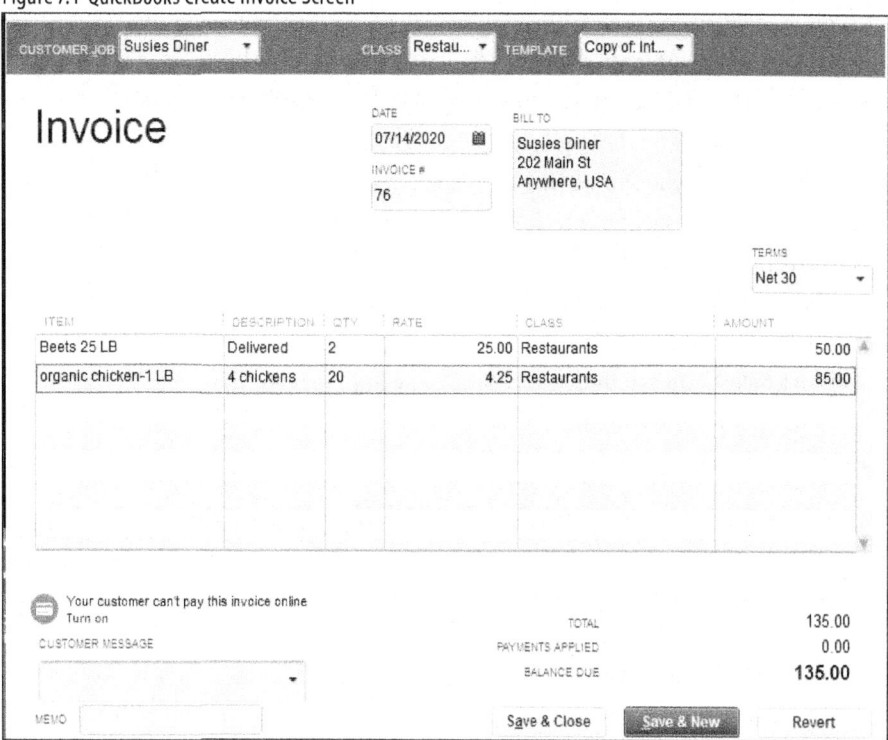

Figure 7.4 QuickBooks Create Invoice Screen

Table 7.1 Item Grouping Options

Option One	Option Two

Bunch Herbs
    B30Dill
    B30Parsley
Bulk Herbs
    1Dill
    1Parsley
	Dill
	    B30Dill
	    1Dill
	Parsley
	    B30Parsley
	    1Parsley

DATA ENTRY

Using Your Computer to Find Filed Records

lYour computer bookkeeping system can make it easy to find historical information. For example, perhaps you want to know "How much did I get paid per pound for my six steers last year?"

In your bookkeeping system, run a profit and loss report for the year, and look at the detail for the account Live Animal Sales. If this is where you record steer sales, you should be able to see the transaction, which you can open for the details of where and when the animals were sold (in this case, October, 20XX at Equity Livestock Sales). You can then track the hard copy receipt with the detail you are looking for.

If your files are organized by month, you would check the October 20XX folder. If you file by vendor you'd check the Equity Livestock folder for the detailed receipt. If you file by alphabet you'd find the D-F file for the year.

If you file by account, you probably don't need to open the electronic record, as the receipt should be easy to find in your Live Animal Sales folder. Of course, if this is useful information to have readily available, you could decide to write the per pound price in the "notes" field of your electronic deposit or receipt transaction, and then you could avoid the paper search altogether!

or to use an online backup system. A good computer-wide backup system will save you the trouble of having to remember to act to save all of your critical data.

Periodically, you'll want to back up your financial data in a way that gets it off site, or at least out of your office. A separate memory key that you rotate with another one at a neighbor's house, or that you mail to a relative, can work well.

One simple way to backup is to set QuickBooks to back up to a folder located on your computer called Backups. QuickBooks doesn't really approve of backing up to the same drive where your file is located, and that makes sense, but you can set your Backups folder to upload to an online service (such as www.carbonite.com, www.moseypro.com or www.crashplanpro.com/business) every night. You can also get an online backup service that continually backs up your computer whenever it's not doing anything else. Automating like this saves you remembering, and also ensures an off-site backup, very useful in allowing you to maintain your business records in times of tragedy such as a house fire or computer crash.

OTTO'S TIP: *You can set QuickBooks to back up your file every time you close it. This may seem like a lot of work and wasted time, but it's pretty inexpensive insurance. From the File menu choose Save Copy or Backup and follow the prompts to select your choices.*

Utilizing Computer Reporting

To get information back out of your computer bookkeeping program you use the Reports function. In QuickBooks, you'll primarily use the reports in the Company and Financial Section of the Reports menu.

The various reports can give you a good snapshot of the immediate activity of your farm. A simple and useful choice is a profit and loss sorted by either class or job. Either report will show you the totals of all the entries made for any date range you choose, grouped either by class or job.

Depending on how you have set up your accounts, you can find answers to questions like "How much income have we brought home from the farmers' market in June?" or "What have we paid for poultry feed so far this year?" or "What were the total costs we've put into the beef operation this year?" (This last is presuming Beef was one of your classes.) You will want to explore the Reports function in your program to see all the useful things you can learn. Some of these reports will be used to build your annual analyses described in upcoming chapters.

Remember that any one report won't provide you with all of the financial information that pertains to your business. For example, the profit and loss report only reports on income and expense accounts, and doesn't include information about loan payments or draws from the business accounts. You will want to explore all of the report options to decide which will be most useful to your operation.

Summary

QuickBooks and other bookkeeping programs offer several options for tracking the receipt of income and payments made or due. Specific features are appropriate for tracking detail in different types of situations. Reports are automated summaries of the data that you enter into your system, and can be run regularly to help you get a quick snapshot of your financial activity.

From the Farmers

Quick Reports Help You Stay on Track

Matt O'Hayer, Vital Farms

Matt O'Hayer of Vital Farms recommends farmers run a profit and loss report by the 10th of each month for the previous month. "It doesn't help to wait till the end of the year to see that you are losing money all year," he says, "You need the information so that you can make changes." You should look at the bottom line, and compare things like feed costs and other expenses to previous periods to see that nothing is getting out of line.

In the poultry business, Matt feels good if a third of his revenue goes to feed, a third goes to labor, and a third goes to profit and other expenses.

This kind of rough figuring can give him a quick look to see if his major expenses, feed and labor, are on track with his income. "Right now feed costs are really high, but I know that this is temporary. Feed can vary up to 40 or 45 percent of total costs and we can still work with it."

With this rough estimate Matt can quickly see how his income and expenses are lining up.

Making Bank Deposits in QuickBooks

If you are using the Receive Payment and Enter Sales Receipts functions, even though you've told QuickBooks that you brought in money, you haven't told it where you want the money to go. Once you've entered payments, you have to make a deposit. When you use the Make Deposits function, be certain you've selected the correct bank account to make deposits to, and then select the payments you want to deposit.

If you didn't use the Receive Payment or Enter Sales functions, or have additional payments not associated with a previous QuickBooks entry (e.g. a rent check or a refund), you can type those into the deposit screen by hand.

Entering into your Make Deposits screen will record the income into your computer, but you will still need to make out a bank deposit slip and take or mail the checks to the bank.

If you've combined multiple checks into one payment, such as for the farmers' market example earlier, it will work best to do that as a separate deposit. If you have any online payments, such as from PayPal, be sure to enter those, including any item or inventory detail, into your system.

CHAPTER 8
Learning Though Non-Financial Data

Key questions addressed in this chapter:

Why is non-financial data important?

What types of non-financial data might you want to collect?

What are some examples of how non-financial data is used?

We are concentrating in this book on your financial record keeping system, but there are lots of records every farm needs to keep that fall out of the realm of financial systems. Each specific type of farming operation will have unique types of non-financial data that will be useful. It will be impossible for us to list all of the types of data needed on every farm, but we will give some general ideas to help you understand how non-financial data can help in your decision making.

There are many sources of sample record keeping forms for numerous types of non-financial data collection. For a start on where to look, see our Resources section. Your area Extension office can be a great source of templates. You may also look up the specific record name or even "farm record keeping" in your favorite computer search engine to find an array of sample forms. Many of the following types of data can be simply kept using a record notebook or computer spreadsheet program, such as Excel.

In Chapter 16 we will explain the process of enterprise budgeting. You will need to collect a variety of non-financial data to do these analyses.

Production Yields

Whether you are a dairy farmer, a potato grower, an egg producer, or run a vegetable CSA, knowing how much of each product is being produced gives you valuable information about productivity and profitability. In your financial data you will be tracking

OTTO'S TIP: *Those planning of running certified organic operations will collect most of the information we list in this chapter for those certification records. For sample record keeping forms, see ATTRA, attra.ncat.org.*

total income, and some of you will track income by each type of product (item) you sell. But, most farms will also benefit from tracking actual yields. Yield data can be associated with additional information, such as which field, bed, date of harvest, barn, or animal yielded what quantity over what particular period of time. The secret to useful production data is to think about what data will be useful to you, what accompanying data will be needed, how often it should be collected, and where an effective collection point should be.

For instance, if you want to track the number of eggs your laying hens produce, you may create a simple chart that is posted in the washing area, and is filled in daily with the date, number of eggs collected, and perhaps egg house collected from if your operation is large. Diversified small scale vegetable producers may track harvest of each crop by pound or bunches with a sheet tacked up in the packing shed that is filled in each harvest day. This list may indicate which field or bed was harvested, the size of the harvest crew, and notes on any field or crop conditions. Dairy producers may use Dairy Herd Improvement (DHI) equipment to measure each cow's yield on a monthly or bimonthly basis.

Those with crops that get harvested in large batches over short periods, such as steers, hogs, or lambs that get shipped, or field crops, will have an easier, but no less important task. These records may indicate live or hanging weight per animal sold, or total bushels harvested per field. Tracked data may also include where the product was sold or stored.

Whatever tracking system you set up, it must be easy to use, accessible to those that need to use it, and create data that is easy to transfer and collate. You can calculate your productivity (see sidebar on page 66), and compare from period to period to see general trends. Changes in yields can indicate needed management changes. Keeping track of yields by seed variety or breed of animal can help you make choices when adding or expanding in the future.

Production Base

How big is each of your fields or beds? How many calves are you feeding? How many trees of each variety are you harvesting from? How many cows are going through the parlor at each milking? How many row feet of raspberries are you picking from?

This may seem simplistic and obvious, but knowing your production base is very valuable, and in many operations, changing information. This will affect your analysis of profitability when you put these numbers with income and expenses. Data such as field sizes probably won't change often, while numbers of animals being fed may change frequently.

If you are experiencing animal losses, you will want to know as soon as possible so that you can change your management. A weasel in the henhouse can cause catastrophic losses, but can be dealt with if your animal inventory tells you that something is invading your flock. From loss figures you can figure mortality rates, which can be improved by management.

Feed, Fertility, and Other Inputs Used

In your financial data you will track the costs of feed, fertility, and inputs used, but it is also valuable to track actual amounts used. Fluctuations in quality and price will

> ## From the Farmers
>
>
>
> Non-Financial Records are Important Too
>
> **Jackie Hoch**
> **Hoch Orchard & Gardens**
>
> *On the cooler door of Hoch Orchard and Gardens is an Excel spread sheet with columns labeled Area, Variety, Date, and Volume. Jackie Hoch instructs each of her employees and interns each year exactly how to record their harvest information on the sheet.*
>
> *"It is very important to design your record keeping systems to mirror what you want to enter into the computer," Jackie says. "Think about what you need to know, and organize it so that it is really easy for someone to do data entry." Jackie adds that "Notebook entries have some value, but if the information isn't organized it is hard to get much back out."*

From the Farmers

Calculating Mortality

Andrea Gunner, Rosebank Farm

Andrea Gunner knows that loss is an important factor for poultry producers, and can almost always be corrected through management.

Andrea figures loss by taking the number of chicks received from the hatchery and subtracting from that the number of birds she sent to the processor, giving her the number of birds that were lost.

The number of birds lost divided by the total number received gives her the percent mortality. (2,000 chicks received – 1,852 chicks processed = 148 chicks lost. 148 chicks lost divided by 2,000 chicks received equals 7.4 percent loss. 2,000 - 1,852 = 148. 148/2,000 = 7.4 percent mortality).

In this batch of 2,000 birds, 7.4 percent didn't make it to processing. Higher than she'd like, Andrea is working to lower the figure with her management.

Productivity

Productivity = total number of units produced/production base

- 800 pounds strawberries picked/ .014 acre bed = 5,714 Lbs/acre

- 42,000 pounds of milk per month / 25 cows = 1,680 pounds of milk per cow per month

- 175 eggs per day / 200 hens = .875 eggs per hen, or 87.5% productivity (lay rate)

---

interfere with your ability to make generalizations about amounts used by looking only at costs. Once again, a tracking system must be set up that fits the particular needs of your operation.

Applying lime to a field can be a one-time notation, per field, of pounds applied per acre. The amount of creep feed used to start calves, piglets, or lambs can be pounds fed per week for an entire age group. However, the larger your operation grows, the more carefully you will want to track specific amounts of feed, fertility, or inputs used. The multiplier effect can add up quickly as your operation grows when simple mistakes are made.

This data will again be important in your ability to assess profitability per enterprise, and to identify any opportunity for change to improve it. It will also be useful in non-quantifiable ways, as it will help you to see trends over time. Are soil tests showing that your fertility is improving, allowing you to apply less of certain nutrients? Tracking inputs will show trends that can reflect improvement (or deterioration) in your management over time.

Animal Weights and Growth

Those raising any kind of animals will generally want to track starting and ending weights so they can calculate feed utilization and efficiency. These numbers can then be compared to previous years or batches, or to industry standard benchmarks. Those raising smaller animals may choose to weigh randomly selected growing stock on a weekly or monthly basis. Those with larger animals will track weights when the animals are sold, and do a calculation to find average rate of gain and ultimately, the feed cost per pound of gain (see sidebar on page 67). If this changes up or down over time, it can indicate a needed management change.

Reproduction Rates

Animal producers will also want to track the reproduction rate of their breeding herd or flock. Generally this will be some kind of annual record keeping system. Tracking reproduction allows you to manage the genetic lines of your herd or flock, and track broader management issues such as feed quality or other things which may affect reproduction rates on a broad scale. Those raising large animals will keep health sheets on each animal, which include a distinct animal identification, veterinary, health, and reproduction data.

Labor

Labor is generally one of the largest inputs into a farming venture. It is extremely valuable to track the labor spent on each enterprise. Although this can be very time intensive, data will be critical in assessing productivity and profitability if crops are assessed at the enterprise level. Time spent considering effective methods for tracking your and other worker's paid and unpaid labor helps in developing consistent habits. It is best to develop a system, either a modified time sheet, a notebook, or a cell phone app which is used daily by each person working on the farm to describe what they have done that day.

If you have a crew, it is useful to develop consistent ways to identify areas of the farm and types of work. (For instance: "Jamie: 2 hours: hoeing beets: bed 12," entered onto a spreadsheet for each worker with columns labeled: hours, activity, crop, location, gives you data that can be used to plan staffing needs and pricing.) It is the ideal to track your own and other family member's labor, even if you are not being paid an hourly wage. Fluctuating labor rates from year to year may indicate troubles with worker training or other factors that may affect efficiency. We will discuss labor more in Chapter 22.

Simple Narratives

Many farmers find it useful to keep simple narrative diaries about farm activities. Best if done on a daily or weekly basis, these may be notes about weather, equipment, field conditions, harvest and planting dates, and other farm impressions. Notations in a simple notebook kept in the tractor or a pocket, or an entry in a computer log can be invaluable in adding depth to management decisions.

The trick to a successful system is to find one that you will actually use, be it a clipboard in the shed, a calendar in the kitchen, a notebook in your pocket or a cell phone app. Find one that feels comfortable and commit to using it. If your production data tells you that your soybean yields were half what they were the previous year, and your notebook tells you that it rained every day in September, you have evidence that helps you understand even years down the road what impacted that crop.

Notes relating to marketing can be invaluable, too. For instance, take a notebook to the farmers market and write down memorable comments from customers. These can be used to not only improve your products, but also in marketing if they show you in a positive light. You may also find it useful to track when you run out of a given item each market day—a potential indicator of expanded market opportunity.

Summary

Although in this book we focus on tracking and analyzing financial data, non-financial data is also very important. Different types of operations will need to track different kinds of data. Setting up systems that collect useful information and are simple to use are key. Non-financial data can be combined with financial data for useful analyses.

This is not an exhaustive list of types of non-financial data you will want to keep, but perhaps helps you see the types of information that may be useful to track. We recommend that you find other farmers, or information about operations similar to yours, to find out what kind of non-financial data will be most useful for your specific enterprise.

Useful Livestock Calculations

Total Weight Gain = ending weight – starting weight

Average Daily Gain = ending weight – starting weight / number of days of growth.

Feed per Pound of Gain = Total pounds of feed consumed per animal / total weight gain. (This is much more difficult to figure for grazing animals.)

Feed Cost per Animal = pounds of feed fed per animal x price of feed per pound

Feed Cost per Pound of Gain = feed cost per animal / total weight gain

---

From the Farmers

Keep a Regular Written Narrative

Carmen Fernholz, A-Frame Farm

Carmen Fernholz's dad told him many years ago to sit down every winter and write about the kind of farming year he'd had. Carmen followed this advice, expanding to weekly, or daily notes about farm conditions and activities.

He keeps a small notebook in his tractor and will write about the weather, what he is planting where and when, any cultivation activity, and other thoughts about what is going on.

These kinds of records are required by the organic standards, but Carmen goes beyond the basic requirements. "I write about soil conditions, how the equipment is working, and how things were in the field. When I review the notes in winter, I can see what I was thinking, what was going on when I wrote down that I needed a tine weeder or a new cultivator. I'd forget all the detail if I didn't write it down."

Carmen transfers his notes into his computer weekly, and reviews them annually. He says that an Excel spread sheet, a WORD document or even notes in an Outlook calendar will work well. "Whatever works for you" he says.

"By looking back at my notes over the years, I've learned that every year from mid-June through mid-July we have a dry spell. Now I know that I should plant my fall crops in mid-August, to be sure that they get a little rain before going into the fall." While Carmen might have figured this out from experience, he now has proof rather than relying on memory.

From the Farmers

Know the Key Statistics for Your Operation

Matt O'Hayer, Vital Farms

As the experienced overseer and advisor for several farms, Matt O'Hayer of Vital Farms knows the key things that Vital Farms farmers must track to assess each farm's profitability and management success. In pastured egg production, Matt says there are three key numbers to track:

How many animals you have (in this case, laying hens). It seems crazy, but this is a number that is not very easy for egg producers to know, but is very important in assessing profitability and animal welfare. No matter what kind of livestock operation you have, if you are feeding those animals you need to know how many there are. To count laying hens, Matt recommends the farmers go into the henhouses at night when the birds are on the roosts and count using a red headlamp. These counts are done at the end of each month, "just like a regular inventory," Matt says. This number is key in assessing feed consumption/conversion, and lay rates.

How much feed you are feeding. Visiting lots of farms every year, Matt is amazed at how many don't know how much feed they are feeding. "Since feed is the number one cost in an egg operation, and will consume 30-50 percent of your revenue, it is key that you are very careful how much you feed." Over-feeding of laying hens will produce super large eggs, which don't sell well, and cause prolapses, leading to pecking and even death. Underfeeding will reduce the lay rate. Other animal species will have other types of problems, but all have ideal amounts they should be fed at their different life stages. Matt recommends any livestock producer go online and find the production manual for the specific breed you are raising. "These manuals are based on years of science, there is no reason we need to second guess the science," Matt says. To measure feed, he suggests that you weigh the exact amount recommended for the stage of growth your animals are in and mark a line on feed buckets. However, he cautions that you should regularly re-weigh, as different batches of feed will weigh differently, due to slight variations in the grind. "If you are feeding $7,000 worth of feed, and your weight is off by 10 percent, that means you are losing $700 in feed costs alone, not to mention the other problems you are causing."

Know your per animal production rate. With eggs the final product in a laying operation, obviously the number of eggs produced per bird is a key profitability factor. The Vital Farms farmers write down the total number of eggs collected each day and plot the numbers on charts or in Excel. The rate of lay is related to the amount of feed, as well as the age of the birds, and how they are managed. Close tracking of the lay rate allows the farmers to respond quickly to optimize production. Matt says that if the birds are on especially good pasture, he may be able to reduce the feed from 25 pounds per 100 birds to 23 pounds per hundred birds and still keep the ideal lay rate of 85-90 percent (total eggs per day divided by the total number of hens). Feeding two pounds less per hundred birds will be a big cost savings when a flock has 400 birds. (4 x 2 lbs x 35 cents/lb = $2.80 per day or $86/month).

From the Farmers

Tracking Labor Pays

David Perkins, Vermont Valley Community Farm

Managing production for 900 CSA boxes each week, David Perkins of Vermont Valley Community Farm will occasionally track labor for specific activities, especially if he is seeing problems. At their large scale of operation, even small variations or inefficiencies will quickly add up. "This year the beets came up extra slow, and so the weeds came first. We had to do 100% hand weeding, costing us $3,500 in labor for beet weeding alone; meaning very expensive beets."

The knowledge this kind of tracking provides helps with future management decisions. "Knowing when to declare defeat is important. If the weeds outgrow the beets again we will till in the weedy beets and consider options: replant, transplant the next planting, or possibly try to trade some of our potatoes for another farm's beets." he says. VVCF is a well-established potato producer, with very efficient growing methods. "Knowing what you do best, and making informed management decisions when things start to go wrong are important for success."

SECTION THREE
THE BIG PICTURE: ORGANIZING BASIC FINANCIAL INFORMATION

Up to now we have talked about the daily and weekly work of collecting and organizing your financial information. Now we change focus and concentrate on a series of annual reports that use the data you have collected to show various overviews of your farm's financial position. While reports such as the profit and loss run from your bookkeeping program can tell you where you spend your money and if you spend more than you take in, you must create an annual balance sheet, income statement, and statement of cash flows to fully understand your financial situation. These standardized reports are common to all businesses, and sound familiar to any established farmer, as they are the bedrocks that farm financial management is built on.

In this section we want you to concentrate on the elements that go into creating each of the statements, and what each statement tells you about the financial health and activities of your operation. They should be created at least annually, but more often for review purposes or for specific needs, such as for obtaining loans and preparing taxes. Comparing the statements from year to year and/or comparing to other farms will leave you with a lot of information useful in making management decisions.

The information you collect in your bookkeeping system provides the data that builds each of the statements discussed in this section. The statements are generally developed by hand (using a computerized spreadsheet program is most efficient), allowing you to fully understand the numbers going in and to make the needed adjustments so the statements accurately reflect your incomes, expenses, and asset balances.

To aid in your understanding of the standardized financial statements we have created a sample farm for a mythical farmer named Otto B. Organic. The University of Minnesota Center for Farm Financial Management financial analysis software program "FINPACK" (cffm.umn.edu) was used to set up Otto's financial scenario, create statements, and run ratios, which we'll talk about in the next section. We invite you to refer to Otto's statements and figures as you follow the details of this and the next section.

CHAPTER 9
Owning and Owing: The Balance Sheet

Key questions addressed in this chapter:

Why is the balance sheet useful?

What goes into making a balance sheet?

How do you determine and track the items that make up a balance sheet?

Your balance sheet is the most basic financial statement for your farm operation. Simply put, your balance sheet is a snapshot of your farm's financial position at a particular point in time. It's sort of a financial report card. It contains everything you own, everything you owe, and what would be left if the farm had to be sold.

All of the things that you own as part of your farm business are categorized on the balance sheet as "assets." All of the dollars the farm business owes to others, or would have to pay out if the farm were to be sold, are considered to be "liabilities." The difference between assets and liabilities is considered to be "owner's equity" or "net worth." It represents your investment in the farm.

The balance sheet is useful for a number of reasons. First, it shows the farm's "solvency," or the extent to which the farm's assets would be able to pay its liabilities if everything was sold. If there would not be enough farm assets to cover all of its liabilities, the farm would be considered to be "insolvent."

Second, the balance sheet allows you to calculate your farm's "liquidity" and net working capital position. Liquidity is the ability of the farm to cover the financial obligations that are due right now, or that will come due within a year, using only the farm's cash or other short-term assets. Liquidity is an important indicator of the farm's financial strength. Strong liquidity allows you to withstand unexpected setbacks or to take advantage of unexpected opportunities that might pop up from time to time.

Third, comparisons of balance sheets from different periods can be used to monitor the farm's financial progress over time. This lets you know if the value of your investment in the farm is growing or shrinking.

Fourth, the balance sheet can be used in combination with other financial statements to evaluate many different aspects of the farm's financial performance. Put the balance sheet and the income statement together and you can calculate a series of profitability ratios which will tell you if the farm is generating an adequate return on the capital invested in the farm. The balance sheet combined with the statement of cash flows allows you to determine the farm's "capital debt repayment capacity," which is an important indicator of the farm's ability to handle financial risk, and important when you approach a lender to ask for a loan.

Finally, the balance sheet shows some key relationships between assets and liabilities. For example, it indicates how the farm's debt is structured, which is very useful in troubleshooting cash flow problems.

We'll start our balance sheet discussion with an overview of the document and the parts that make it up, and then give you detail on how to create your own balance sheet.

Farm Balance Sheets are Different From Other Business' Balance Sheets

Farm balance sheets look different than those from other businesses due to some differences in the way farm financial status is tracked. In agriculture, assets are usually listed on the balance sheet at their current market value, or what somebody would pay for those assets if they were sold today. It doesn't matter what you paid for that tractor; if you could sell it today for $2,000, it appears on the balance sheet with a value of $2,000. This is called a "market value" balance sheet.

Most other businesses use a "cost basis" balance sheet. Each asset is listed on the balance sheet at its original cost minus the amount that the asset has depreciated during the time the business has owned it. It doesn't matter what that tractor is worth today; if it was purchased eight years ago for $5,000 and depreciated $500 each year since (for a total depreciation to date of $4,000), it appears on the cost basis balance sheet with a value of $1,000.

There are logical reasons why a market value balance sheet is used in agriculture. It is simpler to develop, since you don't have to keep track of when each asset was purchased and how much it has depreciated over the years. Also, the balance sheet is often developed at the request of the farm's lender, who needs it for credit analysis purposes. The lender needs to know what the farm assets are worth right now as collateral to support a loan request, not what they cost ten or fifteen years ago.

Finally, a market value balance sheet allows for a more accurate comparison of one farm's financial performance to another's. For instance, one farmer may have purchased her land 40 years ago for $300 per acre while her neighbor purchased his land last year for $4,000 per acre. It would be impossible to make a reasonable comparison of the two farms' financial performance unless asset values were assigned comparable values.

At Times a Cost Basis Balance Sheet is Useful

Even though it is much more common to use a market value balance sheet in agriculture, there are good reasons to use a cost basis balance sheet, too. A cost basis balance sheet takes market value changes out of the equation, which allows you to see how the financial performance of the farm business alone, rather than broad market trends such as real estate values, impact your owner's equity. If the farm was profitable and the profits

BALANCE SHEET

Tracking Asset Value Changes in Your Bookkeeping System

Changes in value of assets, such as adjusting for market value changes or depreciation, can be made in your computer bookkeeping program on an annual basis. Doing these adjustments will assure that your balance sheet and other reports will reflect your most current information.

Your tax accountant can give you a depreciation table for your assets. He or she can recommend a monthly or annual "depreciation expense" that can be entered by using the General Journal function in your bookkeeping program.

If you enter depreciation into your program, it will show up in your generated reports. You will have to keep in mind that depreciation, although real, is not a cash transaction, and so, though it will show on a profit and loss statement as an expense, will not actually be dollars out the door for that year.

For this reason, many people choose not to track depreciation through their bookkeeping program, but make adjustments only in the balance sheet and tax records.

There's an old joke about the perfect hog building. It should pay for itself in five years and self-destruct in ten.

were kept in the farm business, your owner's equity will have increased. If the farm was unprofitable and you took on debt to cover the shortfall, your equity will have decreased.

Similarly, a cost basis balance sheet allows you to more accurately track your farm's financial performance from year to year. It takes into account the fact that rust and rot will cause machinery and buildings to depreciate in value over time. It does not hide poor financial performance behind a screen of rapidly rising land values. A cost basis balance sheet will give you a truer picture of your farm's financial performance.

A cost basis balance sheet allows you to account for a purchased asset that doesn't add any marketable value to the farm. For example, you might spend $10,000 for pasture fencing but, if the farm were to be sold, the new fence may not be worth anything to a potential buyer. In fact, the fence might even lower the value of the farm if the new buyer has to pay to have it removed. However, you made the initial investment in fencing with the intent of generating profits from grazing livestock. You want to track that investment on your balance sheet as long as it still has useful value to you.

Deciding Which Balance Sheet to Use

Many farm balance sheet forms allow you to develop a market value and a cost basis balance sheet side-by-side on the same form. It is ideal to do it this way. However, don't let the perfect get in the way of the pretty good. It is most important to pick the style of balance sheet that you're comfortable assembling each year and then stick with it.

OTTO'S TIP: *If you don't make market value adjustments into your computer bookkeeping program for your assets, the reports function will generate a cost basis balance sheet.*

Update Your Balance Sheet Every New Year's Day

It is important to complete your balance sheet on the same date each year. Doing so takes seasonal variations out of the picture and allows for valid comparisons from year to year. This is especially important for farm operations, as assets such as crop inventories can vary widely across seasons. You can certainly update your balance sheet more often, even quarterly or monthly, if you find the information useful.

To accurately assess financial progress, you need a beginning and ending balance sheet for each year. If you complete your balance sheet as of January 1 every year, you will have what you need. A January 1 balance sheet also corresponds with the tax year. You can put your beginning and ending balance sheets together with the Schedule F (Profit or Loss from Farming) from your federal tax return, and with those documents do a full financial analysis of your farm. The federal government will force you to complete your Schedule F; if you can force yourself to update your balance sheet you'll have the two key documents you'll need to analyze your farm's financial performance.

Updating your balance sheet every year will let you see how your investment in the farm has grown over time. This is particularly important in years when your cash flow hasn't been good, and you feel like you're working yourself half to death and getting nowhere. Often you'll be able to see that you've increased the value of your farm significantly even if the farm checking account balance hasn't changed much.

Having an annual balance sheet for every year of your farming career will likely be extremely helpful if you ever want to transfer the farm to one of your children. You'll be able to see how much the farm was worth in the year your daughter or son joined the operation, and what it's worth the year in which the transfer is going to take place. A portion of the change in the farm's value over that time can likely be attributed to their efforts and can be taken into account as a "sweat equity" contribution in the transfer process.

How the Balance Sheet is Structured

No matter which type of balance sheet you choose, the structure will be the same. Assets are listed on the left side of the page, or on the top, liabilities are listed on the right, or on the bottom. Just below the liabilities is a section to calculate the owner's equity.

The balance sheet usually consists of only one side of a single page. However, there are often a set of "schedules" behind that page which provide richer detail about each of the asset and liability categories on the balance sheet.

Assets

On a farm balance sheet, assets are broken into three categories based on their useful life: current assets, intermediate assets, and long-term assets. This is another difference between a farm balance sheet and a balance sheet for a non-farm business. Businesses outside of agriculture usually only have two classes of balance sheet assets; current and non-current.

Current assets are defined as cash, anything that is likely to be converted into cash, or anything that will be used up within a year on the farm. Current assets include savings and checking account balances, prepaid expenses such as seed or fuel, feed and crop inventories, market livestock inventories, and accounts receivable. You should only include accounts receivable that are likely to be collected. Current assets also include the value of growing crops.

Some current assets, such as corn and soybean inventories, have per-bushel values that change significantly during the year. You should pick an average price per bushel for the year, and use it for both the beginning and ending balance sheets. Any value difference for the crop should come from a change in the number of bushels, not the price per bushel. The values used for growing crops, including vegetables, herbs, etc., are usually based on the cost of the crop inputs used to plant the crops; not what the crops should be worth at harvest. Calves or feeder livestock such as steers should be valued using the same method as corn and beans; use an average value at given market weight (e.g. 10 steer calves weighing approximately 500 lbs @ $120/cwt = $6,000). Tomato plants in a greenhouse would be considered growing crops, whereas raspberry plants or apple trees would be intermediate assets because they have a life longer than one year.

Accounts receivable are a class of current assets that can sometimes present a challenge. If you reasonably believe that you will be able to collect a debt within the next 12 months, it should be included as a current asset. If the person or business that owes you the money has filed for bankruptcy protection, or if the debt has already been uncollectable for more than a year, you should probably not include it. You will want to detail out what each of these debts owed to you are so that you will later understand what your assumptions were with each account.

OTTO'S TIP: *Accounts receivable are the payments that you are expecting from deliveries of product, or sales that have not yet been paid. In your bookkeeping program these are generated through invoices.*

Intermediate assets are assets with a useful life of more than one year but less than ten years. This includes machinery, equipment, perennial plants, breeding livestock that you intend to own for more than a year, and titled vehicles such as pickup trucks. It can also include items that are not easily converted to cash, such as stock in a cooperative or the cash value of a life insurance policy.

Long-term or "fixed" assets are those that have a life longer than ten years. The two main fixed assets on most farm balance sheets are: 1) land; and 2) buildings and improvements. These two assets need to be listed separately because buildings and improvements are depreciable, while land is not. Buildings include livestock buildings, greenhouses, machine sheds, and other functional structures. Improvements are items such as fencing, non-portable irrigation systems, ponds, soil conservation enhancements, and other similar capital investments.

There is one building on many farms that needs to be treated differently than other farm buildings: the farm house. It needs to be considered a nonfarm asset for several reasons that we'll discuss below.

Liabilities

Liabilities are also broken out into current, intermediate, and long-term categories. However, liabilities are categorized according to how soon the debts need to be paid.

Current liabilities include accounts payable and other debts that are past due, credit card balances that are carried forward from month to month, short-term notes that are due within a year such as an operating loan, and the portion of the principal on intermediate or long-term debts that is due within the next year. Any interest that has accrued on debt should also be listed as a current liability. Other items that should be listed under current liabilities are labor expenses, property taxes, or rent payments that have built up or "accrued" but have not yet been paid.

Intermediate liabilities are typically debts that will need to be paid off within the next ten years. Often these will be loans made for the purchase of machinery, titled vehicles, or breeding livestock.

OTTO'S TIP: *Accounts payable are bills that you owe; outstanding obligations at the time that you created the balance sheet.*

Long-term liabilities are debts that will be paid off in more than ten years, such as a farm mortgage or a land contract, or construction loans.

In addition to these three liability categories, if you are using a market basis balance sheet there also needs to be an allowance for "contingent" liabilities. These are liabilities that only become true obligations after a triggering event. For instance, the sale of a farm or any other intermediate or long-term assets will likely create an obligation to pay capital gains taxes, repayment or "recapture" of depreciation that was claimed over the years to reduce income tax liabilities, and possibly to pay a commission to a real estate broker. Ordinary income taxes that would result from the sale of current assets are also included as contingent liabilities. Contingent liabilities are confusing and a bit hard to calculate, so are often left off of farm balance sheets. Ignoring contingent liabilities is a common mistake.

OTTO'S TIP: *It is common to ignore contingent liabilities, but not wise, as they are real expenses you will eventually have to pay if you ever sell any of your farm assets. Or, you can avoid paying contingent liabilities by dying and letting the assets pass through your estate.*

So, if you shouldn't ignore the contingent liabilities, how should you account for them on your balance sheet? Technically, they should correspond to asset sales that would trigger them. For instance, income tax liabilities that would be triggered by the sale of crop inventories should be listed as current liabilities, capital gains tax liabilities that would result from sale of machinery should be listed as intermediate liabilities, and so on. Basically it would be income tax on sales of current assets, capital gains on longer term assets such as machinery or land, and depreciation recapture on sale of assets that have been depreciated to a value below market value.

However, a simpler way to account for contingent liabilities is to just use a percentage of the total assets. A reasonable ballpark estimate would be a contingent liability equal to 15 percent of the total assets on the balance sheet. This can simply be listed as "contingent liabilities" in its own line in the balance sheet.

Separating Personal Assets from Farm Assets

There are several reasons to separate personal and business assets. First, in order to claim a tax deduction (such as depreciation) for an asset, you have to be able to prove that the asset is being used exclusively in the business. Second, if you were sued or if you were

Management of Liabilities and Taxes

Farmers often implement management strategies to minimize each year's income tax liabilities. They will prepay expenses in years when they would have a large income tax liability, and put off buying supplies in years when tax liability is low. They will use accelerated depreciation on recently purchased machinery to reduce the current year's tax liability.

In reality, the tax liability is not averted; most of it is just being pushed off to sometime in the future. This kind of management isn't bad or good, but must be recognized and adjusted for when creating financial statements that compare different years' activities or to other farms or standards.

OTTO'S TIP: *You don't have to switch liabilities from one category to another as they move closer to maturity; they should stay in the category where they started. In other words, when your farm mortgage has less than ten years left until it is paid off, it is still considered a long-term liability and should continue being listed as a long-term liability on the balance sheet.*

forced to seek bankruptcy protection, some assets could be protected from being seized and sold depending on how they are classified. Finally, when you calculate profitability ratios such as rate of return on assets, your net farm income is going to be divided by all of your farm assets. If your home is included in the farm assets, you are essentially forcing it to generate a profit. It's going to make your farm look less profitable than it really is.

Separating business and personal assets is more difficult for farmers than it is for most other businesses. Not many business owners outside of farming live in their place of business. At a minimum, the farm should have its own checking account. All farm income should be deposited in that account and all farm bills should be paid out of it. Smaller operations can get away with not doing this, but purchases and activities should be closely tracked in a bookkeeping system as to if they are "farm" or "personal."

The challenge becomes greater with capital assets such as vehicles and the farm house. The value of the farm house should not be included as a farm asset; it should be listed as a personal or nonfarm asset. A vehicle that is primarily used for farm purposes should be considered a farm asset. However, a car that is mainly used to drive to an off-farm job with occasional trips to pick up farm supplies would be considered a personal vehicle. You should think of the separation in terms of the assets you would need if you were no longer farming. You would need a house in which to live, furniture and appliances, and a car to drive. So, those assets should be considered personal—not farm—assets.

If you have not yet started your farm operation you might wonder why you would need to develop a balance sheet at all, much less worry about splitting farm assets from personal assets. Again, one of the main purposes of the balance sheet is to use it in combination with your income statement to calculate various profitability ratios. These ratios can be calculated as an analysis of the last year's performance, and can help you assess if your planning was on track, or if things need to be tweaked. Useful ratios can also be developed using a projected income statement for the first few years after start-up to show you what to expect in the future.

OTTO'S TIP: *You can separate household finances from farm in your computer bookkeeping system by using different account groupings, or by using Class or Job functions, creating categories such as Farm and Household.*

The farm balance sheet you develop before starting should include any personal assets that you intend to devote to the farm operation, as well as any existing debt that the farm will be expected to cover. You may be investing some of your savings into the farm. Perhaps you have a truck, tractor, or other equipment that will become part of the farm operation. Maybe there is an existing loan against the truck that will be paid out of the farm's cash flow after start-up. All of these things should be listed on your beginning farm balance sheet.

How to Assemble the Balance Sheet for Your Farm

Now that you know the elements of a balance sheet and why it is important to develop one each year, you're probably anxious to start putting yours together. You could grab a yellow legal pad, draw a vertical line down the middle of the pad, write "Assets" on the top of the left column, "Liabilities" on the top of the right column, and start listing everything you own and everything you owe in their respective columns. Within an hour or less you could have a good estimate of your farm's financial position.

If you want a more formal document suitable for submission to a lender, there are many sources that can provide you with a blank balance sheet form. Your county Extension agent, your county Farm Service Agency office, or your lender will have forms available. We have a simple template for you in Appendix C. We also have collected several resources on the website connected to this book at mosesorganic.org/fearless-farm-finances. You can search the web for "farm balance sheet form" and find dozens of different forms that could be printed off and filled out. Your lender may have a worksheet that they recommend you use. If you use a computer with Microsoft Excel, open the program and click File>New>Templates, then look for the balance sheet. If you use a financial software program, it will have a balance sheet report function. You will most likely need to export the balance sheet report from your program into a spreadsheet so that you can adjust it.

Whichever form you decide to use, you will find it helpful to use supporting schedules (or worksheets) that tie to the main balance sheet. In the same way that your farm's Schedule F ties to the Form 1040 when you do your income taxes, the supporting schedules contain more detailed information that is then summarized on the balance sheet. For instance, your machinery schedule may list twenty separate implements, each with its own value, but only the total value of all machinery shows up under "Intermediate Assets" on the balance sheet. Do the schedules first. They will help you organize the information you will need to bring forward onto the balance sheet.

Be sure to write the date on your balance sheet. It is a very crucial piece of information that can easily be overlooked as you dive into the numbers.

As mentioned above, it is ideal to have a balance sheet that is prepared as of January 1 each year. However, this doesn't mean that you have to spend New Year's Day in the barn counting hay bales. You'll want to wait until you receive your end-of-the-year bank statements to fill in asset numbers anyway. Just try to complete it as close to the first of the year as you can.

Economic Depreciation vs Tax Depreciation

"Depreciation" is a way of accounting for the wear and tear that, over time, depletes the value of many capital assets such as machinery, vehicles, buildings, breeding livestock, and other assets that eventually rust out, rot out, or die. Land is not generally considered to be a depreciable asset, although it certainly can lose value due to market conditions or poor husbandry.

There are two types of depreciation: 1) Economic depreciation; and 2) Tax depreciation. Economic depreciation takes into account the initial cost and the expected useful life of the asset, and deducts a portion of the cost from a business' income statement each year of its life as a depreciation expense. It's a more realistic way of portraying how the value of a building or piece of equipment is depleted over time when it is used in a business.

Tax depreciation is similar except that the depreciation may be accelerated as a way to reduce the business' income tax liability. As a result, an asset may be completely depreciated for tax purposes long before the asset wears out. Farmers and other business people commonly take advantage of Section 179 of the IRS tax code, which allows businesses to fully deduct the purchase price of qualifying assets during the tax year. The maximum

Continued on next page

Developing the Asset Side of the Balance Sheet

Once you've found a format that you like, you are ready to start gathering information to put into it. It is usually best to start with current assets. Again, current assets include cash, or anything that could be converted to cash or that will be used up on the farm in less than a year.

Gather your most recent bank statements and locate current balances in checking and savings accounts. Remember to take into account checks that you have written but that haven't cleared the bank yet. Your bookkeeping system can help you with these current balances.

Take inventory of feed, crops, seed, fuel, and other items that you have in storage to either be sold or used up within a year. Do you have growing crops in the ground that will be harvested within the next year? The value of the inputs you invested in those crops should be included in current assets. Take inventory of steers, lambs, market hogs, or other market livestock that will be sold in the year ahead.

Finally, think about any money that is owed to you and that you reasonably believe you will be able to collect.

The current assets category tends to be the most challenging part of the balance sheet because everything is changing on a daily basis. For instance, one day the milk check comes in the mail and it instantly changes from an account receivable to an increase in the checking account balance. The next day, you pay some bills and the checking account balance disappears. You cut first-crop hay and within a week the value of your crop inventory doubles. Don't get too stressed out about it. The point is to capture a representative picture of your current assets at one particular point in time.

Move next to your intermediate assets. Start this section by taking inventory of all of the machinery and equipment being used in the farm operation. If you carry insurance coverage on your machinery you may have already developed an inventory for your insurance agent. It is best to list the machinery and equipment inventory on a supporting schedule. The more significant pieces should have their own lines on the schedule, while the smaller pieces may be lumped together. For instance, each tractor would be listed separately with make, model, age, condition, and value. However, an air compressor, air tools, welder, and table saw might all appear on a line entitled "shop tools." Where you draw that threshold of significance is entirely up to you. If you have a small farm operation, you might consider a $500 roto-tiller to be a significant piece of equipment. A large farm might not list anything with a value of less than $5,000. In accounting terms this is known as your "capitalization limit."

Have the same person value the assets from year to year so that the values are comparable.

OTTO'S TIP:

That takes us to the subject of values. In our experience, most farmers have a better sense of the market value of each piece of machinery they own than they do of anything else on the farm. If you are using a market basis balance sheet, simply use the values you would be able to get for each piece of machinery if you were to sell it or trade it in right now.

If you are using a cost basis balance sheet and this is the first time you've put it together, you can use current market values as a starting point. In future years, subtract economic depreciation from the established values. Theoretically, you could go back and find the original purchase price for each piece of machinery and take off the tax depreciation you've claimed over the years. The challenge with this is the fact that many farmers take advantage of Section 179 of the tax code, which allows greatly accelerated depreciation. Under this, new equipment and other qualifying property can often be fully depreciated the first year, leaving you with a balance sheet value of zero.

Other assets that need to be included in the category of intermediate assets are the value of breeding livestock, and items such as stock in cooperatives or cash value of life insurance policies tied to the farm business.

The valuation of long-term assets is similar to that of intermediate assets. However, you need to separate the value of depreciable assets (primarily buildings) from the value of non-depreciable assets (land). You might ask, "Why bother splitting these values apart? The buildings don't have a value apart from the land." The reason for splitting the values is to fairly assess the contribution the buildings add to the value of the farm real estate. Too often, farmers spend hundreds of thousands of dollars on buildings that add virtually nothing to their farms' asset values. The real value of farm buildings is generally in the capacity they provide for increasing the farm's profitability and net cash flow.

As mentioned previously, the value of the farm house should not be included on the farm balance sheet; it should be considered a personal asset.

Intermediate and long-term assets typically don't change a lot from one year to the next unless you buy or sell equipment, construct a new building, buy additional land, or expand or reduce the size of a breeding livestock enterprise. Aside from those more significant events, it is best not to make big changes in values from year to year.

Table 9.2 on page 81 shows a sample balance sheet from our mythical farmer, Otto B. Organic. The summary in Table 9.1 below tells you a little about Otto's farm. We will be using Otto's numbers throughout this section and the next to highlight the concepts presented.

Table 9.1 Otto B. Organic's Farm Summary

Crop & Livestock Production	Otto B. Organic
207 acre farm	
90 acres feed corn, 160 bu/acre = 14,400 bu	
27 acres corn silage, 24 ton/acre = 648 ton	
90 acres alfalfa hay, 4.5 ton/acre = 405 ton	
80 dairy cows, 20,000 lbs/cow = 1,600,000 lbs	

Depreciation ... continued

allowable Section 179 deduction is $500,000. The use of this deduction can substantially reduce or eliminate a business' income tax liability. However, while it can provide a significant amount of immediate tax relief, it will reduce future years' depreciation deductions.

While the Section 179 deduction is useful for tax management, you must be aware of its implications when making business management decisions. First, you must be sure to put together your financial statements for farm management purposes using economic depreciation, NOT the tax depreciation that you are claiming under Section 179. If you mistakenly use the tax depreciation numbers in the year you utilize Section 179, your financial statements will make your operation look much worse than it actually is.

Second, when a fully depreciated asset is sold, the seller has to report a gain on the sale and the IRS will "recapture" the excess depreciation that the business initially claimed on its federal tax return, which reduced its earlier tax liability. Recaptured depreciation is taxed as ordinary income, which often means it is taxed at a higher rate than the tax rate on capital gains.

What Does Your Balance Sheet Tell You?

When your lender looks at your balance sheet, he or she will be trying to answer the following questions:

Are you solvent?

How is your debt load structured?

What is your net working capital position (current assets minus current liabilities)?

Do you have a lot of open accounts?

Do you know who you owe, and how much?

If you are planning to borrow more money, how will your balance sheet look after the loan closes?

We will look at the information in the balance sheet in more detail when we look at ratios in Chapter 12.

Developing the Liability Side of the Balance Sheet

To create the liability section of the balance sheet, you'll want to start at the top with current liabilities. First, list all unpaid accounts and other payables (amounts owed by you) that are past-due. Don't include normal monthly expenses; just the bills that are more than 30 days overdue. Be sure to include credit card balances that have been carried forward from one billing cycle to the next. Under current liabilities you will also list any short-term notes, such as an operating loan or an outstanding balance on a line of credit.

Finally, any principal due within the coming year on any longer term debts need to be posted as a current liability. This tends to be one of the more difficult pieces of the balance sheet. Some lenders list on their monthly statements the principal due within the year on term debts but, unfortunately, some don't. You will probably have to call your lender to get these numbers or base them off of the amount of principal you paid the previous year.

Once you finish the current liabilities, intermediate and long-term liabilities are pretty straight-forward. Intermediate liabilities are generally any debts connected to items with a useful life from one to ten years. Long-term liabilities are those associated with real estate and other long-term assets. One caution: Be sure to subtract the principal amounts that you already listed under current liabilities. You don't want to count those principal balances twice.

Don't forget to include contingent liabilities under the long-term liabilities portion of your balance sheet. Remember, these are taxes, etc., that you will have to pay when a triggering event occurs.

Net Worth

Now that you've completed both the assets and liabilities sides of the balance sheet, subtract the total liabilities from the total assets to determine your net worth position. This shows you the amount of investment you hold in your farm operation. When you have completed balance sheets for two years or more, you can use the net worth positions in combination with your income statement to monitor changes in the performance of your investment in your farm business.

Net Worth = total assets − total liabilities

Summary

Your balance sheet is one of three major financial statements you'll need to analyze the financial performance of your farm. It consists of assets (current, intermediate and fixed) and liabilities (current, intermediate, long term and contingent). Comparing the two will give you your net worth on the date the balance sheet was created.

Considered by itself, the balance sheet provides you with some crucial information. Put it together with the other two major statements, the income statement and statement of cash flows, and you'll be able to see a vivid picture of the strengths and vulnerabilities of your farm business.

In the next chapter we will look at the income statement, which will show you the overall profitability of your operation.

Balance Sheet			Current	Projected	
	Otto B. Organic		1/01/20X1	1/01/20X2	
Assets					
	Current Assets				
		Cash & checking	5,000	5,796	
		Prepaid exp & supplies	1,000	-	
		Accounts receivable	3,000	-	
		Crops			
		Corn	39,600	39,610	
		Hay	39,000	39,774	
		Silage	23,850	24,222	
	Total Current Assets		111,450	109,402	
	Intermediate Assets				
		Breeding livestock	188,000	188,000	
		Machinery	150,000	136,800	
		Titled vehicles	10,000	8,500	
	Total Intermediate Assets		348,000	333,300	
	Long Term Assets				
		Land	840,000	840,000	
		Bldgs & improvements	80,000	76,000	
	Total Long Term Assets		920,000	916,000	
	Total Farm Assets		**1,379,450**	**1,358,702**	
	Personal Assets		**108,000**	**106,500**	
Total Assets			$ 1,487,450	$ 1,465,202	
Liabilities					
	Current Liabilities				
		Principal due on term loans			
		FCS- machinery	17,372	18,259	
		FCS- parlor	8,841	9,386	
		FCS- mortgage	12,224	13,038	
		Accrued interest			
		Operating loan(s)	400	-	
		Operating loan(s)	10,000	-	
	Total Current Liabilities		48,837	40,683	
	Intermediate Liabilities				
		FCS- machinery	57,628	39,370	
		FCS- parlor	41,159	31,774	
	Total Intermediate Liabilities		98,787	71,144	
	Long Term Liabilites				
		FCS- mortgage	287,776	274,742	
	Total Long Term Liabilites		287,776	274,742	
	Total Farm Liabilities		435,400	386,569	
	Total Personal Liabilities		-	-	
	Contingent Liabilities		100,000	100,000	
Total Liabilities			$ 535,400	$ 486,569	
Net Worth/ Equity			$ 952,050	$ 978,633	
Net Worth Change					$ 26,583
Total Liabilities & Net Worth/Equity			$ 1,487,450	$ 1,465,202	
Total Debt to Asset Ratio			36%	33%	

Table 9.2
Otto B. Organic's Balance Sheet

This table shows a sample balance sheet from our mythical farmer Otto B. Organic.

The summary in Table 9.1 on page 79 shows you a little about Otto's farm.

We will be using Otto's numbers throughout this section and the next to highlight the concepts presented.

CHAPTER 10
Are You Making a Profit? The Income Statement

Key questions addressed in this chapter:

How do cash and accrual accounting systems differ?

How do you develop an income statement?

What can you learn from the income statement?

No matter what sort of business a person operates, at the end of the year the owner wants to know whether or not the business made a profit. You may know that sales increased, prices were stronger than the previous year, and you often have a few extra dollars in the checking account at the end of each month. None of these observations answers the question: Did this business generate a profit? Or, in other words, did the business generate an adequate return on the investment of your money, your time and your labor? To find that answer, you need to develop an income statement.

Your farm's income statement provides you with a systematic method for calculating "net farm income." Net farm income is a dollar amount that represents the amount of money your farm gave you over the past year in return for the labor, expertise, and capital you invested in it. If net farm income is positive, you generated a profit. If it's negative, you suffered a loss and are going to have to make some adjustments in the farm business next year.

Throughout the year you will be using a bookkeeping data entry system such as we described in Section Two. An income statement allows you to look at the numbers you have entered to compare year to year, and understand if you are making money.

There are two parts to the income statement: revenue and expenses. It is important to note that there are cash and non-cash items in each part of the income statement. Because it includes non-cash revenues and expenses, the income statement does not give you relevant information about cash flow. It serves a much different purpose than a statement of cash flows. This will be discussed in more detail below.

The income statement is sometimes called a "profit and loss statement" or a "farm earnings statement."

OTTO'S TIP:

Cash versus Accrual Systems

Similarly to what we saw with the balance sheet, farm income statements are different than other business' income statements.

In farming, it is typical to use a cash basis accounting system. Income and expenses are recorded when money changes hands. Revenue is recorded when a check is received. An expense is listed when a bill is paid.

Most larger, non-farm businesses use an accrual accounting system. In these, revenue is recorded or "accrued" when a product is shipped and an invoice for that product has been issued to the buyer. This may be before the bill is paid and before the income is actually in the seller's hand. Expenses are typically booked (listed) when a bill is received, rather than when the bill has been paid. The term "accrual" refers to any individual entry recording revenue or expense in the absence of a cash transaction. Accrual systems are preferred by accountants, and are useful in that they show a clearer picture of financial obligations and expectations. Accrual systems can also be useful in managing cash flow.

Cash basis accounting is simpler to use than accrual and gives a farmer some flexibility to manage income tax liability at the end of the year. For instance, next year's supplies can be pre-paid in December to reduce the current year's income tax liability.

While there are certainly advantages to using a cash accounting system, such a system can make it difficult to accurately calculate net farm income.

Cash and Accrual Income Statements in QuickBooks

You will be able to run a report in QuickBooks called the Profit and Loss, or P&L, either as a total of all accounts, or by class or job (if you've used them).

You can adjust this statement to either report by cash or accrual by clicking a button from the Print Reports page. However, if you are not using the Bill or Invoicing functions, you are running basically a cash system and the two reports will be the same.

OTTO'S TIP: *The terms "revenue" and "income" are sometimes used to mean the same thing. Used here, either refers to the amount of money (or its equivalent) received during a given period of time.*

Our goals is for net farm income to be an accurate measure of the farm's performance in a given year. Certain common activities will throw this off. For instance, if a farmer buys a lot of inputs at the end of the year to increase tax deductible expenses, or pushes sales into the following year to reduce taxable income, it makes the farm's annual financial performance look worse than it really was. On the other hand, if a farmer has not been paying his or her bills for months on end, the net farm income might erroneously look really good.

To compensate for these issues, it is necessary to make "accrual adjustments" to a cash accounting system to develop an accurate farm income statement. The income statement described here features cash accounting with accrual adjustments. Thus, it is called an accrual adjusted income statement. The adjustments are easy to make and will give you a more accurate measure of net farm income for a given time period.

INCOME STATEMENT

Income Statements from Your Bookkeeping Program

Your bookkeeping program will be able to run a report that is essentially a basic income statement. It may be called a profit and loss statement.

However, it will be easiest for you to make the recommended adjustments outside of your bookkeeping program. If you can, export the program's profit and loss statement to your spreadsheet program. (To do this in QuickBooks, with the P&L report open, click on the Export button at the top. From the window that opens, choose A New Excel Workbook. After it exports, save the Excel document.)

You can also just transfer key numbers to a spreadsheet if you need to make a lot of adjustments.

It is possible that you can manipulate your bookkeeping program's profit and loss statement to conform to farm income statement specifications, but that will involve several general journal entries. It is complicated enough that we won't go into it here. If you'd like to do this, we suggest that you talk to your accountant to get recommended annual general journal entries.

OTTO'S TIP: *The purpose of the income statement is not to determine how well you managed your farm's income tax liabilities. The purpose is to determine how well you managed your farm business.*

Getting Ready to Develop Your Income Statement

Three documents form the foundation of your income statement: 1) Beginning of the year balance sheet; 2) End of the year balance sheet; and 3) Your bookkeeping program profit and loss report for your fiscal year, or the Schedule F (Profit or Loss From Farming) filed with your most recent federal income tax return. Another helpful document from your federal income tax return is Form 4797 (Sales of Business Property). If you didn't sell any business property during the year, such as breeding livestock or machinery, you probably didn't file a Form 4797.

The accrual adjustments you will need to make to develop your income statement are based off of changes during the year in various asset and liability items on your balance sheet. That is why you need copies of both the beginning and ending balance sheets for the year.

Your Schedule F is a very handy document, as it provides a good summary of cash income and expenses for the year. There is no sense recreating all of this information when you've already done it for the IRS.

Finally, you will need an income statement form to use as a template. We offer a sample in Appencix C. You can find templates on-line, or check the website we have set up at mosesorganic.org/fearless-farm-finances. Find a format you like and stick with it.

In Table 10.1 on page 85 we show Otto B. Organic's income statement. You can refer to it as you follow along in this chapter.

Revenue

The revenue portion of the income statement includes many of the ordinary cash income items you would expect to be included: All cash payments (receipts) taken in during the year for farm products, income from custom work, and income from government payments. Include the gross income you received from the sale of raised or purchased livestock, including breeding livestock. Include any crop insurance proceeds you received. Do NOT include income from the sale of land, machinery, or other capital asset sales.

Revenue Accrual Adjustments

Inventory changes. Revenue on the income statement also includes changes in inventory values from the beginning of the year to the end. For instance, if you had $20,000 worth of hay in your barn on January 1 of the year, and $30,000 worth of hay on December 31 in the same year, you would show the $10,000 of increased value as revenue for that year.

You might think that it makes no sense to show the increased value of your hay inventory as "revenue." You didn't sell it, so it didn't generate any cash income. Maybe you don't even intend to sell it; you're going to feed it to your livestock.

Listing inventory change as "revenue" is the first accrual adjustment on your income statement. The adjustment for changes in inventory does three things: 1) It accounts for the value of the inventory you built up during the year; 2) It helps to offset the production expenses you incurred to build up that inventory; and 3) It takes out the value of inventory that was generated in previous years, but then used up.

In the hay example, you would have incurred costs to either harvest or purchase the hay that went into inventory during the year. If there was not a way to show how you created something of value in return for the expenses you paid, your financial performance would not look as good as it should.

So, what happens if your inventory is smaller at the end of the year than at the beginning? You would show the net change as a subtraction in the revenue section of the income statement. The inventory that existed on January 1, 20X2 should have counted as revenue in the previous year (20X1) when it was created. If you ended the year with a smaller inventory than you had on January 1, you used up more inventory than you added and it shows up as a deduction from revenue. Another way to think of it is that by showing this as a deduction from revenue, you are charging the farm for using up the previous year's production.

The same type of accrual adjustments need to be made for changes in market livestock and breeding stock inventories. Breeding stock is the only non-current asset for which we do an accrual adjustment.

Accounts receivable. Another accrual adjustment on the revenue side of the income statement is any change in accounts receivable from the beginning of the year to the end. Perhaps on January 1, 20X2 you were owed $5,000 for vegetables that were delivered and billed during the fall of 20X1. Your January 1, 20X2 balance sheet would show the $5,000 you were owed as an accounts receivable. Let's assume that your customer paid the $5,000 bill during the year, and on December 31, 20X2 you had also been paid in full for all of the produce you sold during the year and ended the year with no accounts receivable. Your accounts receivable would have declined from $5,000 on January 1, 20X2 to zero on December 31, 20X2, so you would show a negative $5,000 of revenue.

Table 10.1 Otto B. Organic's Income Statement

Income Statement	Fiscal Year
Otto B. Organic	20X1
Cash Farm Income	
Corn	33,600
Milk	256,000
Cull stock	18,480
Misc livestock	3,840
Govt payments	3,000
Gross Farm Income	$ 314,920
Cash Farm Expense	
Seed	8,820
Fetility	20,250
Weed & pest treatments	5,265
Cropinsurance	3,510
Custom hire - crops	5,625
Feed	79,987
Breeding	3,200
Veterinary	9,596
Supplies	19,992
Marketing	5,600
Fuel & oil	6,000
Repairs	10,000
Custom hire - other	6,020
Labor	15,000
Land taxes	4,000
Farm insurance	2,000
Utilities	7,200
Cetification fees	3,000
Interest on loans	26,628
Total Cash Farm Expense	$ 241,693
Net Cash Farm Income	$ 73,227
Accrual Adjustments	
Crops and feed	1,156
Market livestock	-
Accounts receivable	(3,000)
Hedging accounts	-
Other current assets	-
Prepaid exp & supply	(1,000)
Growing crops	-
Accounts payable	-
Accrued interest	400
Total Inventory Change	$ (2,444)
Net Operating Profit	$ 70,783
Depreciation	
Machinery	17,200
Titled vehicles	1,500
Bldgs & improvements	4,000
Total Depreciation	$ 22,700
Capital Adjustment	2,000
Net Farm Income	$ 50,083

Again, it might seem like this doesn't make sense. You collected on $5,000 of unpaid bills and kept on top of collections all year long but you're supposed to reduce your revenue by $5,000?!

Keep in mind that the $5,000 you collected on the previous year's bill would have been mixed in with all of your other cash receipts and shows up as income on your 20X2 Schedule F. However, the fact that those vegetables were grown, sold, and billed out during the previous year means that the revenue should have been recognized in the previous year. The accrual adjustment you are making by showing a negative $5,000 in accounts receivable is a way of recognizing that those vegetables were grown, sold, and billed (and thus accrued) in the previous year. They were not a part of this year's financial performance, even though you collected the money this year.

Farm products consumed at home. The value of any farm products such as vegetables or meat that were taken for home consumption by the farm family should be added to revenue on the income statement. Your farm would have incurred expenses to produce these products, so their value needs to be taken into consideration.

Expenses

In the expense section of the income statement you will include all of the normal cash operating expenses for the farm during the year: feed, seed, fertilizer, hired labor, fuel, real estate taxes, and so on.

You will also include interest that was paid during the year on farm debts. Principal payments on debt are not included. The income statement should only reflect the cost you incurred to use the bank's money during the year. You can almost think of the interest as a rental payment for using the bank's money. Do NOT include the purchase of land, machinery, or other capital assets as expenses. Also, do not include income tax or the farmer's own social security payments as expenses; those are considered to be the farmer's personal expenses, not farm expenses.

Now here come the accrual adjustments for expenses. The basic concept of accrual adjustments is the same on the expense side as it is on the income side; we want to isolate the expenses related to this year's production from those of last year and next year.

Expense Accrual Adjustments

Value of growing crops. First, you need to consider any changes in the value of growing crops. Remember that the value of a growing crop is based on the initial cost of the inputs already invested in the crop. If you have value in a growing crop at the end of the year, it represents cash expenses that are invested in something that you didn't sell or harvest as inventory. We need to essentially push those expenses into the year in which the revenue from those crops will show up in the income statement, by sending those expenses into next year. By the same token, we need to accept the expenses tied up in growing crops at the end of last year as an expense in the current year, if you expect to harvest of sell that crop in this next year.

Here's how the concept works in practice. Let's say you had 20 acres of winter wheat in the field on January 1, 20X2. The value of the expenses tied up in the growing crop was $1,400. You harvest and sell the crop during 20X2. In the fall you only plant 15 acres of winter wheat and on December 31, 20X2 the value of that growing crop was $1,050. You want to accept the $1,400 of expenses this year (20X2) and put the $1,050 of expenses for the fall crop off until next year (20X3). $1,400 - $1,050 = $350. Thus, the expense accrual adjustment for value of growing crops in the current year is +$350. In other words, you'll recognize $350 more in expenses due to the fact that you have a smaller investment in growing crops at the end of the year than you did in the beginning of the year.

Prepaid expenses or prepaid supplies. Changes in prepaid expenses are treated in exactly the same way as changes in the value of growing crops. Farmers often prepay expenses such as fertilizer or seed in December as a way to manage income tax liability. In order to fully understand your profit, however, those expenses need to show up in the year in which they are used to produce a crop, which is not necessarily the year in which they were paid.

So, we accept the prepaid expenses on January 1, 20X2 as expenses for the year 20X2, and push forward the prepaid expenses on December 31, 20X2 as costs for next year (20X3). If the January 1, 20X2 prepaid expenses are higher than those of December 31, 20X2 the difference is added to this year's expenses. In this case, the farm was worse off at the end of 20X2 because it had fewer prepaid expenses than it had at the beginning of the year. If January 1, 20X2 prepaid expenses are less than those on December 31, 20X2 the difference is deducted from the 20X2 expenses. The farm is better off because it increased its prepaid expenses during the year.

Accounts payable. An accrual adjustment also must be made for changes in accounts payable. Accounts payable on January 1 represent unpaid bills from last year. We want to make sure that the farm was charged for those bills last year, not this year. If those bills end up being paid during the current year, along with all of the other cash farm expenses, we need to make an accrual adjustment to eliminate that amount from this year's expenses. For example, if accounts payable on January 1 were $1,000 and on December 31 were zero, you would make an accrual adjustment of -$1,000. In other words, you reduce the current year's expenses by $1,000. The farm was better off because you cleared up its accounts payable during the year.

Table 10.3 on page 88 shows Otto's record of how inventory has changed for the year. The figures in the last column, titled Change, are what show up in the Accrual Adjustment section of Otto's income statement in Table 10.1 on page 85. Table 10.2 shows the inventory numbers used to develop Table 10.3.

Depreciation. The next expense item to be considered is depreciation. Depreciation is a non-cash expense item, but represents a true cost to your

> **Accrual Adjustments: Positive or Negative?**
>
> When making accrual adjustments, think about whether the changes from the beginning of the year to the end of the year ultimately made your farm better or worse. For example, if you weren't able to pay some of your bills during the year, and thus increased your accounts payable, the increase in accounts payable ultimately hurts your farm and should result in a deduction from net farm income.

Table 10.2 Otto's Inventory Summary

Crop & Livestock Summary				
Corn			beginning	total
	Produced	bu		14,400
	Sold			
	corn	bu		5,600
	price	$/bu		6
	Fed	bu		8,798
	Inventory	bu	6600	6,602
Hay				
	Produced	ton		405
	Fed	ton		400
	Inventory	ton	260	265
Silage				
	Produced	ton		648
	Fed	ton		640
	Inventory	ton	530	538
Milk				
	no. cows	each		80
	Produced	lbs		1,600,000
	Price	$/cwt.		$ 16.00

INCOME STATEMENT

farm business. It is a way to account for the fact that capital assets such as machinery or buildings are slowly being worn out as they are used on the farm. The value of these assets declines each year. At some point in the future, they will need to be renovated or replaced to keep the farm operating at its current capacity.

Don't use the depreciation amount from your Schedule F for your income statement. Farmers have the ability to accelerate depreciation for income tax purposes. If you use the depreciation amount that appears in Part II, Line 16 of your Schedule F, it will likely make your farm's profitability look horrible, and won't truly approximate the annual decline in the value of your farm's capital assets.

Here is a simple method you might consider using to determine true "economic" depreciation. For all machinery and any titled vehicles on your farm balance sheet such as a farm truck, take a 15% depreciation charge against its market value. For any farm buildings on the balance sheet, take a 5% depreciation charge. (See the depreciation sidebar on page 78.)

What the Income Statement Tells You: A Few Useful Calculations

Now that you have considered all of your ordinary cash income and expenses, made your accrual adjustments, taken a deduction for depreciation, and subtracted the value of your own labor, you are getting close to the bottom line. There are three "bottom line" numbers that need to be calculated: 1) Net Farm Income From Operations (NFIFO); 2) Net Farm Income (NFI); and 3) Net Cash Farm Income. NFIFO will primarily be used here to calculate profitability ratios. Some people choose to use NFI rather than NFIFO to measure profitability, which is fine as long as you understand that your results will be skewed one way or the other depending on the year.

Table 10.3 Otto's Accrual Adjustments

Projected Inventory Change		Otto B. Organic					
FY 20X1							
Commodity	Beginning Inventory	$/Unit	Beginning Value	Ending Inventory	$/Unit	Ending Value	Change
Corn	6,600	$ 6.00	$ 39,600	6602	$ 6.00	$ 39,611	$ 11
Hay	260	$ 150.00	$ 39,000	265	$ 150.00	$ 39,774	$ 774
Silage	530	$ 45.00	$ 23,850	538	$ 45.00	$ 24,222	$ 372
Total crop inventory change							$ 1,156
Accounts receivable			$ 3,000			$ -	$ (3,000)
Hedging accounts			$ -			$ -	
Other current assets			$ -			$ -	
Prepaid expenses & supplies			$ 1,000			$ -	$ (1,000)
Growing crops			$ -			$ -	$ -
Accounts payable			$ -			$ -	$ -
Accrued interest			$ 400			$ -	$ 400
Total Inventories			$ 106,850			$ 103,606	$ (2,444)

We're going to temporarily set aside the third bottom line number; Net Cash Farm Income. We will get into a discussion of net cash farm income when it is time to work on your statement of cash flows.

Net Farm Income From Operations (NFIFO)—Net farm income from operations (NFIFO) is a way to isolate the income generated as a result of the normal day-to-day work carried out on the farm without including income and expenses that result from out-of-the-ordinary occurrences such as sales or purchases of capital equipment or land. NFIFO is simply your (accrual adjusted) gross revenue minus expenses, not including sales or purchases of capital assets.

NFIFO = (accrual adjusted) gross revenue - expenses

Net Farm Income (NFI)—In contrast to NFIFO, Net Farm Income (NFI) takes into consideration all income and expenses of the farm during the year, whether or not they represent ordinary occurrences. For example, in one out of every ten years you may sell an old tractor and buy a new one. Those transactions are excluded from the NFIFO calculation but will be included—for better or worse—in the calculation of NFI.

To calculate NFI, you need to subtract from NFIFO all capital purchases and add all capital sales during the year. If capital purchases are more than capital sales, your NFI will be lower (and vice versa). For example, Otto's NFIFO for last year is $48,083. We can see in Table 10.4 that he bought a used chopper box for $8,000 and a tractor for $6,000. $48,083 - $8,000 + $6,000 = $50,083 NFI.

NFI = NFIFO - capital purchases + capital sales

Table 10.4 Otto's Net Capital Changes

Otto B. Organic		
Capital Purchases		
Chopper Box	5/8/20X1	8,000
Total Cap Purchases		*8,000*
Capital Sales		
Tractor	4/13/20X1	6,000
Total Capital Sales		*6,000*
Net Capital Changes	20X1	(2,000)

How can you tell if your NFI is strong or weak? The best way is to compare your NFI to the NFI of other farms that are similar to yours. Some farm enterprises, such as dairy, have well-established benchmarks that are documented in searchable databases, which are typically maintained by university faculty. (For more information on databases for benchmarks, see the Resource section.) Other enterprises, dairy sheep production for example, are not so fortunate. For any type of farm, the NFI should be increasing each year, and should represent enough economic return to make you feel it is worth your time and effort to continue the business.

Value of the Farmer's Labor

There is one last, very important expense: The value of the farmer's labor.

It is very common for a farmer to skip over this expense and just figure that any remaining profit after deducting all of the expenses outlined above can be considered "return to labor and management." Please don't do this! From a technical standpoint, profitability ratios must be calculated after deducting the value of the owner's unpaid labor.

More importantly, you are not being honest and fair with yourself when you don't adequately account for the value of your own labor. There are only so many hours in a day—and only so many highly-productive years in a lifetime—that any of us can devote to work. You need to get an adequate return on your investment of your time and labor in your farm, just as it's important to get a reasonable return on your investment of money in your farm.

How much is your labor worth? There are a couple of ways to calculate the value of your unpaid labor. One way is to charge the farm the same pay that it would cost to hire somebody to do your job. Another way would be to estimate what you could earn off-farm in the local area, given your education and experience. If you use the second method, it's reasonable

Continued on next page

Farmer Labor ... continued

to reduce the pay rate you "charge" to the farm, recognizing that there are many tangible and intangible benefits to working on the farm rather than working elsewhere. For instance, you might enjoy building fence on your own farm so much that you'd take $8/hour for it, yet you would charge another farmer $20/hour to do the same work.

The bottom line is that your labor is precious and valuable, and your farm business needs to acknowledge the value of your labor. The value needs to be more than zero.

While the value of your unpaid labor is important, it is not included as an expense on the farm's income statement. If a value of unpaid labor was included on the income statement, it would make comparisons between farms very difficult. Every farmer would put a different value on her wage.

Also, it is common for operators of family farms to take an owner's draw to cover family living expenses. The draw is deducted on the annual statement of cash flows. If we also assigned a value of unpaid labor on the income statement, there's a risk of counting owner's compensation twice, which would make the farm's financial performance look worse than actual.

The value of unpaid labor and management will be deducted when we calculate some of the profitability ratios in Chapter 12.

Net Cash Farm Income – Net cash farm income is simply net farm income with the depreciation added back in. Net cash farm income is not used to calculate any of the profitability ratios but is the first number you will need to develop your statement of cash flows.

Net Cash Farm Income = NFI + depreciation

Summary

An income statement is developed to show you, on an annual basis, or as needed, whether or not your farm is profitable. Measuring profitability is a very important part of farm financial management. It tells you if you are on the right track and signals a warning if you are headed dangerously off-course. It allows you to compare the performance of your farm operation to that of your peers. It can help you set achievement goals for the future. It can help you decide whether to make additional capital investments in the farm; particularly important if additional capital investments would require you to take on debt.

However, as important as it is for a farm operation to be profitable, an unprofitable farm operation can continue to plod along for years as long as its cash flow is positive. On the other hand, a profitable farm without positive cash flow won't be able to pay the bills and can be bankrupt in short order. In the next chapter we will look at cash flow and explain how to develop a statement of cash flows for your farm.

CHAPTER 11
When is the Money Moving? Assessing Cash Flow

The Big Challenge:

Every December you purchase a piece of machinery to minimize your income tax liability. Every May, you run out of cash after paying for all of your spring crop inputs. Some of your bills go unpaid, the balances on your credit cards go up, and you lose sleep worrying about how you are going to make ends meet until you have crops to sell. How can you do a better job of planning, and avoid this situation in the future?

Your statement of cash flows gives you a way of looking back at the past year and determining the extent to which your farm was able to generate enough cash income to cover all of your cash obligations. Some farmers might say, "You don't need to waste time putting together a financial statement to tell you that. If you paid all of your bills, made all of your loan payments, and you've still got money left in your checkbook on December 31, your cash flow was positive."

Unfortunately, there are a lot of things your end-of-year checkbook balance isn't telling you. It won't tell you if you short-changed yourself on family living expenses in order to stretch dollars through the end of the year. It doesn't show if you borrowed more principal than you paid down, or if you had to ask your lender to defer principal payments or restructure a farm loan to free up cash. It can't explain if you had to sell a couple of heifers or a piece of machinery to cover an unexpected bill. The process of developing your statement of cash flows will help you understand, accommodate, and plan for these issues and more.

There are really four questions we are trying to answer with the statement of cash flows:
1) Is the cash flowing in from the farm's normal operations enough to cover all of the farm's cash operating expenses?
2) If you consider any capital assets sold during the year versus capital assets that you purchased, how much did those activities add to the farm's cash flow or take away from it? Are you making investments that prepare the farm to generate even stronger cash

Key questions addressed in this chapter:

Why is a cash flow statement important?

How do you create a cash flow statement?

What does a cash flow statement tell you?

From the Farmers

Using the Cash Flows Statement Effectively

Matt O'Hayer, Vital Farms

Cash flow can be tricky, Matt O'Hayer of Vital Farms says. If you sell an asset or increase your payables you will feel rich and have a lot of money in your pocket, but you may still be losing money on your farm. On the other hand, if you pay down payables or buy an asset, you may feel like things aren't going so well, when you are really doing fine.

"You need to be very careful in how you look at the numbers," he says. "Without the facts you are farming blind. A good financial statement should be an early warning system that allows you to fix a problem before it gets out of hand."

---

flow in the future, or are you selling off productive assets to cover operating shortfalls and thus hurting the farm's long-term prospects?

3) From the beginning of the year to the end, were you able to pay down principal balances on farm loans or did you take on more debt?

4) After paying all of the operating expenses, making all scheduled debt payments, taking an adequate draw for family living expenses, and paying any income tax and social security liabilities, was there enough cash left over to replace machinery that is wearing out, buildings that are deteriorating, and put some money aside to protect the farm if an unexpected event puts a squeeze on cash flow?

The cash flow, unlike the previous statements, often combines home living expenses and farm expenses, as its main goal is to help you manage your money so you can cover your bills. If in your bookkeeping system you separate out the farm from your personal expenses, you will want to combine them together when assessing cash flow, unless each is a separate tax entity.

In Chapter 10 we discussed the income statement and explained how it helps determine the profitability of your farm. In this chapter, we're talking about cash flow. Profitability and cash flow are related, but they hold very different positions of importance in assessing the financial health of your farm. An unprofitable farm that has positive cash flow each year can continue to operate for quite some time.

However, positive cash flow without profitability is a terminal condition. The next generation will not be able to purchase the farm at market value and continue operating it. A profitable farm with negative cash flow can quickly end up on a path towards bankruptcy. Negative cash flow is a critical condition, even if the farm is "profitable" as measured by its income statement. In these respects, being able to understand and control your cash flow is more important than calculating various measures of profitability.

There are three elements to a statement of cash flows:
1) Cash flowing in;
2) Cash flowing out; and, hopefully,
3) Cash that sticks around to be invested back into the farm.

The statement of cash flows ought to seem pretty simple after developing your income statement. We're only dealing with cash in and out so you don't have to adjust for changes in inventories or calculate depreciation.

In this chapter, we will talk about your cash flow as an annual financial statement that assesses the past year's cash flow; the statement of cash flows. However, it is also very useful for you to project, or predict, cash flow on a month-by-month basis for the year ahead. A month-by-month cash flow projection can help you see when you might run short of cash, and when your incoming cash flow can be expected. Most importantly, it allows you to formulate a plan to get you through the months when cash flow falls short. This will create your pro forma cash flow. We discuss cash flow planning in more detail in Chapter 20.

Profitability vs Cash Flow

Profitability and cash flow are related concepts but they give you very different information about your farm operation. Profitability gives you a sense of the economic return you are receiving on the capital you have invested in your farm. Cash flow tells you if the money that flows into your farm is more than the money that flows out.

A farm can be profitable yet have a negative cash flow. This situation can exist when a farm has debt that is structured incorrectly and too much principal is being paid in a relatively short a period of time. It can also exist when a farm is making big capital purchases and paying for them out of operating cash flow. It sometimes happens when a farmer is making investments that won't generate cash inflow for several years such as building up a herd of beef cows. Finally, it can be found on farms where family living draws are very high in relation to income.

A farm can be unprofitable yet have a positive cash flow. A typical scenario in which this is found is a farm that has been owned by one farmer for a very long time, all debt has been paid off, and family living costs are very modest. There may be a lot of assets devoted to the farm but not a lot of income.

A calculation of profitability ratios would show that the farm falls below the benchmarks for profitability. However, the net cash flow is still enough to pay all operating expenses, family living costs, and perhaps even cover a bit of capital asset replacement (e.g. buying a new piece of equipment every once in a while).

Cash flow is absolutely critical in the short run, particularly for beginning farmers or other farmers who have a significant amount of debt that needs to be serviced. Negative cash flow for a period of time can be devastating to a farm business. It can ultimately lead to horrible outcomes such as liquidation of assets, foreclosure, or bankruptcy.

Profitability is important over the long run. A farm that is unprofitable but has positive cash flow can continue to operate for a long time. However, an unprofitable farm is a terminal operation. Nobody will be able to buy the farm at fair market value and continue to operate it as a farm business. The farm will either have to be sold at less than farm market value or pass through an estate as an inheritance to continue as a farm. In some places, the farm could be sold at fair market value and converted to a use other than agriculture, or some other more profitable agricultural enterprise.

Cash flow and profitability are both important for a farm to be a sustainable entity over the course of many years. We will discuss both of these concepts in more detail in Chapter 13.

Statement of Cash Flows vs Pro-forma Cash Flow

A statement of cash flows is a document that looks at the history of how cash has moved in and out of your business. A pro-forma cash flow looks at the same kind of information, but as a projection into the future. Both are important in helping you manage your business. The statement of cash flows will provide valuable information for developing your pro-forma cash flow. In this chapter we will only discuss the statement of cash flows. We look at the pro-forma cash flow in Chapter 20.

Getting Started With Cash Flow

The statement of cash flows will be the most important statement for a new farmer, and will be most helpful done on a monthly basis. It will be the main document a banker looks at when considering a loan application.

Getting Started on the Statement of Cash Flows

As you begin working on your statement of cash flows, start by thinking about cash that moved in and out as a result of operating the farm. Also think about other normal, year-to-year cash flow such as non-farm income, and family living expenses or an owner's draw from the farm. In addition, you will want to consider cash that flowed in or out as the result of any purchases or sales of capital assets, any additional personal investments you or others made in the farm, and loan balances that increased or decreased during the year.

The streams of cash flow are broken into three components, which we will describe in detail in this chapter: 1) Cash flow from operations; 2) Cash flow from investing activities; and 3) Cash flow from financing activities.

Your farm's cash balance on the first day of the business year is listed at the top of the statement of cash flows. The farm's cash balance remaining on the last day of the year is shown at the bottom of the statement as the ending cash balance. Just above the bottom line, you'll calculate the overall net change in cash from the beginning of the year to the end.

Your profit and loss statement from your bookkeeping system or the Schedule F from your federal tax return should bring together a lot of the information you need to create the cash flow statement. You will also want to gather some documents to help you in preparing your statement of cash flows: bank statements from the beginning and end of the year; loan documents for any loans taken or paid down during the year; credit card statements if you carried balances at any time during the year, records of capital asset transactions such as machinery or land purchased or sold during the year; and all of your tax records for the year.

The first line on your statement of cash flows will be your beginning cash balance. This is the sum, as of January 1, of the total amount of your checking, savings, money market funds, hedging accounts, and any other cash that was available to the farm. Again, we are only focusing on cash here so we won't include any other current assets such as prepaid supplies or crop inventory. From here, we'll begin exploring various streams of cash flowing throughout the year.

Table 11.1 on page 95 shows the statement of cash flows from Otto B. Organic's farm.

Cash Flow from Operations

Each stream of cash flow has inflows and outflows. The inflow represented in your cash flow from operations is your gross cash farm income, or all of the dollars received during the year from the sale of products from your farm, custom work performed, government payments received, and other cash generated from farming activities. This is on a cash—not an accrual—basis, so money received during the year for products sold the previous year is included. By the same token, any product you delivered towards the end of the year and for which you weren't paid is not included. Your federal tax return or the profit and loss report from your bookkeeping program will show you your cash inflows in your various income areas. Be sure that your profit and loss is run on a cash, not accrual, basis to get the numbers accurate.

Table 11.1
Otto B. Organic's
Statement of Cash Flows

Statement of Cash Flows	FY 20X1
Otto B. Organic	Annual total
Beginning Cash Balance	5,000
Cash Flow From Operations	
Cash Inflows	
Corn	33,600
Milk	256,000
Cull stock	
Cull cows	18,480
Misc Livestock	
Bull calves	3,840
Govt payments	3,000
Operations Inflows	$ 314,920
Cash Outflows	
Seed	8,820
Fetility	20,250
Weed & pest treatments	5,265
Crop insurance	3,510
Custom hire - crops	5,625
Feed	79,987
Breeding	3,200
Veterinary	9,596
Supplies	19,992
Marketing	
Checkoff	2,160
Milk hauling	2,880
Other marketing	560
Fuel & oil	6,000
Repairs	10,000
Custom hire - other	6,020
Labor	15,000
Land taxes	4,000
Farm insurance	2,000
Utilities	7,200
Certification fees	3,000
Income taxes	6000
Operations Outflows	$ 221,065
Net Cash From Operations	$ 93,855
Cash From Investing	
Capital purchases	(8,000)
Capital sales	6,000
Net Cash From Investing	(2,000)
Cash Flow From Financing	
Operating loan payments	(11,372)
Machinery loan payments	(63,686)
Off-farm wages	20,000
Living/draw	(36,000)
Net Cash Flow From Financing	(91,058)
Net Change in Cash	$ 797
Surplus or Deficit (Ending Cash Balance)	$ 5,797

> ### From the Farmers
>
>
>
> **Cash Flow Analysis is Critical**
>
> Kay Jensen, JenEhr Family Farm
>
> *Setting up an annual cash flow statement is a critical exercise, says Kay Jensen of JenEhr Family Farm. "If you don't map out the cash flow, there is a good chance that at some time of the year you'll run out of money."*
>
> *She notes that this is especially true of those running CSAs, where the majority of the income comes in the late winter. "April and May are always hard. We don't want to borrow against our line of credit, so we need to plan ahead."*

Dairy producers will have a fairly consistent cash flow throughout the year. CSA farms often have big cash inflows during the annual signup period in early spring. Fresh market vegetable and other horticultural operations will see most of their cash coming in during the busy summer production season. Other livestock and row crop farmers will generally see income come in in big clumps, as youngstock are shipped or harvested crops are sold.

You don't need to worry about inventory changes for purposes of the statement of cash flows as you did for your income statement; inventory changes don't directly affect your gross cash farm income. Also, don't include cash generated from the sale of capital assets such as machinery, breeding livestock, or land at this point. Those will be handled in the next section of the statement of cash flows.

The outflow in your cash flow from operations is the total amount of cash operating expenses for the year. Any cash that was paid out during the year for any operating expenses, even those that were incurred in a previous year, are included. These are payments from your checking account and cash purchases. If you had expenses that you were unable to pay during the year, those expenses should not be included. A bill that wasn't paid didn't take anything out of the year's cash flow (however, it does need to be shown as a liability on your balance sheet). We also need to include farm interest paid as part of cash flow from operations. Interest payments are part of the cost of doing business on the farm if you are carrying debt. Finally, any income taxes paid on farm income should be included as cash outflow.

Subtracting cash outflow from cash inflow will give you the balance of cash provided by operations. This can be either a positive or a negative number.

Net Cash from Operations = gross farm income − cash paid out for operating expenses

Otto's Net Cash from Operations = $314,920 - $221,065 = $93,855

> ### Farm Wages and the Cash Flow Statement
>
> If the farm is actually paying a regular, consistent wage to the farmer it should be a considered a normal labor cost and appear as part of the cash outflow from operations. If the farmer is taking a monthly payment (commonly known as a "draw") out of the farm, and the draw fluctuates from month to month depending on the farm's cash flow, it should show up under financing activities.

Cash Flow from Investing Activities

The heading for this component of the statement of cash flows is a bit misleading; it sounds like this is the place to talk about all of the money you made from your investment in a vegetable processing plant or a wind farm. However, "investing activities" in this case refers to your investments in capital assets that are part of your farm such as machinery, land, or breeding livestock. Purchases of these items are thought of as investing activities because they should provide benefits to the farm over the course of multiple years. Sales and purchases of capital assets don't typically occur every year so they need to be considered separately from normal operating cash flow.

Sales of capital assets create the cash inflow for this section of the statement of cash flows. You should include the net cash received for each capital asset. For example, if you sold a piece of land using a realtor who took a six percent commission, the sale should be listed as the cash you received after paying the commission and any other sales expenses. You don't have to account for depreciation of capital assets you sold during the year; cash is your only concern here. If you received a partial payment for something, such as deposit on a purchase or payments towards a sale, include only the cash income that comes in during the year you are tracking.

Purchases of capital assets represent the cash outflow in this section of your statement of cash flows. For each capital purchase made during the year, you will want to include the net cash paid out for the purchase. Even if you took out a loan to pay for the purchase—as is often the case—you should still include the net cash paid to the person or company from which you purchased the asset. If the cash paid to the seller was provided through a loan, include it here as a capital asset expense. The principal amount of the loan will be shown as a cash inflow that will be accounted for in the next section.

Here's an example. Let's say you purchased a tractor for $50,000. You wrote a $15,000 check from the farm checking account, and financed the other $35,000 of the purchase. You will show a cash outflow of $50,000 under Cash Flow from Investing Activities. You will also show a cash inflow of $35,000 under Cash Flow from Financing Activities.

Subtracting purchases of capital assets from sales of capital assets will give you the net Cash Flow from Investing Activities. This can be a positive or a negative number.

Net Cash from Investing = income from sales of capital assets —cash paid for purchase of capital assets

Table 11.2 shows Otto's net cash from investing. This is the detail for the cash from investing section of his cash flow statement.

Table 11.2 Otto's Net Cash from Investing

Otto B. Organic		
Capital Purchases		
Chopper Box	5/8/20X1	8,000
Total Cap Purchases		*8,000*
Capital Sales		
Tractor	4/13/20X1	6,000
Total Capital Sales		*6,000*
Net Capital Changes	20X1	(2,000)

Cash Flow from Financing Activities

Financing for most farm businesses is provided either by lenders or from the farm owner's personal investment of cash into the operation. In this section of the statement of cash flows cash that flows in and out from those sources is taken into consideration.

The first cash inflow from financing activities is the total amount of money that was borrowed during the year. If you tapped your line of credit for $10,000, or ran up an unpaid credit card balance of $10,000, that would be a cash inflow from money borrowed. By the same token, if you bought a new tractor and took out a loan of $35,000 to help pay for it, you would have $35,000 of cash inflow from financing activities (and, as we saw in the previous section above, the purchase of the tractor would create a $50,000 cash outflow under cash flow from investing activities).

Next, you need to subtract the amount of principal you paid on borrowed money during the year. If you tapped your line of credit for $10,000 in April and paid the entire amount off in November, you would have $10,000 of inflow and $10,000 of outflow. If you paid over the course of the year $5,000 of principal on your tractor loan, you would show this $5,000 of principal payments as an outflow.

Table 11.3 shows the detail of Otto's loan payments. The total of $63,686 shows up in his cash flow statement as Machinery Loan Payments.

Table 11.3 Otto's Loan Payments

Otto B. Organic	
20X1 Loan Payments	
	TOTAL
FCS- Machinery	
Principal	17,372
Interest	3,358
Total	20,730
FCS- Parlor	
Principal	8,841
Interest	2,760
Total	11,601
FCS- Mortgage	
Principal	12,225
Interest	19,140
Total	31,365
Total Loan Pmnts	63,686

Handling Credit Card Debt

If a credit card is used the same as cash or as a checking account and interest never accrues, the expenses being paid with the card should be counted under cash flow from operations. However, if it's used as an operating loan with balances carried over from one month to the next and interest accruing, the principal and interest should show up under cash flow from financing activities.

Why Are Living Expenses Listed in the Financing Section of the Cash Flow?

Family living expenses are representative of a return on the farmer's investment in the farm. It goes back to the manner in which a farm is financed. Generally, there are two entities that finance a farm operation: a lender and a farmer. Both need to get paid back for their investments. The farm pays the bank interest payments (cash outflow from operations) and principal payments (cash outflow from financing activities).

The farm might pay the farmer a wage (cash outflow from operations) and should pay the farmer a draw (cash outflow from financing activities). The farmer should eventually be able to draw out their entire investment in the farm over a period of time.

Here's where things may get a bit confusing. You next want to consider net cash income earned through off-farm employment as cash inflow under cash flow from financing activities. You might question whether or not it makes sense to include income from an off-farm job as part of the cash inflow for the farm. It is considered to be cash that is available to be used by the farm operation when necessary, which can help sustain the farm during tough times. This is different than when you are doing enterprise or farm profitability analyses, when off-farm income is not taken into account. (We will talk more about those in Sections Four and Five.)

Generally speaking, you should include net non-farm income unless there is a very clear separation between the farm business and the personal life of the farm family. For instance, if your home is not located on the farm, and the non-farm income covers all family living expenses, you can probably leave the non-farm income off of the statement of cash flows. Also, if your farm is incorporated as a separate corporation (such as an S- or C-Corp or an LLC), you will most likely not include off-farm income. In most instances, however, lenders usually want to see non-farm income included.

The farm should generate enough cash flow to allow the owner to take a monthly family living draw that covers family living expenses. Obviously, if the farm is a part-time occupation it won't likely pay all of the family living expenses. At the very least, the farm owner should be able to pay themselves a reasonable hourly wage for all hours worked on the farm. If all goes well, the farm should provide enough cash flow for the farmer to withdraw his or her investment in the farm over a period of years.

Assuming that personal income from off-farm employment was included as cash inflow, you next need to subtract family living expenses. Many farm families, if they aren't keeping detailed records of their family living expenses, tend to estimate these expenses to be much lower than they really are. Family living expenses include health insurance and other medical costs, food, fuel for non-farm vehicles and for the farm house, clothing, child care expenses, charitable donations, etc. If the farm is a separate corporation you will not include these.

To arrive at the net cash flow from financing activities, you need to follow a few steps. Start with the principal borrowed and subtract the principal that was paid back. To the difference of that equation, add cash inflow from any personal income. Next, subtract any family living expenses or other cash withdrawal by the farm's owner. The result will be your net cash from financing activities.

Net Cash from Financing = (principal borrowed – principal paid back) + (net personal income – family living and/or owner draw)

Do these same summary calculations for the other two sections of the cash flow statement just discussed.

Wrapping Up the Statement of Cash Flows

You want to arrive at two figures on the bottom of the statement of cash flows:
1) Net change in cash; and
2) Ending cash balance

The net change in cash is simply the sum of the net cash from operations, net cash from investing activities, and net cash from financing activities.

Net Change in Cash = net cash from operations + net cash from investing activities + net cash from financing activities

Otto's Net Change in Cash is $93,855 - $2,000 - $91,058 = $797

By adding the net change in cash to the beginning cash balance at the top of your statement of cash flows, you will find what your ending cash balance should be. You will want to compare this number to the actual amount of cash you have on hand as of December 31 to make sure you haven't missed any cash flow entries along the way.

Ending Cash Balance = beginning cash balance + net change in cash

Otto's Ending Cash Balance is $5,000 + $797 = $5,797

What Can We Learn From the Statement of Cash Flows?

Ultimately, what you want to know from the statement of cash flows is how cash flows into the farm operation, how it flows out, and how much you were able to grab and keep as it flowed through. Looking at the top and bottom lines, you would obviously want to see a larger ending cash balance than beginning cash balance. However, without exploring each of the three sections of the statement, beginning and ending cash balances don't tell us much.

If you compare your statements of cash flow over several years you would hope to see that net cash flow from operations has been increasing each year. You would also hope to see that the net cash flow from operations was always positive and was greater than net cash flow from investing or financing activities. This means that the actual production on your farm is making money.

Moving down to the cash flow from investing activities, it would be good to see periodic purchases and sales of capital assets. It shows that you are generating adequate cash flow to upgrade and improve your operation, which should lead to greater cash flow from operations in future years. However, if you are making capital purchases primarily as a way to avoid paying income taxes rather than to improve operating efficiency or cash flow, that raises a concern. Another concern is if it appears that you have been systematically selling off needed capital assets in order to raise enough cash to cover operating or family living expenses. This means that you are unable to maintain your farm's infrastructure over the long-term and may be risking your future as a farmer.

As you look at the cash flow from financing activities, you can feel good if over the years you have generally paid down more principal than you have added to term debts. However, there may be years in which you are taking on more debt to finance capital investments that in turn are increasing cash flow from operations. Increasing debt isn't necessarily a bad thing if it improves your farm's cash flow and profitability.

You'll want to study what's happened to off-farm income over time. Would your operation be in jeopardy if you lost your off-farm employment? If your goal was to eventually give up your off-farm job, are you making progress toward your goal? Are family living expenses going up or down at a reasonable rate? If they are going up, are they eating up cash you need to maintain farm operations? If they are going down, have you been skimping on family living to cover farm operating expenses? Finally, are you able to draw out in cash each year some of your initial investment in the farm?

You can see that simply breaking your farm's cash flow out into three separate streams gives you a much better sense of how cash can be managed in ways that can reduce financial risk. It allows you to manage cash in ways that provide better, more tangible returns on your investment in the farm. In Chapter 12 we will introduce you to a number of ratios which will help you to see trends as you compare your cash flow and other numbers from period to period. These ratios will also allow you to compare your financial situation to other similar farms.

Summary

The statement of cash flows helps you understand the flow of cash in and out of your farm business. It is important to see if you are bringing in enough to cover your expenses. It helps you recognize the buying or selling of large capital items, which will affect your cash flow both now and for years in the future. The statement of cash flows includes money paid or taken in from loan activity, and will generally take into account income from off-farm work. The cash flow statement helps you understand if you are making progress on paying back loans, reinvesting in the farm, and if you are putting money away for emergencies or other contingencies.

SECTION FOUR
ANALYSIS AND DECISION-MAKING USING YOUR NUMBERS

Now that you have your standard statements, the real analysis can begin. In this section we begin by helping you understand ways to assess your farm's financial performance in terms of liquidity, solvency, profitability, debt repayment capacity, and financial efficiency. By combining various numbers from your key statements into a series of equations, you get some simple values that help you easily compare the farm's financial activity from year to year, or to other similar farming operations.

The statements created in the previous chapters are tools with which you can assess your farm's profitability. There are several ways to look at profitability, which is different from making a profit. Once you understand your farm's profitability, you can make targeted changes that will increase it.

Next we take you into the realm of using your farm financials to make important decisions. Should you buy that extra 40 acres the neighbor wants to sell, or talk him into renting it to you? Would it be more profitable to increase the herd by 10 cows, or to instead raise the steers? We all have impulses that lead us into these decisions. Following impulses in many instances isn't wrong, but supporting those gut feelings with real numbers is a good idea. In this section we show you how to prove, or disprove, those instincts.

Once you decide you want to add an asset, or if you are starting up an enterprise or operation, or if you are looking for an operating loan, you very likely need to develop a relationship with a lender. A lender explains to you exactly what lenders are looking for, what you should expect from them, and how to prepare materials for them to enhance your success in asking for a loan.

CHAPTER 12
Comparisons Tell a Story: Ratios

Key questions addressed in this chapter:

Why are ratios useful?

Which ratios help you understand your liquidity?

What ratios help assess solvency and profitability?

Which ratios help you understand your cash flow position?

What do ratios tell you about your farm's efficiency?

It is a very common and useful practice to take the numbers found in the balance sheet, the income statement, and the statement of cash flows, and put them together in various equations to assess the financial situation of a farm. These equations, termed ratios, can then be compared from year-to-year, compared with those of other farms or businesses that are doing similar things, or simply used to determine the financial strengths and vulnerabilities of the farm.

Ratios are at times more useful than straight numbers in making comparisons, as they take out some of the variables that can interfere, such as the size of an operation. Your lender will use ratios when assessing your operation for a loan, and they will be very useful for you if you are considering changes on the farm.

It is a good idea to choose a particular subset of farm financial ratios that seem useful to your situation and monitor them at least annually. Do these ratio calculations in an Excel spreadsheet or with paper and pencil in a record book. We recommend that you set up a system that you can add to in upcoming years, so that you can track key ratios and keep a close eye on the financial trends in your operation from period to period.

It can take time to get used to creating and analyzing ratios for your own farm. A local advisor, such as your lender or an Extension agent can help you more deeply understand all of the implications of your ratios. Ratios will point to where you need to take a closer look at something. Further analysis, such as an enterprise analysis (discussed in Chapter 16), can then be used to tease out where the problems are, and lead you to the next questions.

You generally won't be making decisions based on any one ratio. Ratios support each other and verify problems.

OTTO'S TIP:

We will include here calculations of the ratios from our sample farmer, Otto B. Organic, and conclude with a discussion of what we can learn from his numbers. Refer to Otto's balance sheet on page 81, income statement on page 85, and statement of cash flows on page 95 to see where the numbers for his ratios are coming from.

The following ratios use numbers taken from the balance sheet, income statement, and the statement of cash flows.

For a worksheet on ratios, see Appendix E. Also included is a simple chart showing typical ranges for the most commonly used ratios.

OTTO'S TIP:

Where Did These Particular Ratios Come From?

Prior to the farm crisis of the 1980s, farm accounting and financial analysis was done in a haphazard manner. There were no commonly accepted principals being used by farmers or their accountants, lenders, and other financial professionals, which made objective and consistent financial analysis of farms virtually impossible.

The 80s farm crisis caused a group of farm financial professionals to come together and draft a set of financial guidelines for agricultural producers. An organization called the Farm Financial Standards Council (FFSC) was created to promote uniformity and integrity in financial reporting and analysis for agricultural producers.

Their recommended guidelines, and the 21 farm financial ratios that the FFSC has developed, have been widely adopted by accountants and lenders across the country. In this book, we have done our utmost to adhere to the FFSC guidelines.

What You Can Learn From the Balance Sheet

The balance sheet can tell you a number of different things about your farm. A single balance sheet can be analyzed to assess your farm's working capital and solvency positions, the appropriateness of debt structure, and the overall financial risk of the operation. Beginning and ending balance sheets can be compared to each other to determine your farm's financial progress during the year. If you get in the habit of updating your balance sheet every year on January 1, you'll be able to track your financial progress over the long run. Finally, the balance sheet can be combined with the other financial statements to calculate many different ratios that indicate areas of financial strength and vulnerability in your farm business.

Liquidity – Current Ratio and Working Capital

Current Ratio: How are you set for paying this year's obligations?
Beginning with your balance sheet, take a look at current assets and current liabilities. Dividing current assets by current liabilities will give you the farm's current ratio. The current ratio is a way to quickly rate short-term financial risk. It gives you a sense of how easy or difficult it will be to pay all of the farm's obligations within the next year using current assets. It gauges your potential for having cash flow problems.

$$\text{Current Ratio} = \frac{\text{current assets}}{\text{current liabilities}}$$

Generally, a current ratio greater than 2:1 is considered adequate. You should have enough cushion to cover a large, unexpected expense. A strong current ratio can also allow you to take advantage of opportunities that arise, such as discounts for early payments on bills.

A current ratio of 1:1 is risky. This means that you have just enough current assets to cover the liabilities you already know you will have to pay this year. If anything unexpected pops up, you could be in trouble. Keep in mind that current assets include many items in addition to cash, such as crop and feed inventories, market livestock, accounts receivable, and prepaid supplies. If you suffer any sort of financial setback, you may be

RATIOS

Benchmarking (comparing farming operations)

We have presented a lot of information in this book related to developing financial statements and how to calculate financial ratios. But what does an operating profit margin ratio of 15 percent or an asset turnover ratio of 0.25 really indicate? Are these good numbers compared to other farming operations like yours?

Benchmarking is the comparison of your financial ratios to an industry group or a similar group of farming operations. The livestock and dairy industries have compiled large data bases of numbers from current farming operations. Farm business associations often compile and share aggregated numbers by major geographic region. By comparing with similar operations you can learn a great deal about your farm. Unfortunately, if you are a fruit or vegetable grower, there aren't any industry data bases or summaries, so your numbers must be compared to a calculated budget or a set of ideal financial statements compiled by a land-grant university or other reliable source.

The major advantage of using financial benchmarks is the ability to point to where your financial strengths and weaknesses are compared to the larger group. Additionally, your financial benchmarks can often lead back to issues of concern in your production.

Continued on next page

---

forced to sell off inventories or go out and collect a debt to be able to generate enough cash to cover your liabilities.

A current ratio of less than 1:1 means that you don't have enough assets to cover what you owe. If you are in this situation you are in trouble with cash flow, and need to look at ways to remedy the problem.

$$\text{Otto's Current Ratio is } \frac{\$111{,}450}{\$48{,}837} = 2.28$$

Working Capital: How much do you have above what you owe?
By subtracting current liabilities from current assets you can determine your working capital. Working capital is simply the dollar value of uncommitted current assets. It is a particularly useful number when it is taken in context of the farm's annual income and expenses.

Working Capital = current assets − current liabilities

$$\text{Otto's Working Capital is } \$111{,}450 - \$48{,}837 = \$62{,}613$$

Working Capital to Gross Revenue Ratio: How much cushion do you have relative to your gross income?

Dividing your working capital by your farm's gross income gives you the farm's working capital ratio. The working capital ratio tells you how much working capital you are holding in relation to the size of your farm business.

$$\text{Working Capital to Gross Revenue Ratio} = \frac{\text{working capital}}{\text{gross farm income}}$$

$$\text{Otto's Working Capital Ratio is } \frac{\$62{,}613}{\$314{,}920} = .199$$

Your working capital should be greater than 15% (0.15) of your annual gross farm income. If your working capital ratio is much lower than 0.15, you will be in a vulnerable position if your gross farm income drops or expenses take a sudden jump. A low working capital ratio might prevent a farmer from taking advantage of an unexpected opportunity that arises, such as a big discount for prepaying for seed or soil amendments.

Common Liquidity Problems

Some of the most serious financial problems farmers encounter show up in an analysis of current ratio and working capital. Sometimes debt is not structured appropriately, and the farm is trying to pay for an intermediate or long-term asset as if it is a current liability. This can happen when a farmer pays cash or uses the farm operating loan to buy a piece of machinery. He or she is either using up their cash, or is creating a current liability that needs to be paid off within the year.

In some cases it becomes apparent that the farm operation is only able to keep its liquidity strong by capitalizing credit card debt and other short-term obligations. In other words, the farm is essentially spreading out payments for its annual operating expenses over a longer period of time by taking out term loans. This just creates bigger problems in the future as it erodes the overall equity of the farm.

Sometimes looking more closely at the composition of the farm's current assets reveals a more accurate picture of the farm's true liquidity, or the immediate availability of current assets to be used for current liabilities. For instance, it is not uncommon to see much of the working capital for a livestock operation tied up in feed inventories, which can't easily be turned into cash without causing a disruption in production. While working capital may appear to be strong, in reality these are not assets that can be quickly and easily converted to cash in order to pay bills.

Another challenge in assessing liquidity is putting values on current assets. Do we use the market price of corn today, or the forward price being quoted for delivery three months from now when we plan to sell it? Should we use today's price and then discount it to allow for the risk that the price might go down over the next three months? The values we assign to current assets could make a big difference in our liquidity position.

Solvency—Assets, Debt and Equity

Debt to Asset Ratio: How much of what you own is under debt? Next, take a look at total assets, total liabilities, and owner's equity. Divide total liabilities by total assets to calculate your debt to asset ratio. The target for debt to asset ratio should be 0.50 or less. The lower your debt to asset ratio, the greater your ability to withstand a severe financial shock or a long-lasting slump in the farm economy.

$$\text{Debt to Asset} = \frac{\text{total liabilities}}{\text{total assets}}$$

$$\text{Otto's Debt to Asset ratio is } \frac{\$535,400}{\$1,487,450} = .36$$

Should your goal be to reach a debt to asset ratio of zero? Not necessarily. To answer that question you need to know the profitability of your farm. It may make sense to pay interest on borrowed money if it allows you to generate even more profit. For example, if you can borrow money at 5 percent and your farm generates 8 percent return on assets, it makes economic sense to keep some debt in place. Your debt-to-asset ratio is simply another indication of the financial risk in your farm on the day the balance sheet was prepared.

Benchmarking ... continued

For example, you compare your pork operation to an industry standard and find out your asset turnover ratio is better than the average, but your operating profit margin is worse. You review the calculations going into those financial ratios and determine that your gross revenue is higher than average (leading to a higher turnover ratio), but your operating expenses are higher than average as well (leading to lower operating profit margin). You review your operating expenses and notice your feed costs are much higher than average because your feed efficiencies are lower. You can now talk to your pork production expert or other members on your advisory team to determine how to increase feed efficiency, which will lead to lower overall production costs and a higher operating profit margin.

The same procedure could be used for the other financial ratios, as well as many of the other types of benchmark data sets available. However, benchmarking is not without limits. First, the operations that you are comparing to must be similar to yours. Dairy financial benchmarks are different from beef, which are different from grain farms, etc. Organic operations are likely to be significantly different from non-organic operations.

Second, you need to make sure the formulas within the calculations are the same. For example, some data bases use gross revenues for some of the financial calculations (such as turnover ratio) whereas other data bases may use the value of farm production. The resulting ratios are substantially different. Comparing your numbers to one that was calculated using a different formula will lead to incorrect comparisons. The key is to contact the keepers of the benchmark data you are using, explore the exact components of the formulas, and compare their formulas to yours.

Benchmarking can provide a vast amount of information to help you better understand and evaluate your farming operation. Just make sure the comparisons are the same so you don't come up with wrong conclusions.

We have included 2015 Minnesota farm statistics in Appendix F, a sample bechmarking tool.

RATIOS

Equity to Asset Ratio: How much of the farm assets are paid for?

The flip side of the debt to asset ratio is your equity to asset ratio. The target equity to asset ratio is 0.50 or more. In other words, your equity in the farm should be more than 50 percent of the value of the assets. The more equity you have, the greater your resilience during tough times.

$$\text{Equity to Asset} = \frac{\text{total equity}}{\text{total assets}}$$

$$\text{Otto's Equity to Asset ratio is } \frac{\$952,050}{\$1,487,450} = .64$$

Debt to Equity Ratio: How does the debt investment compare to your owner investment in the farm?

The next ratio to consider is the debt to equity ratio. Dividing total liabilities by owner's equity yields the debt to equity ratio. It's the number of pennies of debt for every dollar of equity you have invested in your farm. You want to reach a debt to equity ratio of 0.45 or less. As the debt to equity ratio goes down, your share of the ownership of the farm increases. If you think about it, all of the assets used in the farm business have to be financed by somebody. The portion financed by lenders shows up on the balance sheet as liabilities. The portion financed by you shows up as owner's equity. The lender's stake in your farm should be smaller than yours, and getting smaller over time.

$$\text{Debt to Equity} = \frac{\text{total liabilities}}{\text{owner's equity}}$$

$$\text{Otto's Debt to Equity ratio is } \frac{\$535,400}{\$952,050} = .56$$

There are times when debt to equity ratio will be higher than 0.45. At farm start-up or during a period of farm expansion, the ratio could be significantly higher than 0.45. The important point is that, aside from those out-of-the-ordinary events, the ratio should go down from year to year. If it doesn't, you need to examine the farm business more closely.

Common Solvency Problems

Occasionally, a farm will experience relatively long periods of time when cash flow is negative. After using up all of their working capital and any available operating credit to keep the farm going, the next step is to take on additional intermediate or long-term debt in order to free up cash. This process of converting equity to cash can create a big solvency problem.

Another solvency problem can appear when the market value of assets declines. Machinery and buildings eventually wear out or become obsolete. Land values can drop, as they did in the 1980s. Asset values can sometimes decline faster than the principal balances on the loans used to purchase them. All of these things can cause solvency problems.

Major life events can cause solvency problems. When a farm couple divorces, the spouse who remains farming often needs to take on debt to buy out the ex-partner's ownership interest in the farm. (One farmer we know who had just gone through a divorce said he loved his farm so much that he bought it twice!) The same issue arises with the dissolution of a farm partnership or LLC. Sometimes the debt burden resulting from a buyout is so large the farm can't survive.

Income Statement Comparisons that Help Assess Profitability

Rate of Return on Assets: Is the farm a good investment?

The first income statement ratio to calculate is rate of return on assets (ROROA). The ROROA can be thought of as the interest rate that is being earned on all of the assets being used in your farm business. This includes your investment of equity and your lender's investment of debt capital.

Net farm income from operations (NFIFO, from page 89) is used in the calculation of ROROA, with two slight adjustments. First, because the goal is to calculate a rate of return on both your and your lender's investment in the farm, you need to temporarily eliminate the interest expense in the net farm income. You do that by adding the interest expense back to NFIFO. If you don't add back the interest, the lender's return on investment will be accounted for twice.

Second, since ROROA is a calculation of the rate of return on the capital invested in the farm, if the farm does not pay you wages that were included as labor expenses on the income statement, you will also need to add in a reasonable expense for the value of your unpaid labor and management. This is done by subtracting the value of your unpaid labor and management from the net farm income. If you did include family wages or a salary for your labor, you don't need to make this adjustment.

So, what is the value of your unpaid labor and management? There are a couple of ways to figure it. The first is to consider what you (and other family members if they provide unpaid labor to the farm) would be able to earn in your area if you were to take an off-farm job. A second way is to total up the amount of money or other items of value that you withdraw from the farm business in a typical year to cover family living expenses. Perhaps you withdraw $1,500 per month in cash to pay for groceries, health insurance, and household expenses, and the farm also provides you with meat to fill your freezer. You would total the value of everything and use that figure as the value of unpaid labor and management. (For more on labor see Chapter 22. For more on the value of unpaid labor and management, see Chapter 10)

Finally, consider ROROA to be a calculation of the rate of return on a cost basis for the average amount of total assets used in the farm operation during the year. Therefore, cost basis balance sheets should be used when calculating ROROA. To get the average amount of assets, simply add together the total assets on the beginning and ending balance sheets, and divide by two.

Here is the formula for calculating ROROA:

$$ROROA = \frac{NFIFO + \text{farm interest paid} - \text{value of unpaid labor/management}}{\text{average total farm assets (cost basis)}}$$

RATIOS

$$\text{Otto's ROROA is } \frac{(\$48,083 + \$26,628 - \$36,000)}{\$1,487,450} = .026$$

What would be considered a healthy ROROA? The ROROA should be higher than the interest rate on borrowed money and higher than the rate of return you could expect to receive from an alternate investment. If you are paying seven percent interest on farm loans, you should have a ROROA that is higher than seven percent.

If the ROROA is lower than the interest rate being paid on farm loans, it does not make economic sense to continue borrowing money to invest in this farm business. Why would you borrow money at seven percent interest to generate a ROROA of four percent? If the ROROA is higher than the current interest rate or expected return from alternative investments, it probably makes good business sense for you and your lender to keep making strategic investments in your farm.

To convert your ratio to a percent, multiply the total by 100. For instance, Otto's ROROA is .026 in integers, or 2.6 percent.

OTTO'S TIP:

Rate of Return on Equity: Another way of looking at the farm as an investment. The second balance sheet ratio to consider is rate of return on equity (ROROE). The ROROE is essentially the interest rate you are receiving on your investment in the farm. The calculation of ROROE is simpler than that for ROROA. You only need to subtract the value of your unpaid labor and management from net farm income, then divide that number by the average value of your equity in the farm during the year. You will get your average equity number by adding your equity (from your balance sheet) from the end of the year to that at the beginning of the year, and dividing by two.

Here is the formula for calculating ROROE:

$$\text{ROROE} = \frac{\text{NFIFO} - \text{value of unpaid labor and management}}{\text{owner's average farm equity}}$$

$$\text{Otto's ROROE is } \frac{(\$48,083 - \$36,000)}{[(\$952,050 + \$978,633)/2]} = \frac{\$12,083}{\$965,342} = .0125$$

Your ROROE should be higher than your ROROA, and thus should be higher than the interest rate on borrowed money or the expected return from an alternate investment. A person with no farm debt will have a ROROE equal to their ROROA. A farmer with a lot of borrowed money and relatively little equity will often have a ROROE that swings wildly from one year to the next. In a good year, their ROROE might be 15 percent or higher. In a bad year, it can be negative by a similar percentage. For that reason, a farm investment decision should never be made solely by considering ROROE. It also points out the wisdom of strengthening your equity position in the farm during good years rather than borrowing additional capital to buy more assets in an attempt to avoid paying income taxes.

Operating Profit Margin: How efficient is your farm?
Calculating your operating profit margin is a way to assess the operating efficiency of your farm business. Put in the most simple terms, it tells you the percentage of the value of your annual gross farm production that ends up as net income. The actual calculation is a bit more complicated but should not be too much of a challenge after you've made your accrual adjustments.

To calculate operating profit margin, go back and get the first part of the calculation for ROROA: NFIFO + farm interest paid – any value of unpaid labor and management. The resulting number is considered to be the return on assets. You want to divide this return on assets by your gross farm revenue (accrual adjusted).

Here is the formula for Operating Profit Margin:

$$\text{OPM} = \frac{\text{NFIFO} + \text{farm interest paid} - \text{any value of unpaid labor/management}}{\text{gross farm revenue (accrual adjusted)}}$$

$$\text{Otto's OPM is } \frac{(\$48{,}083 + \$26{,}628 - \$36{,}000)}{(\$314{,}920 - \$2{,}444)} = \frac{\$38{,}711}{\$312{,}476} = .124$$

What is a "good" operating profit margin? It depends on the type of farm enterprise you operate. For a farm that produces raw commodities such as corn, soybeans, milk, or finished cattle, an operating profit margin of 25 percent or higher would be considered very strong. A farm that grows vegetables for sale through farmers' markets or a CSA might consider a 25 percent operating profit margin to be low. Businesses that sell direct to the consumer typically have higher operating profit margins than a farm business that sells commodities.

Earnings Before Interest Taxes Depreciation and Amortization (EBITDA)
The calculation of EBITDA is new to agriculture but has been commonly used in other business settings for years. The concept behind EBITDA is that every business has its own unique way of financing its operations, managing its tax liabilities, and depreciating its capital and intangible assets.

It is very difficult to compare the financial performance of one business to another similar business if interest expenses, taxes, and depreciation are deducted before arriving at bottom-line earnings. One farm might be 100 percent financed with owner equity and have zero interest expense, while the next farm carries hundreds of thousands of dollars in loans and pays tens of thousands in interest each year. EBITDA allows for another way to measure and compare farm earnings.

To calculate EBITDA, you need to start with NFIFO. This eliminates any distortion in income caused by the purchase or sale of machinery or other capital assets. To NFIFO add farm interest paid, income taxes paid, and depreciation expense. (The "A" in EBITDA, Amortization, is not commonly found in production agriculture. It is an expense similar

Labor Ratios

The standard ratios used in agriculture do not include any labor statistics. However, for diversified small farms labor is one of the primary expenses. For this reason, you may want to track certain labor ratios from year to year or month to month.

Standard labor ratios in another high labor industry, retail sales, include:

Direct Labor to Sales DLS = direct labor costs / total gross sales

Direct Labor to Expenses DLE = direct labor costs / total expenses

Net Income per Hour of Labor = net income / number of labor hours

Each of these could be figured at the farm level or at the enterprise level. If you see dramatic increases in these ratios over time, it may indicate labor inefficiencies (or improvements, in the case of Net Income per Hour of Labor).

---

to depreciation but is used to allocate the cost of an intangible asset, such as a patent, over the course of its useful life.)

Here is the formula for EBITDA:

EBITDA = NFIFO + farm interest paid + income taxes paid + depreciation expense

Otto's EBITDA is $48,083 + $26,628 + $6,000 + $22,700 = $103,411

How do you know if EBITDA is strong or weak? Because EBITDA is such a new measure in agriculture, good benchmarks have yet to be established. In other businesses, EBITDA is often used as one of a number of ways to estimate the value of a business. For example, a business might be worth four to seven times its EBITDA.

Common Profitability Problems

Profitability problems often stem from making capital investments that are too large to be supported by a farm's income. Capital investments tend to add significant overhead costs such as depreciation and debt service, which forces the farm to generate a lot more net income to achieve an adequate level of profitability.

Operating expenses that are too high can cause profitability problems. Labor costs, feed costs, and interest expenses are three categories that can be relatively high on some farms. A small change in one of these categories can have a big impact on the bottom line, while a large change in a minor expense category will barely register.

Sometimes the manner in which profitability is calculated can cause a problem. For example, we typically use market basis balance sheets in agriculture. If market values of assets have been increasing, as they did with land over the past 15 years, using a market basis balance sheet when calculating ROROA and ROROE will make it very difficult to show an adequate level of profitability. It's also common to leave out the value of the farmer's unpaid labor and management when calculating profitability, which will inaccurately inflate ROROA and ROROE.

Cash Flow Ratios

There are several measures that you will want to calculate to evaluate your operation's cash flow. However, to calculate these measures you will not only need your statement of cash flows, you will also need to re-visit your income statement and your balance sheet.

Capital Debt Repayment Capacity (CDRC): How much debt can you actually handle? The first cash flow measure to calculate is your capital debt repayment capacity. This dollar amount represents the highest annual total principal and interest payments you could possibly pay given the amount of income generated both on-farm and off-farm. To start the calculation of capital debt repayment capacity, you need the net cash farm income number from your income statement. To this add your non-farm income. Then subtract family living expenses and income taxes/social security paid. Finally, add the interest that was paid on term debts (remember that interest was deducted as an operating expense to arrive at net cash farm income, which is why we need to add it back in here).

Here is the formula for calculating Capital Debt Repayment Capacity (CDRC):

CDRC = Net Cash Farm Income + non-farm income – family living expenses – income tax/SS + interest paid on term debts

> Otto's CDRC is $73,227 + $20,000 - $36,000 - $6,000 + $26,628 = $77,855

Capital Debt Repayment Margin (CDRM): How much borrowing capacity do you have left after making debt payments?

The capital debt repayment margin is simply the total dollar amount of your capital debt repayment capacity that remains after you make all of your scheduled principal and interest payments for the year and make payments on any remaining operating debt that was carried forward from the previous year. Sometimes remaining short-term debt balances will be amortized or spread out over three or four years, as it would likely cause an unmanageable demand on available cash to try to pay it all off in one year.

Here is the formula for calculating Capital Debt Repayment Margin (CDRM):

CDRM = CDRC – scheduled principal and interest payments – annual payment on remaining operating debt

> Otto's CDRM is $77,855 - $63,686 - $0 = $14,169

Capital Replacement Margin (CRM): Do you have enough money available to replace equipment and buildings?

If your farm business is going to continue to grow and evolve from year to year, you will need to have enough excess cash flow to regularly reinvest in capital assets and still have something left over to save for a rainy day. Typically, capital assets are purchased with a combination of cash and borrowed funds. Picking the right balance of cash and credit is primarily determined by your comfort level. The capital replacement margin gives you the ability to determine if there is any rainy day cash remaining after you devote some of your net cash flow to replacement of capital assets that are wearing out.

To calculate capital replacement margin, start with the capital debt repayment margin (CDRM) calculated above. From CDRM, we want to subtract an allowance for replacement of the farm assets that rust and rot such as machinery, vehicles, and buildings. We're going to earmark a bit of our available cash for replacement of depreciating assets. Some good thumb rules for annual replacement allowance are 15% of the value of machinery and vehicles, and 5% of the value of buildings and other improvements. If you don't currently have any loans for any of these depreciable assets and didn't purchase any during the past year, the annual replacement allowances represent the cash needed for capital replacement.

RATIOS

Otto's Assets

Otto's machinery and titled vehicles = $145,300 x .15 = $21,795. Otto's buildings and improvements = $76,000 x .05 = $3,800. $21,795 + $3,800 = $25,595 capital asset replacement allowance.

He made $26,213 principal payments on machinery and parlor and paid a net $2,000 for new equipment for a total of $28,213.

Since his capital asset replacement allowance is $25,595 and he is already devoting $28,213 to capital asset replacement, his allowance is more than covered and no additional cash is needed.

If you used cash to buy depreciable assets, or you're making loan payments on depreciable assets, you're already using some of your available cash for capital replacement. Subtract the cash purchases and principal payments on loans for depreciable assets from the annual replacement allowances. This will tell you how much cash—if any--is still needed for capital replacement. Subtracting any cash needed from CDRM gives you the remaining capital replacement margin.

Here is the formula for calculating Capital Replacement Margin:

CRM = CDRM − unfunded net capital replacement allowance

$$\text{Otto's CRM is } \$14,169 - \$0 = \$14,169$$

Term Debt Coverage Ratio (TDCR): Will your banker think your loan load is reasonable?

Term debt coverage ratio is a benchmarking measure that helps you determine whether or not your total debt load is too high relative to your cash flow. It is one of the main indicators used by many lenders to make loan decisions. Once you've calculated your capital debt repayment capacity, it's easy to calculate your term debt coverage ratio; you simply divide your capital debt repayment capacity (CDRC) by your total scheduled principal and interest payments for the year.

The formula for Term Debt Coverage Ratio (TDCR) is:

$$TDCR = \frac{CDRC}{\text{scheduled principal and interest payments}}$$

$$\text{Otto's TDCR is } \frac{\$77,855}{\$63,686} = 1.22$$

Your term debt coverage ratio needs to be at least 1.0. If TDCR is less than 1, you won't even be able to make your scheduled principal and interest payments, much less have any cash available to pay for replacement of capital assets or have any dollars left over to put in a rainy day fund. Generally speaking, we would like to see a TDCR of 1.3 or more. That would suggest you'll have enough cash to put into the replacement of capital items and still have something left over for a major unexpected expense.

Term debt coverage ratio is particularly important to beginning farmers. Beginning farmers usually start out with a lot of ambition and energy, but not much cash. To accomplish their farming goals, they often need to borrow a lot of money relative to the income potential of their farms. The lender wants to have a sense of comfort that farm loans are going to be paid back. TDCR is a way for the lender – and you – to assess the financial risk of your business plan. The lower your TDCR, the more likely it is that your loan could eventually wind up in default.

Replacement Margin Coverage Ratio (RMCR): Are you investing enough back into your farm?

Replacement margin coverage ratio is similar to term debt coverage ratio except that it not only considers your ability to make your principal and interest payments, but also takes into account any cash needed for replacement of capital assets.

The formula for Replacement Margin Coverage Ratio (RMCR) is:

$$RMCR = \frac{CDRC}{\text{(scheduled principal and interest payments + unfunded net capital replacement allowance)}}$$

$$\text{Otto's RMRC is } \frac{\$77,855}{(\$63,686 + \$0)} = 1.22$$

Replacement margin coverage ratio is a way to formally account for cash that is needed for replacement of depreciating assets. As previously noted, some farmers would prefer to pay cash for capital replacement and others have no problem financing capital purchases. A farmer who has a relatively low debt load and likes to pay cash for replacements will probably find RMCR to be a more useful ratio than will a farmer who is more highly leveraged.

Common Cash Flow Problems

Most farm cash flow problems relate to the fact that production, market prices for farm products, and cost of farm inputs can all fluctuate wildly from one year to the next. If crop production falls short, market prices drop, or the cost of feed goes up, we're going to have cash flow problems.

High debt loads can make cash flow problems much worse. Principal and interest payments can place a big demand on your farm's available cash. That's why lenders tend to focus on cash flow more than anything else when making a loan decision. They don't want you to take on a debt load that is unmanageable when the farm economy takes a dip. While some lenders only look as deep as term debt coverage ratio (TDRC) to assess cash flow, others will use replacement margin coverage ratio (RMCR) to make sure there is enough cash available to replace depreciating assets and maintain the farm's capacity over the long run.

Debt structure can sometimes cause a cash flow problem. A common example is a farmer using the farm's operating loan to buy a piece of machinery. The operating loan generally needs to be paid off within a year. If it is used to buy machinery, the machinery is now on a loan that must be paid back in less than twelve months, which is a huge demand on the farm's cash this year. The machinery should instead be transferred to a term loan with a more-typical five-year amortization schedule.

While most farm families don't live an extravagant lifestyle, family living costs are another demand on the farm's cash. Family living costs can be difficult to track because they

RATIOS

From the Farmers

Analysis Programs Can Help: FINPACK

Carmen Fernholz, A-Frame Farm

The University of Minnesota Center for Farm Financial Management financial analysis software program "FINPACK" (cffm.umn.edu) is "absolutely worth the money, especially for a new farmer," Carmen Fernholz says. You can pay an annual fee for a personal version, which includes a free trial version and numerous training resources.

Carmen says that the program, requires that he input his own data, forces him to get comfortable with his numbers, and adds to his familiarity and understanding of the reports that are generated.

The program offers a diversity of annual financial reports and projections, including balance sheets, monthly and annual cash flows, and overall financial analysis, including comparisons to previous years.

There are sections of the program for budgeting, and making projections if you are considering specific farm changes or want to compare the financial possibilities of one potential crop to another.

With an over 15-year history, FINBIN reports also offer very valuable comparisons to the data from more than 3,000 active farms (finbin.umn.edu). Carmen appreciates these

Continued on next page

tend to be paid in small increments several times a day, 365 days per year. Sometimes family living costs are covered by off-farm employment. If the off-farm job comes to an end, it can cause a cash flow problem on the farm.

Efficiency Ratios

The efficiency ratios described in this section use information from all three financial statements to help you determine how efficiently assets are being used on the farm to generate income. These ratios can point out areas in which your financial performance is being hindered as well as areas of strength. An important point with the financial efficiency ratios is to consider them as a package rather than placing too much weight on individual ratios. You are better off to fall in the average range for all of the ratios than to be strong in one and very weak in another.

Asset Turnover Ratio: How much gross income is your farm generating for the amount of assets being devoted to the farm?

The asset turnover ratio (sometimes referred to as the asset turnover "rate") is a measure of how efficiently your farm assets are being used to generate revenue.

The formula for Asset Turnover Ratio (ATO) is:

$$ATO = \frac{\text{gross farm revenue}}{\text{average total farm assets}}$$

Otto's ATO is $\frac{\$314{,}920}{\$1{,}379{,}450} = .228$

An ATO of 45 percent or higher is considered to be strong. An ATO of 45 percent would say that you are generating $45 of annual gross farm income for every $100 of assets being used in the farming operation.

ATO is a useful ratio, but you need to be a bit cautious in the weight you put on this figure, because there are situations that can skew the number one way or another. For instance, a beginning farmer with few assets who rents land, buildings, and machinery could have an ATO much higher than 45 percent. On the other hand, a late-career farmer who owns many acres of land and sheds full of machinery and generates only a modest level of income could have a very low ATO. The values we use for farm assets can make a huge difference in the ATO, too.

Operating Expense Ratio: Are your operating expenses too high, too low, or about right given your farm's gross income?

The operating expense ratio shows the percentage of your gross farm income that is being used to pay for operating expenses. It helps you determine whether your operating expenses are too high for the amount of gross income your farm is able to generate each year. The calculation for operating expense ratio takes out the interest paid on farm debt and also excludes depreciation.

The formula for Operating Expense Ratio is:

$$OER = \frac{\text{total farm operating expenses (excluding interest and depreciation)}}{\text{gross farm revenue}}$$

$$\text{Otto's OER is } \frac{\$241{,}693 - \$26{,}628}{\$314{,}920} = .6829$$

An OER of 80 percent or less is generally considered to be appropriate for most farm operations and an OER of less than 60 percent is considered to be strong. The OER for a beginning farmer who rents many of his or her assets will often be higher than the OER of a farmer who is making principal and interest payments for assets. This is because rent payments show up as operating expenses while the costs associated with ownership of assets, principal and interest payments are not considered in the calculation.

The OER is a ratio that is most useful when monitored over time. The OER should not vary by more than 5% from one year to the next. If it varies more than this, it is worth digging deeper into your numbers to make sure everything is accurate. It's also important to watch the OER when you are making plans for a major change in your farming operation. For example, if you put together projections for a big farm expansion and show that OER would drop by 10%, you might be overly optimistic in your expectations of your farm's financial performance.

Depreciation Expense Ratio: How much of your gross farm income is needed to cover capital equipment that is rusting or rotting?

The depreciation expense ratio looks at the depreciation expenses your farm is incurring and compares them to your gross farm income. It gives you a sense of whether you own too much equipment, or have an excessive amount of money tied up in buildings relative to the gross income of your farm.

The formula for Depreciation Expense Ratio is:

$$DER = \frac{\text{depreciation}}{\text{gross farm income}}$$

$$\text{Otto's DER is } \frac{\$22{,}700}{\$314{,}920} = .0721$$

An average DER over time of 15 percent or less is appropriate for most farms. However, there might be years when DER is higher than 15 percent. Perhaps you are just starting up a dairy operation and have purchased all of your cows. Purchased cows are depreciable assets (cows you raised yourself from your own calves are not depreciable) so your depreciation expenses in the first few years will be very high. DER is a ratio that needs to be considered in the context of your other measures of financial efficiency, as well as your cash flow ratios, to determine whether it is telling you something important about your financial situation.

From the Farmers...continued

comparisons, especially now that many organic farmers participate, which allows him to see if his numbers are better or worse than others —and where parts of his operation could be improved.

Carmen especially appreciates FINPACK reports for assessing how his individual crops are doing, and for long range planning. He looks at the enterprise reports, especially the comparisons year to year, and asks "What were the factors that made corn or oats more profitable this year? How much were my energy costs, my seed costs, etc.? Where could I fine tune next year?"

Information that he gets from the FINPACK yearly reports helps him to decide questions such as if it makes more sense to plant more oats or barley, flax or alfalfa the next year.

It's important to use true, economic depreciation rather than tax depreciation to calculate DER. If you use tax depreciation, your DER is likely to show big swings from year to year.

Interest Expense Ratio: How much of your gross farm income is being used to pay interest on borrowed money?

The interest expense ratio compares the total interest being paid on farm debt to your farm's gross income. It helps you see whether your total yearly interest expenses are too high in relation to your farm's annual gross income.

The formula for Interest Expense Ratio is:

$$IER = \frac{\text{farm interest paid}}{\text{gross farm income}}$$

$$\text{Otto's IER is } \frac{\$26,628}{\$314,920} = .0846$$

An IER of 10 percent or less over time is generally considered to be about right. If your IER is much higher than 10 percent, you will want to look at the possibility of refinancing debt at a lower interest rate if possible, or consider selling assets to reduce your debt load.

Net Farm Income Ratio: How much of your gross farm income is left for you after paying all of your expenses?

The net farm income ratio gives you a sense of how much of your gross farm income remains as profit that can compensate you for your contribution of unpaid labor and management (assuming you didn't deduct the value of your unpaid labor), as well as your equity investment in your farm.

The formula for Net Farm Income Ratio is:

$$NFIR = \frac{\text{net farm income}}{\text{gross farm income}}$$

$$\text{Otto's NFIR is } \frac{\$50,083}{\$314,920} = .1590$$

Your NFIR should be at least 10 percent and preferably greater than 20 percent. This is a ratio that can vary depending on the type of farm operation you have and the amount of unpaid versus paid labor you employ on your farm. If you are a small-scale farm growing high-value crops and have little or no hired labor, your NFIR probably should be greater than 20 percent. If you run a large scale dairy operation with a great deal of hired labor, a NFIR of 8-10 percent year in and year out might be considered quite good.

Summary

Ratios comprised of numbers from your balance sheet, income statement, and statement of cash flows are a quick analysis tool that can be used to compare your farm's financial activity to previous time periods, to other farms, or to compiled industry data or benchmarks. If you fully utilize ratios they can help you see where your farm management is excelling or lacking and needs to be adjusted.

Key Ratios

Now that we have overwhelmed you with information, let's simplify things a bit. If you were to just concentrate on the most key ratios, which should you pick?

From our many years of experience of working with diversified farmers, we recommend that you focus on the following seven ratios:

1. Can you pay your bills? The current ratio divides current assets (ready cash and crops) by liabilities (what you owe). If you don't have enough to cover your bills you're in trouble.

2. Can you pay your debts? The term debt coverage ratio divides your ability to repay by the amount that you owe in loan payments. If you need a loan in an emergency this indicates how your banker might feel about it.

3. Are you solvent? The debt to asset ratio divides what you owe by what you own, and indicates how much "room" you have to borrow. How much of what you own is under debt?

4. Are you at the right scale? The asset turnover ratio is one indicator of how efficient you are being. Do you have the right amount of equipment to do the job? It is easy to structure things to make this look really good (by renting everything) so be careful. ATR = Gross farm revenue divided by average total farm assets.

5. What is your per unit profit? The operating profit margin will show you if your operating expenses are too high, or your prices too low. Again, if you rent a lot this will look very low. Look at this in combination with the asset turnover ratio.

6. What percent of your revenues do you keep? If you want to make $40,000 a year, but your net farm income ratio is only 10 percent, then you'll need to bring in $400,000 in gross income. 20 to 40 percent is a goal for a smaller diversified farm, with the higher number more likely for those running on owner labor. (NFIR = net farm income divided by gross farm income)

7. Are you paying too much for operations? What kind of sales do you need in order to cover your expenses? The operating expense ratio divides total farm operating expense by the gross farm income.

Tracking these seven ratios for your farm from year-to-year should give you a good base of information for decision making.

Paul Dietmann has a Chat with Otto About his Financial Ratios

We asked author Paul Dietmann what Otto can learn from his ratios. The following is a conversation Paul would have with Otto.

Liquidity Ratios

Current Ratio: 2.28. I'd want to see a current ratio greater than 1, and prefer that it be above 2, so a current ratio of 2.28 is strong. However, the vast majority of Otto's current assets (92%) are in the form of crop inventories. I would ask Otto if all of his stored crops will be needed as feed, or if he has excess inventory that could be sold to generate income. If the farm experiences a significant, unexpected cash shortage and he needs all of his crop inventories for feed, these assets could not be sold to generate cash without causing major problems for the dairy. I recommend that Otto begin building a more substantial cash reserve. Building up a cash "rainy day" reserve is not an easy thing to do for most farmers. There are always better uses for cash on the farm than to leave it sitting in a savings account accruing interest at a .25% rate. However, it is really important to have cash available when something inevitably goes wrong on the farm.

Working Capital: $62,613. Not a bad level of working capital. However, most of Otto's working capital appears to be tied up in inventories of crops that are needed for feed and not intended to be sold. This could present a challenge if he runs into financial trouble.

Working Capital Ratio: .199. A farm's working capital ratio is considered to be okay if it falls between .10 and .25. At .199, Otto's working capital ratio is right in the middle of the adequate range.

Overall, Otto is doing a good job maintaining his working capital. My major recommendation would be to build a larger cash reserve to lessen the likelihood that he will have to sell off feed inventory to generate cash when things are tight. We don't have a good benchmark for the amount of working capital that should be held in the form of cash, but $5,000 seems awfully low for a farm with gross revenue of $315,000. If this was my farm, I don't think I'd be comfortable with less than $25,000 in cash.

Solvency Ratios

Debt to Asset Ratio: .36. The lower the debt to asset ratio, the better. Ideally it is less than .60 and preferably less than .30. Otto's debt to asset ratio is .36, which is fine. His ratio suggests that he is not too highly leveraged and has some borrowing capacity available to him if he needs it.

Equity to Asset Ratio: .64. The equity to asset ratio is the flip side of the debt to asset ratio; the higher the equity to asset ratio, the better. It should be higher than .40, and preferably more than .70. At .64, Otto has a substantial amount of equity in his farm.

Debt to Equity Ratio: .56. A farm's debt to equity ratio is another way of describing how the farm is being financed. It tells us how many pennies of debt are owed for each dollar of the owner's equity investment in the farm. We want it to be less than 1.50, and would rather see it below .43. Otto's ratio of .56 tells us that, for each dollar of equity he holds, he has 56 cents of debt. That's pretty good.

Otto has built up a respectable level of equity in his farm. He does not have an excessive amount of debt. I would recommend monitoring these ratios each year to ensure that they are heading in the right directions.

Continued on next page

A Chat with Otto ... continued

Profitability Ratios

Net Farm Income: $46,083. Net farm income needs to be a dollar amount that Otto is comfortable receiving in exchange for his labor, his equity investment, and the risk he is taking with his money by having it tied up in the farm. If Otto loves farming and is satisfied with $46,083 of Net Farm Income, I would not argue with him.

Rate of Return on Farm Assets: 2.6%. The general rule of thumb is that rate of return on assets (ROROA) should be higher than the interest rate being paid on farm loans. At first glance, it seems that Otto's ROROA is relatively low. However, we need to keep in mind that his balance sheet is based on market values for farm assets. If land values in Otto's area, for example, are increasing at the astronomical rate they have been rising across the Upper Midwest, his low ROROA could be the result of a big increase in asset values rather than from a shortage of net farm income. We need to consider some of the other ratios to determine whether or not his low ROROA is a cause for concern.

Rate of Return on Farm Equity: 1.25%. The rate of return on equity (ROROE) can be thought of as the interest rate the farm owner is receiving for his or her equity in the farm. It should be higher than the ROROA. In other words, the farm owner should get a higher return for their assets invested in the farm than the return being generated on all of the assets invested in the farm. Otto's ROROE is less than half of the ROROA for the farm. This suggests that there are some profitability issues with his farm. I always worry more about cash flow than I do about profitability, at least in the short run. If we find that Otto's cash flow is good and he's happy, those are the most important factors to consider.

Operating Profit Margin: 12.4%. The operating profit margin can vary depending on the type of agricultural enterprise. Commodity producers typically have smaller operating profit margins, but they also produce relatively high volumes of commodities in order to generate adequate levels of income. No matter what type of enterprise, the operating profit margin should exceed 15%. Farms that grow specialty crops or value-added marketing strategies can exceed 25%. Otto's operating profit margin of 12.4% is low. Combined with the other profitability ratios, it indicates that there are profitability issues in need of further attention.

EBITDA: $103,411. EBITDA is a measure of farm earnings that excludes the impacts of financing, depreciation, and tax management strategies being used by the farm owner that can skew the earnings. It's a relatively new measure in farm financial management but has been used for years in other businesses as a tool to estimate the value of businesses. For instance, a business might be valued at five to seven times its annual EBITDA. Using these example multiples, Otto's farm would be worth $517,055 to $723,877, which is significantly less than the $1,379,450 market value of the total farm assets on his balance sheet. The discrepancy between EBITDA and the market value of farm assets suggests that, at least in this particular year, earnings are too low to justify the value of the assets tied up in the farm. If Otto wants to sell his operation to the next generation and have them continue operating the dairy, he will have to sell the farm assets at a significant discount from their market values.

Otto's profitability ratios are of some concern. There is a large misalignment between the earnings being generated by his farm and the farm assets that are being used in the operation. Was this simply a bad year that doesn't reflect the farm's long-term earning potential? Have asset values become over-inflated? Are there assets that are underutilized and could be sold to reduce the total capitalization of the farm? We need to dig deeper to find the root causes of his profitability problems.

Continued on next page

A Chat with Otto ... continued

Repayment Capacity Ratios

Capital Debt Repayment Capacity: $77,855

Capital Debt Repayment Margin: $14,169

Capital Replacement Margin: $14,169

There are no rules of thumb for the three figures above, as each farm has its own unique financing, cash flow, and capital replacement needs. In Otto's situation, the maximum amount of debt that he could possibly service using his current household cash flow – his capital debt repayment capacity – is $77,855. His total annual principal and interest payments on existing debt are $63,686, which leaves him a capital debt repayment margin of $14,169. Is that enough margin? It seems like Otto might be cutting it close, particularly when we consider that $20,000 of the cash inflow available to the farm is coming from off-farm income. If the farm loses that off-farm income, there won't be enough cash flow to cover its scheduled principal and interest payments.

Using Otto's balance sheet, we calculated an allowance of $25,595 needed for replacement of depreciable capital assets. Between his cash outlay for purchase of machinery and the principal payments made during the year on loans for depreciable assets, he spent $28,213. He doesn't need to use any more of the farm's cash to replace stuff that's rusting, rotting or wearing out as he's already exceeding the needed allowance. Otto is left with a capital replacement margin of $14,169. We need to look at the cash flow ratios below to determine whether this is strong or weak.

Term Debt Coverage Ratio: 1.22. A term debt coverage ratio of 1.2 is considered to be the lowest a farm can get before falling into a precarious cash flow condition. At 1.22, Otto is right on the edge. I would be concerned about his cash flow and would work with him on a plan for improvement. Perhaps a loan needs to be reamortized or other changes need to be made to free up a bit more cash flow.

Replacement Margin Coverage Ratio: 1.22. Otto's replacement margin coverage ratio is the same as his term debt coverage ratio because he is already covering his capital asset replacement needs without having to devote any more cash to it. We generally want to see a replacement margin coverage ratio of at least 1.1 and preferably more than 1.4. Otto's replacement margin coverage ratio is not strong but not dire either.

Otto's cash flow condition appears to be precarious, although he ended the year with no operating debt, which is unusual for a farm that's struggling with cash flow. I would like to gather more details to see if there was something out of the ordinary about this year's cash flow. For instance, does the cash flow look tight because he made extra principal payments on term debts?

If this was a typical year, it would not take much to throw Otto into a really bad position. I would recommend that he consider a variety of options to make improvements such as debt restructuring, sale of unused assets such as surplus feed or machinery that isn't used very much, cutting big production expenses such as purchased feed and hired labor costs, boosting farm income, and more.

Continued on next page

A Chat with Otto ... continued

Financial Efficiency Ratios

Asset Turnover Ratio: .22. The asset turnover ratio should be greater than .30; higher than .45 would be considered strong. Otto's asset turnover ratio of .22 is more evidence that the earnings from the farm are low relative to the amount of farm assets being utilized. Are there any unnecessary farm assets that could be sold?

Operating Expense Ratio: .6829. An operating expense ratio of less than .80 is generally considered to be okay and less than .60 is strong. Otto's operating expense ratio of .6829 indicates that his operating expenses are reasonable relative to the farm's gross income.

Depreciation Expense Ratio: .0721. Otto's depreciation expense ratio of .0721 is fairly strong. We don't want to see a depreciation expense ratio higher than .15. Otto's ratio suggests that his buildings and equipment are mostly depreciated, and he hasn't made many capital purchases or improvements in the past year. Even though the ratio is considered to be positive, it may also be an indication that he has been deferring necessary capital investments because his cash flow has not been very strong.

Interest Expense Ratio: .0846. An interest expense ratio of less than .10 is considered to be good. Otto has an interest expense ratio of .0846. This tells us that he is not paying an inordinate amount of interest, his loans are probably aged a bit (he's paying less interest and more principal), or his interest rates are low.

Net Farm Income Ratio: .1590. A net farm income ratio greater than .10 is thought to be okay and greater than .20 is pretty good. Otto's net farm income ratio of .1590 is really not bad. It tells us that he's generating an adequate amount of net farm income relative to his gross farm income.

Otto's financial efficiency ratios have not given us much more information than we already knew. He has a lot of money tied up in farm assets and is not generating enough gross income to fully justify the investment. His net farm income is really not bad, although it appears that some of his operating expenses are high. His interest and depreciation expenses are not out of line. The most serious challenge Otto appears to have is with his cash flow.

CHAPTER 13
Factors That Improve Profits

Key questions addressed in this chapter:

What key factors improve profitability?

What other profitability improvements might you look at on your farm?

For many people the main goal of farming may not be to make a profit, but most of you will need to be profitable in order to stay farming.

So far in this book we've helped you understand if your farm is making a profit, and how to use your financial records to understand more deeply what is going on in your operation. These understandings lead to the next step: making decisions that help you to make your farm more profitable. Sometimes small changes can make a big difference in your farm profitability. Below are some thoughts and suggestions.

Broadly speaking, there are two key ways to improve profitability. The first is to increase your profit margin per unit while selling the same number of units. The second is to increase unit sales while maintaining the same profit per unit (assuming of course that the profit margin is positive to start with). The first way focuses on making your farming operation more financially efficient. This can be measured by looking at the operating profit margin. The second way emphasizes utilizing your farming assets more effectively, and could be measured by a financial ratio such as asset turnover.

Improving financial efficiency (profit per unit) can be accomplished in a variety of ways, including:

Reduce overhead costs. Some might call these "fixed costs." We don't like to use the term fixed costs because if a cost is fixed, it suggests that nothing can be done to change it. A farmer can get rid of equipment that is not used very much. He or she could sell a piece of unproductive land. Loans can be renegotiated when interest rates are low. Perhaps a building could be segmented into areas that are heated and not to cut down on overhead; heating large buildings costs more than heating something the right size.

Reduce variable costs, particularly the variable costs that constitute the largest portions of operating expenses. For a dairy or livestock producer this means first taking a hard look at feed costs, which typically make up more than 50 percent of operating expenses. For a fresh market vegetable producer it means examining labor costs. A small decrease in a large operating expense category makes a big impact on profitability. A big change in a minor category (for example, reducing the cost of ear tags by 60 percent on a dairy farm), has almost no impact on profitability.

Increase your price per unit sold. This is a simple, often looked over solution to increasing profit margin per unit. Farmers often "undervalue" their product or compare their farm product incorrectly to a product that isn't necessarily comparable. For example, comparing your farm raised product to one that is commercially grown, shipped thousands of miles, and sold through a major grocery store chain is not a fair comparison. In Chapter 19 we'll discuss prices in depth. Increasing unit price for an underpriced product can bring in increased profit without lowering the number sold. If you believe your customers cannot or will not pay more for your products, then you have to ask yourself, do I have the right customers?

Increasing sales while maintaining your profit margin can be accomplished through the following:

Increase production, but only if overhead and variable costs are held constant. Perhaps you can do this by choosing more hardy crop varieties, or those that produce higher yields. This can be where many dairy producers run into trouble; doubling the size of their herds and simultaneously tripling their overhead costs by adding buildings, new equipment, manure storage, feed storage, etc.

Increase sales by more accurately matching production with marketing, step up marketing to complement an increase in production. Carefully plan production based on projected sales to minimize any spoilage, shrink, or customer returns. Adding production that makes your farm compost piles or donations to the local food bank bigger won't improve your farm profitability. Utilizing your farm assets effectively to match up production and sales, however, will.

Using Your Operating Profit Margin and Net Turnover Ratio to Manage Profits

In Chapter 12 we introduced you to the standard ratios that you can use to assess what is happening financially on your farm. Let's assume you looked at your asset turnover ratio and operating profit margin and you want to improve them. How do you go about doing that?

$$\text{Asset Turnover} = \frac{\text{value of farm production}}{\text{average farm assets}}$$

To improve your asset turnover ratio you can do any of the following:
- Keep producing all the same products, but increase yields on some or all of them
- Change the product mix to products that yield more
- Increase the percentage of what you produce that is sold
- Look at sharing assets (such as machinery), leasing instead of owning, or custom hiring your field work needs; this lowers your average farm asset value and increases your asset turnover ratio
- Think of other ways that you can increase the number of units produced with your existing farm asset base

From the Farmers

Weak Links

Lauren Langworthy, Blue Ox Organics

"It is important to discover the weak links in your chain—you might be producing all that you need to grow, but if you aren't selling all of it, you won't be making the money you need. Think about where along the line your problem is—putting more acres into production might not be what helps."

From the Farmers

The Value of Guesses

Kay Jensen, JenEhr Family Farm

Kay Jensen points out the importance of using numbers to make decisions. Recognizing that doing the research to make a decision might stall us with the time or lack of information, she sees great value in making guesses. "We can't be afraid of making guesses, and then verifying," she claims. She recommends you use the best information you have to make a good guess, and then track things as they unfold to see how close you were. "If your guess is way off, usually it isn't a big deal," she says. "The next time you will have more information to make a better guess." Starting with a guess is better than not making an informed decision at all.

Profit versus Profitability

When we ask a farmer what their farming goal is, they may very well say that they want to make a profit. Ending up with extra money after you've paid your bills at the end of the year is a good thing. But, perhaps a better answer is that you wish to run a profitable operation. So, what is the difference between making a profit and running a profitable operation?

When you say that you have made a profit, have you considered all of the pieces that make a sustainable agricultural lifestyle? Have you taken into account the need for an equipment replacement reserve, so that when your tractor breaks for the last time you can replace it? Do you have a cash reserve set aside so that you can hire a relief milker when your daughter gets married and you want to take a day off to celebrate? Is the farm paying you back for the financial investment that you initially made in it? Will the farm provide money for retirement?

All of these things are important considerations in assessing whether your farm is financially sound. We don't want your farming to be just about making a profit. We want you to have a profitable farming operation, which allows you and your family to lead a sustainable lifestyle.

Farm Operating Profit Margin =

$$\frac{\text{NFIFO} + \text{farm interest paid} - \text{any value of unpaid labor}}{\text{gross farm revenue (accrual adjusted)}}$$

To improve your farm operating profit margin you could do any of the following:
- Reduce production input costs, as long as that doesn't reduce yields
- Change product mix to those products that have a higher profit margin
- Reduce leasing expenses
- Reduce labor requirements and costs (for instance, look at u-pick or other ways of outsourcing labor)
- Reduce material inventory
- Change your marketing outlets to those that have a higher profit margin
- Think of other ways that you can increase the profit received per unit while maintaining the number of units produced

You will notice that some of the ways to improve one ratio actually works against another ratio. For example, leasing farm machinery decreases the need to own it—which reduces the total value of farm assets—which increases the asset turnover ratio. However, leasing is an operating cost—which reduces net farm income—which reduces the operating profit ratio. (Note that the interest paid on a loan to purchase equipment is also an operating cost. Be aware of this as you make comparisons.) So don't make a management decision solely on how it affects one particular financial measure. Rather, make a management decision such as leasing because it makes the most sense for your overall farming operation.

The question now becomes, if you do want to increase your operating profit margin or asset turnover ratio through product mix or reduction in production, how do you go about it? It is difficult to make decisions on, for example, product mix while looking at only your whole-farm records. The choices you make could be incorrect. For example, you could accidentally replace a high margin crop (or enterprise) with a lower margin crop (or enterprise). For this reason, we suggest you make those decisions based on crop (or enterprise) budgets for your farm, as we'll describe in Chapter 16.

Other Profitability Tips

Every farm, like every business and household, has places that can be tightened up to make the dollars last longer. We include here some suggestions.

Equipment that matches your scale. If you have a lot of oversized equipment, you're carrying too much overhead. However, if it is undersized, you will struggle to balance how much work can be done in a day with the number of hours you can hang on to a tiller. Finding a balance can make a difference in your success and profitability.

Smart credit card use. Utilization of rebates and points are good (especially for gas), but plan to pay credit card charges off every month, or you start to lose quickly in interest payments. Don't finance large debts with credit cards, but use them wisely to manage cash flow.

Labor flexibility. It's nice not to have everybody at work every day. Consider the composition of your labor force and try to find people that can be as flexible in their hours as the farm labor needs are.

Spend more money up front to save money in the long run. Fuel efficient vehicles may do this. Investing in good equipment that will serve your needs, and not break down, will as well.

Buy in bulk. Check into buying supplies on sale and in bulk, and storing them, to take advantage of deals.

Group activities. When you go to town, do everything that needs doing. Keep a list. Order once from your farm supply catalog, not three times, by being organized in tracking what you need. An incredible amount of labor and mental energy can be wasted by doing many small things frequently, rather than larger batches less often. Consider this when planning anything you do — from managing batches of animals, to making trips to the barn, to entering information in your computer. There is a delicate balance, however, between grouping things in efficient work units and waiting too long, when tasks become too large or commitments overdue.

Utilize a team of advisors. This team could include production experts, health experts for livestock enterprises, input suppliers (feed or crop for example), lenders or financial experts, lawyers, marketing advisors, and others depending upon your farming operation. Look at this team as a group of unpaid board of directors that helps analyze your business and gives you advice on your options. They should all be familiar with your farming operation and others similar to yours. Each member should be willing to visit you at your farm on an annual basis (at a minimum). Unless they know your farming operation well, the advice they give you may not fit your farm.

Avoiding Train Wrecks

We've all seen it: a seemingly successful farm (or other business) suddenly appears on the auction block, leaving neighbors stunned and surprised. What happened, everyone asks?

In order to not have this be you the neighbors are talking about, you must learn to recognize early warning signs of when your farm business is going awry. The financial information you have learned to collect and analyze in this book should give you the information you need to head off a train wreck before it is inevitable.

If you start to see (or feel) the following, you should question your operation's sustainability and explore the deeper causes and potential solutions to the issues:
- A current ratio below 1:1
- A term debt coverage ratio below 120 percent
- Noticing that your checkbook isn't stretching far enough
- Regularly carrying open accounts (bills due) past 60 days
- Opening a lot of credit card accounts
- Forgoing necessary inputs
- Selling inventories to raise cash
- Accepting lower than market prices

Maximize Net Income Through Price, Not Production

If you sell 100 bunches of parsley for a dollar each, and those parsley bunches cost you 75 cents each to produce and market, you've made a profit of $25.00. If you want more money in your pocket at the end of the day, you might try to get that by selling more parsley. If you sell 200 bunches, you'll have $50.00 net profit. Sales x (price - cost of production) = profit.

However, another option might be to raise your price. You may sell less parsley, but you'll make more profit on each bunch. Say you raise your price to $1.50 each, and you sell only 67 bunches — you'll still have $50.00 in your pocket at the end of the day, plus you'll have had less hours picking parsley to get it. This allows you more time to do something else that could also bring in a profit.

It is possible a price increase will limit your customer base. To make this change sustainable you must decide if a given market has a large enough group of customers that will support your higher price. We will talk about the elements of pricing in Chapter 19.

From the Farmers

Improving Profitability

Hans Breitenmoser, Breitenmoser Farm

As a large operation, Breitenmoser Dairy Farm spends a lot on supplies. Hans Breitenmoser has learned that having a key employee that keeps her ears and eyes tuned to inventory, need, and prices can save him a lot of money.

"Laurie has been with the farm since 1991, and is very frugal. She knows exactly how long a particular vaccine or other supply will last, and buys on sale or using volume discounts to get the best deal." Hans has found that paying close attention to this expense area makes a significant difference in his bottom line.

It will be a pivotal moment when you realize that all you are doing is forestalling disaster by trying to stretch money farther than it can go. When in this position you have to be very careful to not make decisions that back you farther into a corner. Troubles can accumulate, making it harder to make good decisions. The best thing to do is to get help. Acting early rather than later is one of the hardest, but best things a farmer can do to forestall disaster when troubles start to accumulate.

Before you see major trouble, the following practices can help ease rough spots:
1. Figure your costs of production
2. Make adjustments in expenses, in places that really matter
3. Consider selling excess assets or inventory
4. Talk to consultants or your management team to get their suggestions for change
5. Do a detailed financial analysis

If major trouble has caught you by surprise, there is more you can do:
6. Talk to your lender immediately about your concerns
7. Consider a line of credit to consolidate bills and avoid short term credit costs
8. Change amortization on term debts, stretch out your loan payments or ask for payment deferrals (your ability to do this will depend on your lender)
9. Consider capitalizing your current liabilities—take out a short term loan to pay what you owe
10. Consider asking relatives to invest capital in your business
11. Ask your lender if they will write down a portion of your debt (Farm Service Agency—FSA—can consider this)
12. Undergo bankruptcy as a last resort

Hopefully if you are on top of your numbers and recognize trouble before it gets too deep, you will be able to head off any potential train wreck and keep your farm viable.

Summary

There are two key ways to improve your profitability in any business: increase your profit margin per unit while selling the same number of units, and increase unit sales while maintaining the same profit per unit (assuming of course that the profit margin is positive to start with). We offer several tips to consider for improving profitability. Looking at your asset turnover ratio and farm operating profit margin will help you understand ways to improve your profitability.

There are warning signs that can be monitored to keep your farm from veering off the deep end. We offer a list of actions that can be taken to help avoid financial disaster.

Managing Through Difficult Times:
What is Your Level of Profitability and Survivability?

By Tom Kriegl, University of Wisconsin-Extension farm financial analyst (retired)

The following checklist can help farm families get a sense of the financial risk their farm business has, and understand where they fit on a "profitability continuum." This simple scale points out the prices paid for the choices that are made. The "profitability" levels described range from one to ten, with ten being the most desirable and one being the least desirable. Those finding themselves below level seven are especially urged to seek more in-depth financial analysis help.

- *Level 10*

Level 10 is where farm income exceeds all farm costs, including the opportunity cost of unpaid labor, management and equity capital. Economists call this "economic profit." It is rarely achieved.

- *Level 9*

Level 9 is where farm income exactly equals all farm costs, including the opportunity cost of labor, management, and equity. Economists call this "normal profit." Profitability levels below normal profit are not considered profitable by economists.

- *Level 8*

Level 8 is below normal profit but is high enough for farm income to exceed farm costs, provide a comfortable level of family living, and allow some increase in family savings over and above the increase in equity that occurs when loans on assets are paid. However, owners are not fully compensated for all the opportunity cost of their labor, management, and equity.

- *Level 7*

Level 7 differs from Level 8 in that there isn't enough farm income to increase family savings over and above farm equity increases that result from normal loan repayment.

- *Level 6*

Level 6 differs from Level 7 in that business expenses cannot be paid while maintaining a satisfactory standard of living unless savings or non-farm income is used.

- *Level 5*

Level 5 differs from Level 6 in that business expenses are paid, but family living is very restricted even if there is non-farm income. By Level 5 there are little if any savings (other than declining equity) left to fall back on. Equity can provide staying power, but can erode quickly at this and lower levels.

- *Level 4*

Level 4 differs from Level 5 in that despite the belt-tightening of Level 5, loans are refinanced to defer principal payments as long as possible so other bills can be paid. This can accurately be called "mortgaging the future." (Note: Sometimes refinancing occurs at an earlier step.) Money for family living is very restricted, even if non-farm income

Continued on next page

Level of Profitability ... continued

is available. In the 1970s and early 1980s, inflating asset values allowed many family farms to regularly borrow more money despite continued low levels of profitability. At this level, options are few and chances of recovery decline rapidly. Owners should seriously consider liquidation to preserve whatever equity may remain, tand pursue another career.

• *Level 3*

Level 3 differs from Level 4 in that there is not enough money to pay even the restructured principal payments, although the family severely restricts personal expenses to pay mounting business expenses. Unpaid bills accumulate. If it hasn't already occurred by now, most of the non-farm income is being used for the farm instead of for the family. Equity is declining very rapidly while debt is increasing with equal speed. Once again, owners should seriously consider liquidation to preserve whatever equity may remain.

• *Level 2*

At Level 2 there isn't enough money to pay all current business or other expenses despite non-farm income and loan restructuring. Unpaid bills pile up with ever-increasing speed, and liquidation is imminent.

• *Level 1*

At Level 1 not only is income less than expenses, but debts also exceed asset values, and the business ends if it hasn't already. Many struggling businesses will end during levels 2, 3 or 4 due to overwhelming financial, emotional and/or physical stress. Salvaging as much equity as possible and transitioning out of farming is often the best strategy prior to reaching this point.

Levels eight to ten should be the goal (especially when entering the farm business) although few farms achieve levels nine or ten. Most farms bounce between levels five, six, seven, and eight from year to year with variations in weather, price, and other factors. But most farms do have a level at which they typically operate more than at any other level.

The more one relaxes their standard of profitability below economic profits (Level ten) the greater the risk that is assumed, and the easier one falls to the next lowest level. The lower the level of profitability, the faster the business and family can move in the wrong direction. Below level seven, the likelihood of business success decreases substantially.

Those that find themselves at level six or lower owe it to themselves and their family to seek financial advice soon. Of course, farm families above level six can also benefit from financial advice, and often do.

At level five or lower improvement is difficult. Transitioning out of farming while maintaining equity may be a more realistic goal for those who are at level five or below.

Many farm families have a number of non-business goals that interfere with maximizing profitability. This isn't necessarily bad, but too often the level of profitability that farm families are willing to accept places them under great risk, not only of falling short of business goals, but falling short of personal goals of improved family living and security. Financial analysis can help farm families understand the price they pay for the choices they make.

The University of Wisconsin Center for Dairy Profitability develops and delivers effective interdisciplinary education and applied research to dairy farms and dairy industry service providers resulting in sustainable profitable decisions, and a healthy and progressive dairy industry. For more information, visit them on the web at cdp.wisc.edu.

CHAPTER 14
Should You Buy That Tractor? Farm Investment Analysis

Deciding whether or not to make a significant capital investment can be one of the toughest decisions farm owners have to make. When we say "capital investment" we're referring to the purchase of a farm asset that has a life of more than one year. Land, buildings, machinery, breeding livestock, and perennial plants such as fruit trees are all examples of capital investments.

Often, an investment in a piece of farm machinery, a building, or land means taking on debt that will put a claim on part of your farm's cash flow for a number of years. It is depressingly common for farmers to make investment decisions that literally destroy their financial well-being (and often their family relationships) without their ever considering whether the investment made any economic sense at all.

Doing a few basic calculations can help you avoid making poor investment choices. We'll be upfront in telling you: if the numbers don't work, don't do it. On the other hand, there are, of course, non-economic considerations that may come into play, pointing to a "no" on an investment decision even if the numbers make sense.

Breaking Down the Decision: Start With a Few Questions

It helps to break an investment decision down into manageable pieces. We'll look at a series of questions that you should consider if you are thinking of making an investment.

First, do you absolutely have to make the capital purchase, or are there other feasible ways to achieve what you want to accomplish? Take land as an example. For many logical reasons, most farmers would like to own the land on which they are growing crops or producing livestock. However, land is extremely expensive. Unless you happen to have a pile of cash that you can use to buy the land outright, you will have to enter into a mortgage that will take a huge bite out of your farm's cash flow for the next 20 to 30 years. In the first few years after the purchase, the mortgage interest alone could be three or four times the amount you would pay each year to rent the land. It often makes much better economic sense to rent land, particularly in the early years of your

Key questions addressed in this chapter:

What options do you have when considering an investment?

What should you look at to assess the cost of owning something?

How can you figure out if a particular investment will pay?

How do you compare two different investment options?

INVESTMENT ANALYSIS

Acquiring New or Replacing Existing Machinery and Equipment

That new (or new to you) tiller or tractor you just purchased will wear out and need replacement in the future. How you acquire that new or replacement piece of equipment will affect your financial statements. There are three primary methods for acquiring machinery and equipment; purchase, rent/lease, and custom hire. Each method has advantages and disadvantages both from a financial and tax standpoint.

Purchase is by far the most common; you fully control how the asset is used and the quality of performance. You provide the labor and assume responsibility for the repairs and maintenance. If you borrowed money you can deduct the interest paid on the loan as well as the depreciation expense for tax purposes. The principal part of your payment affects your cash flow, but is not tax deductible (you have depreciation instead).

Under a rent/lease arrangement you still have control over how the asset is used, except there may be restrictions on the amount of use over your rent/lease period. You provide the labor and normally assume responsibility for the repairs and maintenance while it is under your control. The difference between a rental and lease arrangement is the length of time you retain

Continued on next page

farming career when cash flow is tight and there are multiple competing claims for any extra dollars you might have available.

The next question to ask: Could you hire somebody to perform a particular farm task more cheaply than you could own or rent the capital assets you would need to do it yourself? This is an easy question if you're thinking about an out-of-the-ordinary project such as hiring a bulldozer to clean out a fence line. It becomes more complicated if the job is something that needs to be done every year or multiple times each growing season. Commodity farmers may need to decide whether or not to buy a new planter, hay harvesting equipment, or a combine. Fresh market vegetable growers may need to make decisions about building a new greenhouse, packing shed, or purchasing a refrigerated truck. We will look at what these decisions involve a little later.

Once you have decided that hiring the work done is not feasible, the third thing you need to decide is whether or not you can afford to own the asset you need. It may (or may not) make more sense to rent it. There are some advantages to leasing. The annual rental expense is completely tax deductible, while only the interest paid on a loan for a farm asset can be claimed as an expense. The annual expenses for which you are responsible (maintenance, repairs, etc.) are usually more predictable with a leased asset than with an owned asset. Often, little cash is required upfront to enter into a lease, as a result it doesn't take a bite out your current assets. Annual lease payments are sometimes significantly less than yearly principal and interest payments would be on the same piece of equipment, which means there is less of a drain on the farm's cash flow. Leasing is a shorter term commitment, and if your farm needs change you can more easily adapt your assets to your needs. On the other hand, you will not be building up an equity position with a leased asset. These should be enough reasons for a farmer to take a serious look at leasing before buying a capital asset.

OTTO'S TIP: *Did you know that you can lease a building that is constructed on your own farm? There are leasing companies specializing in agricultural structures that will pay for construction according to your specs and then enter into a long-term lease with you. In some situations, the low capital requirement and tax advantages of a facility lease may make economic sense.*

If you decide that leasing an asset is not appropriate in your situation, the fourth question is to decide if the purchase is a sound business investment...is it a wise use of your available cash? This will require a bit of number scratching and, in particular, calculating the "Net Present Value" (NPV) of the investment.

NPV is a very useful—and not terribly complicated—tool that can be used to evaluate any investment. To calculate NPV you will need to know the upfront cash outlay for the asset, the potential impact on farm cash flow over a specific number of years, and the likely value of the asset at the end of that period of time. These numbers can be put together to determine the positive or negative value of the potential cash flow relative to the cost of the asset. If the value is positive, it probably makes sense to make the investment. If it's negative, you will probably want to skip the capital purchase.

If you have several capital assets you would like to purchase but only enough cash to make one investment, one more calculation can help you make the most logical choice. This calculation is the Internal Rate of Return (IRR).

IRR takes the NPV one level deeper, not only telling you whether the present value of an investment is positive or negative, but actually quantifying the rate of return on the investment. By lining up all of the investment choices side by side and comparing the IRR of each, you can pick the "best" alternative that will likely give you the highest rate of return.

The ability of the IRR to compare multiple alternatives at the same time is much different than the partial budget's ability to compare only two alternatives (which we'll discuss in Chapter 17). If you have four alternatives for example, the IRR would be a much simpler method to compare than conducting six, side-by-side partial budget comparisons.

Let's look a little more closely at the things that you need to consider in making investment decisions.

Figuring the Cost of Ownership

To decide whether it makes the most sense to either buy or rent the asset, or to hire somebody to perform work for you with their assets (commonly known as a "custom hire" arrangement) you will need to first assess the true cost of ownership. Ownership costs include:

Depreciation. This is not a cash expense but needs to be taken into account when you own something. With the exception of land, most other farm assets will lose value over time. Depreciation is a calculation that considers the amount of an asset's initial cost that is "used up" each year.

Interest. The interest paid on a term loan used to buy a capital asset is an expense, but the actual principal amount paid is not. You can think of interest as the rent you are paying on borrowed money. Your principal payment is simply the way you are giving back the money you borrowed.

Repairs. Depending on the type of asset you buy, repairs can be a very significant expense. These will be the significant fixes made to your asset.

Equipment ... continued

control; rental agreements are normally short (hours, days, or maybe months), whereas lease agreements usually cover multiple years. The rent/lease payment is fully tax deductible. Because you do not own the asset, you cannot depreciate the asset for tax purposes.

Custom hiring is becoming more widespread. This is where you pay for an operator to perform a particular farming operation. The custom hire operator provides both his or her labor and equipment. You have no control over how the asset is used except for the particular farming operation you are hiring to be performed on your farm. You also don't often have much control on when the operation is actually started and completed or the quality of work that was done. You are normally not responsible for any repairs or maintenance for the custom operator's equipment. The cost of the custom operation is fully deductible. Again, because you do not own the asset, you cannot depreciate the asset for tax purposes.

Which asset replacement method you choose will depend upon your financial ability to borrow money or spend available working capital, on your access to custom hire operators, the type of equipment and duration needed, the importance of the timing of the farming operation, and how often the equipment will be used.

Equipment that is used often for multiple operations throughout the year that are timely is usually purchased. Purchase of expensive, single-purpose equipment may be delayed through rent/lease or custom hiring. How fast you replace or add new equipment is up to you and your financial ability. If your financial ability indicates that purchase is not possible at the moment, look at other ways of acquiring needed farm equipment.

Maintenance. Maintenance includes all of the routine things you need to do to keep a capital asset in good working condition. It could include greasing machinery, painting a building from time to time, and other work you expect to do during the time you own an asset. If you don't keep up on maintenance, you will end up experiencing higher repair costs.

Insurance. You will want to insure your assets against casualty loss and any liability that might result from the use of the assets. This is not usually a significant expense unless it is an asset that is used off of the farm, such as a truck.

Labor. Any additional labor cost that will result from ownership of an asset—and you wouldn't incur if you lease or custom hire—needs to be included.

Fuel and Oil. Obviously, some capital assets such as a new building will not require gasoline, diesel fuel, or oil. However, you may have to pay for LP gas or electrical service, which should be counted as expenses.

Taxes. If the capital asset you purchase is land or a building, you will have to pay property taxes. In some states, personal property taxes are assessed on various types of assets.

The costs of ownership for any asset you are considering adding or changing should be estimated and totaled on an annual basis. The total annual cost should then be divided into whatever increment makes the most sense to use for comparison with other types of use, such as renting or leasing. For example, it might be best to break the cost of building ownership out on a monthly basis. A tractor might be considered on a per-hour basis, as your local machinery dealer will probably quote you an hourly rate if you inquire about leasing a tractor. For other equipment, it might be appropriate to break the costs per-acre if your custom operator charges by the acre.

The important point is to be honest with yourself about the real, total cost of ownership. If you leave out the depreciation, for instance, you will skew your analysis sharply in favor of ownership.

Once you've figured out the true cost of ownership, you need to decide whether or not renting or custom hiring are practical, economically feasible options. Is it even possible to rent what you need? If so, is renting less expensive than owning the asset? Is it available within a reasonable distance from your farm? If you're thinking of hiring a custom operator, will they be able to do your work in a timely manner? If your hay likely won't get harvested until two weeks after it's in prime condition, the economics of ownership could be significantly different.

If you've done an honest calculation of the full cost of ownership of a particular asset, and then compared the ownership cost with the cost of renting or custom hiring, and concluded that there is a clear economic advantage to ownership, that might be as far as you need to go with your investment analysis. However, if the ownership advantage is marginal or if you are trying to decide between several different capital investment options, there are some additional calculations you can do to help you make a choice.

Analyzing a Single Investment

You have decided that it might make sense to buy a particular asset but you want to know whether or not the asset is likely to give you a positive return on the dollars you invest. In other words, will you be better off or worse off in the future for having invested your cash today?

To answer the better off/worse off question, we need to calculate the net present value (NPV) of the benefits you will receive from owning the asset over a number of years. Calculating NPV is similar to calculating compound interest. If you invest $100 today at a five percent annual compound interest rate, you can calculate that you will have $105 one year from now, $110.25 two years from now (you earned some interest on your interest), and so on until you eventually withdraw your money.

The value of money changes over time due to factors such as interest rates, inflation, market volatility, and other risks from year to year. A dollar today is considered to be worth more than a dollar in the future because when the dollar is in your hand, you have the immediate potential to use it in any of a number of different ways. If you are going to give up that current potential by tying your dollar up in an investment, you probably will expect some sort of financial incentive to do so. You wouldn't give up your dollar today to only get back a dollar two years from now, but you might give it up today to get back $1.10 in two years' time. This concept is referred to as the "time value of money."

Thinking about the example above a bit differently, we know that at an expected five percent interest rate, the $110.25 you are going to receive in two years is worth as much to you as the $100 you are prepared to give up or invest today. When we calculated forward, the five percent represented a "compound" rate. When we calculate how much the $110.25 in the future is worth in today's dollars, the five percent is considered a "discount" rate. That's the essence of the NPV calculation. If you know how much you can expect to receive in the future and can estimate the discount rate, you can figure out the maximum amount you could afford to invest today.

For the NPV calculation, we need to know the initial cash outlay required for the investment. We need to calculate some estimates of net cash flow for each year that you intend to use the investment. We need to estimate which year you will stop using the asset and how much the asset is likely to be worth at that time. Finally, we also need to decide what discount rate to use. We'll crunch those numbers together and compare the result to the initial cost of the potential investment. If the result is higher than the initial cost, the investment makes economic sense. If the result is negative, it doesn't.

An example will illustrate how the NPV calculation works. Let's say you have some underutilized pasture land and are considering the addition of a beef cow-calf enterprise. You are thinking of buying ten beef cows for $1,000 per head, for a total investment of $10,000. You estimate that you will keep each cow for four years, your net cash flow from the sale of calves will be $150/cow each year (total annual net cash flow from the enterprise will be $1,500), and each cow will be worth $500 as a cull cow at the end of the fourth year.

Valuing an Asset

A significant danger in investment analysis is over-estimating the value of an asset after it's been put into use, particularly if it's a highly specialized asset such as an on-farm food processing facility. If something unexpected happens and you need to sell your farm, the asset may have no value to the next owner and your entire capital investment could be lost. It's extremely important to generate the return on your investment from annual cash flow and not to rely on the residual value of the asset when you're done using it.

INVESTMENT ANALYSIS

A simple analysis suggests that the cows will pay you back $11,000 over the course of four years (3 years x $1,500/yr = $4,500, + the 4th year's $1,500 + $5,000 cull value = $11,000). Getting $11,000 back for your initial $10,000 investment seems like a fairly good return. However, when we adjust for the time value of money by calculating the NPV of the four years of cash flows, we get a much different view of the investment.

We already have most of what we need to do the NPV calculation for the beef cow investment. We know how much we'll have to invest upfront to buy the cows ($10,000). We estimated the annual cash flow from owning the cows ($1,500). We have a good idea of what the cows will be worth four years from now ($5,000). What we are missing is the discount rate.

There are different ways to decide what discount rate to use. The most common is to simply use the interest rate you would pay on a loan to purchase the asset. Some people prefer to use the current rate of inflation plus the prime lending rate. Some will establish a personal hurdle rate; they won't invest in anything unless they can expect an eight percent return, for example.

We believe that it is wise to consider the riskiness of the investment and increase the discount rate accordingly; the higher the risk, the higher the discount rate. When investment bankers talk about risk, they are looking at the possibility that an investment won't pay off, or won't pay off as well as they hoped. You need to take the same thing into account when you make an investment. At the time of this writing, a farmer with good credit could expect to pay six percent interest on a loan to purchase a small herd of beef cows. We will add one percent to account for some risk in the enterprise and will use a discount rate of seven percent in our example.

You can calculate the NPV using a formula but we find it much simpler to use a table that gives you the present value of $1.00 at various discount rates and time periods. We've included an NPV table for your convenience in Appendix G. Using data from a present value table we are able to do our NPV calculation as shown in Table 14.1.

Table 14.1 Net Present Value of four years of cash flow from a $10,000 beef herd investment at 7% discount rate

Year	Investment	Net annual cash flow	Discount factor (from table)	Net Present Value
0	$10,000			
1		$1,500	.935	$1,402.50
2		$1,500	.873	$1,309.50
3		$1,500	.816	$1,224.00
4		$6,500	.763	$4,959.50
Total	$10,000			$8,895.50

In this case, the NPV of the cash flow generated by the ten beef cows is $8,895.50, which is less than the initial investment of $10,000. If the NPV of the cash flow was $10,000, the return would be equal to the discount rate: 7%. Since the NPV is less than $10,000, it tells us that the return on our initial $10,000 investment is less than 7%. If you won't accept less than a 7% return on your investment, you shouldn't buy the cows.

Comparing One Investment to Another

You now understand how to evaluate a single capital investment opportunity to decide whether or not it makes sense. How do you decide between two or more investment opportunities that might require a different upfront investment, and may have much different cash flow patterns and time horizons for ownership? To do this, we need to go a bit further than the NPV and calculate an "Internal Rate of Return" (IRR) for each potential investment. The IRR for a potential investment is essentially the discount rate at which the NPV of a stream of cash flows is equal to the initial capital investment.

To give you a better sense of how this works, let's take another look at our beef cow example. We saw that at a discount rate of seven percent, the NPV of the stream of cash flows was less than the initial investment. In other words, we know that the initial $10,000 investment does not yield a seven percent internal rate of return. If it did yield a seven percent IRR, the NPV of the cash flows would have been $10,000 rather than $8,895.50. The beef cow investment gives us something less than seven percent (Table 14.2).

OTTO'S TIP: NPV and IRR are based on net cash flow rather than net income. Principal and interest payments on a term loan that was taken out to purchase the asset must be included in the cash flow analysis.

Depending on how precise you want to be, there are different ways to calculate IRR. You could use a financial calculator or an Excel spreadsheet if you really want to see some decimal points (search "IRR calculator" on the Microsoft website). Otherwise, you can just go back to your present value table and try different discount rates until you arrive at a NPV that is close to the initial investment. To demonstrate, let's run the beef cow example using a three percent discount rate instead of seven percent

Since the NPV of the cash flow is a bit more than $10,000 using a three percent discount rate, we can see that the IRR on the beef cow investment is slightly more than three percent.

Now we'll look at an alternative investment possibility that is competing with the beef cows for your dollars. Let's say you are considering the purchase of a high tunnel for fresh market vegetable production. The initial investment is $10,000 and you calculate that it will add $2,000 of net cash flow per year to your farm. You plan to use it for seven years, at which point it will not have value.

Since this investment is competing with the beef cows, which are projected to give us slightly better than a three percent IRR, we will use a three percent discount rate for our initial NPV calculation. Since the NPV of the hoophouse investment is significantly more than the $10,000 initial investment (Table 14.3), we can see that the IRR must be significantly higher than three percent. In fact, if you try various discount rates you'll find that the IRR for the hoop house investment is more than nine percent.

If you are trying to decide between buying a beef cow herd and buying a hoop house, you'd be much better off financially to choose the hoophouse – assuming, of course, that you were prepared to utilize its full potential with your labor and markets!

Table 14.2 Net Present Value of four years of cash flow from a $10,000 beef herd investment at 3% discount rate

Year	Investment	Net annual cash flow	Discount factor (from table)	Net Present Value
0	$10,000			
1		$1,500	.971	$1,456.50
2		$1,500	.943	$1,412.50
3		$1,500	.915	$1,372.50
4		$6,500	.888	$5,772.00
Total	$10,000			$10,018.50

Table 14.3 Net Present Value of seven years of cash flow from a $10,000 hoophouse investment at 3% discount rate

Year	Investment	Net annual cash flow	Discount factor (from table)	Net Present Value
0	$10,000			
1		$2,000	.971	$1,942
2		$2,000	.943	$1,886
3		$2,000	.915	$1,830
4		$2,000	.888	$1,776
5		$2,000	.863	$1,726
6		$2,000	.837	$1,674
7		$2,000	.813	$1,626
Total	$10,000			$12,460

INVESTMENT ANALYSIS

> ### Don't Exaggerate!
>
> When calculating additional net cash flow from an investment, take care not to exaggerate numbers! You want to focus here on net cash flow that results directly from the change in your operation that the investment will provide.
>
> For example, if you are looking at a new hoophouse on your vegetable farm, you estimate the income that the additional produce would provide, then subtract out the produce you would have produced on that land otherwise. Then, calculate the annual operating expenses associated with your investment. For the hoophouse, that might include seeds, fertilizer, labor, plastic, and irrigation supplies. Your income minus your expenses becomes your net cash flow for this project.
>
> You don't need to include overhead expenses in this analysis, because they won't change due to the investment; in other words, you don't need to include things like property taxes in the decision about purchasing a tractor.

NPV and IRR are simple yet powerful and important tools to use when evaluating capital investment opportunities for your farm. They allow you to make objective comparisons between alternatives and help you invest your money where it will do the most good for your farm operation.

Making Capital Investments on a Rented Farm

Maybe you've been leasing a farm and have been reluctant to invest in any capital improvements because you're afraid you'll lose your investment when the lease ends. Or, maybe you plan to purchase the farm you're leasing because you would like to proceed with capital improvements but think it wouldn't make sense while you're renting.

If you have a multiyear lease on your farm, it may actually be economically beneficial to make capital improvements even if you receive nothing for them at the end of the lease term. The key is to generate enough positive cash flow during the lease term to give you an adequate IRR if there is no residual value at the end. This is where the IRR calculation can be extremely helpful. Making investments now on a leased farm might very well put you in a much better financial position to own a farm in the future.

If you decide to forgo making capital improvements until you own the farm, you may find that you'll need to use all of your available cash for the down payment on the real estate and will have nothing left to invest in capital improvements. Your overhead costs may be higher, and your ability to improve cash flow will have been stifled. Please don't make that decision without first thinking through all of your options with the help of the IRR calculation.

Many highly successful retail businesses choose to lease real estate on a long-term basis rather than own it. They don't want their capital tied up in real estate, they prefer to invest it in the interior infrastructure that allows them to efficiently serve a large number of customers, and in inventory that turns a 15-20% profit numerous times each year. They are maximizing their IRR on invested capital.

Other Factors to Consider

Making investments in equipment, landscaping, buildings, livestock, or other assets should almost always involve a series of double-checking and second-guessing. Even if the numbers work, there are still social and lifestyle filters that should be applied before making an investment decision.

OTTO'S TIP:

In reviewing the draft of this book, one farmer commented that doing all of this analysis "takes the fun out of buying something new." Author Paul Dietmann, with many years experience assisting farmers in desperate financial trouble, responds: "Facing bankruptcy at the end of a long series of poorly considered investment decisions tends to take the fun out of farming too!!"

From a financial perspective, we make investment decisions to improve our financial circumstances: we buy a new tractor to make our farm more profitable by allowing us to get our field work done more quickly during a wet spring, or we buy a new hoophouse to extend our cropping season and expand our sales season.

But in a lifestyle-intensive business like farming, your investment decisions can have a much broader impact. If you take on debt to buy that new tractor, you can easily figure out your monthly payments on the loan, and how that affects your bottom line; but it's a bit harder to figure out how the stress of additional loan payments might affect your or your partner's ability to sleep at night. Or, if you buy a new hoophouse, it might improve your farm's profitability, but you might suddenly be expected to keep delivering vegetables right through Thanksgiving, when you usually go to visit your mother a day's drive away.

Invest in Weak Links: Choosing the Right Solution

It's all too easy to go after an obvious solution that doesn't really address the problem, to invest in order to have the feeling that you are doing something to solve a problem, or to make purchases that end up backing you into a financial corner. Watch out for the "buy something" cure.

You'll always be able to come up with reasons to buy something that you want. If you start to get the itch to buy a new tractor, you'll find all sorts of problems this will solve: "If I had a new tractor, I could cover more ground faster. I could unload pallets of supplies from a semi more easily. My tractor would start more easily on cold mornings." But, these might not be important enough reasons to make the investment. You'll want to take a well-rounded look at your situation to decide if a purchase is the correct action.

Try writing down the problem you want to solve other than "making more money." Maybe describe an operational problem that you are having, like lack of space to pack vegetables for the CSA, or not delivering the frozen cuts of meat on a timely basis in the summer. Describe it in broad terms that don't necessarily point to the answer. Then do some brainstorming about what might be influencing that problem. Work hard to be honest and open in this brainstorming process, so that you don't end up simply justifying your desire to buy something that you've decided you want.

A chain will always break at its weakest link, so making the rest of the chain stronger won't affect its overall strength until you make the weakest link stronger. For instance, it doesn't do any good to invest in a better transplanter to put out your vegetable transplants more quickly if you have a problem with deer eating all of your vegetables.

Weak links aren't always obvious, and they don't always involve money to strengthen them. Maybe your employees are unhappy, so you think that giving them a raise will make them happier, but the real problem lies with your management skills. In this case, your solution would better lie with getting training about managing people, perhaps through books or classes, or maybe a mentoring relationship with an excellent manager.

> ## Buying to Save Taxes
>
> A common way for farmers to solve income tax liability issues at the end of the year is to buy depreciable assets. If the purchase makes sense from an IRR standpoint, go for it. If all you're doing is eliminating tax liabilities in the short term and driving up overhead costs over the long term, you're likely headed down a bad path.

Each year it's useful to look for the weak links in your enterprises as you put together your budget. Once you've identified any investment needs, sit down and honestly think through all of the potential life impacts that the change may bring. You could even go so far as to make a list of positives and negatives. Using this list in combination with your financial assessment will leave you with the most well-rounded decision.

Summary

Capital investments have some of the strongest impact on a farm's sustainability, as they can have very significant, long term financial and non-financial effects. Calculating net present value (NPV) and internal rate of return (IRR) will help you evaluate if a given investment will offer a positive return, or which investment in a comparison will give the best rate of return.

Other factors, such as pinpointing the actual problem you are trying to solve, and recognizing when you are justifying a purchase that you have already decided you want to make for other reasons, should help you make better investment decisions. Assessing all of the positive and negative impacts of an investment, both financial and non-financial, is important in making the best decision.

CHAPTER 15
Getting the Most from Your Lender Experience

Most farmers find themselves thanking about taking out a loan at some point. You may be looking for funds to cover annual operating expenses, or for a particular asset purchase such as land or a tractor, a land purchase, or an improvement to your operation. In any of these cases, you will want to be well prepared when approaching a potential lender.

It is very important for farmers to develop strong relationships with their lenders. A good lending relationship is an important, multi-faceted resource for your farm operation. Loan officers, once they understand what you are planning to do, can offer key advice drawn from experience in dealing with operations similar to yours. They can help you avoid costly mistakes as you make your borrowing plans. And, they can help you navigate through the turbulent times that are a natural part of agriculture.

From a farmer's perspective, borrowing money can be looked at as a lot like renting a piece of equipment. Instead of renting a machine to help you accomplish a particular task more quickly and efficiently, you are renting the use of money to help you achieve a goal more quickly. Just as using a rented machine can be dangerous if you don't how to handle it, using rented money can be risky too. You wouldn't operate a dangerous piece of machinery without first reading the operator's manual. In many respects, this book you are reading right now can be thought of as an operator's manual for your farm's money.

From a lender's perspective, lending money to a farm is not really selling a loan, it is buying a farm's debt. The lender approaches a debt-buying decision very carefully, and really doesn't want to make a mistake that could prove costly down the road. He or she is making a long-term investment that needs to benefit all parties involved.

Selecting a Lender

It is necessary to find a lender that you like and trust, one with whom you can easily communicate and who understands your operation. This can be a challenge, but a good relationship between you and your lender is necessary to ensure success in your business. To find a lender, first ask other farmers in the area about who they enjoy working with,

Key questions addressed in this chapter:

How do you enhance your success in working with a lender?

What do you look for in a lender?

How can you prepare in approaching a lender for a loan?

LENDERS

Farm Operating Loans or Lines of Credit

For help with balancing the ups and downs of your farm's cash flow, an operating loan or line of credit is a better alternative than asking your vendors to carry you for longer than they planned. An operating loan is much better than using credit cards to provide for short-term credit needs. We recommend that you go to your lender and get approved for an operating loan before you actually need it. If you get into a bad spot, and haven't set this up already, you may have trouble getting it when you really need it.

Operating loans and lines of credit are both intended to be used for annual expenses and completely paid off from annual farm income. An operating loan is typically a one-year loan that helps cover annual operating expenses and is paid off when crops or livestock are sold. A line of credit is a multi-year commitment of a set amount of funds that are available for the farmer to use as needed and paid back down to zero at least once per year.

It often makes sense to set up an operating loan at the same time you are taking out a mortgage. If you do utilize it, make a plan on how you will pay it off before you tap any of the available funds. It used to be common for lenders to approve rolling an operating loan balance

Continued on next page

look for references, and then make an appointment to meet and get to know someone at the lending institution you are considering. The first meeting, the first impression, is important. Come prepared. Remember that both you and your lender have the same goal—supporting a successful farming operation that can meet its obligations.

Look for a lender who
- Understands the type of farm you will be operating
- Asks good questions, is a good listener, and is willing to discuss ideas
- Has experience and experienced staff
- Can clearly communicate with you about the terms and conditions of loans
- Is competitive in his or her area and can meet all of your lending needs
- Is interested in a long-term working relationship with you
- Isn't too quick to say yes. You want a lender who understands that it isn't just important that the loan be paid back; the loan needs to be in your best interests and give strength to your farm business.

Preparing For the First Meeting

Remember, lenders are providing someone else's money to finance your operation and they work in a highly regulated business. While they typically have some authority to use their discretion in making lending decisions, they have standards and criteria they must follow. The following suggestions will help facilitate your new lending relationship.

Don't expect an immediate answer to a loan request. Time is needed to process your application. The larger the loan request, the more time it will take to make a loan decision. Prepare to start working on a loan a few months before you actually need the money.

Have a clear understanding of exactly what you are asking for; how much money and for what period of time. Provide your lender with a clear plan of operation for your project, purchase, or production year, supported with reasonable data. Explain what has happened in the past on your farm, and what you predict will happen in the future. Provide clear and accurate records of income and expenses, as well as production yields if you have them.

The best source of information is your own records, but if you don't have them, county or state averages may be used to predict your yields and future income. If you are starting a farm enterprise that is somewhat unique, reasonable third-party production or financial data might be very difficult to find. Be able to explain where your data came from and why you chose it. Make sure you fully understand your proposal and the supporting information you are presenting, and that you can answer any questions about it.

Know your loan repayment ability. Ask that loans be set up in such a way as to insure that you will be able to meet all of your financial commitments. Communicate with your lender and honor your commitments. If your plans are not working out, contact your lender to keep him or her informed. Lenders don't like surprises. It is in the lender's best interest to have your loan repayment succeed. There may be ways he or she can offer assistance if you are having trouble. However, the longer you wait to let your loan officer know that you're experiencing a problem, the fewer options they will have available to help you.

It is a good idea—but not absolutely necessary--to bring as much of the following information as you can to your first meeting with a lender. Eventually, the lender will likely need all of this info to support a loan decision:
- A recent balance sheet with a complete list of farm personal property such as livestock and machinery inventories. Personal and business balance sheets for the past three years would be preferable (see Chapter 9 for more on balance sheets)
- Income tax returns for the past three years
- Estimates on the cost of any improvements you plan to make to real estate, and/or personal property you plan to purchase
- Estimates of the amount of cash or equity you are able to commit to your need (don't expect a lender to provide 100% financing)
- Month-by-month cash flow projections for at least one year (see Chapter 20 for more on cash flow projections)
- A copy of your signed offer-to-purchase if you are seeking a loan to buy real estate
- Current non-farm income verification such as recent pay stubs
- Samples of earnings from other comparable operations if you don't have your own. These may be hard to get, but if you know someone to ask they can be very valuable.

The Five Cs of Credit

Lenders consider a combination of qualitative and quantitative measures when making a loan decision. These measures are commonly called the "Five Cs of Credit," and include Character, Capacity, Capital, Collateral, and Conditions. We'll describe each of them and explain what they mean to you as a potential borrower.

Character
This element of the lending decision focuses on the borrower. How much experience do you have managing a farm? What types of formal and informal education have you undertaken to help you become a better farmer? Is it likely that you will be able to accomplish the goals you've set for your farm? Do you have a history of following through on your commitments, particularly your financial commitments?

Don't be too modest when talking to your lender about your education, your experience, and your farming accomplishments. You want your lender to have confidence that you know what you're doing and you'll continue to be successful at it.

You also want to be forthcoming about any blemishes in your credit history over the past five years or so. Your credit bureau report and Fair Isaac Corporation (FICO) score play big roles in the loan decision process. Any late or missed payments on financial obligations will appear on the credit bureau report and will hurt your FICO score. Your lender will likely have a minimum FICO score to even consider a loan application, as a borrower's FICO score is considered to be a strong indicator of the likelihood that a borrower will default on a loan. Any recent major derogatory factors such as a foreclosure or bankruptcy on your credit bureau report will likely prevent you from obtaining a loan.

Capacity
Capacity looks at cash flow. It takes into consideration your ability to consistently generate enough cash flow to make your loan payments on time. The cash flow may come from the farm or it may come from off-farm income. The lender will consider all sources of

---

Loans ... continued

forward from year-to-year. Now most lenders require that you pay the operating loan down to zero each year.

An operating loan is typically secured by a lien against growing crops or livestock. When crops and livestock are sold, the operating loan is paid off and the lien is released. Sometimes, after several years of successful experience with operating loans, the borrower can obtain an unsecured operating loan that doesn't require a lien against farm production.

If you aren't able to completely pay off an annual operating loan using the current year's income, your lender may convert the operating loan balance to an intermediate term loan with regular principal and interest payments for several years until the balance is paid off.

However, having your operating loan "termed out" takes away your flexibility in using the operating loan and creates an obligation to make periodic loan payments. It may also prevent the lender from providing additional operating credit in the future.

From the Farmers

Working with a Lender

Lauren and Caleb Langworthy, Blue Ox Organics

Lauren and Caleb Langworthy sat down and penciled out the operation they wanted to create. As they did their numbers they realized that they needed more money to get started, and so they went to the Farm Service Agency to apply for both a farm ownership loan and a seven-year "intermediate loan" to purchase equipment and breeding animals. "Gathering all of the needed paperwork ahead made the time at FSA getting loans go much smoother," Lauren explains.

Document Conversations with Your Lender

You should make a habit of documenting every conversation you have with your lender. At a minimum, make a note about the date and key points covered. If you have a loan portfolio, your lender is probably already doing this for every conversation he or she has with you; it only makes sense that you would take a moment to record your impressions of the conversation, any statements your lender made, and any agreements you came to. You always hope the relationship doesn't go sour, but you never know when you might need a reminder of a particular discussion that you had.

income and all existing financial obligations, and evaluate whether the payments on the new loan are manageable.

A good lender will not only determine whether you have sufficient cash flow to service the new debt; he or she will also calculate whether the cash flow is enough for you to adequately cover all of your family living expenses, to replace machinery and other capital assets that wear out over time, to build up working capital reserves, and to have some money left over to put into savings. It doesn't do you any good to make all of your loan payments but have nothing left when the loan is paid off but junk machinery and collapsing buildings.

Capital

Capital is all about your balance sheet. Are your total assets significantly more than your total liabilities? Do you have enough available working capital to cover unexpected financial setbacks? Are you willing to put up some of your equity as a down payment or as additional collateral to secure the loan?

Lenders look at capital as a key measure of the riskiness of a loan. The more capital that a borrower is willing to invest, the less likely it is that the borrower will default on the loan if they run into a jam. It is not unusual for a conventional lender to require a 30-35% down payment on a loan to purchase agricultural assets.

Capital is often a significant challenge for beginning farmers. When faced with a 30% down payment requirement, someone who has been farming for many years and has a great deal of equity on their balance sheet will typically pledge additional assets rather than putting up a cash down payment. A beginning farmer usually can't just reach into their balance sheet and pull out a free-and-clear 40-acre parcel to use for a down payment; they either need cash or somebody with a strong balance sheet to back them.

OTTO'S TIP: *While a conventional lender may require a 30 to 35 percent downpayment, USDA Farm Service Agency loans will require significantly less.*

Collateral

Collateral is the asset or assets that are pledged by a borrower to secure a loan. In a worst case scenario in which the borrower isn't able to follow through on their loan commitment, the collateral is taken by the lender, sold, and the sale proceeds are used to pay off the loan principal balance.

Because the collateral will need to be sold in the event of a loan default, the loan amount is going to be limited by the market value of the collateral. Lenders typically have guidelines that dictate the maximum loan:collateral ratio that they can approve. The difference between the loan amount and the collateral value represents the costs that would be incurred if the lender had to take legal action to satisfy the loan.

From the Farmers

Penciling Out an On-Farm Expansion

Jackie Hoch, Hoch Orchard & Gardens

An important product of the Hoch Orchard is apple cider. Originally this popular product was processed in a commercial-scale facility on a nearby farm. This processing facility allowed the Hochs to bring their apples and take home cider, but the fruit was pooled with others and the cider was not exclusively from Hoch apples.

In effect, the Hochs sold apples to the processor, and bought back processed cider at a wholesale cost. In 2006, this disconnect led Jackie and Harry to discuss the idea of putting up their own on-farm cider processing facility. There were many reasons an on-farm cidery made sense, but would the numbers work out, and could they get a loan?

Because Jackie kept very good historical records of how many bushels of apples were sold to the cider processor, how many gallons of cider they bought at what price for resale, and how much they were able to resell the cider for, she was able to pretty easily show how much they would save by pressing their own apples into their own cider. In the peak of their reselling activity, Jackie found that they were spending $30,000 per year purchasing cider.

Jackie and Harry figured that they would need about $150,000 to put up their own facility: $50,000 for the building, $50,000 for the pressing equipment, and $50,000 to finish the building and set everything up.

They went to the bank and asked for two loans, totaling about $150,000. They were able to show on paper that the savings from not purchasing cider for resale would pay off their investment in only five years. Jackie says that the bank was happy to support their loans.

She also notes that she and Harry had a strong business plan, and a great relationship with their banker. "We work with our local bank, they know our payment history. We might not have done so well with a larger bank," Jackie says. The project ended up costing them less than they had anticipated, and all of the borrowed money was paid off on schedule. The Hochs are now looking forward to their fifth successful pressing season in their own facility.

Sales Predictions
We intend to produce three lines of cider in the proposed facility: a Premium Hoch Cider made with 100% Hoch apples; a high-end certified organic cider; and continue to sell the Minnesota's Finest Brand, which will be made with purchased apples, and apples that are not utilized by the more expensive Premium Hoch Cider.

Sales History

2001	522 gallons	$1,827 total revenue
2002	628 gallons	$2,338
2003	1488 gal	$5,932
2004	4246 gal	$17,159
2005	6014 gal	$24,474

Projected Total Volumes:

2007	7,000-8,000 gallons
2008	8,000-10,000 gallons
2009	10,000-12,000 gallons

Year	Volume	Line/Brand	Wholesale Price/Gallon	Revenue
2007	6000 gallons	MN Finest	$4.00/gallon	$24,000
2007	2000 gallons	Hoch Premium	$5.50/gallon	$11,000
			Total Revenue	$35,000
2008	4000 gallons	MN Finest	$4.00/gallon	$16,000
2008	4000 gallons	Hoch Premium	$5.50/gallon	$22,000
2008	2000 gallons	Hoch Organic	$7.50/gallon	$15,000
			Total Revenue	$53,000
2009	4000 gallons	MN Finest	$4.00/gallon	$16,000
2009	4000 gallons	Hoch Premium	$5.50/gallon	$22,000
2009	4000 gallons	Hoch Organic	$7.50/gallon	$30,000
			Total Revenue	$68,000

How to Improve your Credit Score

- Always pay all of your bills on time, including utilities, cell phone, and medical bills

- Use no more than 30% of your available credit limit on revolving debt such as credit cards

- Build successful long-term credit relationships. Don't jump from one lender or credit card to another to save a little bit on interest

- Pay down debt, don't just move it around.

- Use various types of credit, and make all payments on time or early.

- Be cautious about applying for new credit, particularly within six months of needing a sizeable loan such as a farm mortgage.

Collateral value can be a big issue for a farmer who needs a loan to purchase very specialized equipment or a structure that may not have much resale value, such as a high tunnel greenhouse. For example, it may cost $15,000 to purchase and construct a high tunnel, but its resale value after one year may only be $3,000 - $5,000. A lender probably won't be able to finance the $15,000 cost without additional collateral being pledged to secure the loan.

Sometimes a loan guarantee from the USDA Farm Service Agency or another entity can be utilized when either capital or collateral are a serious impediment to obtaining a loan. A guarantee takes much of the loan risk off of the lender and transfers it to the guarantee provider. The borrower will still need strong character and capacity to get the loan, however.

Conditions

After the other four factors have been considered, the conditions make up the agreement between the borrower and the lender. The loan amount, interest rate, and length of the loan term will be spelled out. Collateral is identified and public records are searched to ensure that there are no other security interests in it. All other terms of the loan agreement will be spelled out.

As another condition of the loan, the lender may require the borrower to carry insurance on machinery and buildings while the loan is in place. The borrower may be required to submit annual financial documents such as a balance sheet or tax returns. If the collateral used to secure the loan includes crops or livestock, buyers of those products may be required to write checks jointly to the farmer and the lender.

There are several red flags that can cause concern to a lender and may result in loan denial.
- Not fully disclosing your complete and accurate financial information
- Unwillingness to discuss all information. Don't tell a lender only what you think they need to know
- A borrower who is not willing to commit his or her own funds to a project, and expects the lender to finance nearly all of it.
- Insufficient collateral to adequately secure a loan.
- Lack of complete disclosure of all past credit problems, such as bankruptcy, late payments, and collections and judgments. Do not let the lender find out problems after your initial meeting
- Seeking credit far from home, or borrowing from numerous creditors
- Serious personal problems, such as an impending divorce or loss of an off-farm job
- Purchasing anything before credit has been arranged
- Providing an overly optimistic plan that is not supported by reasonable income, expense, and production data

The better a lender understands your business, the more likely he or she will do business with you. The relationship between a borrower and a lender must benefit both. This requires good communication and cooperation between both parties.

Summary

Lenders have the same goal as you in lending you money: they want to see you succeed. In order to be the most successful with your loans, you want to find a lender you feel comfortable with and that has an understanding of your farm business. You want to be well prepared when you approach a lender for funds, and be sure that you understand fully your financial situation and the details of the plan or proposal you are hoping that he or she will fund.

Choosing a Lender

All lenders have some type of risk rating scale based on financial measures that give the lender an indication of whether the borrower has: 1) Sufficient cash flow to make loan payments; 2) Enough working capital and overall equity to withstand poor production periods; 3) Enough profitability to increase net worth when production goes well; 4) Sufficient collateral to pay off the loan in the unlikely event that the borrower is not able make their loan payments; and 5) Other factors to determine how risky issuing the new loan to you will be. Most lenders have a combination of subjective and objective characteristics in their risk rating scale that incorporate the five Cs of credit discussed in the text.

Lenders use the rating scale to determine your loan terms such as interest rate, collateral needed, payback period, and number of payments per year (as well as other terms of your loan). Normally the lower your risk rating score, the better the terms of your loan are. Remember that money is a commodity and every lender has some. It is important that you understand the risk rating scale of your current or prospective lender. With this information you can track both your farm financial measures and your risk rating score. If your score is improving, your loan terms should be improving too.

The more you know about how lenders conduct their business, the better your decision should be regarding how much to borrow from which lender. In addition to understanding their business, you should expect the lender to understand your business. Questions to ask include: How many farming operations like mine borrow money from you? How much do you know about my industry and how farms like mine make a profit? When would you like to come visit my farm and would you be willing to go with me to a conference, workshop, or farm tour to better understand my business and how the various aspects of my industry affect my profitability? We would expect all lenders to visit each farm at least annually and we feel that it is not unreasonable for lenders to attend some professional development training opportunities to educate themselves and gain your business.

NOTES

SECTION FIVE
ANALYZING SPECIFIC ELEMENTS OF YOUR FARM

You now have the knowledge you need to build a number of financial statements that help you understand your farm's financial position. You can see if your farm made money, if you have enough to pay your bills, and what kind of ownership or equity position you have in the farm. This is a good base of financial knowledge.

However, there are even more ways the numbers you collect can be useful. We next explore ways you can track, assess, and analyze various aspects of your farm operation. In this section, we give you tools to answer questions such as: Is my primary enterprise making money, or should I change it somehow? How do my enterprises compare to each other as far as profitability is concerned? Are there other markets that would be a better fit for me? or, How do I know if I am charging the right price?

Some enterprises on your farm won't be as profitable as others. Knowing where each enterprise stands can contribute a lot to decisions about product diversity and balance. Numbers can be generated to answer specific questions, such as the impact of a potential product change or expansion in a particular production line. Partial budgets are a valuable tool in comparing various options for your operation.

With the surge in direct marketing in the last several years, many farmers have numerous marketing options available. How can you decide which one to put your energy into? Chapter 18 on comparing marketing costs will help you answer this question.

And, finally in this section we offer background and tools to help you with product pricing. Farmers use many mechanisms to price their products; we will explore several.

CHAPTER 16
Enterprise Budgets: Where are You Making Money?

Key questions addressed in this chapter:

What is an enterprise budget?

What are some examples of enterprise budgets?

How can you use enterprise budget information to farm more profitably?

In the previous chapters we have looked at ways to organize and analyze data involving your entire farm operation. Although important, whole farm data will only give you a broad overview of the financial aspects of your operation. You will need more detailed information to assess the specific changes that will have the most positive impact.

For example, let's assume you developed your income statement, balance sheet, and statement of cash flow and analyzed them as described in Chapter 12 on using ratios. Perhaps in your analysis you determine that your working capital ratio, operating profit margin, and operating expense ratio are all in the yellow, and approaching red range according to the Farm Finance Scorecard (Appendix E). A little more study leads you to the conclusion that if you manage expenses more effectively without lowering revenue you could lower your operating expense ratio, increase your operating profit margin, and improve your working capital ratio as you increase net income.

These are all great profitability strategies, but where do you start? Which of your enterprises are already providing an efficient and effective source of income, and which enterprises are hurting you financially?

Many farms have a diversity of production lines, or enterprises, that make up the income stream. Even a dairy farm, whose primary product may be commodity milk, may also sell calves, steers, replacement heifers, hay, grain, or other products. Many farms are deeply diversified, and have some flexibility in decision making about the crop or product mix. Looking at your farm production at a closer level is very beneficial in guiding decision making that leads to increased profitability.

The data that you collect through your bookkeeping system, using the mechanisms detailed in Section Two will help you in doing the analyses in this and the next chapter.

What is an Enterprise Budget?

An enterprise budget is an estimate of the costs and economic returns (profit) to produce a particular crop or enterprise. Enterprise budgets allow you to look at detail to make decisions about improving profit, improving your quality of life (such as reducing labor at certain times of the year without reducing profit), or achieving some other business goal.

Creating an enterprise budget forces you to take a close look at each crop or product line—the inputs, the labor, the machinery needed—as it relates to the amount of income you can generate by selling that crop. It will give you information that can help you see where you are making money, and allow you to make informed decisions if you wish to make changes.

The enterprise budget examples used in this book, as well as those received from universities, use generalized numbers that are presented as examples only. Your own actual farm data may differ significantly from those presented. It would be dangerous for you to make any decisions on your farm based on the examples we show here. It is important, and valuable, for you to develop your own enterprise budgets based on your own farm records.

To create enterprise budgets you will need to collect per crop or product line: the specific costs of production, the amount of product produced, how much of your base assets (overhead) were used, and the amount of income generated.

Enterprise budgets are created in spreadsheets or by hand, using data from your bookkeeping system along with other non-financial data you have collected. The types of non-financial data presented in Chapter 8 will be useful here. Formats for enterprise budgets vary in complexity, layout, and assumptions. Templates can be found from most state agricultural universities. We have made some available from our website at mosesorganic.org/fearless-farm-finances, and list them in the Resources section.

An Enterprise Example

Table 16.1 on page 151 shows an enterprise budget for specialty green beans. This budget shows the generalized format that all enterprise budgets can take. Livestock farmers will use the same principle outlined here, but measure their production in pounds (of meat or milk) with the "production area," the number of animals or animal units.

OTTO'S TIP: *We show vegetable examples here, and offer a beef example in Appendix H. This shows the type of incomes and expenses that would be tracked for a livestock enterprise, using the same technique shown in this green bean example.*

From the Farmers

Data Capture

Lauren Langworthy, Blue Ox Organics

Lauren Langworthy uses OneNote, a Microsoft Office program with free online access, to track a diversity of records and activities at Blue Ox Organics. It has proven helpful in tracking inventory and sales for farmer's markets. With the program in the cloud, and accessible from her phone or computer, Lauren fills a chart template with the items and amounts being brought to market as they pack the truck. At the end of market, they enter ending inventories. They track item prices and sales in conjunction with their Square credit card processing (https://squareup.com) at the market or in the evening when they are back home.

Keeping close track of what they sold at each market allows them to compare to previous weeks and years, and make decisions about what to harvest and bring. This increases their harvesting and packing efficiency. Keeping record of weekly sales data over multiple years provides data is useful for future enterprise planning.

"OneNote helps me by keeping all of our information in the cloud, accessible by my phone or computer, and not on the little sheets of paper that were always getting lost. While one of us is driving, the other can use that time to get the work done. We don't need to reenter written data into our system later—saving precious time."

Units of Measurement

Crop farmers may find it easier to use a different unit than a bed for measurement of production area. The use of "bed" will be troublesome for those with non-standard sized beds, or those growing large acreages of crops. It may be more accurate and convenient to use square feet, acres, plants per square foot, or plants per acre as the unit of measurement. Whether using a bed, an acre, or 40 acres, the same principles are used —divide total income and expenses by the number of total units of measurement.

An acre is 43,560 square feet. To determine the acreage of any area, take the length times the width (in feet) and divide by 43,560. For example, a 20 foot by 100 foot bed = 2,000 feet^2 / 43,560 = .046 acre.

Cash Rental Equivalent

An estimate for cash rental equivalent for your particular region can be calculated as a percentage of current land values. In general, many economists assume that land rent is three to four percent of total land value. If you use three percent, which we used in our example, the average land value estimate would be about $5,330 per acre ($160/.03). We recommend you determine average cash rental equivalent using the average land value in your region over the past three to five years.

The enterprise budget is divided into five sections. The first section shows the total dollars of product sold. In this case, the units sold are on a per pound basis ($3.00 per pound) and a bed (4 ft by 100 ft area) basis ($360 per bed). Records should be kept on both a sales unit (in this case pounds) and land unit (in this case bed) basis. We will discuss why this is important later when we discuss product mix.

The second section outlines the cost of planting and growing the crop. These costs are kept separate for two reasons. First, planting costs have occurred whether a crop is eventually harvested or not. Once the seeds are paid for, for example, they are a real cost and need to be included in the budget. Second, there is a delay between the time a crop is planted and when it is harvested and sold. Production expenses have to be covered from borrowing or savings or some other source. Therefore, interest paid on a loan, or lost by tying up savings on pre-harvest expenses, should also be included as a production expense.

The third section is the harvest component of the budget and includes costs associated with harvesting (primarily labor) and harvest packaging. For livestock this would include butchering expense, including the travel involved.

The fourth section includes the cost of ownership. Each farm has assets, such as land, buildings and equipment, included on the balance sheet, which are used in the farming operation as you produce crops or products. The enterprise budget must include some fraction of the asset value to account for costs of ownership in relation to that production.

Calculating Ownership Costs

There are several ways to allocate ownership costs. Whatever method you use for deciding the value of your ownership, you want to use the same technique and assumptions in all of your enterprise budgets so they accurately compare to each other.

In our example, the land use cost is its current cash rental equivalent of $160 per acre. You could instead take the actual land costs of interest expense (land loan only), property taxes, improvements, etc. from your financial statements and allocate those costs to the budget by dividing the total costs by the acreage used by this specific crop. Or you can take a cash rent equivalent, which is the amount of dollars you could rent the land for if you didn't farm it yourself.

For this example, it is assumed that vegetables are grown on 70 beds per acre. So, the $160 per acre annual land rent charge is shared by the 70 beds, or $2.29 per bed.

Machinery ownership can be broken down into variable costs for your machinery (fuel, repairs, etc.), plus the fixed cost of machinery ownership (insurance, storage, etc.). You will allocate the total machinery cost per measurement unit. In the specialty green bean example, we are valuing machinery at what it will cost to replace (refer to your current schedule from your balance sheet for this information). We estimated annual machinery cost to be about $500 per year, or about $7.14 per bed. ($500/70 beds)

The irrigation system is assumed to need replacement every three years, for a total per acre investment of $240. Thus, total ownership costs are estimated at $1.14 per bed per year. ($240/70 beds/3 years). The total ownership cost will be the same for all the crops grown on any of the beds for the farm.

Table 16.1 Specialty Green Bean Enterprise Budget

Per 4 ft x 100 ft bed	Quantity	Unit	$/Unit	Total
RECEIPTS				
Bean sales (Income)	**120**	**lbs**	**3.00**	**$360.00**
PLANTING YEAR				
Supplies				
Seed - cover crop	0.75	lbs	0.60	0.45
Seed	2	lbs	10.00	20.00
Fertilization	6	lbs	0.15	0.90
Labor				
Cover crop	0.05	hrs	12.00	0.60
Bed preparation	0.20	hrs	12.00	2.40
Fertilizer spreading	0.10	hrs	12.00	1.20
Planting	0.15	hrs	12.00	1.80
Irrigation set up	0.25	hrs	12.00	3.00
Weeding	2.00	hrs	12.00	24.00
Interest on Preplant Costs	54.35	dollars	0.035	1.90
TOTAL PREHARVEST COSTS				**$56.25**
HARVEST & PREP COSTS				
Bags (1 lb)	120	bags	0.03	3.60
Labor				
Harvest labor	15.00	hrs	12.00	180.00
Packaging	0.50	hrs	12.00	6.00
TOTAL HARVEST & DELIVERY COSTS				**$189.60**
OWNERSHIP COSTS (ANNUAL)				
Irrigation system				1.14
Machinery				7.14
Land				2.29
TOTAL OWNERSHIP COSTS				**$10.57**
TOTAL COSTS (ANNUAL)				
per crop year				$256.42
per lb				2.14
RETURNS OVER TOTAL COSTS, ANNUAL (NET INCOME)				**$103.58**

From the Farmers

Information-Based Decisions

Sharon Hoerichs, Little Sioux Orchard

Sharon Hoerichs has been making goat soap for a few years now, primarily from ingredients they raise on the farm. However, she does buy lye, a major ingredient. Recently she needed to find a new source of lye, and the best she could find would be $2.00 per pound more than the previous source.

Since Sharon had already done an enterprise analysis/cost sheet in excel, she knew in a minute by plugging in the new price that each bar would only cost her four cents more. "This gives me the freedom in knowing that I can go with this option, rather than spending hours to try to find a better price. It is worth it to me. Without the numbers, I wouldn't have that security."

The fifth section totals up all of the costs per bed. Subtracting these from the income total ($360 − $256.42 = $103.58) gives you the total returns over cost, or, in this example, the net income per bed.

Calculating Break-even Price

The break-even price is the price at which your expenses are being met. This is the base price that you must add planned profit to set your final sales price. You will want to include your labor along with the rest of the production costs in the break-even calculation, as you'll want these costs covered when you are deciding on your final sales prices. A break-even price will be different for each type of market you plan to sell to, as your marketing costs will vary.

To figure the break-even price, take the total costs of production and divide by the total amount of product harvested. You can calculate this on the entire volume or weight produced of a given crop, or by specific unit, such as the previous per bed example. If this was a livestock operation, your unit might be the entire herd, and the break–even expressed in dollars per animal, or it might be one steer or one hog and the break-even expressed as dollars per pound live weight, or dollars per pound dressed weight. (See the sidebar on page 153.)

In our green bean example from Table 16.1, the total costs of production were $256.42 to produce 120 pounds of beans. $256.42/120 = $2.14. This means that if you want to earn a profit on these beans, you must charge more than $2.14 per pound PLUS your costs to market this product. This is the base price you need to cover your costs of production. (We will cover more on marketing costs in Chapter 18.)

You can use the $2.14 per pound number to compare (or benchmark) your costs to other farmers to determine if your costs are higher or lower in comparison. You also can compare your production costs from year to year on your own farm (trend analysis). If your costs are high compared to others or compared to your numbers, then carefully evaluate the individual budget items to determine where the costs are different and why. For instance, if your labor costs are high, perhaps your workers are using inefficient methods. Do you have too much invested in machinery for your scale of production? These are the kinds of issues you should assess to get full value from the enterprise budgeting process.

Break-even Yield

Another interesting number you may want to calculate is the break-even yield, which tells you how much product you need to harvest in order to meet your production costs. To figure this, take the total cost from your enterprise budget and divide by the sales price of the product. For the specialty bean example, your total costs for production is $256.42 per bed. You are selling specialty green beans for $3.00 per pound, so you would have to produce 85.5 pounds per bed to cover your total cost of production ($256.42/$3.00 = 85.5).

Keep in mind that this enterprise budget includes only production cost. Marketing costs must be added to determine the break-even total cost per pound or yield.

Another reason to complete an enterprise budget is to determine what your key costs are. For example, pre-harvest and harvest labor for specialty green beans totaled $219.00 per bed (18.25 hours at $12 per hour), or 85.4 percent of total costs. Labor is one of the important non-financial data collections we talked about in Chapter 8. To do an accurate enterprise budget, you will need to track all labor (paid and unpaid) used to produce a specific product and assign a dollar value.

With labor such a large percent of overall expenses, a change will have a significant impact. You should look at labor needs at all stages of production to see if there is a way to become more labor efficient without lowering yields. In this case, perhaps growing a bean variety with a different growth habit that makes it easier to pick.

All of the other costs combined make up the other 14.6 percent of the costs, and so have a much smaller impact. Supplies in the bean budget total only $21.35 per bed (8.3 percent of total costs). Because of the smaller contribution to total costs, supplies do not need to be looked at as closely as labor. Reducing supply costs by 10% will have a much smaller impact than reducing labor costs by 10%.

Fixed and Variable Costs

Fixed and variable costs are two terms used frequently by accountants, tax preparers, and lenders. The differences between the two terms may not seem all that important at first, but an understanding of what they are and what they can tell you about your farming operation could affect some of the decisions you make in your business.

Fixed costs are those costs that do not change, no matter how much of something you produce, with costs even if nothing is produced. For example, once you purchase a tractor you usually have costs of ownership such as a place to store it, insurance, and perhaps borrowed money to pay for it. The costs of storage (or housing), loan interest, insurance, and depreciation occur whether you use the tractor or not. The only way to avoid the fixed costs on this tractor is to sell it.

Another set of fixed costs would be those concerning the basic running of your farm (overhead costs). General farm building repairs and maintenance, property taxes, farm insurance, and other similar items need to be paid regardless if a product is produced or not. Note that fixed costs are really not "fixed," they just tend not to change as the amount of production changes.

Variable costs are those costs that you, as the manager, have control over and can change at your discretion. These generally

Calculating the Break-even Price for Various Markets

Each break-even price must be customized to incorporate any specialized handling of processing for a given market. For example, a break-even for a dressed steer will be quite different than that for a live sale animal, because the dressed weight price includes the cost of processing, with a lower final product weight. You should choose the calculation that is most relevant to how you sell your products.

Examples:

Break even cost of steer (live sale)

$$\frac{\text{Cost of production (calf value, feed, veterinary, etc.)}}{\text{live weight of steer at sale}}$$

Break even cost of steer (carcass)

$$\frac{\text{Cost of production (calf value, feed, veterinary, processing, etc.)}}{\text{hanging weight of steer}}$$

From the Farmers

Checking Prices Each Year

Andrea Gunner, Rosebank Farm

Andrea Gunner loves to look at numbers, and is amazed at how much she can learn in just a few hours each year. She has set up Excel spreadsheets that she plugs new numbers into each year that help her assess if her prices are covering her costs and bringing in the profits she plans on. With numbers that go back to 1994, she has a lot of food for thought every time she opens her records.

She got word from her poultry slaughter facility that the per-bird processing rate would go up by 25 cents per bird. She was able to sit down in March, plug in the new slaughter cost, and decide what price she needed to charge to still make the profit she was aiming for. It took her ten minutes to figure out that a raise of $0.25 in slaughter price per bird could be offset by a 10 percent increase in her poultry prices.

---

change with the amount of production. The most common variable costs are crop and livestock inputs such as seed, fertilizer, pest control products, veterinary, and feed. Fuel and maintenance (based on use) are variable costs associated with machinery such as the tractor we just discussed.

Labor will be considered either fixed or a variable cost, depending on if the employees are salaried (fixed), work piece rate (variable), or are hired only to accomplish specific production-related tasks (variable).

The importance of the difference between fixed and variable costs comes into play in how they relate to the price you receive for a particular product. Fixed costs will stay the same no matter how much product you produce, whereas variable costs change with the amount produced.

Let's look at an example, where you are growing green beans and selling them at your local farmers' market. You calculated your fixed costs for production and marketing at $0.40 per pound and variable costs at $3.10 per pound. Your season average selling price was $2.75 per pound.

In this case, your selling price did not even cover your variable costs. The money that you brought in from selling your product was below the total of those costs that you control (seed, fertilizer, labor, etc.). You lost $0.75 [$2.75 - ($ 3.10 + $0.40)] per pound for every pound of green beans you sold. By not producing any green beans at all you would lose only your fixed costs, or $0.40 per pound. So in this case, with this low market price of $2.75 per pound, you are losing more money by actually growing and selling green beans than by not growing and selling them at all. Increasing your volume of sales will not help in this situation, as every extra pound you produce will add to your losses, since the selling price of $2.75 does not cover the variable costs of $3.10 per pound.

When prices do not even cover variable costs, a decision needs to be made quickly. Can prices be increased, marketing outlets be changed, production or marketing practices be altered? If not, you need to stop growing the current product now and choose something else that can contribute profit to your farm.

Alternatively, assume your season average selling price for green beans was $3.30 per pound. In this case you would cover all of your variable costs and half of your fixed costs ($3.30 - $3.10 = $0.20, which can be allocated toward covering the $0.40 per pound fixed cost). You could over a short time period (one to two years at most) keep producing green beans. At some point in the future, however, your fixed assets will need to be replaced. If you have not covered those costs there will be no money available from your farming operation for replacement. In this case, you may be able to cover losses by increasing sales volume.

If you believe it is unlikely that changes to your production or marketing plan can increase the sales price or reduce costs in order to cover all costs, then you need to stop growing green beans altogether and choose a different enterprise.

Some CSA producers say that even if a particular product is unprofitable, they may choose to include it in the share box to attract customers. While loss leaders may work in grocery stores where thousands of different products are offered, loss leaders in a share box of only 30-40 items should be approached with care.

The Concept of Economies of Scale

One hidden consequence of fixed versus variable costs is the concept of scale. If you have a large amount of fixed costs (several pieces of large machinery, buildings, land, other equipment) but don't produce very much saleable product, the total of those fixed costs will have a heavy impact on your costs of production. If, however, you are able to maximize the use of all of your fixed assets, by either having a smaller fixed cost base (smaller or no equipment, less overhead), or a larger scale of production, then the amount of fixed cost per unit of production will be reduced.

We are not saying that bigger is necessarily better or worse, but that if you choose smaller scale production, then you should have a correspondingly smaller fixed cost base. Thus, if you want to only grow an acre of mixed vegetables, or milk 35 organic jersey cows, you will be much better off financially if you plan your vegetable production without the purchase of a tractor, and don't plan to construct a large loafing shed. Dividing the ownership costs of a tractor over one acre of production will have a much greater financial impact than dividing those same costs over ten, or even five acres.

You will want to carefully assess the impact of your asset/overhead purchases in relationship to your scale of operation if you wish your farm to be sustainable. The concepts we talked about in Chapter 14 will be useful here.

Economies of scale also comes into play when planning labor as well. If you need to go into the field to do chores, it is possible that work can be more efficient if more units are being served. For example, a poultry farmer found that combining two batches of 125 broilers (each eight weeks of management, for a total of 16 weeks) into one batch of 250 (for a total of only eight weeks of management) took a little more land resource, and slightly more management time per day, but less management time overall, as feeding 250 chickens doesn't take twice as much time as it takes to get set up and feed 125 chickens. Considering such things as clean up time and infrastructure cost, this would also be true of milking cows in a parlor (there is less cost per cow if you are running the maximum number through your parlor, whatever size it is planned for), and many other farm chores.

Changes in production practices that can reduce costs without lowering yields, or increase yields more than the corresponding

Focusing on the Right Stuff

When you are reviewing or analyzing your financial statements, enterprise budgets, or other financial information, a key thing to remember is to focus on the important items.

For enterprise budgets this means focusing on key expenses. Remember enterprise budgets include all labor (including family contributed, valued at the going rate for the area), land rental fee, and machinery and equipment charges. For example, labor expense for many small acreage vegetable producers is 65 to 70 percent of total production expense. Crop inputs, including transplants, are another 15 to 20 percent of the total cost.

For farrow-to-finish pork producers, feed can easily be 50 to 55 percent of total cost, with buildings and other ownership cost contributing another 20 to 25 percent. The primary expense categories for beef finishing enterprises are the cost of the calf (60 to 65 percent or more) and feed and other inputs (25 to 30 percent of the total).

So if you are analyzing your enterprise records and looking for ways to reduce costs, focus on the key expenses. A 20 percent reduction in a key expense that is 70 percent of your total cost will have a dramatic effect on total expenses (and return to management), whereas a 20 percent reduction in an expense that comprises 10 percent of the total or less will have little effect on your return to management.

For whole farm income statements you want to focus on those expenses and income categories that have the largest contribution to your entire farm. For example, if you have multiple enterprises with one of the enterprises contributing 65 percent or more toward your total gross income, focus on that enterprise first. Conversely, if an enterprise impact is small (10 percent or less of the total) analyze it later, if at all.

ENTERPRISE BUDGETS

Choosing Your Size and Profit

We talk about economies of scale in the text, but there are also diseconomies of scale. This shows up in the University of Wisconsin Center for Dairy Profitability's dairy data. The most efficient operations (the ones with the highest profit per cow) are typically those with 50 to 100 cows. The farms with more than 250 show the least profit per cow. The bigger operations have much higher labor costs, higher vet expenses, more land rent (and drive up rents in their local areas by competing for land against other dairies), and higher interest costs.

So, why milk 300 cows if 50 would be more profitable on a per-cow basis? Well, if you net $500 per cow x 50 cows, you earn $25,000. If you net $200 per cow x 300 cows, you earn $60,000. That's economies of scope, not scale. (For more information on dairy profitability see cdp.wisc.edu.)

---

costs, can increase profit. However, without detailed enterprise budgets indicating where changes should be made, and what the result is from the changes implemented, the effect on profit will be a mystery.

Using Your Analysis to Help Determine Product Mix

Enterprise budgets allow you to compare profit and labor use among the various products that you produce. This is very helpful in making decisions about what to concentrate your production efforts on.

We know from Table 16.1 earlier that our specialty green bean example showed profit returns over total costs of $103.58 per bed. Labor use was 18.25 hours. The returns over total cost per hour were $5.68 per bed ($103.58 profit/18.25 hours). Doing enterprise budgets such as this on several of your primary crops allows you to then compare them to each other, which is a very informative exercise.

In Table 16.2 we show the totals from budgets for 13 crops, including the specialty green beans. Shown in comparison like this, you can see a wide range in both economic returns and hours of labor needed for the various crops. A quick comparison shows annual returns over total costs per bed range from $29.21 for asparagus to $524.46 for heirloom tomatoes. Labor hours required per bed vary significantly from 1.55 for strawberries to 18.25 for specialty green beans. It will be useful to you, no matter what you produce, to at some point compare different enterprises on your farm in a table like this. (It is very important to note that since these are generalized estimates, your own numbers may be very different.)

Once you have information like this for your own farm, how you determine your product mix will depend upon whether you consider your land or your labor as the more limited resource. If you feel that you will be limited by the amount of land you can farm, and adequate labor is available, then you should pick those crops that receive the highest returns (or profit) per bed (column one). If you have more land available, but the labor supply is short, then you should pick those crops that receive the highest returns per hour (column three). The choice between columns one and three will affect what you plant.

For example, if these were your numbers and you wanted to maximize profit per bed, then specialty green beans should be in your product mix. The economic returns for specialty green beans ranked fifth among the 13 crops shown, so it is likely that you would choose to grow more specialty green beans than some of the other crops. If you have limited labor and you choose product mix based on column three instead, specialty green beans ranked eleventh out of the 13 crops in profit per hour. If profit per hour is your deciding factor for product mix, it is likely that specialty green beans will have a smaller percentage of your total production than the other crops.

Comparisons of the distribution of labor use are particularly important if multiple crops are harvested at the same time. For example, early harvest crops such as greens, snow peas, and some early green beans all compete for labor at the same time. If you are thinking of making changes, budgets for proposed new enterprises should be developed using estimates and compared to existing enterprises. Additional information, such as time of harvest, or value in a rotation, or strength of the market, can then be combined with the enterprise values to plan your product mix.

As discussed previously, there may be reasons to keep lower profit margin products in your product mix. However, once you understand an item brings in a lower profit, you might want to lower the amount you produce. This would increase your overall profit. For example, if you want to have specialty green beans in your CSA boxes, you could provide half as much (or some other percentage) as you did previously, and substitute a product that has a higher profit margin per unit in its place. Or as an alternative, perhaps you can get specialty green beans from another grower, and include a small mark-up to cover any handling costs on your end.

Enterprise budgets can be developed for any production stream on your farm. Be it raising steer calves versus selling them at three months, choosing a certain breed of poultry, or deciding if sheep or hogs would be a profitable addition to your orchard, tracking and/or predicting the exact income, costs, and labor expenditures for that production stream will be a very valuable exercise.

Comparison of your enterprise budgets will help determine which product mix best allocates the scarce resources (land and labor) for your farm and meets your farm financial goals.

Getting the Most Out of Your Budgets

The question always comes up, particularly for those vegetable farmers that grow a wide variety of produce: How can I be expected to develop 30 or more enterprise budgets? We suggest that you start with the two to three crops that would have the biggest impact on your farm profit (e.g., those crops that customers pass by other farm stands to come to yours for, or those crops that customers buy your CSA share to receive). It is likely that changes to production practices, prices, or product mix may be indicated, which if implemented will result in an increase in operating profit margin or asset turnover ratio.

A second common question is: How do you develop an enterprise budget for a crop or product you have never raised or grown? The preferred source of information is a friend or neighbor that has a similar operation to yours. Do they have production records to indicate what an expected yield could be? Do they have a good estimate of what the key expenses are (particularly labor) and potential market prices?

Table 16.2 Comparison of Economic Returns and Labor for Various Enterprises

	Returns over Total Costs	Hours of Labor	Returns over Total/Hr
Asparagus	$ 29.21	2.95	$ 9.90
Basil	$ 150.07	6.90	$ 21.75
Carrots	$ 43.21	5.35	$ 8.08
Cherry Tomatoes	$ 158.36	11.20	$ 14.14
Eggplant	$ 71.83	6.45	$ 11.14
Specialty Green Beans	$ 103.58	18.25	$ 5.68
Garlic	$ 29.42	7.15	$ 4.11
Greens	$ 97.21	2.80	$ 34.72
Heirloom Tomatoes	$ 524.46	11.20	$ 46.83
Potatoes	$ 51.25	5.10	$ 10.05
Red Raspberries	$ 118.65	6.15	$ 19.29
Snow Peas	$ 42.92	7.65	$ 5.61
Strawberries	$ 49.96	1.55	$ 32.23

Adapted from C. Chase, 2006 Iowa Vegetable Production Budgets, Iowa State University, Iowa State University Extension, Bulletin PM 2017.

From the Farmers

Enterprise Analysis May Not Tell it All
Jackie Hoch, Hoch Orchard & Gardens

Jackie Hoch points out that a lot of different crops can make money. But, there may be other, important, non-financial reasons that a certain crop stays within Hoch Orchard and Gardens' product mix. Strawberries are a good example. Jackie says that they are a less profitable crop than some of the others they grow, but that they are a nice early crop, and helps the farm's workers get settled and learn the farm systems at a less than peak time. "Strawberries are also important in keeping our labeled products on store shelves," maintaining customer name recognition and highly valued shelf space. "We don't grow things that don't make money," Jackie says. But they might grow something that makes less money if there are other reasons that make that product a fit for the farm.

The Hoch's recently decided to expand into livestock—hogs and poultry in the orchard. Each of these are valued in how they are helping to maintain the orchard. "We want to consider all of the values something contributes, including the ecological intangibles. Making the most profit might not be the best basis for a decision for the farm, or for your personality."

Jackie tells another story to reflect this. "HoneyCrisp apples bring in the most money, but they also take the most management. They also are not as good for biological diversity." And so, the Hochs plant a lot of other varieties besides HoneyCrisp.

If there are no friends or neighbors to ask, your local Extension agent or land grant university production expert may be able to help with the production aspects (yields and production costs) of the budget. You also could talk to some lenders or other government agency personnel that are working with the type of crops you are looking at adding. Do some market research to find out what types of markets are available, and what price you can expect to sell your product for within your region.

Developing a process for creating enterprise budgets will take time. You can make adjustments as you become more confident in how you are growing and marketing the new crop. As you are starting out with enterprise analyses, it will be useful to make several different estimates using different prices and costs to determine a range of potential profitability. We recommend that you start small with any new enterprise until you reach a comfort level, and then grow smart, keeping track of changes in profitability over a period of time.

Summary

An enterprise budget is an estimate of the costs and economic returns (profit) to produce a specific crop or enterprise. Enterprise budgets give you the detail you need in order to make decisions to improve profit, improve your quality of life (e.g., reduce labor at certain times of the year without reducing profit), or achieve some other business goal.

Developing enterprise budgets gives you the ability to analyze production practices and/or product mix and determine if changes to either can be made to increase profit. Changes in production practices can vary, but should focus on the key expense items revealed by the budgets. Product mix changes can focus on returns to a land unit, such as a bed or acre, or on labor, depending upon which resource (land or labor) is limited. Your farm data may differ significantly from the generalizations we have presented so it is important that the decisions you make are based on your own farm records.

From the Farmers

Should I Raise More Turkeys or Broilers?

Jody Padgham
Wild Crescent Farm

Jody Padgham of Boyd, Wis. was interested in finding out how well each of her mini-enterprises, organic pasture-raised turkeys and broilers, did in a year. She was thinking that turkeys were more time- and cost-effective, and was considering trying to raise more turkeys and fewer broilers. She did an analysis of her production season, in which she raised 225 broilers and 17 turkeys, each in their own growing group.

Jody was hoping that the less work-per-day turkeys would bring in proportionally more money, but it's looking like that isn't the case. The broilers are, in eight weeks of more daily work, netting $782, while the turkeys, which have to be managed daily from July through the end of November, only bring in $136 above her labor. Dividing by the number of birds in each group shows a net profit (above labor) of $3.48 per broiler and $8.00 per turkey.

By comparing the net income to the gross income she can see the net income ratio, or how much of every dollar of sale is going into her pocket. For Jody's broilers, this is $782/$3,346, or .23 or 23 percent. This means that for every dollar she takes in selling the broilers, 23 cents is profit (above what she pays herself to do the work). For the turkeys this number is $136/$1,257, which is only .11, or 11 percent, meaning 11 cents of every dollar she takes in is profit.

Jody also calculated the net income per hour of labor spent. Here she took her net income and divided by the number of hours she put in. For broilers this number is $783/63 hours, or $12.41. For turkeys this is $136/26.5 hours or $5.13. This means that for broilers, along with the $10 per hour she is paying herself, she is making an additional $12.41, for a total of $22.41 per hour. For the turkeys this total is only $15.13, which, though not as good, still isn't bad.

One thing that she doesn't show in this analysis is that by raising more birds per batch she can make her production more efficient. "I ran these same numbers last year, with a larger overall number of broilers in two smaller batches—one starting in May, the other in July — and the results were very different. I was putting in a lot more labor, and getting a much lower return." If she was raising more turkeys per batch, they might become as cost-effective as the larger group of broilers was. This labor efficiency is an intangible that would have to be estimated through another analysis comparing fixed and variable costs and labor estimates between smaller and larger groups.

After looking at the numbers and ratios Jody decided to continue focusing on broiler production while also trying to get more turkey pre-orders. She was happy to see that for the price she paid for feed (the largest production variable), she had her customer prices about right. Overall she made about $1,813 in income (labor costs + profit), which she feels is pretty good for 225 organic chickens and 17 turkeys.

Jody's Enterprises	(in dollars)		
	Broilers	**Turkeys**	**Total**
Gross Income	3346	1257	4603
# birds raised	225 birds	17 birds	242 birds
Expenses			
Overhead	80	40	120
Labor @ $10.00/hr	630	265	895
Inputs			
Feed	1400	570	1970
Chicks/Poults	214	71	285
Other			
Equipment (amortized)	100	30	130
Supplies (bags, ties, labels)	60	5	65
Marketing	10	5	15
Other (butchering/propane)	20	85	105
Mileage	50	50	100
Total Expenses	2564	1121	3685
Net income (Gross income- Total expenses)	$782	$136	$918

CHAPTER 17
A Tool for Comparisons: Partial Budgets

Key questions addressed in this chapter:

What is a partial budget, and how is it useful?

What goes into a partial budget?

Should you add an enterprise? Change production practices? Change your product mix? Custom hire or purchase machinery? Add a milking parlor or packing shed? Change marketing outlets? Purchase transplants or grow your own? As your farm business matures, you may find yourself wondering about potential change.

An analysis tool useful in helping answer these types of questions is the partial budget. A partial budget lets you analyze a portion of your farming business to see if adjustments to your operation should be made. It allows you to assess how a change in one aspect of the farm operation might impact the rest of the operation. Partial budgeting allows you to compare two alternatives side by side. It does not tell you whether either one of your options is the best alternative available, only that one is comparatively better than the other.

There are several different methods that can be used to organize a partial budget. All of them evaluate the changes in costs and revenues you can expect as you explore production or marketing changes.

The simplest partial budgeting method is to separate the projected changes into positive and negative financial effects. You'll see positive effects if a change increases revenue or reduces costs. Negative effects occur when income is reduced or costs are increased. Adding all of the positive and negative effects together will show you if the net change is financially positive or negative. If the net change is positive, then the proposed change would increase profit; if the net change is negative, the proposed change would decrease profit.

You most likely would decide to implement a financially positive change, and not make a negative change. We use the term "likely" because not all decisions will be based solely on economic returns. Other factors such as quality of life, lower personal labor requirements, environmental considerations, and safety and health, among other issues, should be considered in making decisions and are not easily translated into financial dollars and cents.

A partial budget is often used to evaluate the impact of a proposed change that has not yet been tried, and so farmers often ask where to get numbers to make the estimates.

Unlike an enterprise budget, a partial budget will not include all of the costs of producing the product. In a partial budget we only look at what will change between the two choices. For example, if ownership costs are not affected, they will not be included, since they would be exactly the same for both alternatives within the partial budget analysis. Similarly, if income is not affected by the decision, then revenues should not be included. Costs or incomes with the same values on both sides of the partial budget calculation offset each other so they do not need to be part of the analysis.

The success of partial budgeting analysis is dependent upon the accuracy of the estimates used. It is extremely important that the financial numbers used for the base comparison are from your own farm records, and that the estimates for an alternative consideration are as accurate as possible, based on what you know about your operation. If accurate estimates are not available for the proposed change, we suggest that you go through the partial budgeting process several times, using a range of estimates. The range will show you the variety of different ways that a change may play out.

Finding the Numbers

In creating a partial budget, number estimates might come from an Extension publication or other trade resource, from a neighbor's experiences, from a trial plot on your farm (generally the best source of data), or from other sources that seem reasonable and accurate.

Keep in mind that if estimates are gathered from sources off the farm, you may have to make adjustments to reflect your current production practices and abilities. Comparisons must be made on similar sized units of land (beds to beds, acres to acres, etc.).

Be very careful in making budget estimates. The adage "garbage-in, garbage-out" certainly pertains here.

OTTO'S TIP:

Partial Budget Components

There are seven components to a partial budget: increased revenue, reduced cost, reduced revenue, increased cost, total of positive effects (increased revenue and reduced cost), total of negative effects (reduced revenue and increased cost), and net change (positive minus negative effects). An example of a partial budget analysis outlining the seven components is presented in Table 17.1 on page 162.

Looking at Changing Crops

In the example shown in Table 17.1 a producer is comparing an existing green bean operation to a potential change to salad greens on the same land.

In our example, substituting salad greens for specialty green beans would reduce income by $210 per bed, from $360 for specialty green bean sales to $150 for salad green sales. Labor requirements and input and packaging costs, however, would be lowered by $245.85 - $42.22 or $203.63 per bed, primarily due to the lower labor requirements for salad greens compared to specialty green beans. Total negative effects outweigh total positive effects by $6.37 per bed, indicating that the change from specialty green beans to salad greens would reduce farm profit. Non-economic considerations such as labor (note that specialty green beans need 15.45 more hours per bed than the salad), would have to be thought about before absolutely deciding the change isn't worthwhile.

Table 17.1. Partial Budget Analysis of Changing Product from Specialty Green Beans to Salad Greens

Positive Effects of Changing		**Negative Effects of Changing**	
Increases in revenue		*Decreases in revenue*	
Sales of salad greens	$150.00	Sales of specialty green beans	$360.00
Decreases in cost		*Increases in cost*	
18.25 hrs of labor @ $12 per hr	$219.00	2.8 hrs of labor @ $12 per hr	$ 33.60
Input & packaging costs	$ 26.85	Input and packaging costs	$ 8.62
Total decrease in costs	$245.85	Total increase in costs	$ 42.22
Total positive effects	$395.85	**Total negative effects**	$402.22
Net change	-$6.37		

Expanding Your Production

A second example of how a partial budget could be used is presented in Table 17.2. Let's assume your farm produces vegetables on 4 ft by 100 ft beds. You have developed enterprise budgets for the four or five crops that provide a majority of the income on the farm. Currently, you produce carrots in two rows down the length of the bed. You wonder, what would happen to income and costs if a third row of carrots was planted? You estimate that adding a third row of carrots would increase production by 75 pounds. Given your current sales price of $0.80 per pound, that means revenue would increase $60 per bed. However on the negative side, seed, other crop inputs, and labor are estimated to increase $21.50 per bed. Total positive effects of $60 per bed outweigh the increase in negative effects of $21.50 per bed. If the production change was made, it would increase profit by $38.50 per bed.

If you feel there are no other significant non-economic factors involved, you most likely would determine a third row of carrots would be an easy and profitable production change to implement. (Assuming, of course, that you have a ready market for your increased production, and that you have considered the horticultural and systems issues as well.)

Table 17.2. Partial Budget Analysis of Changing Carrot Production Practices

Positive Effects of Change		**Negative Effects of Change**	
Increases in income		Decreases in income	
Increase in production (75 lb @ $0.80)	$60.00		
Decreases in costs		Increases in costs	
		Increase in labor and input costs	$21.50
Total positive effects	$60.00	Total negative effects	$21.50
Net change $38.50			

Note that economies of scale could come into play, and efficiencies with expanded production, or the potential use of equipment, etc. must be incorporated into the analysis. You must think about all of the potential impacts of a possible change and accommodate them as well.

Comparing Production Methods

A third example of how partial budgets can be used in decision making is in comparing two different production methods. In this example, you are comparing growing your own bedding plant transplants to purchasing them from someone else.

If you purchased transplants you would no longer be purchasing the soil mix, seed, and other supplies necessary to grow your own transplants (Table 17.3). You also would not be providing labor to grow the transplants. For simplicity in this example, no building or equipment costs are included (although if this decision was being made on a larger scale, they would need to be considered).

On the negative side, in this example you would be purchasing the 100 transplants at $1.50 each. Your actual cost would depend upon what type of transplant you were purchasing as well as the size of your purchase order; larger orders normally have lower prices per unit bought.

Based on the transplant cost of $1.50 each, it would not make economic sense for you to purchase transplants because you would pay $133 more than growing them yourself.

Looking at Labor-saving Equipment

A fourth example of how partial budgets can be used in decision making looks at purchasing a new piece of equipment. The purchase decision focuses on the cost of the equipment versus the cost of labor that is saved by the equipment. For this example, you are wondering whether it makes sense to purchase a one-row potato harvester, compared to continuing to pay labor to harvest by hand (Table 17.4 on page 164). You have one acre of potatoes to harvest each year.

The potato harvester would be able to harvest one acre in about two hours versus paying laborers for 100 hours. At $12 per hour, using the harvester your labor cost is $24. Paying $12 per hour, you would no longer have $1,200 per acre hand labor costs if you used the potato harvester.

From the Farmers

Financials are Just Another Tool

Carmen Fernholz, A-Frame Farm

"Financial analyses are just another tool, like a tractor or a combine, which help me get my farm work done," Carmen Fernholz points out.

But, he reminds us, they don't always tell us the full story. There are often additional non-financial factors to consider when making decisions.

"My financial reports on alfalfa may show a lot of red ink in some years, but when I walk the fields, and see the impact on the weeds and future crops, I know that alfalfa is valuable for many reasons on my farm, that it is integral to my management systems."

Carmen cautions to not make farm decisions based on the bottom line alone.

Table 17.3 Partial budget analysis of 100 Transplant Purchase vs Growing From Seed

Positive Effects of Changing		Negative Effects of Changing	
Increases in revenue		Decreases in revenue	
Decreases in cost		Increases in cost	
Labor developing transplants (1 hr)	$12.00	Transplants	$150.00
Supplies	$5.00		
Total decrease in costs	$17.00	Total increase in costs	$150.00
Total positive effects	$17.00	Total negative effects	$150.00
Net change	-$133.00		

PARTIAL BUDGETS

From the Farmers

Analyzing Numbers to Increase Profits

Andrea Gunner, Rosebank Farm

Planning to increase production, raising profitability was a goal at Rosebank farms. Andrea Gunner identified that death losses in their roasting chicken production was costing them a lot. She read about a mineral supplement for poultry that other producers claimed significantly reduced thriftyness-related losses and decreased feed costs by enhancing feed efficiency. This mineral mix, produced in central Pennsylvania, would cost Andrea $125 plus $10 shipping per 50 pound bag. The question she wanted to answer was: Will the positive effects of the mineral mix offset the costs of bringing it to British Columbia?

To answer her question, Andrea did a trial run of birds using the mineral to see how much it affected mortality and feed consumption. The first two batches of birds (which, because of weather, traditionally have higher mortality), experienced losses of 19 and 22 percent without the mineral. The third batch, using the mineral, experienced only 1.5 percent mortality, and subsequent batches had no measurable mortality at all. Previous records kept on Excel spread sheets told Andrea that average mortality for an entire season without the mineral mix were 16.5 percent. The trial year, in which the mineral mix was used for all but the first two batches, the overall annual mortality was reduced to 7.4 percent. She also

Continued on next page

Notice that we didn't include the cost of the potato harvester itself in this budget. The price you paid for the potato harvester was $2,000, and the estimated life of the equipment for accounting purposes is seven years. The term "for accounting purposes" is important because that is how you will determine the depreciation cost of the equipment. The depreciation cost for this equipment is the sales price minus the salvage value (or the price you could sell the piece of equipment for at the end of the seven-year period) divided by the useful life of the equipment.

For this example, you have a $2,000 purchase price minus zero salvage value divided by the seven-year life, which equals an annual depreciation cost of $286 per year. The salvage value of zero assumes your potato harvester is not worth anything at the end of the seven years. This is probably not what would actually happen if you chose to sell your harvester, but it is a conservative approach to making this decision.

$$\text{Annual Depreciation Cost} = \frac{\text{sales price} - \text{salvage value}}{\text{life of equipment}}$$

$$\$286 = \frac{\$2{,}000 - 0}{7}$$

In addition to depreciation costs, you have additional fixed and variable costs associated with your potato harvester. The fixed costs (those that don't vary by usage) would include taxes, storage, and insurance. It is estimated the fixed costs are one percent of the purchase price, or $20 per year. The variable costs (those that increase or decrease with usage) would be repairs and maintenance. The variable costs are estimated at two percent of the purchase price, or $40 per year. Your actual fixed and variable costs can differ substantially from these estimates from year to year. Keeping good records on repairs and maintenance, as well as fixed costs such as insurance and building (storage) costs will allow you to be more accurate when estimating these costs.

The total costs associated with the potato harvester purchase and use would be $370 per year for the one acre of potatoes. The net change would be a positive $830, indicating that you would increase your farm profitability by replacing hand labor for potatoes with a potato harvester. Plus, you'd save your and your helpers' backs!

Table 17.4 Partial Budget Analysis of Changing Product from Speciality Green Beans to Salad Greens

Positive Effects of Changing		Negative Effects of Changing	
Increases in revenue		*Decreases in revenue*	
Decreases in cost		Increases in cost	
Labor (100 hrs @ $12 per hr)	$1,200.00	Labor (2 hrs @ $12 per hr)	$ 24.00
		Depreciation cost	$ 286.00
		Taxes, housing, insurance (1%)	$ 20.00
		Repairs and maintenance (2%)	$ 40.00
Total decrease in costs	$1,200.00	Total increase in costs	$ 370.00
Total positive effects	**$1,200.00**	**Total negative effects**	**$ 370.00**
Net change	**$830.00**		

From the Farmers...continued

found that while using the mineral, each chicken ate measurably less feed.

Now that Andrea could see that the mineral mix had an impact, she needed to find out if the financial impact of lower losses and lower feed use balanced out the increased cost of the supplement. Again using an Excel spreadsheet, and taking average costs and mortality figures from previous years, Andrea was able to figure that providing the mineral cost 17 cents per bird, but that the feed costs went down, from $4.70 to $3.94 per bird. Since all other costs were equal, this gave her a total net cost to produce birds with the mineral mix of $10.24 per bird, and $10.82 without. This alone might have convinced Andrea that this was a worthwhile change, but she also took into account the financial impact of the lower mortalities. This made the difference even more significant, with birds given the supplement costing only $10.50 per bird to produce, and those without costing her $11.41.

Given that Andrea didn't need to make any other changes to use the mineral mix, she was able to make the easy decision to import the 50-pound bags of mineral from Pennsylvania, and actually save money while she was still charging the same price to her customers. Doing the trial run and tracking the real numbers gave her great confidence in making this decision, which at first glance may have looked expensive.

If any part of her carefully calculated costs change over time, she will be able to easily enter new numbers and see what production or pricing changes she needs to make to accommodate them.

With Poultry Mineral Mix			
2010		**Chicken Costs**	
(based on 2,000)		$/MT	$/bird
Chicks (incl freight)			1.74
Apple cider vinegar			0.02
Skim milk powder			0.06
Fertrell's Poultry Nutri-Balancer			0.17
Grit		66.00	0.03
Starter	0.0011814	450.00	0.53
Grower	0.00874884	390.00	3.41
Cracked Grain	0	400.00	0.00
Slaughter			3.25
Bags, Labels & Ties			0.15
H2O2 (4l), 35%, want 2500		42.99	0.01
Thymol (15 ml)		7.99	0.00
Heat		350	0.18
Bedding	0.67	375.00	0.13
Supplies		100	0.05
Building R & M		400	0.20
Fencing R & M		100	0.05
Vehicle		500	0.25
Sub-Total Direct Costs			10.24
Mortality	0.0741	3.44	0.25
Total Direct Costs			**10.50**

Avg Wt	$/lb.	avg cost/bird
5.15	3.95	$ 20.34

Margin	% Costs/Price
9.85	51.59%

Without Poultry Mineral mix			
2010		**Chicken Costs**	
(based on 2,000)		$/MT	$/bird
Chicks (incl freight)			1.74
Apple cider vinegar			0.02
Skim milk powder			0.06
Fertrell's Poultry Nutri-Balancer			0.00
Grit		66.00	0.03
Starter	0.001425	450.00	0.64
Grower	0.0104125	390.00	4.06
Cracked Grain	0	400.00	0.00
Slaughter			3.25
Bags, Labels & Ties			0.15
H2O2 (4l), 35%, want 2500 p		42.99	0.01
Thymol (15 ml)		7.99	0.00
Heat		350	0.18
Bedding	0.67	375.00	0.13
Supplies		100	0.05
Building R & M		400	0.20
Fencing R & M		100	0.05
Vehicle		500	0.25
Sub-Total Direct Costs			10.82
Mortality	0.165	3.55	0.59
Total Direct Costs			**11.41**

Avg Wt	$/lb.	avg cost/bird
5.15	3.95	$ 20.34

Margin	% Costs/Price
8.93	56.10%

Summary of impact	Per Bird	Per Year
Better feed conversion	$0.76	$1,516.90
Lower mortality	$0.33	$663.54
Cost of NutriBalancer	-$0.17	$340.00
Difference to our bottom line	$0.92	$1,832.10

From the Farmers

Equipment Purchase Decisions

Kay Jensen, JenEhr Family Farm

At JenEhr Family Farm a decision to make a purchase is carefully researched. Thinking about the time spent by their crew in transplanting, Kay and Paul asked the crew to track for a week how much time was spent transplanting. With 7 people transplanting for a little more than 7 hours per day, they put in 50 hours a day for five days to transplant 10% of the crop. Given they paid $10 per hour for the work, this 250 hours (50 hrs/day x 5 days) cost them $2,500. Since the crew planted 10% of the crop this week, to plant the entire crop would cost 10 x $2,500, or $25,000 in labor.

Kay says that they could buy a pretty nice transplanter for $25,000. Of course, there would still be labor to use the machine, but it would be drastically reduced, and easier, leaving crew members available to do other work and less tired from the transplanting tasks. Kay and Paul figured out that the transplanter would pay for itself in about 18 months, and so they went ahead and bought it.

Kay also points out, however, that they always map out an exit strategy for every major purchase they make. They prefer to buy from a local equipment dealer, who will readily buy a piece back if it isn't working for them, or if things change and it isn't a good fit anymore. "We set up parameters ahead of time, to gauge when something isn't working. This makes it easier to decide when we're in the thick of a busy season."

You can also use partial budgets to explore different marketing venues. We will talk about this in Chapter 18 on marketing.

Summary

Partial budgeting allows you to compare two alternatives side by side to determine which alternative would increase farm profit. Examples illustrate product mix, production changes, evaluating transplants, and machinery investments. Partial budgets can be used to explore many types of alternative paths, such as custom hire versus ownership, buying feed from one source or another, renting pasture versus buying, etc.

Remember that a partial budget analysis does not tell you whether either one of your options is the best alternative available. Rather, the analysis tells you which one is comparatively better financially than the other. The key to any analysis is getting as accurate numbers as possible for your comparisons. The adage "garbage-in, garbage-out" pertains here, and poor input numbers could lead to a wrong conclusion.

Note: Tables 17.1, 17.2, 17.3, and 17.4 are built from Chase (2006), "Iowa Vegetable Production Budgets."

CHAPTER 18
What is Your Best Market? Comparing Marketing Costs

We began this book remarking that financial management isn't especially popular with farmers. Historically, farm product marketing might be right up there in second place for least favorite tasks. That said, a new generation of farmers seem to be challenging this assumption. There is a lot of excitement about the potentials and growth of a diversity of direct markets. Farmers' markets are growing; we see more direct access to stores, restaurants, and wholesale distributors. Community Supported Agriculture farms[1] (CSAs) are becoming more well known, even in rural areas, and other markets, such as internet and specialty sales, are developing. The commodity market continues to be viable for many crops, including organic production.

It is wonderful that this diversity of markets exists, but how do you decide what market is best for your product, your family, and your farm's bottom line?

There are obviously a lot of social considerations that go into choosing a market, ranging from one as simple as "I hate talking to people," to "We don't have enough labor available to go to two farmers' markets," or "There are already three farms at that market selling grass-fed beef." In evaluating different markets a simple list recording pros and cons, and the various needs for each market can help separate out the feasible from the non-feasible.

But, once you get past the obvious hurdles, and consider various ways of getting over the lesser barriers (Can your chatty daughter be the one that stands at the table? Will the second farmers' market let you hire someone to sell your product? How can you differentiate your beef?), you will want to look at the financial aspects of different markets to see what makes the most financial sense for your farm.

Key questions addressed in this chapter:

How do markets differ in their financial impact?

How can you measure this impact?

If you don't have numbers for specific crops, can you still assess various market potentials?

---

1. Community Supported Agriculture (CSA) farms operate with a group of "members" who pay the farmer a fee, often at the beginning of the season, to grow a diversity of products —most commonly vegetables, but increasingly meats, fruits, and other farm-produced items. The products of the farm are distributed to the members on a regular basis, or as they are harvested.

MARKETING COSTS

From the Farmers

Get Help for Commodity Marketing

Carmen Fernholz, A-Frame Farm

As a diversified organic grain farmer, Carmen Fernholz often has several different products going to market. "The best thing I have done for my marketing is to hire a professional marketing agent. That way, I can concentrate on being a good farmer, and they can concentrate on getting me a good price."

He continues "As producers we are emotionally tied to our production, and bonded to production tasks. It is hard for us to be objective about the marketing of that production."

Carmen works very closely with his marketers, who have their eyes on the commodity market "24/7." The marketers understand the mindset of different buyers, and how that changes over time. "I write their paychecks, and they know they have to bring me a good price to earn that."

Carmen recommends working with marketing pools, available for dairy, some meats, and grains. He works with the Organic Farmers Agency for Relationship Marketing, Inc. (OFARM, ofarm.org) to connect with good marketers.

Diversification is Key

The ways you sell your products can be diversified by where you sell your products. You can sell your vegetables through your CSA in the small town where you buy your farm supplies, or you can take your CSA shares to the big city two hours away. Each market is uniquely different, and though you're using the same marketing model for each, you'd want to approach each market differently.

If you visualize the ways you market your products and the locations where you market your products as two axes of a grid, you can get a snapshot of how diverse your business is, and therefore, how stable it potentially is. Selling through only one farmers' market is kind of like growing just one variety of one crop on your farm—you don't have much stability if something goes wrong with that market. The city could sell the vacant lot or parking lot where it's located, the market could get sued and go out of business because of an accident you had nothing to do with, or a competitor could move in and undercut your prices to such a degree that you can't sustain your business.

The same thing is true if you sell all of your products to just a few customers; one disruption, perhaps through no fault of your own, can have a huge impact on your business.

So, assuming that you want to market in a diversity of markets, how do you know which markets make the most sense for you economically?

Evaluating Income Potential

When evaluating a current or potential marketing venue, it's important to look at its overall income potential and how that fits with the scale and total profits you want to realize from your business.

In other words, if you want to make a full-time living from your vegetable farm, you need to market your vegetables in a location and to a segment of the population that is large enough to provide you with that profit. If you know that you need to sell $160,000 worth of organic vegetables grown on your farm to provide you with the income you want to receive, you probably won't be able to do that in a town of 8,000 people. Likewise, even though you may have read that a rare species of livestock can be extremely profitable, you need to be certain that enough people that you have access to will want these animals before you raise a whole bunch of them.

Before you put significant resources into marketing through a particular method or marketplace, you will want to assess the potential that avenue has for getting you to your goals.

One way to assess potential is to find out how much your target market venue is currently distributing of a particular product, or range of products. At a grocery store, you could ask a produce manager about the volume of produce they sell, then estimate the percentage of that produce that is made up of products you can grow in commercial quality and quantity, and the percentage of the year you'd be able to provide that produce. This will give you a rough idea of what your ultimate potential for that particular market is. Of course, there are other variables that will impact whether you'll be able to provide product to a particular market (such as competitors, quality, or price), but some simple work will give you a ballpark that helps you understand if considering a particular market makes sense in the big picture.

Developing Marketing Budgets

Once you have a set of markets you would like to consider, how do you go about comparing them? One way is to prepare a marketing budget for each potential market.

Start by estimating (or, if you are comparing various current markets, collecting records for), your marketing costs. Marketing costs, as defined in this book, are those costs associated with the marketing and delivery of the product from your farm to your customer. Marketing costs for farm products include post-harvest handling, processing, packaging and storage, as well as the labor to sell, invoice, and deliver the product. Costs associated with coolers or other storage facilities (fixed or portable), as well as transportation units (e.g., vans, trucks, or refrigerated transports) should also be included.

Creating a separate marketing budget as a worksheet in your overall annual budget will be very helpful. Combining the marketing budget with an enterprise budget will allow you to determine the overall profit for each of your major crops. If multiple marketing outlets (e.g., farmers' market, CSA, u-pick, etc.) are used, a marketing budget should be completed for each outlet, allowing you to compare profits.

Determining Your Costs to Market

Let's assume you have a choice between selling your produce at a farmers' market and to a small institutional buyer (care center or hospital). Your production isn't large enough to sell wholesale through larger marketing outlets. Enterprise records on your farm production have been kept and the farm is operating efficiently. Tomatoes will be the crop used for this example. However, these same principles will apply for any direct marketed products, such as apples, cheese, honey, cuts of meat, etc.

After doing an enterprise analysis for this tomato example (such as we outlined in Chapter 16) the break-even production cost is estimated at $0.44 per pound. A total tomato production of 800 pounds (two beds) must be marketed. Two marketing outlet choices are available about 40 miles away from your farm; a twice-a-week farmers' market and a small institutional buyer.

The price you receive at the farmers' market is full retail, whereas the institutional customer is willing to pay only 65 percent of full retail. On average, 95 percent of what you take to the farmers market is sold, with the other five percent being donated to a food bank. Preparation for, traveling to, operating the booth, tearing-down and traveling back for each farmers market takes six hours, twice a week, over the 10-week production season. Pounds of tomatoes taken to market vary by week, but on average 40 pounds of tomatoes are for sale for each market.

The institutional market volume varies weekly, with products ordered two weeks in advance. However, the institutional buyer would purchase all 800 lbs of tomatoes over the growing season. Time to complete paperwork, as well as storage and handling facilities, are the same regardless of the marketing outlet.

From the Farmers

Choosing CSA

Kay Jensen, JenEhr Family Farm

After 20 years of managing a large Community Supported Agriculture (CSA) farm, Kay and Paul of JenEhr Family Farm decided to drop the marketing strategy.

"While the CSA was always good for cash flow," Kay says, "We now question the profitability." She sees consumer needs changing, with CSA member numbers dropping and more interest in customers who want "a grocery store in a box."

Flexibility and Stability

In assessing and planning for markets it is important to take into account the experience and stability of the customer, your history with the customer, the level of control you have over the pricing in the marketplace, and the buyer's (or organization's) level of commitment. The more secure each of these things, the lower your risk in a given market.

MARKETING COSTS

Don't Count Those Markets Before They Hatch

In their first full year of business, a pair of farmers in rural Iowa sold about a third of their vegetables to a new locally oriented restaurant in their town, and another third to a local natural foods retailer. The balance went to a small CSA and a farmers' market in a small nearby city.

That winter, they had very encouraging meetings with the buyers for the restaurant and the store, and anticipated significantly expanded sales at each of them. This was necessary growth in order to meet the farmers' goal of working full time on the farm. About two weeks after the meetings, they learned that the chef at the restaurant had quit, and that his replacement was under great pressure to reduce expenses. A week after that, a meeting between local growers and the natural foods store made it plain that, despite how well things had gone the previous season, community politics were going to cut significantly into their sales.

In the following year, sales at both accounts were slashed in half. Fortunately, the farmers had followed through with connections in a more distant but much larger market, and they were able to make up for the lost sales with new accounts and a significantly expanded CSA. They diverted produce to their farmers' market stand, and doubled the farm's sales there. Overall, sales increased that year by a little over 76 percent.

Sales in their small town continued to decline in the third year as the restaurant went through financial troubles. In the meantime, the farmers expanded their production of high-profit crops in the big city, helping them achieve efficiencies of scale that made those crops even more profitable.

Based on this experience, and discussions with small business people in other industries, they developed a rule of thumb that they would always try to sell their produce in at least three types of markets. They also agreed to never have more than 20 percent of their sales wrapped up in any one customer, so that they wouldn't be left out in the cold if something went wrong.

Table 18.1 presents total estimated cost to produce and market your tomatoes through the farmers' market and the institutional market.

The total estimated cost to produce tomatoes and market them through the farmers' market is $1.97 per pound ($0.44 production + $1.53 marketing). Total estimated cost to produce tomatoes and market them through the institutional market is $0.88 per pound ($0.44 production + $0.44 marketing).

It would be extremely difficult to determine how much labor, supplies, etc. you spent on a particular crop like tomatoes at a farmers' market or for an institution when sales may include 8-15 other items sold at the same time. Therefore, total cost over the entire sales period is calculated for each marketing outlet and then the total is allocated to the relative volume of various products sold. In most cases, total marketing costs are only allocated to the major sellers.

In this example, 15 percent of the total cost of marketing is allocated to tomatoes, and so farmers' market tomatoes need to cover $1,164 of the total cost of the farmers market and $354 of the total marketing cost associated with the institutional buyer. The 15 percent allocation is a guess at what portion of the total volume of sales is tomatoes, and will vary by the core group of products that you sell at each market. In all cases, 100 percent of the costs would need to be allocated to the total of the various products.

So which market will return the most profit? That depends upon what prices you receive for the product in the two markets. We talk more specifically about pricing in the next chapter. However, it is clear that you would need to charge at least $1.97 per pound at the farmers' market and $0.88 per pound for the institutional market just to cover your costs of production and marketing (assuming the 15 percent marketing cost allocation).

Allocating Marketing Costs from Whole-Farm Records

What if all you have are the whole-farm records you keep for filing your income tax returns (Schedule F)? You have not yet done enterprise analyses, but you still want to assess which markets might be best for your products. For taxes you keep records on product inputs (seed, soil mix, compost, feed, vet supplies, minerals, etc.), hired labor, packaging and handling containers and supplies, depreciation on machinery, buildings, fencing and the irrigation system, and land rental. In addition, you have whole-farm records related to marketing expenses (tables, supplies, trucking, processing, vendor fees) and hired labor.

Table 18.1 Comparison of Marketing Costs by Market

Farmers' Market: 20 weeks/40 markets

Transportation vehicle expenses @ $.50/mi, 3,200 miles	$1,600
Labor charges; 2 people @ 12hr/wk, 20wks, @$12/hr	$5,760
Supplies (bags or sacks, other supplies) @ $20/wk	$ 400
Total transaction costs for the season	**$7,760**
Total transaction costs allocated to tomatoes (percent of total sales) – 15%	$1,164
Total transaction costs/lb sold (760 lbs sold)	$ 1.53

Institutional Market: 20 weeks

Transportation vehicle expenses @ $.50/mi, 1,600 miles	$ 800
Labor charges; 1 person @ 4hr/wk (includes selling), 20wks, @$12/hr	$ 960
Supplies (containers, other supplies) @ $30/wk	$ 600
Total transaction costs for the season	**$2,360**
Total transaction costs allocated to tomatoes (percent of total sales) – 20%	$ 354
Total transaction costs/lb sold (800 lbs sold)	$ .44

In this analysis, you will also need to include the value of non-paid labor. Often one of the largest costs on a small farm, you want to include its value when doing market cost assessments.

Let's assume you have a three-acre vegetable farm, keep whole-farm records, and want to evaluate whether it is more profitable to sell your products through a farmers' market or to an institutional buyer. Your sale projections are for total gross revenue of $18,000 per acre if sold direct through a farmers' market. Direct production expenses including depreciation, land rent, non-paid (family contributed) labor are $10,440 per acre (65 percent of sales). Your net farm income goal is $3,600 per acre (Table 18.2).

Given the gross revenue, production costs, and net farm income percentage, the amount of dollars left to market the crops produced can be calculated. By doing the math, you can see that in this case, the marketing cost allowance would be $3,960 per acre, ($7,560 - $3,600) or $11,880 for the 3-acre farm ($22,680 - $10,800). Can you reach your markets for this amount? Are you charging high enough prices and keeping costs low enough so that you have enough money to take your products to market? What markets could you go to to keep within this budget?

Initial Market Choice Evaluation

Let's say that you have several retail and wholesale marketing outlets available within an 80-mile radius of your farm. An urban farmers' market is 80 miles from the farm. You are thinking that about 60 percent of all your product can be sold at this market. The remaining 40 percent will be sold through various other markets. Remember that projected sales volumes and your overall production estimates will not always be the same; you'll have to allow for losses through storage and handling as well as any returns from the farmers' market.

From the Farmers

Labor Helps Decide the Market

Sharon Hoerichs, Little Sioux Orchard

Not everyone is willing to do the extra work that labor tracking involves, but Sharon Hoerichs of Little Sioux Orchard knows that it allows her to make better decisions. "Our first year we were really excited to sell at the farmers' market, but when we figured in our labor, it just didn't pay. It took us a lot of time to raise and pick the vegetables, and then four hours sitting at market to bring home only $30."

They joined a growers' cooperative and were able to send 50-pound boxes of vegetables through that wholesale market, which Sharon says was a lot more profitable for them, primarily because of the reduced labor.

Table 18.2. Revenue, Costs, and Income Per Acre

	Dollars per Acre	Dollars per 3-Acre Farm
Gross revenue	$ 18,000	$ 54,000
Procuction costs	$ 10,440	$ 31,320
Production profit margin (revenue-costs)	$ 7,560	$ 22,680
Net farm income goal	$ 3,600	$ 10,800
Marketing costs (margin-net)	$ 3,960	$ 11,880

MARKETING COSTS

From the Farmers

Market Philosophies

Kay Jensen, JenEhr Family Farm

Kay Jensen of JenEhr family farm uses several baseline philosophies to decide if a given farmers' market is worthwhile. They refer to the farm's mission statement to guide these principles:

• We won't sell at a market that allows farmers' to resell other farmer's products.

• If we are required to be at a market for more than four hours, we must generate at least $150 per hour in sales to make it worth going.

• We know that one person can handle sales up to about $1,000 or $1,200 per day. If sales are higher, we'll need another person, but there is a decision point where we have to closely watch the economics of paying a second person and having the market still be feasible economically.

• The costs of being at the market shouldn't be more than 10 percent of the total income we make. If we have to drive a distance to get there, those costs must be added in. If costs are above 10% this creates real sustainability problems, especially if the sales are really variable week to week.

The total of your preparation, set-up, sales, and tear-down time (including driving to and from the market) are estimated at nine hours. Two people will need to be on site at all times (18 hrs total) because of the potential volume of business at this market. Round-trip mileage is 160 miles. Marketing supplies (bags, boxes, etc.), annual cost for signage, tables, other equipment, and vendor fees is estimated at $50 per day. The farmers' market agreement requires vendors to be on-site 20 weeks per year. Your total marketing costs for this farmers market are presented in Table 18.3.

Table 18.3. Urban Farmers' Market Estimated Costs, per Day

	Unit	Rate	Costs
Supplies			$ 50
Labor – preparation and sales	18 hrs	$12.00/hr	$216
Transportation	160 miles	$0.50/mile	$ 80
Total estimated marketing cost			$346

Your total estimated farmers' market costs for the season would be $6,920 ($346 x 20 weeks). Given that you think you can sell 60 percent of your production here, the estimated marketing dollars you have available for this market would be $7,128 (60 percent of the total allocation of $11,880, from Table 18.2). Since the projected marketing cost is less than the marketing allowance you figured (above), this market would make economic sense for selling 60 percent of your farm's products. Using this market you'd bring back more to your net farm income than planned.

A Secondary Market

A second smaller farmers' market is available closer to your farm. You predict that of the remaining 40 percent of total projected sales, 30 percent (or 75 percent of the remaining sales) can be made through this market. Because of lower sales volume, only one person would be needed each week. Your estimated costs per day are shown in Table 18.4.

The cost per marketing day is substantially less at this market ($131 vs. $346). The annual cost would be $2,620 ($131 x 20 market days). This annual marketing cost is also lower than the allocated marketing cost of $3,564 (30 percent of the total allocation of $11,880, from Table 18.2).

OTTO'S TIP: *Those using a computer bookkeeping system and using the class function to identify specific markets (such as Farmers' Market, or CSA), will be able to extract marketing costs pretty quickly by running a class report. Look carefully at the costs you have included in each market to be sure they are specific to that market, and not overall costs. If you have not segregated costs by the type of market you can do rough figures based on the bills you have paid and the time you have spent.*

Table 18.4. Rural Farmers' Market Estimated Costs, per Day

	Unit	Rate	Costs
Supplies			$ 20
Labor – preparation and sales	8 hrs	$12.00/hr	$ 96
Transportation	30 miles	$0.50/mile	$ 15
Total estimated marketing cost			$131

Assessing an Institutional Market to Sell the Remaining Product

You are thinking that only 90 percent of total production can be sold through the two farmers' markets. Therefore, a third marketing outlet should be explored. Let's assume that there is a local institutional market (care center or hospital) in your area. Changes to the estimates for gross revenue, percentage of production costs to gross revenue, and marketing cost allowance need to be made for this new kind of market, since it will require different pricing. The institutional market will pay a lower price, which we estimate to bring in a 20 percent lower gross revenue. Rather than $18,000 (Table 18.2) you can expect $14,400 per acre.

It is possible that this institution will pay less than 80 percent of your farmers' market price per unit (pound, bunch, etc.). However, it is quite likely that not all of the products you take to the farmers' market are sold. Throwing things away (or giving them to the food bank) will reduce your overall average sales price. And so, the difference between the average farmers' market price (sold and unsold) and the institutional sales price, where 100 percent of what is delivered is sold, is likely to be smaller than the quick comparison between prices per unit.

Production techniques and costs will be the same regardless of which marketing outlet you choose, and remain at $10,440 per acre. Your dollar-per-acre profit goal remains the same as well, at $3,600 per acre. (From Table 18.2) The marketing allowance therefore is reduced to $1,080 ($11,880 - $10,800) for this institutional market for the farm (Table 18.5).

Table 18.5. Revenue, Costs, and Income, per Acre, Institutional Market

	Dollars per Acre	Dollars per 3- Acre Farm
Gross revenue	$14,400	$43,200
Production costs	$10,440	$31,320
Production profit margin	$ 3,960	$11,880
Net farm income (planned)	$ 3,600	$10,800
Marketing costs	$ 360	$ 1,080

The division of production and marketing costs as a percentage of gross revenue changes dramatically for the institutional sales market compared to the direct market. In this example, because of the lower prices paid, but the same cost of production, production costs make up 72.5 percent of gross revenue ($10,440/$14,400) leaving only 2.5 percent of revenues ($360/$14,400) for marketing costs. The question is: Can you keep the costs of selling to this institution to only $1,080 over a 20-week period?

MARKETING COSTS

Because tables, signs, and other farmers' market-specific materials are not needed to sell to the institution, supplies per delivery day are less. However, packaging products will still be needed to deliver institutional products. Labor for preparation and sales would be much less, since set-up, presence at the farmers' market, and tear-down are not required. (Table 18.6).

Table 18.6. Institutional Market

	Unit	Rate	Cost
Supplies			$ 5
Labor – preparation and sales	3 hrs	$12.00/hr	$36
Transportation	30 miles	$0.50/mile	$15
Total estimated marketing cost			$56

The institutional markets are located on a 30-mile roundtrip loop from the farm, resulting in a transportation cost of $15 per delivery. Adding in supplies and labor, this gives you a total estimated marketing cost of $56 per delivery. A 20-week delivery schedule (one delivery per week) would result in a total annual marketing cost of $1,120 ($56 x 20 weeks).

Since you are planning that only 10 percent of your sales will be made to the institution, the marketing allowance would be only $108 (10 percent of the total marketing allowance of $1,080 from Table 18.5). So, it is clear that if only used for 10 percent of your sales, this market is not cost effective.

Next Step

Both the urban and smaller rural farmers' market allowed you to meet your financial goals based on whole-farm records. Unfortunately, you estimated that you could only sell 90 percent of your total projected production at a farmers' market. What should you do now regarding the other 10 percent or your production? There are other outlets, such as a community supported agriculture farming operation, u-pick, on-farm stands, or other market venues that could be analyzed as part of a combination of marketing outlets.

What would happen to marketing costs if three different marketing outlets were served locally? What would happen if you sold products at the two farmers' markets along with the other 10 percent of your estimated production at the institutional market (Table 18.7, page 175)?

Maximizing your sales at the two farmers' markets and filling in the last of the sales to the institutional market allows you to sell all of your products, while still staying under the total annual marketing goal of $10,800. The marketing goal is met in spite of the institutional market costing $1,012 more ($1,120 compared to $108) than its allowance. In this case a combination of the two farmers' markets and institutional sales allowed you to sell all of your products, and still slightly exceed your net farm income goal of $10,800.

Table 18.7. Combination Farmers Market and Institutional Market

	Urban Farmers Market	Local Farmers Market	Local Institutional Markets	Total All Markets
	60%	30%	10%	
Ideal				
Gross revenue	$32,400	$16,200	$ 4,320	$52,920
Production costs	$18,792	$ 9,396	$ 3,132	$31,320
Production profit margin	$13,608	$ 6,804	$ 1,188	$21,600
Net Farm Income Goal	$ 6,480	$ 3,240	$ 1,080	$10,800
Marketing costs (Allocated)	$ 7,128	$ 3,564	$ 108	$10,800
Reality				
Supplies	$ 50	$ 20	$ 5	
Labor – preparation and sales	$ 216	$ 96	$ 36	
Transportation	$ 80	$ 15	$ 15	
Total estimated marketing cost (per trip)	$ 346	$ 131	$ 56	
Total annual marketing cost (per year)	$ 6,920	$ 2,620	$ 1,120	$10,660
Total Marketing allowance	$ 7,128	$ 3,564	$ 108	$10,800
Marketing balance vs. allowance	$ 208	$ 944	$ -1,012	$ 140

Summary

Many farms today have a diversity of market venues to consider. It is highly recommended that you do diversify, as any given market may change significantly with little notice.

Using numbers from your enterprise budgets, you can estimate the costs involved in taking a particular crop to a specific market. You can also evaluate different marketing outlets based on whole-farm records. Whole-farm records are easy to generate compared to enterprise records. However, they still allow you to determine a marketing cost budget based on gross revenue, production costs, and a net farm income goal. Because production costs and the net farm income goal do not vary by marketing outlet, comparisons between different markets focus on how sales revenue changes, relative to prices, along with the costs of moving your product to the buyer.

The examples presented here indicate that you could not market all of your products through one marketing channel and meet your net farm income goal. Clearly, this is not always the case. Some growers thrive by marketing their products through one market such as a farmers' market, community supported agriculture, or other outlet.

However, it is likely that most small-scale growers will have multiple marketing outlets available to them within a reasonable radius from the farm. The net farm income you can expect from those outlets will vary significantly. It is important, therefore, to evaluate each of the marketing outlets available to you as to its potential contribution to your overall farm profit.

CHAPTER 19
Making Assessments About Pricing

Key questions addressed in this chapter:

Why is proper pricing important?

How can you set the right price?

What should prices be based on?

Once you have chosen to direct market your products, you must decide how much to charge for your product. This can be an especially difficult task for those new to farming, or those taking products into a new market. In general, the closer you get to the final retail customer, the higher the price you can expect to charge for your product. And while that looks appealing, you also need to remember why that price gets higher; as you get closer to the final retail customer, costs and risk increase, so your prices should do so as well.

Many new farmers have a tendency to start out pricing their products too low. Several factors might lead to under-pricing. New farmers might not be secure in their belief that they are producing a quality product that is worth a higher price. You may introduce a product to test out a market, and think that a low price is the best way to get new customers. A beginner may not want to take their marketing and product seriously, and decide to "just get a little bit" for the products. Or, a farmer may not have any idea what a fair price for their product is in a particular type of market.

Whatever your pricing rationale, you owe it to yourself and your fellow farmers to charge a fair price in the marketplace. In order to develop a sustainable business for yourself, you must cover your costs of production and marketing, as well as bring yourself a return to profit. Consumers will assume that you are offering the product at a fair price. If you set prices at levels below your costs, other farmers that are also in your market might look as if they are charging unreasonably high prices. This behavior creates downward price pressures in a market, in which everyone loses as your customers have unrealistic expectations of what a sustainable price is. Eventually, only farmers that don't rely on an income will be left to serve customers.

If you start your pricing too low, it can be a difficult process to bring prices up to a sustainable level if you stay within the same market. If your pork chops are $2.99 per pound the first year, and then $4.99 the next (because you discover this is the price you need to charge to make a profit) you will most likely lose customers. However, if you start your business with the pork chops at $4.99, those customers that are drawn to your quality, hand-raised product will more likely appreciate what you are doing and sustain you.

Given the importance of proper pricing, how do you go about setting a price for your product? While there are a variety of ways to price products, all pricing decisions should take into consideration the customer, the competition, and the cost to grow and market the product. Of the three components, cost is the most important. If you do not consistently price your products above their cost to produce and market, your farming business will not be economically sustainable.

A Diversity of Pricing Considerations

Customer-based pricing focuses on how the customer values the product. In assembling this, ask yourself the following: What are the characteristics of your product that encourages customers to choose your product over others (organic, sustainably-grown, locally-grown, pesticide-free, pasture-raised, etc.)? What are the benefits customers attach to those characteristics (healthier food, sustainable community, etc.)? What is the value your customers place on those perceived characteristics and benefits? You may be able to charge a higher price because your customers are convinced your product provides them a higher value.

Competition-based pricing focuses on what the competition is offering, and at what price. To assess this, you must understand how many competitors are in your market, how much product they are providing to your proposed customer base, and where competing products are grown. How much other products might compete with yours will depend upon how similar the product is to yours, and how important any differences are to the customer. For example, your locally-grown, heirloom, freshly-picked, organic vegetable is not the same as one that is a conventionally-grown hybrid, picked a week earlier, and shipped a thousand miles to your local food store.

Although you can see that your tomatoes or broccoli are not the same product as what they've been buying, you need to ask: Is the customer willing to pay more for the differences your product offers? This brings back the issue of customer-based pricing. If the customer doesn't care about the differences, then your price competition will be the well-traveled conventional hybrid.

At this point, you have to make a choice. You can either accept that the customer is unwilling to pay for the differences in your product, and find a different customer that is, or do a lot of work to educate your potential customer pool on your product's difference. Another customer may only view your competition as other local growers, not the commodity product and be willing to pay more. In this case, you want to look at the differences between your and other local products to determine how unique yours is, and then price accordingly.

Cost-based pricing takes into consideration your costs to grow and market the product. Costs must be determined to ensure that your product is being sold for a profit. We discussed enterprise budgeting in Chapter 16. This is important in helping you understand costs of production for each of your products. Only if your products, or at least a majority of them, are sold at a profit is your farm business sustainable. If you consistently

New Products

Given the challenges, how do you determine a market price for a new or unique product? Even if the product is unique, your customer will be buying it to replace (or substitute) for something else. What is the price of the product that is being replaced? How different is your product, and what are the benefits or features that the customer is likely to gain from its purchase?

We recommend that you price based on the ideas in this chapter, focusing on what the customer is willing to pay (how much value is placed on your product), what the competition will allow (remember that although your product is unique, it does replace something on the plate), and lastly (and most importantly) what the product costs to produce and market.

Perceived Value

People don't make purchasing decisions on the basis of price and the qualities of the product alone. You can get a higher price and a bigger share of the market by emphasizing the perceived values of your product in addition to the actual values of your product. Customers show a willingness to pay for things like selection, convenience, quality, service, seasonality, additional information, and the whole farmer image as well as cleanliness, preparation, and freshness.

PRICING

sell your products for less than what it costs to produce and market them, you will be consistently losing money. In fact, the more you produce and sell, the more you will lose!

Cost-based pricing does not take into consideration what a customer is willing to pay, or what the competition will allow your price to be. Therefore a balanced approach to setting prices is to use your break-even price as the lowest price considered, and then determine what your customer is willing to pay, and the competition allows, as the upper price limit. Once you estimate an upper limit, you can work with mark-up or margins to assess your profit potential.

From the Farmers

The Right Price

Kay Jensen, JenEhr Family Farm

At JenEhr Family Farm they set prices based on the cost of production, the markup and what the market will bear. "We set prices so we are in the top 20% at our farmers' market" says farmer Kay Jensen. "Our product is that good, and the price creates an awareness of the higher quality product."

"We develop a pricing philosophy, and stick to it," she explains. A quality product is never offered at a discount, even at the request of late shoppers looking for bargains at the end of the market. "We know the price we need to get to have a sustainable operation. That doesn't change at the end of the day." Any leftover product is taken to a food pantry or added to the compost pile, where it contributes important fertility back to the farm

OTTO'S TIP: *Retailers have long known that there are certain price points around which consumers will or won't notice price variation. How often do we see a price of $4.99, but never $4.87? If you take advantage of these in your pricing, you will get the maximum return in your price range. See Appendix D for a price point chart.*

Price Mark-ups and Gross Margins

Where most customers think about how much a product gets "marked up" from the price a retailer or a wholesaler bought it for, most retailers and wholesalers think about setting prices from a "margin" perspective. The margin is what the seller gets above their cost of purchasing the product, to cover their expenses and their profit. They will want to purchase a product from you at a price that will allow them to add the margin they feel they need, while selling your product at a price their customer will pay.

Grocery store produce departments often use a 40-45 percent margin when they are pricing individual products, but their goal for a gross profit margin—the total value of product sold versus the price it was purchased for—is more like 35 percent due to loss and "shrink." Produce departments have a three to five percent shrink due to spoilage and other factors. The margin on a product has to cover losses, direct expenses related to selling the product, overhead expenses, and any profit.

Wholesale distributors use a lower margin than retail stores because they have fewer risks and less costs; they usually don't occupy prime real estate, and handle product by the pallet or the case instead of by the piece. We show you how to calculate margin in the sidebar on page 179.

If you sell your product to end users (eaters), you are assuming the same risks and many of the same expenses as a retailer, and you should get a similar price, or a similar margin above the cost of production and distribution. At a farmers' market, you pay for real estate in the form of a stall, for an awning and other infrastructure, and for the time that you could be back home weeding your carrots. You put your product on the market taking on the risk that the market will be rained out, or overstocked with a similar product.

Likewise, if you sell your product direct to retailers and restaurants, you should get a price similar to that of local wholesale distributors selling locally-grown products, since you have assumed the same costs for warehousing, order fulfillment, invoicing, and delivery.

How does this understanding of margin affect what you do? The end-seller's preferred margin will dictate how much he or she will pay for your product. If a natural food store wants to sell a tomato for $4.00 per pound, and has a 30 percent margin, it could pay at most $2.80 per pound ($2.80 / 70%). However, even knowing the margin a store is aiming for will not guarantee they will offer a price using this formula exclusively. If the price they offer is not satisfactory to you, you will need to explain why you believe your product should get a higher price. In particular, explain how your product is different (better) than those currently sold.

Each product you sell might not contribute the same margin back to your farm. For example, you should be able to sell early specialty kale at a higher margin than tomatoes in the middle of August. This is where perceived value comes in—scarcity or uniqueness can certainly contribute to a customer's willingness to pay.

As detailed in the discussion of enterprise budgets in Chapter 16, you can have some loss-leaders in your product mix, but overall you want to price products to bring something back to the farm as profit. This allows you to maintain a sustainable operation over time.

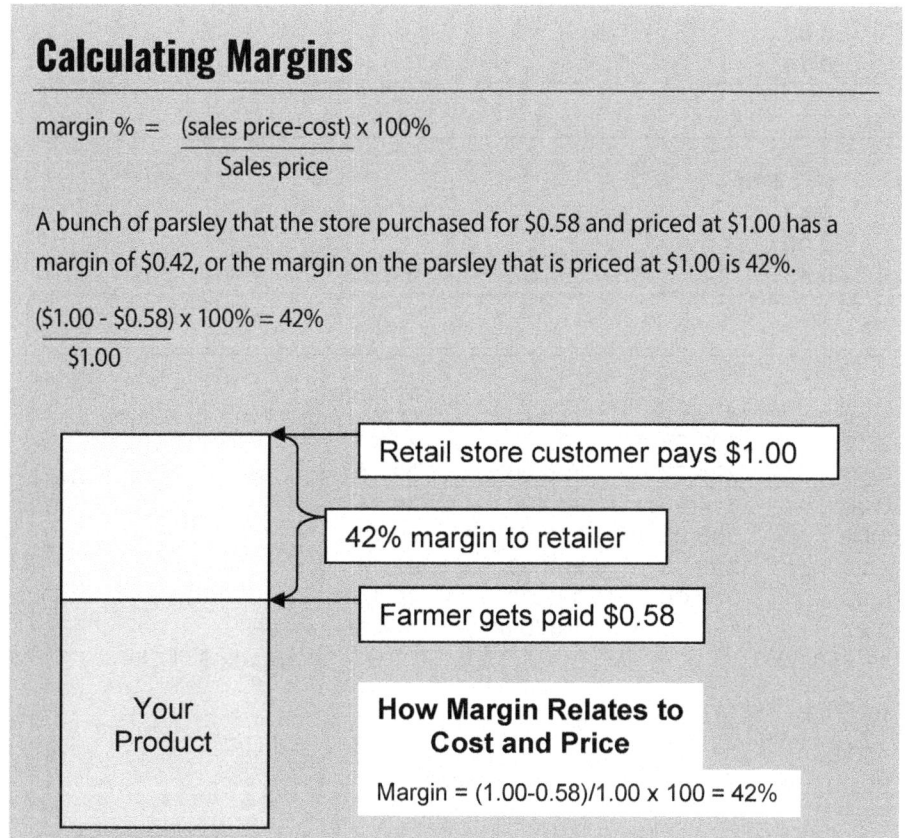

Calculating Margins

margin % = $\frac{\text{(sales price-cost)} \times 100\%}{\text{Sales price}}$

A bunch of parsley that the store purchased for $0.58 and priced at $1.00 has a margin of $0.42, or the margin on the parsley that is priced at $1.00 is 42%.

$\frac{(\$1.00 - \$0.58) \times 100\%}{\$1.00} = 42\%$

Retail store customer pays $1.00

42% margin to retailer

Farmer gets paid $0.58

Your Product

How Margin Relates to Cost and Price

Margin = (1.00-0.58)/1.00 x 100 = 42%

From the Farmers

What is Influencing the Customer?
David Perkins, Vermont Valley Community Farm

David and Barb Perkins at Vermont Valley Community Farm were worried after their third year, as they realized they weren't making enough money to sustain the farm.

Planning for their fourth year, they asked "what do we need financially to make this work?" and raised the price on their CSA shares significantly. That year, sales leaped.

David's conclusion as to why? 1) Either price doesn't matter, or 2) you need to charge enough for people to truly value what you do. He thinks that #1 has more influence than #2.

"Look at everyday advertising," he says, "Ads never sell a product, they try to sell values associated with the product." David claims that at VVCF they aren't selling the vegetables, they are selling the farm. "The vegetables are actually pretty irrelevant," he laughs. "Well, you have to do an excellent job on the veggies, but with CSA, you are selling a relationship, that is what really matters."

VVCF offers a lot of farm events, which add another level of connecting the consumer to the farm. Not everyone comes ("if they all did we'd be in big trouble," he laughs), but it is the offer that counts. "It is important that you invite them," he shares, "Not that they accept it."

From the Farmers

Be Sure You Are Charging the Correct Price

Sharon Hoerichs, Little Sioux Orchard

As part of the regular management on their diversified farm, Sharon Hoerichs annually runs numbers several different ways in Excel spreadsheets so she can be sure her prices are correct and that her management is effective and efficient. She enters all of the expenses for each enterprise, including allocations for fixed assets, and adds calculations for labor. When she analyzed her pastured broiler operation, she looked at the expense per bird as well as the expenses per pound of chicken produced. Using her Excel spread sheet, she could plug in different prices per pound or numbers raised to see how the bottom line profit changes.

2012 Broiler Cost

Birds Processed	610 Birds Sold			547
COST OF BIRDS		# Birds	Total $	$ per bird
Cornish Cross	11-May	275	273.53	.99
Cornish Cross	7-June	330	347.00	1.05
Freedom Rangers	31-May	25	65.00	2.60
		630		
Avg. Price/ Bird				**1.55**

BROODING		Per Bird
Fixed Assets	37.37	0.06
Supplies this year	47.00	0.08
Brooding per Bird		**0.14**

PASTURING		Per Bird
Fixed Assets	408.69	0.43
Supplies this year		0.00
Pasturing per Bird		**0.43**

FEED					Mileage
Verity		# ton	$ / ton	Total	(136 mi @ 14 mg @ $3/gal)
	19-May	2.16	303.55	305.71	29.14
	30-June	0.53	294.53	295.06	29.14
	30-June	0.30	344.90	345.20	29.14
	30-June	1.06	305.25	306.31	29.14
	22-Jul	1.29	296.63	297.92	29.14
	13-Aug	0.63	319.60	320.23	29.14
TOTAL VERITY		5.97		1,870.43	174.86
Verity in pounds		11,940.00			Approx $ .17 lb
Other Feed, etc.		#lbs.	$/ lb.	Total	
Grit		400.00	0.12	47.00	
Bomgaars Feed		80.00	0.26	20.80	
TOTAL FEED		12,429.00		2,113.09	
Feed Consumed / bird		20.36			
Feed Cost / bird				**3.46**	

Continued on next page

From the Farmers ... Continued

PROCESSING		Per Bird
Fixed Assets	436.85	0.72
Labor Paid	225.00	0.37
Processing Hours (6 people * 6 days * 6 hour/day @ $8/hour) – Paid Above	1,503.00	2.46
Bags (.20 ea. *610 birds)	122.00	0.20
Labels (.05 ea. *547 birds)	27.35	0.05
Propane	50.00	0.08
Plastic	50.00	0.08
Other supplies this year	40.00	0.07
Processing / bird		**4.03**

BROODER / PASTURE LABOR		
Daily Care Hours (9 wks, .75 hrs/day @ $8/hour)	378.00	
Per Bird Daily Care		**0.62**

TOTAL Cost Per Bird		**10.23**
TOTAL Cost Per Pound (avg. wgt 4.8 lbs)		**2.13**
Total Cost Per Bird Less Processing		**6.20**

2010 Broiler Income

	Birds Sold	Total Cost	Total Sales	Net
July Sales	252	2578.20	3,488.00	909.80
August Sales	295	3018.13	3,929.00	910.87
TOTAL	547	5596.34	7,417.00	**1,820.66**

From the Farmers

Using Margin to Assess Profits

Andrea Gunner, Rosebank Farm

Margin tells Andrea Gunner how much of her total retail sales dollar is coming back to pay for her labor and her profit. To figure margin, she takes the average weight per chicken (5.15 lbs) times the retail price per pound ($3.95) to get an average income per bird ($20.34). She then subtracts the cost of producing that bird (including the cost of mortality) ($10.50) for the net margin per bird ($9.84). This means that for every bird she sells, she has $9.84 to put toward her labor and profit. (5.15 x $3.95) - $10.50= $9.84.

Sometimes people like to see margin as a percent of sales. In this case Andrea's margin is 48.4 percent ($9.84/$20.34). This means that for every bird she sells, 48.4 percent of that income is coming back into her pocket as profit and return for her labor. The inverse of this figure, the costs divided by the total sales price, gives her the percent of non-labor costs per bird. ($10.50/$20.34= 51.6 percent). Andrea likes to keep this number steady, and so will adjust her prices to her customers if her costs go up and she starts to see this ratio going down.

Summary

Pricing any product can be challenging, but it becomes more difficult for products that you're selling to a new market. Pricing must take into consideration your customers' willingness to pay, your competition, and your costs to produce and market the product. Although all three considerations are important, knowing your costs is the only way to ensure your price will allow you to make a profit.

We discussed how margins enter into pricing decisions. Understanding how margins work helps you to look at a food store price and back into the price the store might be willing to pay you for your product. If you believe your products should get a higher price, you will need to explain what makes your product different (better) than what is currently being sold.

SECTION SIX
THINKING ABOUT THE FUTURE

Now that you've been introduced to ways of organizing, interpreting, and making decisions using your financial data, we move onto ways to use your knowledge to help map out the future.

The creation of a pro-forma cash flow statement is a useful tool in which you use current and historical data to predict the detail of what might happen in a future period. These statements, which also act as annual budgets, show you how realistic and feasible your plans might be. They also help you assess, as the year progresses, how well you are meeting your expectations, or if you need to make any changes in your assumptions.

Monitoring allows you to check in to see how you are doing in relation to the plans you have made. Regular monitoring shows you what aspects of your farm are following your predictions, and what assumptions might need to be changed. Monitoring activity gives you solid information for changing either your operation and practices, or adjusting your budget if things go differently than you expected they would.

Credit: The budgeting and monitoring processes in this book draw heavily from the trainings and books put out by Allan Savory and Holistic Management™. While the presentation here has been modified from that work, we would be remiss to not acknowledge that work.

CHAPTER 20
Annual Cash Flow Planning

Key questions addressed in this chapter:

How will an annual cash flow projection help you?

What goes into an annual cash flow projection, and how do you get these numbers?

What do you do if your cash flow doesn't balance?

What do you do if your projection shows cash-poor months?

In Chapter 11 we looked at the importance of assessing historic cash flow, showing how your cash moved through the previous year. Once you get a sense of this, you can create a new cash flow projection, assessing upcoming plans and adjusting the statement to predict what you expect to happen in the upcoming year. The previous year's statement of cash flows can be used as the basis for next year's pro forma cash flow. The detail of the pro forma will also be built from sets of enterprise budgets, plus other cash flow information such as payments on loans, family living draws, etc. This exercise will basically be creating a cash budget for the upcoming year.

Cash Flow Planning

For some farmers, cash flow planning is filled with hope and wonder. You hope you'll have enough money to pay all of the bills at the end of the month, and wonder what you're going to do if you come up short.

If you don't like riding a financial roller coaster, a month-by-month cash flow projection for the year ahead will help you plot a smoother course.

A cash flow projection is a prediction of all of the cash that will flow into and out of the farm operation during a given period of time. On the cash inflow side it includes money generated from the sale of farm products, government program payments, cash from sales of capital assets such as machinery, income from off-farm employment, and proceeds from new loans.

Cash outflow includes operating expenses, interest and principal payments on loans, funds used for capital purchases, income tax and Social Security payments, and any family living draws taken by the farm owner.

An annual cash flow projection (sometimes referred to as a "pro forma" cash flow or budget) is a very useful planning tool for a farm. You can plot out on a month-by-month basis when cash income will be received and when cash expenses will need to be paid. You will be able to predict which months your cash flow will not meet your needs. Finally, you will be able to plan ahead to cover the cash shortfalls.

The annual pro-forma cash flow statement forces you to do general farm planning. For instance, to know how much you expect to spend on a given expense, such as corn seed, you need some idea of how much seed you are going to use and how much each pound is going to cost. This will lead you to making decisions about where you will get the seed, and when you will plant. Penciling out all of these decisions should make your farming year go more smoothly.

Nearly every farm will have months—possibly even years—when cash flow from operations is negative. Hopefully, the good months will generate enough positive cash flow to offset the negative months. If this isn't the case, it's an indication that the farm operation will need to be subsidized by other sources of cash such as off-farm employment, sales of equipment or breeding livestock, or by taking on additional debt.

If you develop a cash flow projection and predict that cash flow is going to be short in some months, you can make plans to cover the shortage. Maybe you can build up your cash reserves during good months. Maybe you could change your farm enterprises and add one that brings in cash flow during months you would otherwise fall short. Perhaps you could pick up a part-time, off-farm job at key times of the year. You might be able to re-schedule the payments of some bills or term loan payments to more closely match your cash flow. You could set up a line of credit with a lending institution, which can be tapped in lean months and paid off in good months.

Please don't use credit cards to cover cash shortages! If you develop your projection and decide to use short-term credit to bridge your low cash months, work with a reputable lender and apply for an operating loan or a line of credit. The terms will be much better than paying credit card interest rate of 18% or more.

Over the long run, the farm operation should generate enough positive cash flow from operations to pay all of its operating expenses, make loan payments, pay the farm owner a decent draw, and have enough cash left to replace some capital equipment and put a bit into cash reserves. If the operation consistently runs negative cash flows, you should undertake a more in-depth financial analysis and consider making structural changes to your farm business.

Perhaps most importantly, a cash flow budget provides you with a tool to monitor how you're doing throughout the year relative to your expectations, so that you can make adjustments as necessary. The budgeting discussed here is designed to facilitate the monitoring described in Chapter 21. A well planned cash flow budget should give you opportunity to make changes when things don't go according to plan.

Where to Start with a Cash Flow Projection

Detail from specific enterprise budgets (see Chapter 16) can form the basis of your cash flow projection. Your enterprise budgets are a projection of the income, operating expenses, and overhead costs for each enterprise you intend to, or already have on your farm.

New or Old Numbers?

If you have some production history, when you sit down to do an annual cash flow budget you'll decide if you will do it from scratch or based on the numbers generated from past activity.

Working from scratch each year provides a good opportunity to check yourself against reality, and opens up room for creativity. Instead of just doing what you did last year, you can reconsider your expense and income assumptions.

If you know that you spent $12,000 on fertilizer last year, it may be a fair assumption that you'll spend that again. But fertilizer prices change, and if your crop mix has changed, the amount of fertilizer you use might change as well.

On the other hand, it can save time and mental energy to look at previous numbers, asking for each one "what might change this year?" The best method may be to approach each year as a blank slate, then check against previous cash budgets and actual numbers to determine whether your current ideas have a basis in reality.

CASH FLOW PLANNING

What If You're Just Starting Out?

When being encouraged to make a cash flow budget, beginning farmers often come back with two responses: "How am I supposed to come up with these numbers if I don't have any experience?" And "If I'm just starting out, my budget's so small it doesn't matter, so what's the point?"

Our answer? It will be very useful for you to create a beginning cash flow budget. Start by using the best numbers you can get, and know that you'll refine your budgeting process as time goes on. Even if you're starting out small, the practice of budgeting, monitoring, and controlling will prepare you for the times when the decisions you make will have a much larger impact on your financial well-being.

Income in your farming operation will be primarily a function of prices and yields. You can find this data in resources for just about any agricultural enterprise. Vegetable farmers can find yield data in a number of books (for example *Knott's Vegetable Grower's Handbook*, or *Sharing the Harvest*) before you begin to generate your own. Livestock and dairy producers can turn to data reported by university research groups or Extension services, such as the Wisconsin Center for Dairy Profitability. A quick search online with a web browser using terms

Continued on next page

An enterprise budget is really just a mini-feasibility study, looking at the potential (or reality) of generating a profit with a specific enterprise. However, an enterprise budget doesn't tell you anything about the timing of cash flow.

We know the income probably isn't going to show up on Day One, with expenses not paid until sales are complete. The real world is just the opposite, with a lot of upfront expenses before income is generated. The cash flow projection helps us figure out how we're going to pay all of the bills and then survive until the income arrives.

In addition to the enterprise budgets, pay stubs from off-farm employment, tax returns, and bank records all contain information that can be helpful in building your cash flow projection.

OTTO'S TIP: *Those budgeting directly into QuickBooks or another computer bookkeeping program will choose to set up the budget using the Class function to do this enterprise approach.*

Getting Started: Find or Create a Template

There are numerous mechanisms that you can use to create an overall cash flow budget for your farm. Very effective, yet simple cash budgets can be created using pencil and charted paper, following the categories of your bookkeeping system. We offer a simple template in Appendix C.

Those with computers will find that an electronic spreadsheet makes a perfect cash flow budget template. There are template budgets available from state educational institutions and Extension programs. For access to some of these, see our Resources section. These offer excellent guidance for those who may not have a chart of accounts set up yet. The limitation of these is that they are generic per industry, and will not reflect the specific customization of your farm.

You also have the option of creating a cash flow budget from scratch in a spreadsheet program. You will type in all of the accounts and numbers by hand, and then use the spreadsheet formula function to do calculations. To set up the budget, enter all of the active names from your chart of accounts into the first column, and title the columns across the top with the months. Use additional worksheets and the linking worksheets function to get the most out of your spreadsheet budget. (See the sidebar on page 190.) Spreadsheets make great budgets, but must be carefully checked, as they are notorious for hiding (sometimes catastrophic) math errors.

Most bookkeeping software programs have a Budgeting function built in. Explore your program to see how functional it seems. Appendix I shows how to use the QuickBooks Budgeting feature. A limitation of software budgets is that they can be clumsy to use and may not allow you enough flexibility to adapt the budget to your needs. A positive is that if your budget is in your bookkeeping program, then you will be able to easily run regular reports comparing what you expected to what is actually happening. A compromise is to create your budget outside of your program, and then copy the budget back into the bookkeeping program. This allows you to take advantage of the benefits but avoid the pitfalls of the software.

A good way to set up a cash flow budget template is by exporting the basic structure of your bookkeeping program into a spreadsheet program. The advantage is that it will copy your chart of accounts, and should export formulas that will be useful. Exporting to a spreadsheet allows you flexibility in viewing and manipulating the cash budget.

Filling in Your Budget

Now that you've found a budget spreadsheet you like, created your own spreadsheet, or set up your computer bookkeeping program's budget, you are ready to begin creating your cash flow budget. You can approach this with great detail in some portions and less in others.

You'll want to start by planning your income, and then your expenses. You'll put in figures for the amount of money you need to take out of the budget to cover your living expenses, and any profit goals you have beyond them. Finally, you'll determine if your plan works, and make adjustments until it does.

Determining Your Income

Planning your income first will help you avoid the temptation to artificially increase income to meet your expense needs. Most operations have far simpler income allocations than expense allocations—there aren't nearly as many ways to bring money into the farm as there are to spend it—it is harder to fool yourself with income allocation. You will be less tempted, or have fewer opportunities, to artificially adjust them to try to make things fit an optimistic financial picture you hope to end up with.

To keep these allocations real, you might want to create a new detail worksheet for each income account you've created. For example, if you have one income account for CSA, and another for farmers' market, create a new worksheet for each of those. On the worksheet for farmers' market, you might then include a row for each Saturday of the month (since some months have four and some have five), and use a formula at the bottom of the data to calculate estimated monthly totals based on the volume and variety of products you expect to have to sell. You can then transfer or link the monthly totals to the appropriate cells in your master cash flow spreadsheet.

Taking an Enterprise Approach

If you have a number of enterprises on your farm that have different income and expense streams—if you raise both cattle and pigs, for example—or if you want to budget using classes as outlined starting on page 61, you might follow a slightly different budgeting approach.

Instead of creating a new worksheet for different income and expense accounts, you could create a new worksheet for each class, or income and expense stream, and include only the direct expenses associated with each class on a given worksheet. Non-direct (overhead or administrative) expenses appear on a separate worksheet. For example, you would fill in your expected feed costs, labor, vet costs, and processing costs for beef on

Starting ... continued

such as "grain yields" will bring you numerous university-produced documents to look at. (See the Resources section for more suggestions).

Price data should be gathered from the places you plan to sell your products. If you are planning to sell into a commodity market place, you can look at historical data collected by the USDA Agricultural Marketing Service (AMS), in your local agricultural newspaper with area auction prices, or from university Extension services in your area.

If you plan to sell to retail markets, such as grocery stores or restaurants, you may be able to get information about prices they are paying just by asking. You can scout stores to check prices, but remember that there will be one or two markups above the price you sell to the store buyer or wholesale distributor for and what you see on the shelf.

If you know the standard margins the industry uses to determine retail prices, you can figure out what local distributors are probably paying for equivalent products. (See the section on margin pricing starting on page 178.)

If you plan to sell direct, such as at a farmers' market or from the farm, explore similar products in your area that use those types of markets. Be sure to take into account any quality difference that you may offer. See

Continued on next page

CASH FLOW PLANNING

Starting ... continued

Chapter 19 on pricing for more information.

Expense information can be gleaned both from raw calculations – this many trips to farmers' market times this much gas per trip – or through production budgets available online and in print from a number of state Extension services.

As you go through the process of estimating line items for your budget, avoid the temptation to bump up yields and productivity, or to make unrealistic cuts to expenses. Relying on hope as a strategy can be a temptation throughout the budgeting process.

If you plan to make $3,000 at every farmers' market throughout the summer to make your overall income goals, you must have a solid plan on how you will make that money. You will need to know how many feet of radishes and tomatoes you need to grow and sell, when you need to plant them, and what it will take to harvest them and deliver them to market.

---

one sheet, and the same for hogs on another. These would then be transferred or linked to your main cash flow spreadsheet.

Determining Your Expenses

Expect to spend far more time on expenses that you did on income. Particularly if your operation is new, growing or changing, plan to spend serious effort here with research and decision-making.

Detail worksheets can prove invaluable in this process. They can help you work from small pieces of manageable data up to big, unseemly financial numbers. For example, to determine how much expense you will need to fuel your delivery truck, you could multiply the number of miles in your delivery route by the number of times you make that trip each month, then divide by the miles per gallon for your vehicle and multiply by the price of fuel.

You will want to go through this kind of thinking and calculation for each expense item for each month. Track these "mini-calculations" in your budget worksheets. You probably won't need a separate worksheet for each item, but can group several together on one page, such as "marketing calculations" or "overhead calculations." Table 20.1 shows what a background worksheet might look like.

An advantage to this sort of cash flow justification is that it later provides a record of what you were thinking when you came up with a given number. This allows you to quickly determine the impact of changing circumstances, and make appropriate budget or activity adjustments if needed. For example, if you had calculated fuel costs for deliveries at $3.00 per gallon and they suddenly jump to $4.00, you can quickly plug those numbers into your spreadsheet to determine their impact during the rest of the year.

Some expenses will, thankfully, stay more or less constant on an annual basis, and won't change unless you make very major changes in your operation. These include loan payments and property taxes.

Whether you are working in your bookkeeping budget program or in a spreadsheet, you should now have a very basic income and expense cash flow budget set up. Now you will sum your incomes and your expenses, for a Gross Income figure (called Gross Profit in QuickBooks) and a Total Expenses figure. Subtracting the expenses from the gross

Table 20.1 Sample Worksheet for Freight

Freight	Jan 11	Feb 11	Mar 11	TOTAL Jan - Dec 11
Number of Mondays	5	4	4	52
Charge per week	150	150	150	
Total Freight	750	600	600	7,800

OTTO'S TIP: *If you are budgeting within your computer bookkeeping program, you can create worksheets in a spreadsheet program to support what you are entering into the bookkeeping program. After you export your completed budget from your bookkeeping program into a spreadsheet for later manipulation, you can cut and paste the supporting worksheets into the tabs behind your master spreadsheet.*

income gives you Net Ordinary Income. Next we will explain some additional budget items you will want to track outside of the main body of the typical budget. If you'd like to peek ahead, we have a view of a sample cash flow budget (Table 20.2) on page 191.

Add Rows for the Rest of Your Cash Flow

Those working in their bookkeeping budgeting program will now want to export their resulting budget into an Excel spreadsheet. There are additional calculations that will be useful beyond your bookkeeping program's budgeting capabilities. Those already in a spreadsheet will now add to that document.

You probably spend money on things that fall outside of your income and expense accounts, and you need to include those in your budget as well. Investments in assets, and the cash that flows in and out of your farm as part of financing your operations also need to show up in your cash flow budget.

The last row of your master budget to this point should be Net Income. This represents the amount of cash you've brought in above operating expenses. Two rows below this section start another section titled Other Cash Flows. It is useful to set up a nested structure for these accounts, and to use the same names for accounts that you use in your bookkeeping system. Sections under Other Cash Flows include Operating Activities, Investing Activities, and Financing Activities.

First, create a subsection called Operating Activities, with a row for each very short-term income or expense that you need to account for in your planning, such as payroll liabilities and credit card financing. At the bottom of this section, create a calculation to total the changes this section will make to your cash flow.

The next subsection, titled Investing Activities, includes the investments made by the farming business, not the money you put into it from outside of the business. You'll again want to use the same names as the asset accounts in your bookkeeping program, and create a calculation that totals the changes this section makes to your cash flow.

Financing Activities include all of the ways the is business financed, and pays for financing. Create a line for each loan you are obligated to pay and/or expect to receive money from. If you receive money from a loan, you enter a positive number in that row.

From the Farmers

Cash Flow Statements

Lauren and Caleb Langworthy, Blue Ox Organics

Each year Lauren and Caleb Langworthy of Blue Ox Organics create cash budgets for each of their enterprises by month: lambs, winter CSA, and wholesale vegetables. Each of the enterprises are on a spreadsheet tab and their results automatically feed into master budget where the whole picture comes together.

"If it looks like we're causing a cash problem for ourselves, we can try pushing an expense forward or backward to ease the pressure." Income is a little harder to move, but can be managed by rethinking portions of an enterprise. For instance, planting additional successions of salad mix for fall harvest can bring in money when payments for hay are needed. "We found an annual budget, with one big number for each account, wasn't very helpful for planning. It's been more important to have the right money at the right time."

Using Excel Worksheets

Whether you have exported from your bookkeeping program or created a template from scratch, if you are designing an Excel spreadsheet to use for budgeting you will want to know about using worksheets.

In Excel, each spreadsheet file can contain multiple worksheets. If you think of the spreadsheet as a file folder, each worksheet is like a sheet of paper in the file folder, except that data on each worksheet has the magical ability to be linked to another worksheet in the same folder. The worksheets are accessed from the tabs at the bottom of the open screen. You can easily create and name as many worksheets as you need. Using worksheets that are all connected to your main or master budget, rather than multiple spreadsheets, helps keep your information easy to find and well organized.

Linking Worksheets

It is easy to link data from one worksheet to another. Use this function when you are doing background calculations that are later summarized for a broader view, such as sub-budgets for small equipment purchases to go into the equipment line of your budget. The best thing about linking is that if you make changes in your detail sheets, the link will bring those changes into the master sheet, which will be useful as you are making adjustments to get your budget to balance.

In the detail worksheet, select the cell you want to link from. Click the Copy button on the Home tab (or right-click). Switch to the master worksheet, and click the cell you want the detail to show in. On the Home Tab (or by right-clicking), select Paste Special and choose Paste Link.

You can link an entire range of cells—for example the row of cells with totals for the calculations you ised to determine total fertilizer expenses for each month—by selecting the source cells and clicking the copy button. Swtich to the destination sheet, and click the cell where you want the upper left cell of the range of cells to be located. Then paste the link as described above.

Overall Budget

You can see all of the formulas in your spreadsheet by holding down the Control key and pressing the tilde key. The tilde (~) is the squiggly line above the n used in Spanish. On U.S. keyboards, it is usually found in the upper left corner of your keyboard, above the tab key. Control + tilde will return your spreadsheet to the normal view.

Bruce's Bison Budget		2012
		total
Infrastructure		
	small equipment	155
	fencing	2000
	building repair	1500
Feed		
	hay	2000
	grain	1500
	mineral	300
Labor		
	Bruce	
	Sally	
Processing		
etc		

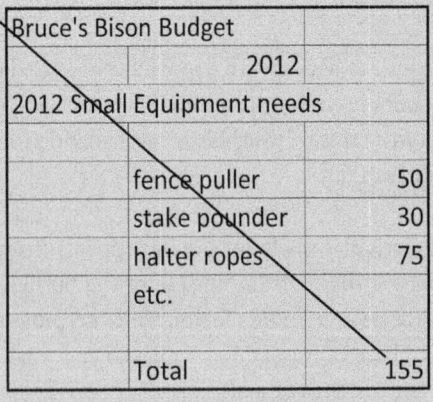

Bruce's Bison Budget		
	2012	
2012 Small Equipment needs		
	fence puller	50
	stake pounder	30
	halter ropes	75
	etc.	
	Total	155

If you are making a payment, you enter a negative number. Include principal and any interest expense together for this cash flow budget.

Financing Activities also includes money you put into the business, such as money from an off-farm income. A computer bookkeeping program probably refers to these as Owner Investments. If you don't pay yourself a salary, but do take money from the farm, this is also the place to account for that, as an Owner Draw. Create a calculation that totals the changes this section makes to your cash flow.

The sum of your Operating Activities, Investing Activities, and Financing Activities will be your Total Other Cash Flows, so you'll create a row with a calculation for that.

Skip another row, and create a row titled Net Cash Increase for the period. This will be the sum of Net Income and Total Other Cash Flows. The next row is titled Cash at Beginning of Period; for January this is manually entered.

Create a final row called Cash at End of Period, which is the sum of the Net Cash Increase and Cash at Beginning of Period.

Table 20.2 Sample Excel Budget (Collapsed view)

Summary	Jan 11	Jan 10	Feb 11	Feb 10	Dec 11	Dec 10	TOTAL Jan - Dec 11	TOTAL Jan - Dec 10
Ordinary Income/Expense								
Income								
FARMING	11,198	5,370	23,973	15,349	13,875	10,688	156,103	141,584
INCOME - NON-SALES	0	0	302	0	0	13	646	598
Total Income	11,198	5,370	24,275	15,349	13,875	10,701	156,748	142,182
Total COGS	840	0	0	84	0	0	1,140	231
Gross Profit	10,358	5,370	24,275	15,265	13,875	10,701	155,608	141,951
Expense								
INFRASTRUCTURE	1,363	280	270	1,732	263	293	8,646	8,549
LABOR	2,685	2,307	2,858	2,584	3,249	3,995	55,953	63,916
MACHINERY & EQUIPMENT	0	51	-2	59	0	105	7,973	3,750
OPERATIONS	1,945	339	1,413	891	1,118	2,162	22,184	17,385
OVERHEAD	1,604	2,203	1,814	2,844	1,119	1,647	22,855	25,592
SALES & PROMOTION	887	2,188	974	522	21	245	4,717	4,526
Total Expense	8,483	7,368	7,327	8,631	5,770	8,447	122,328	123,718
Net Ordinary Income	1,875	-1,998	16,949	6,634	8,105	2,255	33,280	18,233
Other Cash Flows								
Operating Activities	0	0	0	0	0	0	0	0
Investing Activities	0	0	0	0	0	0	0	0
Financing Activities	-1,204	0	-1,204	0	-898	0	-15,615	0
TOTAL CHANGES IN OTHER CASH FLOWS	-1,204	0	-1,204	0	-898	0	-15,615	0
NET CASH INCREASE								
Net Income	1,875	0	16,949	0	8,105	0		
Total Changes in Other Cash Flows	-1,204	0	-1,204	0	-898	0		
Cash at Beginning of Period	0	0	671	0	10,459	0		
CASH AT END OF PERIOD	671	0	16,416	0	17,665	0		

CASH FLOW PLANNING

In February and subsequent months, the Cash at Beginning of Period will be the sum of the Net Cash Increase for the current month, plus the Cash at the End of Period for the previous month.

In Table 20.2 we show a sample Excel monthly cash flow budget. This was built from an export of a QuickBooks chart of accounts in the collapsed view, showing the overall income and expense summary categories. This table shows only the beginning and end of the budget year, we have hidden the middle months of the budget. This table shows two years of budgets side by side, a previous budget (xx10) and the current budget (xx11). We have expanded the detail of lines 22 through 34 in chart 20.3 on page 194.

OTTO'S TIP: *To hide columns in an Excel spreadsheet highlight the columns you wish to hide, right click on your mouse and select Hide. To unhide, highlight the columns on either side of what is hidden—in table 20.2 these are columns O and BA —right click and select Unhide. Non-sequential column identifiers (in this case letters) tell you that columns are hidden.*

Profit Goals

In Chapter 3 on planning we discussed the importance of determining how much profit it will take to support the quality of life you desire. In your bookkeeping system, unless you pay yourself a salary, the money you take out of your business is called an Owner Draw. Budgeting for an Owner Draw and keeping that money separate from your business expenses can be an excellent way to promote fiscal conservatism in both your business and your personal life.

In the Owner Draw row of your spreadsheet put in the amount you want to take out of your business each month. Creating a separate worksheet might be helpful in determining how much you need to take out, or reminding yourself why you thought you could get by on so little, or actually needed so much. Detail on your owner draw worksheet will outline your personal and family needs, such as rent or mortgage, food, health costs, home utilities, transportation costs, entertainment, etc.

OTTO'S TIP: *A good way to manage Owner Draw is to decide how much you want to take annually, and divide that number by 12. On the first of each month transfer that amount from the farm checking account to your personal checking account. For instance, if you'd like to make $30,000 per year, on the first of each month you'll transfer $2,500.*

Reserve Funds

As part of your profit you may want to set up a regular deposit to any of a number of reserve funds. Reserve funds are virtual set asides of amounts that you wish to designate for specific uses. Perhaps the most important of these would be a depreciation fund, so that when an asset, such as a tractor or other piece of equipment, has reached the end of its life, you have the money to replace it without having to borrow.

Using a worksheet in your spreadsheet file, list all of the assets that will eventually need to be replaced in one column. In the next column, put the replacement cost of the item. In the third column, put the number of years you expect the item to last. In the fourth column, set up a formula to divide the replacement cost by the number of years the item will last. This depreciation worksheet will be an important living document that should be updated regularly.

The sum of the fourth column is the theoretical amount you need to set aside each year to cover asset replacements. You could choose to remove this money from your available cash by investing it in a tax-free income-generating investment until you need it, or you could invest it in your business in such a way that it generates additional profits that can cover those expenses later.

Other reserve funds you may wish to save for could include a land investment fund if you have your eyes on buying new property in the future, or a building expansion fund if you are planning an upcoming on-farm development. Your reserve fund line in your master spreadsheet, based on the detail from your worksheets, will be a negative number indicating in each period how much cash you are taking out of the farm and moving into reserve for later.

OTTO'S TIP: *Those who take their taxes to an accountant should be able to get a depreciation schedule from him or her.*

The Bottom-Bottom Line

You now should have a spreadsheet that has income lines and totals at the top, expense lines and totals in the middle, with a sum of Net Cash Flow. Below that will be the section titled Other Cash Flow with lines totaling your Operating Activities, Investing Activities, and Financing Activities. The sum of these is the Total Other Cash Flows. After that is a line titled Net Cash Increase. At the bottom will be your Net Cash at the End of Period. You now have your draft cash flow budget.

Table 20.3 on the next page shows a sample of the detail of accounts added beneath the Net Ordinary Income (below line 20 in Table 20.2).

CASH FLOW PLANNING

Table 20.3 Budget Liability and Equity Details

Projected Cash Flow August - December xx11					Jan xx11	Feb xx11	Mar xx11
OTHER CASH FLOWS							
	Operating Activities						
		Payroll Liabilities					
		Credit Card			0	0	0
	Total Operating Activities				0	0	0
	Investing Activities						
		Buildings and Greenhouses			0	0	0
		Machinery and Equipment			0	0	0
	Total Investing Activities				0	0	0
	Financing Activities						
		Current Liabilities					
			Accounts Payable		0	0	0
			26351 Crop Note		0	0	0
			2033116 Overdraft Protection		0	0	0
		Total Current Liabilites			0	0	0
		Long Term Liabilities					
			26597 BegFarmer Loan		-583	-583	-583
			25451 Mach & Eq Loan		-526	-526	-526
			15457 Farm Mortgage		-95	-95	-95
		Total Long Term Liabilities			-1,204	-1,204	-1,204
	Total Financing Activities				-1,204	-1,204	-1,204
TOTAL CHANGES IN OTHER CASH FLOWS					-1,204	-1,204	-1,204
NET CASH INCREASE							
	Net Income				1,875	16,949	74
	Changes in Liability and Equity				-1,204	-1,204	-1,204
	Cash at Beginning of Period				0	671	16,416
CASH AT END OF PERIOD					674	16,416	15,287

Adjusting to Meet Your Goals

If your Net Cash Increase at the end of the year (in the far lower right corner) is negative at this point, it means that you won't meet your profit goals with the budget as it is and you will need to make adjustments. Since you've already closely calculated your income, you will probably need to tighten up your expenses.

First, look for expenses that you can trim. If the adjustments are going to require changes in behavior or spending patterns, make certain that all of the decision-makers understand and agree with the changes. It might be helpful to write down justifications for why you think you can get by on less.

Any worksheets used to calculate your expenses can provide a good reality check against the fantasy world of big numbers. A calculation detailing the number of expected trips to town, with the expected price of gas, makes it more difficult to fool yourself into adjusting numbers without reason. Be sure to go back to your detail worksheets to make your adjustments and then transfer to the overall budget, to preserve accurate information about what goes into each number.

Find the items that account for the largest percentage of your expenses to determine where you might start trimming. Dive into the major expenses in each of your expense categories, looking for realistic ways to cut. For example, a ten percent reduction in an $80,000 payroll bill has a lot more impact than squeezing money out of the $3,000 spent on casual labor for extra weeding.

Checking Your Cash Flow

Once you have your cash flow projection complete, look it over to see how the cash flows throughout the year. If there are months where the cash you have on hand is less than zero, or too close for comfort, look first at whether you can adjust the timing for any income or expenses to close that gap. If that doesn't work, this is the time to set up a line of credit at the bank, before you run into problems.

Completing the Pro-Forma Cash Flow Budgeting Process

If you now have a cash flow budget that works, you can be proud of yourself. Budgeting is as much an art as it is a science, and you will get better at it the more you do it.

Those who created their cash flow budget in a spreadsheet have the option of taking the income and expense numbers and entering them into their computer bookkeeping Budget function. This will allow you to not only check for formula errors, but also allows you to regularly run reports comparing your budget to your actual activities, helping you assess how you are doing throughout the year.

Summary

Annual cash flow projection, or budgeting, gives financial structure to your planning, and provides a mechanism for checking back throughout the year to see how close your reality is coming to your dreams. It is also important in estimating if you will have enough money at the right times to cover your costs, and allow you to plan to make adjustments ahead of time if needed.

You have several options to set up a cash flow budget—most bookkeeping programs offer a budgeting program, or you can use a budget template or a spreadsheet. Whatever form you choose to use, we explain how to make estimates and collect numbers, which can be especially difficult for those just starting out. Income and expenses must be estimated, and then adjusted as your numbers are compared and a net income projected. Adjustments might be necessary as you see the way cash is predicted to flow throughout the upcoming months.

MONITORING & CONTROL

CHAPTER 21
Plans vs Reality: Monitoring and Control

Key questions addressed in this chapter:

Why is monitoring important?

How are monitoring systems set up?

What do you do if your monitoring tells you something is going wrong?

Many of you started your farming operation based on a business plan (either formal or informal) that laid out your goals (both economic and non-economic), a timeline to reach your goals, and some measurements that told you when those goals would be met. As part of your ongoing planning process, you develop an annual pro forma cash flow budget (just discussed in Chapter 20) and use the budget prep process as an annual planning tool.

The next step to fully use that annual pro forma cash flow budget plan is to monitor it by keeping track of your progress. This involves regularly assessing if you are heading in the right direction and can still expect to achieve the goals you have set. In an assessment you can judge it things have gotten off track, or if circumstances have changed, and you can decide to change your timeline or path, or even your end goals so things even out.

Ideally, every month you will compare your actual cash flow to your plan (your budgeted cash flow) to assess your financial status relative to your annual goals. This requires a budget that lays out expectations for monthly progress. It also requires that you regularly enter data in your bookkeeping system. Recognizing the value of, and having a

OTTO'S TIP: *Doing the work is more important than having all of the numbers one hundred percent accurate. It is unlikely that the difference of a few dollars, or even a few hundred dollars, will make or break your operation. However, catching a big discrepancy early on will make a big difference. So, do the monitoring work even if your numbers aren't perfectly up-to-date, and don't stress out trying to get everything exactly right.*

196

commitment to periodically assessing your performance relative to your plan provides an incentive to keep up with the weekly work of financial data entry.

Monitoring progress should lead directly to actions that control negative deviations and adjust for positive developments, and a recognition of when things are working right.

Monitoring

Monitoring your financial progress consists of comparing your planned financial performance to your actual performance. You'll look at the dollar amounts for each major-level account you created in your chart of accounts, and note any negative deviations from your cash flow budget. You'll also monitor any positive deviations for potential impacts downstream—for example, if you've sold a lot more halves of beef than you expected, you might need to increase your budgeted expenses for trucking to the locker.

The following discussion of the physical processes builds on the spreadsheets described in Chapter 20 on the creation of an annual pro forma cash flow statement, or budget.

Getting the Information Together

Each month you'll want to evaluate your financial performance for the month and for the year to date.

If your budget is a spreadsheet it is easiest to do monitoring if you create a new spreadsheet that holds both the projected budget and the actual data from the period that you want to monitor. This allows you to compare your activity for each month, and for the totals year-to-date. If your budget is in your computer program, you will want to export it to a spreadsheet so you can make comparisons. (See the sidebar on page 198)

To get actual data to compare to your budget, those with computer bookkeeping systems will run a profit and loss statement for the period you want to compare. Those using a paper system will compare the final figures in their General Journal for a period to their budget.

If your budget is simple you may be able to make comparisons by looking from one report to the other (one print of the budget and one print of the actual numbers), but if there is any complexity at all it is nice to collect all of the numbers together on one sheet, so that you can circle or highlight any figures that stand out, and should be explored or followed up on.

Even those using a computer program may find it easiest to hand enter actual numbers for a given period into a copy of your budget spreadsheet, which is what those using a paper system will do. Some may find this less stressful than trying to get everything to match up while cutting and pasting numbers.

Balance Sheet Changes

Now you must track down how much each account in your balance sheet has changed during the period that you are monitoring. Financing and investing activities don't show up on a computer bookkeeping program's profit and loss report, so you need to find that

Computer Reports

Those with computer bookkeeping programs start by generating two reports that set you up to compare your actual financials to your cash flow budget. The profit and loss report provides information about your income and expenses, and a balance sheet report provides data about your investing and financing activities, including loan payments, owner draws, and asset purchases.

If you have entered the income and expense portion of your budget into your bookkeeping program, you should be able to run a Budget to Actuals report.

To do this in QuickBooks, go to Reports then Budgets and select Budget vs Actual. Follow the prompts to build your budget report. You can export this report to an Excel spreadsheet, where you will be able to then add the rows that you added below your net income line when you created your budget.

Exporting from QuickBooks

One way to get actual and projected numbers onto one sheet is to export the profit and loss report to a new Excel spreadsheet. After export, copy the data and paste it into a copy of your budget spreadsheet, into a column next to the budget column you are comparing to.

When pasting into a column for comparison like this, you must be sure that all of the accounts are represented, and the same in both documents. If you added any accounts as your year progressed, these must also be added to your budget spreadsheet.

For example, if, midyear, you decided to buy a new breed of cattle and started tracking those expenses under the account "Longhorn Expenses," but didn't budget for this, then the extra account line will cause your account lists in your Excel budget and bookkeeping program to no longer match up. You can adjust for this by adding any new account lines into your budget in the appropriate place whenever you add a new account line in your bookkeeping program.

---

information through different means. You can generally get this information from bank, loan and credit card statements.

Those with computer programs will run a balance sheet report for the last day of the period before your period starts (the last day of the previous month, when monitoring monthly), and another for the last day of the current period. The difference between the two is the amount of change that you will add into your monitoring sheet.

Because you haven't budgeted for changes to the amount of assets you own, you don't need to enter that data on the monitoring worksheet. Only enter changes for the accounts included in your budget, unless you've added additional accounts for a new loan or similar change.

Control for Deviations

Now, go through the monitoring worksheet and look for numbers that don't support your plan: income numbers that are too low, and cash outflow numbers that are too high. By tracking both monthly and year-to-date information, you can catch when small monthly deviations turn into more serious issues.

If you have grouped accounts in your chart of accounts into general categories (see page 50) you can save yourself a significant amount of time and concern by only comparing higher level account totals rather than itemized detail to look for the deviations.

In other words, if your account structure looks like Table 21.1, you might look at the overall total for Total Computer Expense and not worry about the individual line items of repairs, hardware, and software.

Table 21.1. Chart of Accounts Detail

```
OVERHEAD
    Cell Phone
    Computer Expense
        Computer Repairs
        Hardware
        Software & Online Services
    Total Computer Expense
```

If something is not going according to budget, make a plan to correct for it. Focus on the larger deviations, and try to discover the causes. Make a plan to control expenses that are too high, or to bring income back in line with expectations. It will be helpful to go back into your bookkeeping data to double check that you have categorized all of your income and expenses as you had planned to.

In the event that income is down significantly, you may need to re-plan your expenses. Sometimes, you will need to reevaluate your entire plan, even going back to scratch to create a new budget for completing the year.

If expenses are down in one account, but up in another, don't use that as an excuse to ignore your deviation from budget. You want to take some time to understand why things are different than what you had planned, and if you need to adjust anything to fix the deviation.

Serious deviations from the budget may present one of the greatest dangers to farm relationships and farm stability. Dealing with them before they spiral out of control, or before it's too late to do anything about them, provides an excellent opportunity to avoid aggravation at the end of the year. Regular monitoring allows you to adjust your plans and do what is necessary to bring the plan back on track.

Deviating from your plan, at times, could be intentional as part of a management decision. For example, you may be a livestock producer that finishes your beef on a corn-based ration. Corn prices suddenly drop like a rock, to the point where they are lower than it costs you to produce and market your own corn. You decide it is time to purchase an additional year's worth of grain and have it milled into feed and stored at your local cooperative. This extra purchase was not part of your budget, but by making this purchase you lowered your cost to produce and market your finished beef and increased the beef enterprise's profitability. The point here is that not all deviations from your budget are negative and unplanned. There are times where it makes economic sense to take advantage of market opportunities when they arise.

OTTO'S TIP: *QuickBooks, and other bookkeeping software have a feature that makes it easy to explore the detail behind an account total. From any report, double click on the dollar total for the account and it will open a detail view of all the transactions that make up that total. Clicking again on an individual entry will open up the detail of the specific entry. If you made an error in assigning an account to any transaction, you can change it here. Once you have modified a transaction, hit Refresh or Update on your report and it will incorporate the changes.*

Monitoring Control Worksheet

A useful tool for tracking deviations from your budget is a Monitoring Control Worksheet. Whenever you sit down to compare your budget to actual activity you can list significant items that are going "adverse to plan," or opposite to the way you'd hoped, such as incomes that are too low, or expenses that are too high. You might set a threshold which indicates when an item should be listed—such as a 10 percent deviation, a $500 difference, or other threshold that makes sense for the scale of your operation.

The control worksheet pressures you to put thought into what is going differently than you expected, and make a plan as to what you will do about it. You may decide to do nothing, or to wait to see if there is a correction later, but recognizing that you have some plan is an important management tool.

Monitoring Control Worksheet				
Item	How much was it off?	Why is it off?	How will you change it?	When was the change made?

Additional Monitoring

It is always good to look ahead to the budget plan for the upcoming months to identify what you need to do so things you've planned will happen later in the year. You can assess if there is a new need for action now to prepare for something coming up. Regular monitoring also provides an opportunity to recognize changed circumstances that might impact your budget plans in the months to come.

Summary

Monitoring allows you to track your progress in relation to what you had planned. It gives you a chance to make changes in your future expectations if things aren't turning out the way you had predicted. Monitoring allows you to make adjustments in your current and future activities so that you can end up the year in good shape.

SECTION SEVEN
OTHER FACTORS THAT AFFECT YOUR FINANCIAL SITUATION

There are a few other things that will come up as you are managing your farm financial situation. One of these is labor; how to count it, who to pay, how to report it. Labor issues are extremely complex, and overseen by both federal and state laws, but we would be remiss in not at least introducing some of the key concepts to you here.

The way you choose to legally structure your business has an impact on some of the financial responsibilities, and certainly on tax reporting. We share with a brief overview of the various ways you may choose to organize your farm's business structure.

Any successful farmer will eventually need to think about farm transition—be it passing a farm on to another generation, to a new, unrelated farmer, or through a sale or estate. We will review some basic considerations to think about for your planning.

CHAPTER 22
Who Does the Work on Your Farm?

Key questions addressed in this chapter:

How is labor tracked, and why does it matter?

Who is classified as an employee on a farm?

How do you manage paying yourself and employees?

It generally takes a lot of manual labor to make a farm work. In fact, on many farms labor will be the largest input into the operation. Farmers often debate whether to actually pay themselves for the time they put into the farm. It is a common argument that whatever profit is left at the end of the year is the money earned for the time put in. For a simple operation, this argument can work.

However, it should be the goal of a sustainable farm to not only pay for the labor that is put into the operation, but to also generate a profit at the end of the year that will pay the owner back for their initial investment, and be available for improvements, savings, equipment replacement, and other investments. Keeping your payment for labor separate from your profit helps you assess if your farm is truly sustainable and able to afford needed investments.

Whether you are actually paying yourself and others by the hour, as salary, or by taking an owners draw, you will be well served by keeping track of the productive hours being put into your farm.

Putting a value to the labor on your farm is useful for a number of reasons:
- When setting your prices you will want to include a value for your and any other labor. This assures that you cover the real costs of producing this crop, and is especially important to price more labor-intensive crops appropriately.
- If you are doing enterprise analyses to determine if one crop is more profitable than another, the value of labor may be an important determining factor.
- Some useful ratios that help you assess and compare your profitability require that you include the value of your labor.

How actual payments for labor are allocated and tracked can get confusing pretty quickly, especially if you have other people helping on the farm. You may have people working on your farm who fall into a few different labor classifications. The way you view and pay these different classes of workers is regulated by both state and federal laws. These laws are very complicated, particularly for farms, and you must carefully follow them.

We will give a brief overview here to help you understand how paid labor fits into your financial records, but it is critical that you look into state and local laws pertaining to labor before you actually start paying anyone to work for you on the farm. Farms have been lost to labor violations and the significant fines that can be tied to them.

OTTO'S TIP:

The book "Legal Guide for Direct Farm Marketing" by Neil Hamilton of Drake University is a great resource for all laws pertaining to farming, including labor issues. Available online at http://directmarketersforum.org/the-legal-guide-for-direct-farm-marketing, updated in 2011.

Who is an Employee?

You probably work on the farm yourself. As the farm owner you may consider yourself to be self-employed, and not an employee of the farm. But, you do have the choice of considering yourself as an employee and having the farm pay you a salary or hourly wage. Your tax accountant can help you figure out which makes the most sense for your operation. There are other ways you can pay yourself, we will talk about those below.

Many farmers also have family members that work on the farm. You may decide to pay your spouse and children as employees (and take deductions to pay taxes), but most states allow immediate family members to work without conforming to labor laws, such as paying minimum wage, if the farm is wholly owned by a spouse or parents. If you pay your family to work on the farm, you will want to track any payments as a labor expense.

However, even if you don't pay them, it would be beneficial to track how much time everyone is contributing to the farm business, and the equivalent "value" for that time, as this will be important for enterprise or pricing decisions. You should set up a tracking system in a notebook or spreadsheet program independent of your bookkeeping system to tally any unpaid hours.

Some farmers have people who occasionally volunteer, such as CSA members doing labor trades. These workers fall into a grey area. If you have many people participating in this way, you must explore the laws in your state to see what compensation rules apply.

You may also have a class of people that you call "interns," a blend of paid worker, volunteer, and student. Again, these folks fall into murky territory as far as labor law is concerned. But, for our purposes of keeping good financial records, you will want to track any payments, (even if they are called "intern stipends" or something along those lines), in the labor section of your bookkeeping records.

From the Farmers

Planning Labor

Lauren and Caleb Langworthy, Blue Ox Organics

Before the start of each farm year at Blue Ox Organics, Caleb and Lauren Langworthy create a spreadsheet listing each enterprise's monthly labor needs. While the weather will have some effect on the exact date any task gets done, they block out rough estimates for when things like cultivating, seeding, harvesting, shearing, lambing, haying, etc. will need to be done.

This allows them to see any potential trouble spots where more labor is needed than time and hands available. To mitigate these labor crunches, they can often adjust an enterprise or task forward or backward. If there is no way to move labor needs and a crunch still exists, they have advance warning to budget for extra help on the farm.

LABOR

How Much Are You Worth?

When calculating the profitability of a particular crop, you will want to use a value for labor that is based on your productivity relative to the other workers on your farm, or the market rate for getting the particular work done. If a farm laborer gets paid $12 per hour in your area, and you are doing farm-laborer type work, you should "bill" or allocate that enterprise at a rate of $12 per hour for your time.

If you pay more money to more productive workers, you might choose to value your labor more if you are more productive. If you are doing farm management type work for your farm, you should value your time at a higher rate.

When you are using numbers to evaluate the profitability of a given enterprise, don't get caught up in whether you are getting a fair return on your investment of management expertise and capital by allocating a particular dollar amount for your physical participation in a project – the returns to management and investment come out of your overall farm profits, not the profitability of any one enterprise.

As with family, if your interns are putting in a lot of labor that is not paid by the hour, you will benefit from tracking how many hours they are actually putting in on the farm. However, as learners, interns may be much less efficient than an experienced paid worker, so this difference should be taken into account when making pricing or other enterprise decisions.

OTTO'S TIP: *Those selling products across state lines must be particularly diligent in doing labor law homework, as you are required to follow the laws of the state you are selling into, or federal law, whichever is more stringent.*

Contract Labor

You may occasionally hire someone to do something special on your farm, many times using their own equipment. This might be a custom harvester, a website designer, the artificial inseminator, or someone to do milk relief when you occasionally take a day off. If this person only comes to your farm occasionally, also offers the same services to other farmers (e.g. they don't work for you exclusively), and meets other specific criteria he or she will generally be considered to be a "contractor." Contractors are self-employed or work for another business, but are not considered your employees. The distinction is important, as you don't have employment law obligations to contractors in most situations.

Any contractors paid over $600 for services in a given calendar year must be provided an IRS 1099-misc form reporting the amount they were paid for their services. This form goes to the contractor and the Federal government by January 31 for the previous year's payments. For detailed information, contact the Internal Revenue Service (irs.gov 800-829-4933).

OTTO'S TIP: *There are some situations where workers' comp is required for contractors, such as construction. As some farmers also do construction on the side, it is good to be cautious here.*

Paying Yourself

If you are the farm owner, you may choose to not include payments to yourself in a "labor" line in the chart of accounts. Many farmers take an owners draw, which is considered an equity payment, but not an expense. The amount of the draw will show up on the balance sheet, but not the income statement. You will want to be sure, however, to include the amount of draw you take when you calculate a cash flow statement. The owners draw is generally not figured on an hourly basis related to the number of hours worked. It is more commonly based on farm profits and family cash needs.

Regular Employees

People that you pay to regularly help out on the farm are "employees." If you have employees you must study up on state and federal employment laws. Agricultural workers have specific laws that regulate their time and work. There are numerous special cases and exemptions that come into play.

In general, you have several areas of responsibility when you have employees. First, you must assure that they have a safe working environment and are trained to not only do their job but also how to stay safe. Second, you must comply with wage and hours laws. You must also withhold and then transfer payments for federal and state taxes. You may be required to purchase workers compensation insurance for any covered employees, and may be required to pay into your state's unemployment compensation fund. There are also very complex rules for migrant laborers. You also must comply with federal agricultural child labor laws involving hazardous work, even for your own children.

Federal law dictates that farms over a specific size (having roughly seven workers in any calendar quarter) must pay farm workers at least the federal minimum wage. Many states, however, are more stringent and require at least the state minimum wage be paid when the farm has just one employee. Federal and most state laws allow at least a portion of a wage to be paid out as food or lodging in certain situations. These laws change state to state, so be very careful to do research before you employ anyone. Overtime pay is not required for agricultural labor when the worker is performing farming tasks, but come into play if your employee is giving tours, sells at the farmers market, or does something else that is not commonly considered "farming."

If you hire employees, you must obtain a federal Employee Identification Number (EIN). This connects you to your employees through the withholding and reporting of state and federal taxes. You must file a federal form W-4 (withholding) and state tax form, as well as keep on file a federal I-9 form (employment eligibility) for each employee.

You want to explore the tax reporting requirements for both your state and the Feds. You will deduct taxes from employee paychecks, and then deposit the accumulated taxes into an authorized financial institution, such as your bank, for transfer to the IRS. You must complete and hand out W-2 forms reporting wage history for the previous year for each employee every January, and submit copies with a W-3 form (which compiles all of the W-2 data) to the IRS. Tax deposit periods can be as frequently as weekly, or as infrequently as annually, depending on how much tax liability you have. Regularly submitted reports to the Feds will reconcile these tax deposits. Penalties are stiff if you miss a filing, so be sure that you understand this well.

OTTO'S TIP: *The website farmcommons.org offers a wealth of up-to-date information about all aspects of farm law, including how to navigate complex employment laws.*

WWOOFERS

World Wide Opportunities on Organic Farms (WWOOF) started in the United Kingdom in 1971, and now extends to 120 countries worldwide. Organic farmers sign up to receive visitors who stay for any period of time, visiting and potentially working on the farm in exchange for room and board and education about the farm. There is no screening process by the organization, although complaints about either farmers or WWOOFERS are taken seriously, with a "3-strikes-you're-out" policy. The U.S. organization recommends WWOOFERS help with tasks for 5-6 hours per day, up to 5.5 days per week. No pay is exchanged. Labor laws still apply to any situation where people are working on your farm, including WWOOFing. https://wwoofusa.org/about. 415-621-3276

A WOOFER host comments: "Our first year hosting WWOOFERS has been awesome. Life was so enriched for us. We hosted a total of 11 over the year. We would welcome any of them back. As hosts, we tried to offer tasks to our guests that we thought would add to their WWOOFING experience, like milking, cheese-making, carpentry, even decorating, etc. But sometimes our guests just enjoyed doing mundane things. But honestly, perhaps more importantly than getting projects and chores checked off the list, was the cheerful, inspiring exchange of ideas, favorite books, artwork, philosophers, countries, and ways of preparing food."

LABOR

Contractors and QuickBooks

Payments to contractors can be tracked using a Contract Labor or Custom Hire line in your chart of accounts. QuickBooks has a feature that allows you to assign certain categories of payments (such as custom hire) as eligible for 1099 reporting. To set these up, from your main QuickBooks screen click on the Edit tab, then scroll to Preferences. Scroll down to Tax:1099 and click on the Company Preferences tab. From this screen you will be able to select the accounts that you wish to associate with each of the 1099 categories.

You also must set up which of your contractors will get 1099s through the QuickBooks Vendor Center. As you set a vendor up, click on the Additional Info tab. There you will see a Vendor Eligible for 1099 checkbox. When you check this, QuickBooks will ask you to add the person's tax id number, which will be their social security number or business tax number (which you get by sending the contractor a blank W-9 form to fill out, also available from the IRS). The IRS can help you understand how to set this up and decide who you must send 1099s to each January.

Workman's Compensation is insurance administered by states to cover medical payments, lost wages etc. if an employee is injured while working on your farm. With rates based on the numbers of injuries industry-wide, it is expensive for farmers. Workers' comp is also very valuable in protecting the farm from a liability lawsuit. Again, explore your state laws to understand the requirements.

Many bookkeeping software programs offer a payroll feature which makes paying employees and keeping up with government tax payments and reporting straightforward, once you understand which laws you need to operate under. However, if you do payroll using a bookkeeping program, you may pay an additional software fee, and be locked into paying annual fees to upgrade tax tables. This can add up to a hefty ongoing software expense.

Many small businesses find it valuable to hire an outside entity to manage payroll. Though the fees for this service may seem steep, putting the responsibility for compliance with the many payroll reporting laws into the hands of experts may well be worth the investment.

OTTO'S TIP: *While payroll companies are valuable for payroll reporting compliance, they aren't liable in situations such as a farmer not paying at least the minimum wage, buying workers' comp, etc.*

Summary

Farms are very labor-intensive. There are numerous reasons to track the labor that goes into running your farm, whether it is paid or unpaid. People doing work on your farm may fall into several different labor categories, many of which are governed by state and federal laws. It is important that you fully understand all of the laws pertaining to labor before you start to involve anyone other than yourself and family members on the farm. Contact your state Department of Labor to find which laws apply to your situation.

From the Farmers

Tracking Labor

Kay Jensen, JenEhr Family Farm

Producing a large diversity of vegetables, fruits and pastured chickens on 110 acres of certified organic land, there is a lot of manual labor at JenEhr Family Farm. Managing that labor properly has a lot of impact on the farms profitability.

Farmer Kay Jensen says that their 14-person staff fill out daily timecards on 8 x 11" charts that detail the time and the job that was being performed. She has chosen to track the type of work (e.g. weeding, transplanting, harvesting) rather than the enterprise, as she finds this more useful in making decisions.

"I require all of my staff to wear a watch on their wrist," she laughs. A cell-phone won't cut it. "I want them to tack when they start and stop a row, so we can see how long a given task is taking." While they don't need this detail with every task, they will check it frequently.

With 20-years of experience, Kay and Paul know how much money they need the crew to produce for them per hour. If it is taking longer than expected for a given task, Kay says they look at three things (in this order):

1. Has the staff gotten the right training? Do we need to retrain?

2. Maybe the field or crop isn't right—is it too weedy, or is the crop not yet ready (e.g., the radishes too small to make a proper bunch)?

3. Is this crewmember just too slow on this task, do they need to be moved to another job?

"We'll time things in 10 or 15 minute increments, and look to see if the whole crew isn't producing, or if just one person is struggling."

Social Security

If you are married and your farm is organized and filing taxes as a sole proprietorship, only one person will have social security benefits related to the farm income associated with their name. This means that one of the members of the couple will not be accumulating anything in a fund with their name on it.

For this reason, some accountants recommend that one of the spouses be paid as an employee, with taxes and social security being taken out and paid by both the farm business and the "employee." The farm can also choose to file taxes as a partnership to achieve the goal of building a social security account for both parties. We recommend that you talk to your accountant to decide what is best in your own situation.

CHAPTER 23
Business Structure Decisions

Key questions addressed in this chapter:

Why do you need to consider how your business is legally structured?

What questions will lead you to decide on different business structures?

What do you do once you decide on a structure?

One decision that must be made when establishing a new farming business is: What structure or organizational form should it take? Many people refer to this as choosing a farm "business entity." The choice of business structure will affect how liability plays out and how the business files its taxes.

Most beginning farming operations start out as sole proprietorships or partnerships. These business entity choices are the easiest. Farmers do not have to do anything formal to launch a sole proprietorship. Any person who sells a product or service will automatically form a sole proprietorship (if one person owns the business) or a partnership (if more than one person owns the business), if no other business structure is chosen.

However, the sole proprietorship and partnership are just two of a few business entity options and they may not be the best at meeting the farmers' business and personal goals. It will be worthwhile for all farmers to understand all the options available to them.

OTTO'S TIP: *Caution: Are you already a corporation? If you are already a corporation, and thinking of change, don't do anything until and unless you consult a tax professional. There can be serious tax implications when changing to another entity. While it can still be useful to go through the process of determining the best entity for you, if you decide on another entity be sure you consult with your accountant or tax attorney before switching.*

Many Extension offices and farmer training programs publish charts that compare the characteristics of each entity option. While these are helpful it may be more useful to answer some basic questions about the farm business you have and intend to have to determine which organizational structure would best fit your farming operation.

Below are the most popular farm business structure options. There are other options, such as the limited partnership, but these are rarely utilized for new farm businesses.
- Nonprofit Corporation
- Sole Proprietorship
- General Partnership
- Limited Liability Company (LLC)
- C-Corporation
- S-Corporation
- Cooperative

The following questions will help farmers identify potential options for their business. In all cases, farmers should do additional research to confirm their choice. Speaking with an accountant, tax preparer, and any financing entities may be a part of that process.

1. Are you comfortable never being able to sell the farm business at a profit?
If you are comfortable with this, the option of forming a nonprofit corporation may be open to you, although you need to clear a few more hurdles. Nonprofit entities are only eligible for tax benefits if they also receive nonprofit status from the Internal Revenue Service. Farms are only eligible for this status if they are exclusively organized for charitable or educational purposes, (the most common grounds for tax-exemption, there are also others). If you envision a farm business that can return profit back to you over time, the nonprofit corporation is not a suitable business entity.

Farmers answering No to this question should avoid the nonprofit corporation business entity.

2. Are you okay with having separate personal and business bank accounts and doing paperwork in order to protect your personal assets from liability, as well as gain potential tax benefits?
This question is designed to determine if a farmer should stick with the simple sole proprietorship/general partnership or if the farmer should consider an entity that offers what is called "limited liability." Limited liability companies (LLCs) and S- or C-corporations offer limited liability. Before anyone gets too excited, it's important to point out exactly what limited liability entails. If you select a business entity with limited liability, then the farmer's personal assets are protected from business liabilities. This is especially valuable for your personal assets such as stocks, vacation property, or other personal resources. For many farmers, the vast majority of their assets are farm assets—tractors, equipment, and the like. The bad news is that a limited liability entity does not protect business assets from business liabilities. All the farm business's assets can be lost if a farm LLC or corporation incurs a liability. (This is why farm businesses carry insurance.)

The second point of caution is that having an LLC or corporation comes with costs. Farmers must do annual paperwork, file entity taxes, and maintain separate bank

Is Your Nonprofit a Corporation?

Most nonprofits are corporations. But, not all. It's possible and legal to form a nonprofit association, which isn't a corporation. That means the people involved do not have the benefits of a corporation - the members of the nonprofit (or directors) have their personal assets at risk if the nonprofit incurs a liability. However, you can't get 501(c)(3) status from the IRS unless you form a corporation, so that motivates people to form one.

BUSINESS STRUCTURE

Prepare Good Organizing Documents

After deciding on a business entity, the next step is for the business owner(s) to write the organizing documents that back up the business entity choice. This is especially important where the farm has more than one owner.

The organizing documents can have a dramatic impact on several things: your ability to make management decisions, your and other owners' liability for decisions or actions, your personal income taxes and self-employment taxes, and the ways you can transfer ownership.

Many farmers do not take the next step of writing careful, thorough organizing documents. They are missing out on the opportunity to control very important matters over the life of the farm business.

---

accounts between personal and business. If you are not willing to do these things, the protection offered by the LLC or corporation is degraded.

Farmers answering No to this question should focus on a sole proprietorship or general partnership.

3. Do you plan to seek funding from venture capitalists or to "go public" (meaning selling shares to the public)?
This question helps identify farmers best suited for a C-Corporation. C-Corporations are created as corporations at the state level and the "C" designation indicates the method of taxation through the IRS. Owners of C-Corporations often experience higher taxes overall than corporations designated as for "S" taxation. Very few farmers will have plans to go public, so this is not a common option.

Farmers answering Yes to this question should focus on a C-Corporation.

4. Is "one member, one vote" important to you as a strategy for how owners govern the business, regardless of actual ownership percentage?
Farmers answering Yes to this question should focus on a cooperative. Cooperative businesses are founded on the principle of one member, one vote, and farmers may find other advantages to forming a cooperative. Cooperatives can be organized with different individuals as the owners: the farm workers, or farm customers, or someone else. The various options are worth exploring. A good resource is University of Wisconsin Center for Cooperatives. (www.uwcc.wisc.edu)

5. Will the farm business have more than 100 owners, owners who are not United States citizens, or owners who are not "natural persons" (as in, are a trust or an LLC)?
This question helps farmers identify if they should explore an LLC as opposed to an S-Corporation. S-Corporations may not have more than 100 shareholders (owners), and all shareholders must be natural persons who are U.S. citizens.

6. Does the farm business anticipate offering different types of ownership, such as different priority for return of one's investment, different bases for receiving distributions, or different eligibility for voting?
This question also helps farmers identify if they should explore an LLC as opposed to an S-Corporation. S-Corporations cannot create more than one class of shareholder. If you are looking to create different "levels" of ownership, you may need to create different classes. Thus, farmers answering Yes to this question should focus on an LLC.

If you have made it through each of these questions without identifying the right focus for your farm, you should explore both the LLC or the S-Corporation. In many situations, there is no clear "correct" answer between the LLC and the S-Corporation.

In some situations, the taxation structure of the S-Corporation can be advantageous. However, LLCs can choose to be taxed like an S-Corporation, so the factor doesn't mean you should form an S-Corporation necessarily.

Many farmers have heard that an LLC is easier to manage than an S-Corporation. It is true that under many state laws, LLCs do not have to follow some specific rules, like holding an annual meeting or taking meeting notes. However, LLCs should be doing these things anyways as a best business practice. LLCs that do not hold annual meetings or maintain meeting notes risk degrading the protections the LLC offers. Because the LLC and S-Corporation operate very similarly, many farmers choose between the two based on their (or their tax preparer's) personal preference or experience.

These questions are designed to help farmers identify a business entity to focus on as they explore their options in depth. Discovering the best entity choice requires more research and careful consideration.

For a much more detailed flowchart to identifying the best potential business entity for an individual farm, and extensive detail about each entity option, see Farm Commons' *Farmers' Guide to Choosing a Business Entity*. (farmcommons.org/resources/farmers-guide-choosing-business-entity). You will also find detailed information on how to write solid organizing documents for any farm business entity (including sample documents),

Selecting a business entity is just the first step. Farmers should pay close attention to drafting a solid partnership agreement, operating agreement, or bylaws for the entity. These organizing documents are important because they give the entity legal legitimacy. From a practical perspective, these documents help you make important decisions such as allocating responsibility, determining how profits are distributed, outlining how people enter or exit ownership, and setting out rules for transfer of ownership. These are the important issues on which many farm businesses succeed or fail. It is well worth the time to create a careful, thorough organizing document that prevents problems.

Summary

A few basic questions can help farmers identify the best business entity to further explore for their farm. The ultimate choice should be made after doing further research, especially for farms already organized as a corporation and farms in Midwestern states. All farmers should strongly consider creating detailed organizational documents, such as an operating agreement. Farm businesses with more than one owner especially have a lot to gain from good organizing documents.

> **Caution: Anti-corporate Farming Laws**
>
> Farmers in Midwestern states who are considering forming an LLC or corporation must look in to their state's "anti-corporate farming" laws. These laws restrict some LLCs and corporations from owning or managing farmland. Details on the state laws are available in Farm Commons' *Farmers' Guide to Choosing a Business Entity*.

CHAPTER 24
Exiting the Farm: Transfer and Sale

Key questions addressed in this chapter:

What farm transfer options are there?

What must be considered in making farm transfer decisions?

While the majority of information presented in this book is directed toward those just setting up farming systems, we would be remiss to not include a few notes about the issues involved in selling or transferring a farm operation. All good things will come to an end, or at the least, continue under someone else's stewardship after you are done or gone. A little knowledge at the front end can avoid some expensive difficulties on the back end.

Farms will be transferred for numerous reasons and in many ways.
- As a farm owner, you can decide to sell all or some of the farm assets, either to a family member or to someone else
- While still living, you can give all or a portion of your assets away
- You can set up a trust or other entity to manage the farm assets before and/or after death
- You might die leaving a will directing assets to one or more people or entities
- You might pass on without a will or plan, and state law will dictate what happens to the property you owned
- You may go through a divorce, forcing a sale of farm assets to split the property between spouses
- You may encounter serious financial issues that precipitate an exit from farming
- You might decide to scale back, and, while still living on the property, sell off most of your farm assets and stop farm operations

Since most farms are set up with a huge amount of sweat equity, and are often a family's residence as well as place of business, there are often significant emotional as well as financial investments in the farm. A farm transfer, through selling, gifting or death, will ideally be carefully planned to incorporate the emotional as well as financial needs of everyone involved.

Given the investment that has been made in the farm, there are many things to consider in setting up a smooth transfer. Most critical are plans on how to:

- Transfer labor
- Transfer management duties and decisions
- Transfer assets: land, buildings, animals, labels, markets
- Explore and manage potential trouble spots

Things that will impact decisions about the transition will be the size of the farm and assets, the mix of farm and non-farm in the family's income and asset stream, and the farmer's overall goals and retirement needs.

Business Structure Makes a Difference

As we explored in Chapter 23 on Business Structure, how your business is legally structured has many implications, including on farm transfer.

Your legal structure will dictate who is allowed to make the legal decisions about the property. The legal owners in a sole proprietorship, a partnership, or a LLC, or the stockholders in a C- or S-Corp are the ones who can transfer property, generally speaking. Business structure will also impact how tax responsibility is allocated in a transfer. Legal structure will also affect if a transfer can take place gradually over time, or as a one-time transaction.

OTTO'S TIP: *Sometimes, only specific people within the business can transfer property, not all owners.*

As you set up your farm business, thoughts of transfer in the future might help you decide which legal structure best fits your overall plans. Some may find that changing the legal structure (for instance from a sole proprietor to a LLC) as you look toward a farm transfer may smooth the transition. Information in the Business Structure chapter or the Resource section will help you understand some of these considerations.

OTTO'S TIP: *Defining "Estate"*
When a person dies, all of that person's property (including real estate, personal possessions, and money) is pooled together in the person's "estate." The legal plans for handling the estate after death will determine what happens to the assets. Any debts owed by the deceased person may be collected from the assets of the estate—usually before any distributions are made to the heirs or beneficiaries.

What's in an Estate Plan?

An estate plan is a written document. It should be updated periodically and at a minimum, include the following:

- A Multigenerational Family Tree that includes social security numbers and contact information for each family member.
- An inventory of farm and non-farm assets and how each is titled.
- Farm and non-farm liabilities.
- A description of insurance polices that includes: ownership; name of the insured; face value; cash value; date of transfer, if any; and contact information.
- Retirement accounts including: IRAs, Roth IRAs, and any others.
- Location of important records including: will, trust, deeds, powers of attorney, durable power of attorney for health care, stock certificates, insurance policies, and partnership or other business operating agreements.
- Estimate of retirement needs including a retirement budget with housing, health, and living costs.
- Estimate of retirement income including: current estimate of social security benefits, IRA distributions, investment, rental, farm, or other income that will provide cash for retirement needs.
- Plan for succession of operating business including: assets to be transferred to respective heirs and method of transfer, such as buyouts or gifts; proposed schedule of transfer (by will/trust or annual gifting); summary of any buy-sell agreements; annual gifting plan; history of annual gifting.
- The plan for transfer of non-farm assets including non-farm real estate, stocks, bonds, and insurance proceeds.
- The plan for transfer of farm land.
- Wishes with respect to personal property.
- Budget for transition expenses: insurance premiums, professional fees, annual expenditures, periodic appraisals, and any other expenses.
- Names and addresses of personal representative/trustees.
- List of professional farm service providers, including: accountants, attorney, financial analyst, insurance agents, and brokerage firms.
- Charitable giving wishes.
- Attachments to the estate plan should include:
- Copy of Will, Trust, Durable Power of Attorney, and Durable Power of Attorney for Health Care.
- Gift tax returns.
- Copy of business agreements including the operating agreement or partnership agreement.
- Copies of deeds

From "A Legal Guide to the Business of Farming in Vermont" Updated Sept 2015 Univ. of Vermont Extension www.uvm.edu/farmtransfer/?Page=legalguide.html

Make a Plan

If at all possible, we recommend that you make an estate plan. Those who are comfortable with planning might do some thinking about eventual transition as they are in the process of setting up their farm operation, or as a part of annual planning. However, most will wait until a farm transfer is on the close horizon to make the needed decisions.

Formalizing the estate planning process, ideally working with an advisor or set of advisors, can take some of the strain off of what can be a very emotional set of decisions. Lawyers are often willing to help with estate planning, accountants can offer useful advice. Outside entities, such as non-profits, state Ag departments or university Extension staff often have advisors or trainings on farm transfer available. There are several useful websites and written resources available that will help (see the Resources section).

It is easy to remember that an estate contains assets, but it also contains debt. Anyone planning their estate transfer must also consider how outstanding debt is managed as assets transfer. It is also wise to consider what will happen if you become disabled, incapacitated or otherwise unable to continue farming.

Family Transfer

Those transferring the farm from an older generation to a younger have many considerations, both financial and emotional, to take on. Communication and finding common goals can be challenges. Utilizing outside advisors and/or a written planning guide can sometimes help relieve tension by creating structure for the decision-making. A well thought out transfer can take a year or more to plan. Expect to put a fair effort into meeting with all involved parties, including all family members if feasible, enough times to feel comfortable about the decisions being made.

The older generation may find it easiest to let go of responsibility for the labor as the first step in a farm transfer. Ideally, after taking on the work, the new generation will start to take on management decisions. Next will be a transfer of the farm assets, either gradually or in one or a few steps. A timeline for these transitions will help clear misunderstanding.

Important in discussions and decision making is if the farm is operating at a level that can not only support everyone through the transfer phase, but can also fulfill the goals of the new operators.

If a labor transition takes place over a long period of time (as in a youth working their way into the farm and adulthood), it is most fair to give some value to the investment in time that is being made. This may be cash or a wage, but could also be livestock shares or an equity position in the farm, which will help ease the eventual farm transition, as the younger farmer will have some portion of investment already made.

The transfer of management responsibilities can be very difficult and create a lot of tension. New and old ideas can collide. Some farmers have succeeded by portioning off sections of land or the operation for the new farmer to fully manage, so he or she gets experience in making financial decisions and builds an asset base. With technology making many farming operations less physically demanding, the timing of management transfers can be delayed as the older generation keeps at it into their 80s and 90s. It is ideal to let the younger generation take on management long before this, so they can run the farm the way they chose while in the prime of their lives.

Identifying the Challenges

There are a number of challenges common in a family transfer. First, the transition often takes too long. The younger generation may get impatient and frustrated waiting for the parents to cede control over the farm. If the frustration becomes too great, they may exit the farm altogether, leaving the older generation with more work than they can handle.

A second issue can arise when the older generation has children that chose to leave the farm while other children decided to stay on the farm. It's natural for parents to want to treat all of their children equally. However, a child who farms with his or her parents is usually making many unpaid sweat equity contributions to the farm over the years that add significant net worth to their parents' balance sheet. Is it fair for their sweat equity to be divided among their non-farming siblings?

Communication is an enormous challenge for many farm families. Even though they are working together every day and talking about crops and livestock, they sometimes have a hard time talking about the big issues that deeply affect all of them. The parents' may have a transfer plan in mind or even in writing, yet they never discuss it with their children. The younger generation may have grave fears about their farming future, yet don't discuss their concerns with the parents. A child who left the farm may have a strong desire to return, but doesn't express their wishes to the rest of the family.

It can be extraordinarily difficult for families to work through a farm transfer without some outside assistance. Every member of the family has a vested interest in the outcome. Even with the best of intentions, people's motives can be questioned. It can be

FARM TRANSFER

very beneficial to ask a trusted, experienced, disinterested third-party to help the family negotiate the transfer. An outside advisor can raise key issues, ensure that every member of the family has an opportunity to speak their mind, facilitate civil discussions, and can share strategies that have worked for other families. An Extension agent, technical college instructor, or staff from your state's department of agriculture are all potential facilitators for a farm transfer.

Asset Transfer

Whether a farm is transferred to a younger family member or to an outside party, the assets must eventually change hands. The options and considerations involved are dependent on the way the business is legally structured and how fast the transfer will take place.

There are several creative strategies to consider when transferring assets to a younger generation. For example, ownership of a share in equipment or livestock could be traded for labor contributed by a young farmer. Farmers considering this option should do careful tax planning, as there are income tax implications when a person works for ownership in a business.

If transferring assets rather than shares of ownership are the best strategy, another option is for the older farmer to sell an older piece of equipment to the younger farmer, who can then trade it in on the purchase of a newer model that they then own. This kind of plan allows the new farmer to spread out the timing of expensive purchases while getting set up with what he or she needs to run the farm.

OTTO'S TIP: *If the young farmer isn't personally selling any farm products, he or she wouldn't file a Schedule F. They might be building up farm assets without generating farm income.*

Selling on Contract or Lease with Ownership Transfer

Selling equipment on contract or lease are more complex strategies. If the sale is to a closely related party, the capital gains are all due and depreciation is recaptured the year of the sale. However, if the sale is to an unrelated party, selling the equipment on contract can spread the capital gains liability over the life of the contract. The payment schedule on any installment contract must carry an interest rate that is at least equal to the "Applicable Federal Rate" (AFR). The interest income is taxable to the seller in the year it is received.

A lease with option to purchase is another story. Lease payments are taxable income to the owner, and the machinery stays on his or her balance sheet and depreciation schedule. Lease payments are a deductible expense for the renter. The lease has to contain an option to buy the asset at fair market value at the end of the lease term. If the buyout is at less than fair market value, the IRS could treat the transaction as an installment sale instead of a lease and tax it as such.

Working for Assets

There are issues to consider when a new farmer works for another in exchange for shares in assets. Ownership of the asset needs to be clear. It shouldn't appear on both farmers' balance sheets at 100 percent value. It can be listed on each party's balance sheet at a percentage less than 100 percent (75 percent:25 percent for example.) However, it's likely that neither party would be able to use the asset as collateral to secure a loan if they don't have 100 percent ownership interest in it.

No lender wants to try to repossess 75 percent of a tractor if the farmer stops making loan payments on it. Also, if a lender already has a security interest in the asset, the older farmer doesn't have the right to transfer any ownership without the lien holder's permission.

If you don't know whether there is a lien against an asset, ask your lender.

Sometimes farmers don't really know what's been pledged as collateral. For instance, FSA usually takes a blanket lien on ALL personal property and doesn't release it until the loan is entirely paid off.

Another possible option is for the owner of a farm asset to sell it and reinvest the proceeds in a "like-kind" asset that is then leased to the younger farmer. Like-kind property exchanges are permitted under Section 1031 of the Internal Revenue Code and thus are often called "1031 exchanges." A like-kind exchange defers the taxable gains that would ordinarily be due on the sale of assets held in a business.

While the most common use of a like-kind exchange is selling one piece of land and buying a different piece of land, it can be used for other assets as well. Let's say the senior farmer owns a line of machinery with a fair market value of $500,000 that has been completely depreciated. The machinery doesn't meet the needs of the younger farmer. An outright sale would trigger a very large tax liability. However, the farmer might instead choose to reinvest the sale proceeds in other, similar farm business assets that the younger farmer can utilize, and then enter into a lease agreement for the use of the new assets. The tax liability will be pushed off to some point in the future, allowing the older farmer to reinvest more dollars today.

There are some very specific rules pertaining to like-kind property exchanges that, if not properly followed, could trigger immediately taxable gains. Be sure to get professional advice if you are exploring this option.

Both breeding and raised livestock can be sold in parts or as a whole. However, if there is some kind of joint ownership of a breeding herd your business will look like a partnership and must be treated as such for tax purposes.

Giving Assets Away

Assets may be given as gifts to anyone you wish, related or not, but must follow IRS gift tax rules. As of 2017, the annual limit to give a gift (cash or other assets) without having to report the gift is $14,000 per person. If a gift to an individual exceeds $14,000 in one year, the person making the gift must report it to the IRS.

However, that doesn't mean the person making the gift will have to pay tax on it. The IRS allows a total lifetime "unified credit" or gift tax exemption of $5.25 million. A portion of the giver's unified credit would be applied to the amount of the gift that exceeds $14,000. The $14,000 does not count against the taxpayer's unified credit.

Some farm families will coordinate their gifts at the end of the year to maximize the effects of the annual exclusion. For instance, an older farm couple could each gift $14,000 to their child (total of $28,000) on December 31. They could each also gift $14,000 to their child's spouse (another $28,000) on December 31. They could then each gift their child an additional $14,000 (another $28,000) on January 1, and $14,000 each to the child's spouse ($28,000 more). Using this strategy, the older couple will have gifted $112,000 to the next generation in two days without exceeding the annual exclusion.

The IRS requires that the value of gifts other than cash be assessed at fair market value. Keep good records documenting how the value of non-cash gifts was determined.

For a farm asset, the value of a non-cash gift will be the asset giver's basis in the item. If the receiver of a gift later sells the asset, they must pay tax on the difference between the

> ### Recapturing Depreciation
>
> Any assets that have been depreciated, such as buildings, equipment or livestock, must have the depreciation recaptured at the sale of the asset.
>
> When a taxpayer sells an asset for a gain after taking deductions for depreciation, depreciation recapture is used to tax the gain. Because the taxpayer received a deduction from ordinary income for the depreciation of the asset, any gain the taxpayer receives, up to the depreciation amount, must be included as ordinary income to offset the earlier deduction.

selling price and the basis value at the time the gift was received. Rules governing this come from the Internal Revenue Service, and may change over time.

If you sell your farm, or some of your assets, at less than market rate, the IRS will consider the difference between the market rate and what you sold the asset for as a gift, and you will be liable to pay gift tax on that difference if it exceeds the amount of the lifetime unified credit.

If you make contributions to 501 (c)(3) charitable organizations, you may get a tax break on the donation. Check with a tax accountant for details.

You won't get a tax break on charitable contributions if you don't itemize deductions on your tax form.

OTTO'S TIP:

When cash or other assets are gifted, they simply disappear from the giver's balance sheet. If the recipient uses a market basis balance sheet, the gift should appear on the balance sheet at its fair market value. (Keep in mind that there might also be a contingent liability for taxes that would become due if the asset were to be sold.) If the recipient is using a cost basis balance sheet, the gifted asset should appear at its tax basis value.

If your farm business is organized as an LLC or corporation you have the option of giving away "shares" of the business. This can be useful if you want to slowly transfer ownership and management over time. Any assets involved should be appraised before they are transferred, and a letter documenting the value and the transfer of ownership interests should be retained in the business' files.

Often, shares in a closely held, family corporation will be valued at a discount relative to the total market value of the assets owned by the corporation, because there is a very limited market for the shares. For example, the farm may own assets with a total value of $1 million, but the total value of the shares in the farm LLC is only $750,000. Very few people would be interested in buying shares in the farm LLC. Transferring shares rather than tangible assets allows more assets to transfer without going over the unified credit.

Once again, a gift tax form must be filed by the giver in the year the transfer is made if the value of the gifted ownership interest exceeds the annual exclusion. Farmers must mind the annual and lifetime gift tax exclusions. The gift tax rules apply when gifting ownership as well as assets.

Selling your Farmland

Selling a farm outright, to either a relative or someone else, will have tax implications on any capital gains, which is the difference between the farm asset basis and the sale price. There are special tax rules for sales to family members. There is some exclusion up to a limit if the property is used for your primary residence. There are also like-kind exchange allowances if you use farmland sale proceeds to buy a new property for productive use within 180 days of the sale date. In this case, the original basis will be transferred to the new property, and capital gains paid on the total when that property is sold. But, these laws can change, so please, always check with a tax accountant before you make any final decisions.

Many farms choose to sell their land though a land contract, which is a private agreement of terms over a period of time with the buyer. We recommend that you consult a lawyer to set up a binding contract for any land contract agreement. A land contract will spread the capital gains liability out over time, as it will be reported in installments. However, a land contract also puts the seller in the role of the lender, which can be particularly difficult if the property is being sold to the seller's son or daughter.

Conservation Easements

Some farmers choose to put their land into a conservation easement. This is a sale or donation of the development rights to a conservation organization, such as a land trust, which limits development in perpetuity while still allowing agriculture and forestland use. Farms may have to meet certain criteria to qualify for a conservation easement.

A farmer can decide to donate the rights to the land trust, and claim a charitable deduction on its value. The land trust can also purchase the conservation easement, which is registered in the town land records like a deed, and restricts use. An appraiser will value the land before and after the conservation easement is in place to determine the value of the easement. If the property is sold or transferred, the easement goes with the transfer. The farmer's balance sheet should be updated to reflect the reduction in value of the real estate.

If there is a mortgage on the farm, the lender will need to do a partial release of lien to complete the sale of the easement. Depending on the outstanding principal balance on the mortgage, the lender may require a certified appraisal of the land. Most land trusts are familiar with this process and will help coordinate with your lender.

If a conservation easement is placed at the time of a sale transfer to a new owner, a donation to the land trust can be made by either the buyer or the seller, and may be decided by who can make best use of the tax deduction.

Trusts

Those making an estate transfer plan should consider the use of a trust. Relevant types of trusts include charitable remainder unitrusts and revocable living trusts.

A trust is a relationship where property is held by one party for the benefit of another. The trust will be created by a "settlor" and the property will be transferred to a "trustee." The trustee holds the property for the trust's beneficiaries. The trustee may be an individual, a company or a public body. The settlor will turn over some of their rights, as the legal ownership of the property transfers to the trustee, who is obligated to act for the good of the beneficiaries. This will create tax implications during the settlor's lifetime. Trusts

---

Basis and Capital Gains

"Basis" is the base value of an asset, and is generally what you paid for it minus any accrued depreciation (relevant to buildings or equipment, but not land, which does not accrue depreciation). The basis will change to the appraised value when the asset is sold. If the asset is transferred, such as through a gift or pre-death inheritance, then the basis won't change.

For instance, if your grandfather bought land for $200 an acre in 1955, and it was never sold or passed through an estate, the basis is still $200 in 2017. However, when you sell it in 2017 for $4,000 per acre the basis will rise to that amount, and you will pay capital gains tax on the difference between the $200 and the $4,000. Assets that pass through an estate are allowed a step-up in basis to the fair market value at the time of the owner's death.

are also set up to manage property in the case of the settlor's absence, such as controlling what happens after their death.

In a charitable remainder unitrust, (CRUT) the farm or other assets are put into trust while the farmer is still alive. The farmer or other beneficiary (the settlor of the trust) receives a designated fixed percentage of the value of the assets each year (between 5 and 50 percent of the net fair market value) while he or she is still alive. At the time designated when the trust is set up (generally the death of the settlor), the remaining value of the trust is given to a designated charity. At least 10 percent must be left at the time of final transfer.

Because the CRUT is set up to give the asset to a charity, these trusts can be used to save on income, gift or estate taxes. The tax laws are complex, however, and so before final decisions are made, we recommend you consult a tax specialist.

Revocable living trusts are often used to transfer property to surviving spouses, and can dictate how property control will be maintained. They are sophisticated and complex tools which take a lot of effort and expense to set up and manage. Again, consult an attorney for details on how to set up a revocable living trust.

Death and Taxes: Estate Tax

In the case of property transfer upon the death of an owner, liability for estate taxes will generally come into play. Estate tax laws seem to change frequently, as they are fertile ground for tax reformers.

A will outlines who the deceased owner wishes the property to pass to. If there is no will, the state will step in to manage the property transfer per state law. When property passes through an estate, the basis will be reassessed at the time of death of the holder. As noted above, long-time family farms can be caught with a significant tax burden if the basis has not changed for a long time, which is often the case. The use of a revocable living trust or other transfer strategy can help moderate any estate tax burden.
Most families will have farming and non-farming heirs, which can create strife at the time of farm transfer. Ideally conversations have been had and an equitable plan designed to relieve burden on the heirs at the passing of the older generation. Many farmers have found it very challenging to have farming and non-farming heirs work together as owners and decision makers of a farming operation.

If an heir has been on the farm, contributing sweat equity, that contribution can be recognized when valuing the assets to be split.

OTTO'S TIP:

As of this writing, the estate transfer of farm property valued below $5.45 million ($10.9 million for a couple) are exempt from state and federal estate taxes.

Managing Debt in Estate Transfer

While it might be fulfilling to decide who will take on farm assets once you are done or gone, you must remember that your farm debt is also passed on.

Normally, creditors must be notified of a farm owner's death, and they collect their debts out of the estate before the assets are divided amongst the heirs. While technically the heirs are not personally liable for the deceased person's debts, it is possible that all of the estate's assets will be used up and nothing left for the heirs to take.

Some estate plans call for the farming heirs to buy out the non-farming heirs' ownership interests in the farm assets. Depending on how the plan is structured, it could cause the farming heirs to have to take on a level of debt that is simply unsustainable.

Even if the farm asset transfer isn't entirely consumed by debt, taking over a farm encumbered with a large debt load is a huge, and potentially impossible task for a new generation coming into a farm operation. If your goal is to have a viable future to leave your heirs, you will want to carefully manage debt during your lifetime and plan for disposal of excessive debt at the time of your death.

It can be potentially very destabilizing to have the full balance of a loan paid at the time of farm transfer. Some loan programs allow an incoming farmer to take over the loan obligation and payments when the farm is transferred during the original borrower's lifetime. The original borrower may or may not continue to be liable for the loan balance. The situation is more complex when the borrower dies, and will be managed in relation to the specific lender and unique situation at the borrower's death.

Summary

Planning for your transfer away from the farm operation is a critical step in ensuring that what you build has the potential to sustain beyond your involvement. Creating an estate plan is a valuable process that should consider the needs of all family members. Whether a farm is sold, given away, or transferred through an estate, there are numerous considerations to explore.

Managing the farm well under your ownership, including understanding and managing the farm's financial situation and profitability and being responsible with debt, are the most important factors in ensuring you pass on a strong legacy in your farm transfer.

From the Farmers

Farm Transfer Story

Bob Scharlau, S & S Grains

Bob Scharlau, a lifetime beef and grain farmer, as well as co-owner of S&S Grains, LLP in Arcadia, Wisconsin, recently transferred his fourth generation family farm.

With their children not wanting to farm, Bob and Connie looked for non-related farmers to take over their 200 acres of certified organic crop land, two houses and some obsolete farm outbuildings. Bob wanted to find farmers that would keep the land organic. It took seven years and three attempts to find the right match. There were several lessons learned in their transition story.

As they started exploring options for their farm transfer, Bob and Connie soon realized that the only organic enterprises that could cash flow the debt a new farmer would take on would involve livestock, especially dairy. They advertised widely to find a new family interested in a place to start an operation.

After several months, a family inquired looking to raise all natural pork. They worked out a trial agreement, and converted the old dairy barn to a hog farrowing facility. Bob rented one house, the land and equipment to the new farmers, while they explored how everyone liked the situation, and if a bank would fund the transfer. Staff from the University of Wisconsin helped facilitate the situation. However, after two years the young family decided they wanted a different farm, and gave three months' notice they were leaving.

With no one renting the land, Bob planted organic crops and baled hay, since he didn't want to take on animals again. The Scharlau's advertised again.

A second family, currently renting their parent's certified organic farm 10 miles away, decided to try Bob's farm. Already owning some cattle and equipment, there were reasons that it wouldn't work for them to take on their parent's farm. They rented one of Bob's farm houses and the land, and raised crops for the dairy cattle, which they were still milking 10 miles away. The plan was that they arrange for financing to buy Bob's farm and put up a new dairy barn. Unfortunately, neither government loan programs or local banks were supportive of the plan to build new infrastructure, claiming the debt load would be too high. This family also left, buying a smaller farm with existing dairy buildings that a local bank was willing to finance.

By this time five years had passed in their transition story. Bob did another year of cash cropping. Throughout the years the Scharlau's saw a lot of interest in their organic farm, primarily from people wanting a home in the country within 40 miles of Minneapolis, with five to 20 acres that they could try growing vegetables on. But, Bob and Connie really wanted

Continued on next page

From the Farmers...continued

to sell the farm to people that wanted to make a living farming, and so they kept advertising: through MOSES, Land Stewardship Project and Organic Valley publications.

In year six a young man who had looked at the farm four years earlier contacted Bob again. This young man had been working for an organic dairy farmer who had paid him partially in organic calves and cows, and rented him the land. The young man had recently gotten married, and they were renting a house in town while they farmed on the rented land. All was going well, until the dairy farmer's daughter got married, and the son-in-law decided he wanted to farm.

With six months to find a new farm, the young farmer again contacted Bob. Since he could bring 150+ head of cattle, some machinery and years of experience running a successful operation, the bank was willing to finance 60 acres, the farm buildings, and the construction of a new parlor and free stall barn. Bob worked out that the additional 120 acres could be sold via land contract, which would help spread out the farm sale income and tax liability over several years. This transfer is now in place, and Bob and Connie, as well as the new farmers, are very pleased with the outcome.

Bob has a few tips from his experience to share:

- *In the family for four generations, much of Bob's land had always been transferred before the owners died, and so still had a tax basis of only $1.00 per acre. Selling at $3,000 per acre, Bob and Connie had a huge capital gains tax bill to pay. Bob notes that if either he or Connie died before the sale, the basis would be readjusted to current value for the survivor, and the tax bill much lower, but they wanted to sell now, before one of them died. This meant they needed to pay the tax.*

- *Part of the land was in Connie's name, and she decided to donate her parcel to the Lutheran Church to put into a charitable remainder trust. The church then sold the land to the new farmer. This allowed Connie to take a tax deduction, and saved them capital gains tax on that parcel while helping both the church and the new farmer, as well as give a monthly income to Connie.*

- *Bob reminds us that any of us could probably sell to the big guy in the neighborhood, looking to increase his land base. However, supporting new, younger farmers trying to start out in farming is a worthwhile and fulfilling alternative. It just takes a little creativity and time.*

- *Helping new farmers create equity by working for shares in cattle or crop sales, or utilizing land contracts, will help them get approved for a loan or spread out debt.*

- *And Bob's final point: This all takes time. Don't wait until you're on the way to the nursing home to start the transition process!*

Conclusion: A Few Final Words

We've put this book together to explain the most important concepts that you need in order to succeed with your farm financial management. Your ability to use them will grow as you become familiar with the ways that your numbers work together, and start to understand your farm's financial trends over time. Just like in farming, a thorough understanding of farm financial management will take time to develop.

Each farmer will have unique goals for maintaining their farm. But, each will most likely have the goal of maintaining—keeping a sustainable farm operation thriving for as long as they wish to manage it—as a key factor. While farms can sustain without good financial management, it is more assured they will sustain if the financial picture is understood and used to make management decisions.

We offer below a few keys to success in farm financial management:

- Use this book to understand the big picture, and how numbers fit together to tell the story of your farm's situation.

- Every farmer will collect data for annual tax filing, which creates the base of a farm financial system. From there, systems can be elaborated to facilitate study of the detail of how your farm is sustaining financially.

- You can start slow, and set up financial systems as you need them, in ways that make sense for the particular questions you need to answer to be a good manager of your operation.

- Consider relying on an accounting expert to help you set up a computer bookkeeping system. They will ask you questions to customize their work, and fit your answers into a framework that can give you the kind of reports you will need. The standardized system they set up should be helpful to any financial professionals, such as a tax accountant.

- Remember that good cash flow does not mean strong profitability. Cash in the bank at the end of the year might not reflect the farm's long-term sustainability.

- Consider tracking the detail needed to do analysis of particular enterprises on your farm, to help you understand where you are making or losing money. It will take time to analyze numerous lines of production on diverse farms, choose a few per year, specifically those that have the highest impact. The information you gain can help you make decisions to increase profitability.

- Try figuring out a few ratios, such as the "key ratios" we list on page 117. Looking at how these change year to year will give you a lot of useful knowledge. Figuring these early in your farm tenure will give you very interesting information to reflect on as your operation develops over time.

- As we detail in Chapter 13 on improving profits, there are warning signs that a farm is in financial trouble. Pay attention to these signs, and go for help before it gets too late. As we point out, your lender, accountant, and farm service providers want you to succeed. It is in their best interest, too, to have your farm be profitable. They may have valuable help that can be drawn on with an honest conversation about any financial trouble brewing in your operation.

- A good system isn't effective if it isn't used. If you don't use the numbers to help you make your business decisions, it isn't worth taking the time to collect them.

And finally, don't forget why you are farming. We hope that the guidance we have given you in this book allows you to set up simple financial tracking systems that free you up from having to guess about your farm's financial position. You will gain information to help you make management decisions, which can be used to guide your farm toward your goals. As an ideal, a good financial management system will relieve stress and create opportunity for you to better enjoy those aspects of farming that brought you to it in the first place.

We wish you long-term, sustainable financial health for your farm enterprise.

Please look for accompanying resources on the MOSES website, at mosesorganic.org

NOTES

APPENDICES

Appendix A	Iowa Custom Rate Survey.	228-231
Appendix B	Paper Record Keeping Forms, OSU	232-239
Appendix C	Simple Financial Statement Templates	240-242
Appendix D	Retail Price Points	243
Appendix E	Farm Finance Scorecard	244-247
Appendix F	2015 Farm Business Management Report Summary . .	248-249
Appendix G	Net Present Value (NPV) Table	250-251
Appendix H	Sample Livestock Enterprise Budget.	252-253
Appendix I	Using the QuickBooks Budgeting Function	254
Appendix J	Financial Skills Trouble Shooting Concepts	255

APPENDICES

Appendix A: 2016 Iowa Farm Custom Rate Survey

2016 Iowa Farm Custom Rate Survey

Ag Decision Maker

File A3-10

Tillage	Average Charge	Median Charge	Range			Number of Responses
Chopping cornstalks, / acre	$11.85	$11.90	$7.00	-	$19.00	53
Moldboard plowing, / acre	18.80	19.00	12.00	-	25.00	27
Chisel plowing, / acre	16.45	16.00	12.00	-	22.75	44
Disk/chiseling, / acre	17.80	16.75	10.00	-	25.00	54
Vertical tillage, / acre	16.05	16.70	8.00	-	21.00	58
Subsoiling (8 to 15 in. deep), / acre	20.35	20.00	15.00	-	27.50	44
V-ripping (over 15 in. deep), / acre	20.15	20.00	12.00	-	30.00	36
V-ripping with tandem disk, / acre	23.15	23.25	14.00	-	35.00	62
Disking, tandem, / acre	14.25	14.80	8.00	-	20.35	76
Disking, heavy or offset, / acre	18.45	18.00	13.00	-	25.50	31
Harrowing or dragging, / acre	8.95	9.00	5.00	-	13.00	23
Soil finishing, / acre	14.00	14.00	10.00	-	18.00	59
Field cultivating, / acre	14.05	14.10	8.00	-	21.00	87
Rock picking, / acre	14.90	15.00	10.00	-	20.00	20
Cultivating, conventional, / acre	13.50	14.50	8.00	-	20.00	31
Cultivating, ridge-till, / acre	16.45	16.40	11.50	-	22.75	14
Rotary hoeing, / acre	10.65	11.00	5.00	-	15.00	37
Land rolling, / acre	7.45	7.00	5.00	-	12.00	54

Machine Rental (operator, tractor, and fuel not included)	Average Charge	Median Charge	Range			Number of Responses
Tractor, / horsepower, / hour	$0.22	$0.20	$0.10	-	$0.33	22
Grain drill, / acre	10.50	10.00	8.00	-	15.00	12
No-till soybean drill, / acre	12.30	12.00	9.00	-	18.00	13
Corn head for combine, / acre	9.85	9.05	5.00	-	15.00	17
Soybean head for combine, / acre	9.40	10.00	6.00	-	13.25	16
Grain cart with auger, corn, / acre	6.70	6.50	4.50	-	10.00	15
Grain cart with auger, soybeans, / acre	6.00	5.60	4.00	-	8.20	14
Grain wagon, / bushel	0.08	0.08	0.04	-	0.12	11
Grain truck (semi), / bushel, / round trip	0.12	0.11	0.07	-	0.19	13
Grain auger, / bushel	0.06	0.06	0.05	-	0.08	10
Grain vacuum, / bushel	0.08	0.08	0.02	-	0.12	19
Grain cleaner, / bushel	0.08	0.08	0.07	-	0.08	7
Liquid manure spreader, / hour	38.65	40.00	30.00	-	45.00	7
Solid manure spreader, / hour	45.35	42.90	35.00	-	50.00	8
Skid loader, / hour	57.70	55.05	20.00	-	85.00	20
Dry bulk fertilizer applicator, / acre	3.70	3.75	2.00	-	5.00	14
Liquid fertilizer applicator, / acre	4.95	5.20	3.50	-	6.00	8
Anhydrous fertilizer applicator, / acre	4.80	5.00	2.00	-	8.00	19
Power washer, / hour	41.65	42.55	30.00	-	50.00	10
Generator, / hour	44.35	45.25	38.75	-	50.00	9
Tub grinder, / hour	199.20	200.00	150.00	-	220.00	9

Appendix A: Custom Rate Survey...continued

Page 2 *2016 Iowa Farm Custom Rate Survey*

Planting, Drilling, and Seeding	Average Charge	Median Charge	Range		Number of Responses
Planting					
- with fertilizer & insecticide attachments, / acre	$19.90	$20.00	$12.00 -	$30.00	75
- without attachments, / acre	18.55	18.00	12.00 -	28.00	78
- with splitters & attachments, / acre	20.70	21.00	12.00 -	32.00	46
- no-till planter, / acre	20.15	20.00	12.00 -	33.50	78
- no-till planter with splitters, / acre	20.85	21.00	15.00 -	30.00	49
- ridge till planter, / acre	22.40	22.00	17.00 -	29.00	14
Extra charge for seed shut-offs, / acre	2.30	2.50	0.00 -	5.00	64
Extra charge for variable rate seeding, / acre	2.70	3.00	0.00 -	5.00	51
Seed tender, / acre	3.15	3.50	0.00 -	6.00	46
Drilling soybeans, / acre	16.40	15.50	12.00 -	23.00	35
Drilling soybeans, no-till, / acre	18.40	18.25	13.00 -	28.00	54
Drilling grass seed, / acre	16.40	16.00	10.00 -	25.00	43
Drilling small grain, / acre	16.10	16.00	10.00 -	22.00	31
Seeding grass, broadcast with tractor, / acre	12.25	12.00	8.00 -	15.00	20
Seeding grass, broadcast with ATV, / acre	14.70	14.90	8.00 -	20.00	18
Spraying (materials not included)					
Ground, broadcast, tractor, / acre	$6.80	$6.50	$5.00 -	$10.10	60
Ground, incorporated, tractor, / acre	11.80	11.15	6.50 -	20.00	21
Ground, broadcast, self propelled, / acre	7.35	7.00	5.00 -	15.00	111
Ground, banded, tractor, / acre	10.95	11.00	8.00 -	13.65	12
Ground, road ditches, / hour	63.70	65.00	20.00 -	90.00	38
Aerial, / acre	10.60	10.00	7.00 -	15.00	40
Fertilizer Application (materials not included)					
Dry bulk - applied, / acre	$4.90	$5.00	$2.00 -	$8.00	57
- strip-till, / acre	17.15	17.00	7.00 -	25.00	21
Liquid - spraying, / acre	6.65	6.50	4.00 -	11.00	35
- strip-till, knifed, / acre	15.10	15.00	12.00 -	21.00	13
- side dressing, / acre	11.15	12.00	6.00 -	15.00	33
Anhydrous - injecting, with tool bar, / acre	12.25	12.00	7.00 -	20.00	82
- injecting, without tool bar, / acre	11.10	11.00	7.00 -	18.00	48
Spreading lime, / ton	6.35	6.50	3.00 -	11.30	31

Harvesting, Drying, and Hauling Grain	Average Charge	Median Charge	Range		Number of Responses
Corn combining, / acre	$34.75	$35.00	$23.00 -	$55.00	121
- with chopper head, / acre	40.10	39.50	26.00 -	57.00	64
Soybean combining, / acre	34.05	34.00	25.00 -	52.00	108
- with air reel, / acre	35.55	34.50	28.00 -	50.00	28
- with draper head, / acre	38.10	38.35	29.00 -	50.00	63
Small grain combining, / acre	31.55	30.00	25.00 -	40.00	18
Complete harvesting (combine, grain cart, haul to farm storage)					
- Corn, / acre	49.70	50.00	30.00 -	85.00	62
- Soybeans, / acre	46.40	47.00	30.00 -	70.00	60
Added charge for GPS mapping, / acre	2.45	2.50	0.00 -	5.00	49
Picking ear corn (seed corn), / acre	36.85	37.00	34.00 -	39.00	7
Picking ear corn (farm use), / acre	29.95	29.50	25.00 -	35.00	12
Drying corn (includes fuel, electricity, labor)					
- continuous flow dryer, / point per bushel	0.047	0.050	0.018 -	0.070	23
- bin dryer, / point per bushel	0.054	0.054	0.040 -	0.070	10
Handling grain by auger, / bushel	0.061	0.060	0.010 -	0.100	56

Appendix A: Custom Rate Survey...continued

2016 Iowa Farm Custom Rate Survey — Page 3

Harvesting, Drying, and Hauling Grain (cont.)	Average Charge	Median Charge	Range	Number of Responses
Hauling grain				
- grain cart, corn, / acre	$6.45	$6.25	$2.00 - $11.00	69
- grain cart, soybeans, / acre	5.70	6.00	2.00 - 10.00	68
- to farm storage, wagon, / bushel	0.071	0.070	0.020 - 0.140	40
- farm storage to market, wagon, / bushel	0.087	0.080	0.050 - 0.150	33
- to market, truck, (5 miles, 1-way trip), / bu.	0.099	0.100	0.050 - 0.180	71
- to market, truck, (25 miles, 1-way trip), / bu.	0.163	0.150	0.100 - 0.300	63
- to market, truck, (100 miles, 1-way trip), / bu.	0.325	0.327	0.120 - 0.510	30
Harvesting Forages				
Hay - mowing, / acre	$12.30	$12.00	$6.00 - $18.00	32
- conditioning, / acre	11.70	11.00	10.00 - 14.00	15
- mowing/conditioning, / acre	14.00	14.00	8.00 - 21.00	36
- raking, / acre	6.55	6.65	3.00 - 10.00	38
- windrowing, / acre	14.20	14.05	11.00 - 17.00	14
- tedding, / acre	7.20	7.00	5.00 - 10.00	19
Swathing hay or small grain, / acre	13.20	13.50	12.00 - 13.75	7
Hay baling - small square bales, / bale	0.66	0.70	0.35 - 1.00	28
- large square bales, / bale	9.75	10.00	8.00 - 12.00	17
- large round bales without wrap, / bale	10.70	10.50	8.00 - 14.00	21
- large round bales with wrap, / bale	12.35	12.50	9.00 - 16.00	51
Straw or corn stalk baling				
- large round or square bales w/o wrap, / bale	12.05	12.00	10.00 - 14.00	17
- large round or square bales with wrap, / bale	13.70	13.50	11.00 - 16.00	38
Picking up with accumulator, / large square bale	3.30	3.00	3.00 - 4.00	7
Moving large round bales to storage, / bale	2.85	2.90	1.75 - 4.00	14
Moving large square bales to storage, / bale	3.05	3.00	2.50 - 3.15	9
Hauling rd bales by truck or trailer, / bale, / loaded mile	0.09	0.03	0.01 - 0.19	10
Silage - chopping, / hour, / head row	44.60	28.75	13.33 - 100.00	8
- chopping, / ton	7.10	7.00	5.00 - 10.00	10
- chopping, haul, fill silo, / hour, / head row	67.15	30.00	16.67 - 133.33	5
- chopping, haul, fill silo, / ton	8.45	8.50	7.50 - 9.25	9
Filling silage bags, / foot of bag	11.00	11.00	9.00 - 13.00	7
Haylage - chopping, / ton	9.10	9.00	7.50 - 11.25	9
Earlage or snaplage - chopping, / acre	54.50	55.00	42.00 - 65.00	11

Custom Farming (tillage, planting, pest control, harvesting, and hauling to farm, no drying)	Average Charge	Median Charge	Range	Number of Responses
Corn, / acre	$129.95	$130.00	$70.00 - $190.50	59
Soybeans, / acre	116.15	115.00	60.00 - 170.00	57
Small grain, / acre	93.55	92.50	80.00 - 110.00	12

Farm Labor Wages for Operating Machinery	Average Charge	Median Charge	Range	Number of Responses
Spraying or harvesting, / hour	$16.60	$16.00	$11.00 - $25.00	81
Other operations, / hour	15.05	15.00	10.00 - 20.00	85

Appendix A: Custom Rate Survey...continued

2016 Iowa Farm Custom Rate Survey

Miscellaneous Services (labor, fuel, and equipment included)	Average Charge	Median Charge	Range		Number of Responses
Removing snow (loader), / hour	$78.10	$75.00	$35.00 -	$110.00	43
Removing snow (blade), / hour / foot of blade	5.35	5.85	0.88 -	9.38	14
Removing snow (blower), / hour / foot of blower	10.30	12.50	1.38 -	17.00	21
Grinding, mixing feed, / ton	10.60	10.50	9.75 -	11.50	8
Tub grinding hay, / hour	208.85	200.00	180.00 -	250.00	11
Spreading liquid manure, injected, / 1000 gal.	13.30	13.50	10.00 -	17.00	22
Applying liquid manure w/ drag line, / 1000 gal.	12.65	11.65	9.50 -	17.00	14
Loading solid manure, / hour	77.60	75.00	60.00 -	110.00	13
Loading, spreading solid manure, / hour	120.25	120.00	100.00 -	150.00	13
Power washing, / hour	43.25	42.00	35.00 -	50.00	19
Building fence, barbed (no materials), / hour	15.60	15.00	14.80 -	18.00	7
Building fence, barbed (no materials), / rod	15.00	14.50	11.00 -	18.00	10
Building fence, woven (no materials), / hour	17.45	16.50	15.00 -	20.00	7
Building fence, woven (no materials), / rod	15.35	14.75	11.00 -	20.00	8
Scouting crops, / acre	4.25	4.00	2.00 -	7.45	26
Scouting crops with drone, / acre	2.60	2.25	1.00 -	4.00	6
Soil testing, / sample	5.60	6.00	2.50 -	7.00	12
GPS grid soil testing, / acre	7.20	7.00	4.00 -	10.00	22
Managing stored grain, / bushel	0.06	0.05	0.01 -	0.10	19
Vacuuming grain, / bushel	0.09	0.08	0.02 -	0.15	33
Shearing sheep, / head	3.70	3.50	3.00 -	4.00	9
Livestock hauling with trailer, / loaded mile	2.90	2.95	2.00 -	4.00	13
Livestock hauling w/ straight truck, / loaded mile	3.35	3.45	2.75 -	4.00	8
Livestock hauling with semi truck, / loaded mile	3.75	3.80	3.50 -	4.00	12
Bulldozing, / hour, / foot of blade	12.45	12.15	7.08 -	18.00	20
Digging post holes, / hole	3.70	3.55	3.00 -	5.00	10
Driving steel fence posts, / post	2.60	2.50	2.00 -	4.00	11
Driving wooden fence posts, / post	3.85	4.00	3.00 -	5.00	11
Building terraces, grassed back, / foot	3.15	3.15	2.75 -	3.50	12
Building terraces, narrow base, / foot	2.55	2.50	2.00 -	3.00	9
Trenching, / foot	1.40	1.45	0.75 -	2.00	16
Tiling, tiling machine (excluding materials), / foot	1.10	1.15	0.50 -	2.00	22
Tiling, tile plow (excluding materials), / foot	0.72	0.75	0.30 -	1.05	24
Back hoeing, / hour	94.45	95.40	50.00 -	150.00	32
Clearing land, / hour	133.70	138.65	95.00 -	175.00	16
Building ponds, / hour	147.05	145.00	133.10 -	175.00	14
Chain sawing, / hour	57.85	60.00	25.00 -	75.00	19
Welding machinery, / hour	52.15	50.00	30.00 -	75.00	26
Mowing CRP or pasture, / acre	17.45	16.00	12.00 -	25.00	42
Mowing fence rows, ditches, / hour	68.75	70.00	25.00 -	100.00	42
Mowing lawns, / hour	38.55	40.00	18.00 -	60.00	31
Chopping brush, / acre	33.95	31.00	25.00 -	50.00	16
Using truck scale, / load weighed	5.60	4.75	2.00 -	10.00	14

Bin Rental	Average Charge	Median Charge	Range		Number of Responses
Bin dryer, / bushel dried, (no fuel or labor)	$0.074	$0.069	$0.040 -	$0.150	12
Storing grain, bin rental, / bushel / month	0.024	0.020	0.015 -	0.040	20
Storing grain, bin rental, / bushel / year	0.159	0.150	0.090 -	0.300	36

APPENDICES

Appendix B: Paper Record Keeping Forms

RECEIPTS

Month _____ Year _____ Page A-6a

Date Line	Details Of Transaction		Sale of Livestock & Other Items Bought For Resale	Raised Market Livestock & Livestock Products (calves, dairy products, etc.)			Crop Sales			Line
	Amount Received	From Whom Received / Item, Units, Weight, Price, etc.					Wheat	Other: ____	Other: ____	
			1	2	3	4	5	6	7	8
1										1
2										2
3										3
4										4
5										5
6										6
7										7
8										8
9										9
10										10
11										11
12										12
13										13
14										14
15										15
16										16
17										17
18										18
19										19
20										20
21										21
22										22
23										23
24										24
25										25
26										26
27										27
28										28
29										29
30										30
A	End of Month: Total Each Column and Transfer to Page B-4a									
31	Non-Cash Receipts Included Above									
32	Total Receipts to Balance With Check Register (line A – line 31)									

Source: Oklahoma Farm and Ranch Account Book, OSU Ag Exrension http://agecon.okstate.edu/

Appendix B: Paper Forms...continued

RECEIPTS — Page A-6b

	Crop Sales (continued)		Ag Program Payments	CCC Loans Under Election or Forfeited	Disaster & Crop Insurance Proceeds	Custom Hire	Other Farm Income Refunds, etc.	Non-Taxable Farm Receipts		Sale of Breeding Livestock, Equipment, Buildings, Land	Non-Farm Taxable Receipts			
Other:	Other:	Other:						All Farm Loans Received	All Other Non-Taxable Receipts		Rent & Royalty	Interest & Dividends	Other Taxable Non-Farm Receipts	
9	10	11	12	13	14	15	16	17	18	19	20	21	22	

Rows 1–30 (blank)

B = Total columns 1 through 22 (A must equal B)

Source: Oklahoma Farm and Ranch Account Book, OSU Ag Exrension http://agecon.okstate.edu/

APPENDICES

Appendix B: Paper Forms...continued

EXPENSES

Month _____ Year _____ Page A-8a

Line	Date	Check Number	Amount Paid	Details of Transaction		Cost of Livestock & Other Items Bought For Resale	Car & Truck Expenses	Chemicals: Herbicide & Insecticide	Conservation	Custom Hire	Employee Benefits	Feed	Fertilizer & Lime	Freight & Trucking	Gas, Fuel & Oil	Line
				Items, Units, Weight, Price, Etc.	From Whom Purchased											
1																1
2																2
3																3
4																4
5																5
6																6
7																7
8																8
9																9
10																10
11																11
12																12
13																13
14																14
15																15
16																16
17																17
18																18
19																19
20																20
21																21
22																22
23																23
24																24
25																25
26																26
27																27
28																28
29																29
30																30
A	End of Month: Total Each Column and Transfer to Page B-5a					1	2	3	4	5	6	7	8	9	10	
31	Non-Cash Expenses Included Above															
32	Total Expenses to Balance With Check Register (line A – line 31)															

Source: Oklahoma Farm and Ranch Account Book, OSU Ag Exrension http://agecon.okstate.edu/

Appendix B: Paper Forms...continued

EXPENSES — Page A-8b

Line	Insurance: Farm	Interest: Farm Mortgage	Interest: Farm (Other)	Labor Hired	Pension & Profit-sharing	Rent or Lease	Repairs & Maint.	Seeds & Plants	Storage & Warehousing	Supplies	Taxes: Farm Property	Utilities	Vet, Breeding & Med	Other Expense: Fees, Dues & Misc. Expense	Capital Purchases: Breeding Livestk, Equip. Bldgs, Land	Loan Principal Payments	Non-Farm Expense
1																	
2																	
3																	
4																	
5																	
6																	
7																	
8																	
9																	
10																	
11																	
12																	
13																	
14																	
15																	
16																	
17																	
18																	
19																	
20																	
21																	
22																	
23																	
24																	
25																	
26																	
27																	
28																	
29																	
30																	
Col	11	12	13	14	15	16	17	18	19	20	21	22	23	24	25	26	27

Vehicles, Mach., Equip. / Other (col. 15)

Farm Share / Non-Farm (col. 22)

B = Total Column 1 through 27; (B must equal A)

Source: Oklahoma Farm and Ranch Account Book, OSU Ag Exrension http://agecon.okstate.edu/

APPENDICES

Appendix B: Paper Forms...continued

CASH INFLOW (Receipts Summary)

YEAR: _____ Page B-4a

Line	CASH RECEIPTS: (From A-6a and A-6b)	JAN	FEB	MAR	APR	MAY	JUN	JUL	AUG	SEP	OCT	NOV	DEC	Line
1	Sale of Purch. Lvst													1
2														2
3														3
4														4
5														5
6	Wheat													6
7														7
8														8
9														9
10														10
11														11
12	Ag Program Pymts													12
13	CCC Loans													13
14	Disaster & Crop Ins													14
15	Custom Hire													15
16	Other Farm Income													16
A	OPERATING RECEIPTS (Sum lines 1 thru 16)													A
17	All Loans Received													17
18	Other Non-Taxable Receipts													18
19	Sale: Capital Assets													19
20	Rent & Royalty													20
21	Interest & Dividends													21
22	Other Taxable Receipts													22
B	TOTAL CASH INFLOW (Sum lines A and 17 thru 22)													B

A= Sum lines 1 through 16:

B= Sum lines A and lines 17 thru 22. Carry the "Total Cash Inflow" for each month to page B-5a, line B.

Source: Oklahoma Farm and Ranch Account Book, OSU Ag Exrension http://agecon.okstate.edu/

Appendix B: Paper Forms...continued

CASH INFLOW (Rec

YEAR: ____

Line	CASH RECEIPTS:	Sub-Total For Period To	Sub-Total For Period To	Sub-Total For Period To	Year End Total
1	Sale of Purch. Lvst				
2					
3					
4					
5					
6	Wheat				
7					
8					
9					
10					
11					
12	Ag Gov't Program Pymts				
13	CCC Loans				
14	Disaster & Crop Ins				
15	Custom Hire				
16	Other Farm Income				
A	OPERATING RECEIPTS (Sum lines 1 thru 16)	*	*	*	*
17	All Loans Received				
18	Non-Taxable Receipts				
19	Sale: Capital Assets				
20	Rent & Royalty				
21	Interest & Dividends				
22	Other Taxable Receipts				
B	TOTAL CASH INFLOW (Sum lines A and 17 thru 22)	*	*	*	*

Source: Oklahoma Farm and Ranch Account Book, OSU Ag Exrension http://agecon.okstate.edu/

APPENDICES

Appendix B: Paper Forms...continued

Page B-5a

CASH OUTFLOW (Expenses Summary)

YEAR: _____

Line		JAN	FEB	MAR	APR	MAY	JUN	JUL	AUG	SEP	OCT	NOV	DEC	Line
B	TOTAL CASH INFLOW (From B-4a)													
	CASH EXPENSES													
1	Lvst Purch for Resale													1
2	Car & Truck Expenses													2
3	Chemicals													3
4	Conservation													4
5	Custom Hire													5
6	Employee Benefits													6
7	Feed													7
8	Fertilizer & Lime													8
9	Freight & Trucking													9
10	Gas, Fuel & Oil													10
11	Insurance: Farm													11
12	Interest: Farm Mortgage													12
13	Interest: Farm (Other)													13
14	Labor Hired													14
15	Pension & Profit-sharing													15
16	Rent or Lease													16
17	Repairs & Maintenance													17
18	Seeds & Plant													18
19	Storage & Warehousing													19
20	Supplies													20
21	Taxes: Farm Property													21
22	Utilities													22
23	Vet, Breeding & Med													23
24	Other Expenses: Fees, Dues, Misc.													24
C	OPERATING EXPENSES (Sum lines 2 thru 24)													C
25	Capital Purchases: Breeding Livestk, Equip, Bldgs, Land													25
26	Loan Principal Payments													26
27	Non-Farm Expenses													27
D	TOTAL CASH OUTFLOW (Sum 1, C, and 25 thru 27)													D
E	NET CASH FLOW (B - D)													E
F	ACCUM NET CASH FLOW													F

C=Sum lines 2 through 24; D=Sum lines 1, C, and 25 through 27; E=Line B - line D; F=Current line E + previous line F.

Source: Oklahoma Farm and Ranch Account Book, OSU Ag Exrension http://agecon.okstate.edu/

Appendix B: Paper Forms...continued

FEARLESS FARM FINANCES

Page B-5b

YEAR: _____

CASH OUTFLOW (Expenses Summary)

Line		Sub-Total For Period ___ To ___	Sub-Total For Period ___ To ___	Sub-Total For Period ___ To ___	Year End Total
	TOTAL CASH INFLOW				
	CASH EXPENSES				
1	Lvst Purch for Resale				
2	Car & Truck Expenses				
3	Chemicals				
4	Conservation				
5	Custom Hire				
6	Employee Benefits				
7	Feed				
8	Fertilizer & Lime				
9	Freight & Trucking				
10	Gas, Fuel & Oil				
11	Insurance: Farm				
12	Interest: Farm Mortgage				
13	Interest: Farm (Other)				
14	Labor Hired				
15	Pension & Profit-sharing				
16	Rent or Lease				
17	Repairs & Maintenance				
18	Seeds & Plant				
19	Storage & Warehousing				
20	Supplies				
21	Taxes: Farm Property				
22	Utilities				
23	Vet, Breeding & Med				
24	Other Expenses: Fees, Dues, Misc.				
C	OPERATING EXPENSES (Sum lines 2 thru 24)	*	*	*	
25	Capital Purchases: Breeding Livestk, Equip, Bldgs, Land				
26	Loan Principal Payments				
27	Non-Farm Expenses				
D	TOTAL CASH INFLOW (Sum 1, C, 25 thru 27)	*	*	*	
E	NET CASH FLOW (B - D)				

Line 25 sub-columns: Vehicles, Mach, Equip | Other
Line 27 sub-columns: Farm Share | Non-Farm

* This cell should be totaled horizontally and vertically. A discrepancy indicates an error in posting or totaling.

Source: Oklahoma Farm and Ranch Account Book, OSU Ag Exrension http://agecon.okstate.edu/

APPENDICES

**Appendix C:
Simple Financial
Statement
Templates:
Balance Sheet**

FFF Simple Balance Sheet				Current Year	Next Year	
Assets						
	Current Assets					
		Cash & checking				
		Prepaid expenses & supplies				
		Accounts receivable				
		Crops				
			Corn			
			hay			
			Silage			
	Total Current Assets					
	Intermediate Assets					
		Breeding livestock				
		machinery				
		Ttiled vehicles				
	Total Intermediate Assets					
	Long Term Assets					
		Land				
		Buildings & improvements				
	Total Long Term Assets					
	Total Farm Assets					
	Total Personal Asets					
Total Assets						
Liabilities						
	Current Liabilities					
		Principal due on term loans				
			Machinery			
			Mortgage			
		Accrued interest				
			Operating loans			
	Total Current Liabilities					
	Intermediate Liabilities					
		Machinery loan				
		Other loan				
	Total Intermediate Liabilities					
	Long Term Liabilities					
		Mortgage				
	Total Long Term Liabilites					
	Total Farm Liabilities					
	Total Personal Liabilities					
	Contingent Liabilities					
Total Liabilities						
Net Worth/Equity						
Net Worth Change						
Total Liabilities & Net Wort/Equity						

Appendix C: Simple Financial Statement Templates: Income Statement

FFF Simple Income Statement	Fiscal Year	
Cash Farm Income		
Row crops		
Milk		
Cull stock		
Misc livestock		
Meat sales		
Vegetables		
Other		
Govt Payments		
Gross Farm Income		
Cash Farm Expenses		
Seed		
Fertility		
Weed & pest treatments		
Crop insurance		
Custom hire- crops		
Feed		
Breeding		
Veterinary		
Marketing		
Fuel & oil		
Repairs		
Supplies		
Custom hire- other		
Labor		
Land taxes		
Farm Insurance		
Utilities		
Certification fees		
Interest on loans		
Total Cash Farm Expenses		
Net Cash Farm Income		
Accrual Adjustments		
Crops and feed		
Market livestock		
Accounts receivable		
Hedging accounts		
Other current assets		
Prepaid exp & supply		
Growing crops		
Accounts payable		
Accrued interest		
Total adjustments		
Net Operating Profit		
Depreciation		
Machinery		
Titled vehicles		
Bldgs & improvements		
Total Depreciation		
Capital Adjustment		
Net Farm Income		

Appendix C: Simple Financial Statement Templates: Cash Flow Statement

BadgerLand Financial	Paul Dietmann												
ANNUAL CASH FLOW PROJECTION		Jan	Feb	March	April	May	June	July	Aug	Sept	Oct	Nov	Dec	TOTALS
BEGINNING CASH														
CASH IN-FLOW														
	Livestock income													
	Crop income													
	Government payments													
	Crop insurance proceeds													
	Custom work income													
	Sales of capital assets													
	Proceeds from new loans													
	Off-farm income													
	Other income													
	TOTAL CASH IN													
CASH OUT-FLOW														
	Livestock purchases													
	Car and truck expenses													
	Chemicals													
	Custom hire													
	Feed													
	Fertilizer & lime													
	Fuel & oil													
	Insurance													
	Labor hired													
	f machinery & equipment													
	Land rent													
	Repairs & maintenance													
	Seeds & plants													
	Supplies													
	Property taxes													
	Utilities													
	Vet & breeding													
	Professional fees													
	other expenses													
OPERATING OUT-FLOW														
	Capital purchases													
al and Interest payments														
	Family living draw													
	TOTAL CASH OUT													
	ENDING CASH													

Appendix D: Retail Price Points

Retail Price Points		
Major Price Barriers	Minor Price Barriers	Retail Price Points
		0.49
1.00		0.99
		1.29
		1.39
	1.50	1.49
		1.69
	2.00	1.99
		2.49
	3.00	2.99
	4.00	3.99
5.00		4.99
	7.00	6.99
	8.00	7.99
10.00		9.99
	13.00	12.99
15.00		14.99
	17.00	16.99
	18.00	17.99
20.00		19.99
	23.00	22.99
25.00		24.99
30.00		29.99
40.00		39.99
50.00		49.99
		69.99
75.00		74.99
		89.99
100.00		99.99
		119.99
		129.99
		139.99
150.00		149.99
		159.99
		169.99
		179.99
		189.99
200.00		199.99

Pricing Using Retail Price Points

Major Price Barriers are the trigger points at which all customers will notice a price variation. *Minor Price Barriers* are where some customers will react, but not all.

Most customers will feel the same regarding a product priced at $1.52 as at $1.69. Reseach shows that you will not sell significantly less of a product priced at $1.69 than the same product priced at $1.52.

Since most customers won't notice or care, you can make more revenue by taking advantage of these "pricing gaps."

Retail Price Points are those prices that will gain you the most return for customer satisfaction. For effective pricing, figure your ideal price, and then move it to the next higher price point.

APPENDICES

Appendix E: Farm Finance Scorecard, University of Vermont

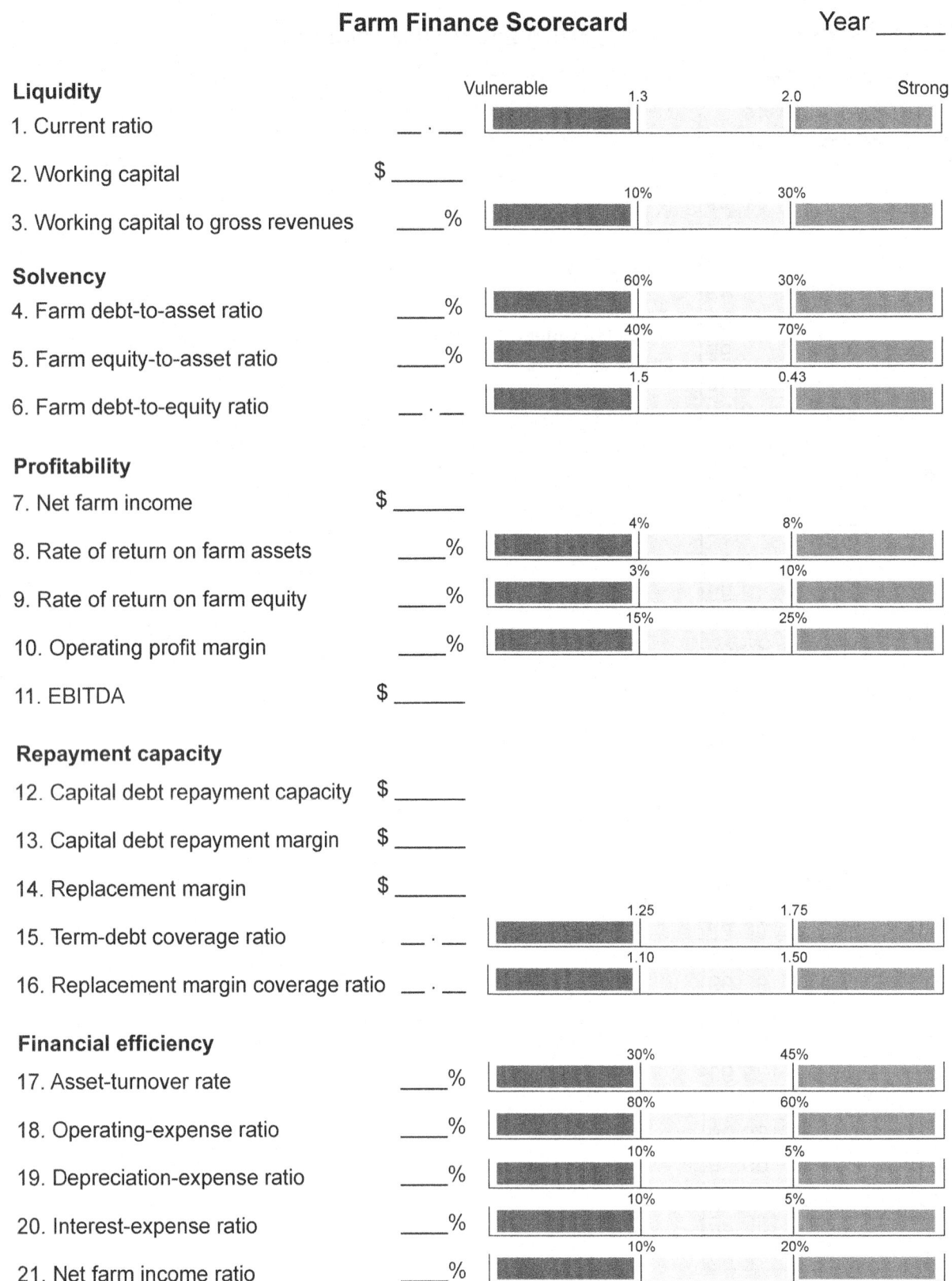

Appendix E: Scorecard...continued

Farm Financial Ratios and Guidelines

From the balance sheet

Liquidity
- is the ability of your farm business to meet financial obligations as they come due – to generate enough cash to pay your family living expenses and taxes, and make debt payments on time.

1. Current ratio
   - measures the extent to which current farm assets, if sold tomorrow, would pay off current farm liabilities.

2. Working capital
   - tells us the operating capital available in the short term from within the business.

3. Working capital to gross revenues
   - measures operating capital available against the size of the business.

Solvency
- is the ability of your business to pay all its debts if it were sold tomorrow. Solvency is important in evaluating the financial risk and borrowing capacity of the business.

4. Farm debt-to-asset ratio
   - is the bank's share of the business. It compares total farm debt to total farm assets. A higher ratio is an indicator of greater financial risk and lower borrowing capacity.

5. Farm equity-to-asset ratio
   - is your share of the business. It compares farm equity to total farm assets. If you add the debt-to-asset ratio and the equity-to-asset ratio you must get 100%.

6. Farm debt-to-equity ratio
   - compares the bank's ownership to your ownership. It also indicates how much the owners have leveraged (i.e., multiplied) their equity in the business.

From the income statement

Profitability
- is the difference between the value of goods produced and the cost of the resources used in their production.

7. Net farm income
   - represents return to 3 things,
     - Your labor,
     - Your management and
     - Your equity,
   that you have invested in the business. It is the reward for investing your unpaid family labor, management and money in the business instead of elsewhere. Anything left in the business, i.e., not taken out for family living and taxes, will increase your farm net worth.

8. Rate of return on farm assets
   - can be thought of as the average interest rate being earned on all (yours and creditors') investments in the farm. Unpaid labor and management are assigned a return before return on farm assets is calculated.

9. Rate of return on farm equity
   - represents the interest rate being earned by your investment in the farm. This return can be compared to returns available if your equity were invested somewhere else, such as a certificate of deposit.

10. Operating profit margin
    - shows the operating efficiency of the business. If expenses are low relative to the value of farm production, the business will have a healthy operating profit margin. A low profit margin can be caused by low product prices, high operating expenses, or inefficient production.

11. EBITDA
    - Earnings Before Interest Taxes Depreciation and Amortization. Measures earnings available for debt repayment.

APPENDICES

Appendix E: Scorecard...continued

From the cash-flow statement

Repayment capacity
- shows the borrower's (i.e., your) ability to repay term debts on time. It includes non-farm income and so is not a measure of business performance alone.

12. <u>Capital debt repayment capacity</u>
    - measures the amount generated from farm and non-farm sources, to cover debt repayment and capital replacement.

13. <u>Capital debt repayment margin</u>
    - is the amount of money remaining after all operating expenses, taxes, family living costs, and scheduled debt payments have been made. It's really the money left, after paying all bills, that is available for purchasing or financing new machinery, equipment, land or livestock.

14. <u>Replacement margin</u>
    - the amount of income remaining after paying principal and interest on term loans and unfunded (cash) capital purchases.

15. <u>Term-debt coverage ratio</u>
    - tells whether your business produced enough income to cover all intermediate and long-term debt payments. A ratio of less than 1.0 indicates that the business had to liquidate inventories, run up open accounts, borrow money, or sell assets to make scheduled payments.

16. <u>Replacement margin coverage ratio</u>
    - A ratio under 1.0 indicates that you did not generate enough income to cover term debt payments and unfunded capital purchases.

From all the financial statements

Financial efficiency
- shows how effectively your business uses assets to generate income. Past performance of the business could well indicate potential future accomplishments.

It also answers the questions:
- Are you using every available asset to its fullest potential?

- What are the effects of production, purchasing, pricing, financing and marketing decisions on gross income?

17. <u>Asset-turnover rate</u>
    - measures efficiency in using capital. You could think of it as capital productivity. Generating a high level of production with a low level of capital investment will give a high asset-turnover rate. If, on the other hand, the turnover is low you will want to explore methods to use the capital invested much more efficiently or sell some low-return investments. (It could mean getting rid of that swamp and ledge on the back 40 and getting something that produces income.)

The last four ratios show how Gross Farm Income is used. The sum of the four equals 100% (of Gross Farm Income).

18. <u>Operating-expense ratio</u>
    - shows the proportion of farm income that is used to pay operating expenses, not including principal or interest.

19. <u>Depreciation-expense ratio</u>
    - indicates how fast the business wears out capital. It tells what proportion of farm income is needed to maintain the capital used by the business.

20. <u>Interest-expense ratio</u>
    - shows how much of gross farm income is used to pay for interest on borrowed capital.

21. <u>Net farm income ratio</u>
    - compares profit to gross farm income. It shows how much is left after all farm expenses, except for unpaid labor and management, are paid.

Appendix E: Scorecard...continued

Liquidity

1. Current ratio
   = Total current farm assets
   / Total current farm liabilities

2. Working capital
   = Total current farm assets
   − Total current farm liabilities

3. Working capital to gross revenues
   = Working capital / Gross farm income

Solvency (market)

4. Farm debt-to-asset ratio
   = Total farm liabilities / Total farm assets

5. Farm equity-to-asset ratio
   = Farm net worth / Total farm assets

6. Farm debt-to-equity ratio
   = Total farm liabilities / Farm net worth

Profitability

7. Net farm income
   = Gross cash farm income
   − Total cash farm expense
   + / − Inventory changes
   − Depreciation

8. Rate of return on farm assets
   = Return on farm assets / Average farm assets
       Return on farm assets
       = Net farm income
       + Farm interest
       − Value of operator labor & management

9. Rate of return on farm equity
   = Return on farm equity / Average farm net worth
       Return on farm equity
       = Net farm income
       − Value of operator labor & management

10. Operating profit margin
    = Return on farm assets
    / Value of farm production
        Value of farm production
        = Gross cash farm income
        + / − Inv change of crops, mkt lvst,
            brdg lvst & other income items
        − Feeder livestock purchased
        − Purchased feed

11. EBITDA
    = Net farm income
    + Interest expense
    + Depreciation and amortization expense

Repayment capacity

12. Capital debt repayment capacity
    = Net farm income
    + Depreciation
    + Net non-farm income
    − Family living & income taxes
    + Interest expense on term loans

13. Capital debt repayment margin
    = Capital debt repayment capacity
    − Scheduled principal & interest on term loans*

14. Replacement margin
    = Capital debt repayment margin
    − Unfunded (cash) capital replacement allowance

15. Term debt coverage ratio
    = Capital debt repayment capacity
    / Scheduled principal & interest on term loans*

16. Replacement margin coverage ratio
    = Capital debt repayment capacity
    / (Scheduled principal & interest on term loans*
    + Unfunded capital replacement allowance)

Financial efficiency

17. Asset-turnover ratio
    = Value of farm production
    / Average farm assets

18. Operating-expense ratio
    = (Total farm operating expense excluding interest
    − Depreciation)
    / Gross farm income

19. Depreciation-expense ratio
    = Depreciation
    / Gross farm income

20. Interest-expense ratio
    = Farm interest
    / Gross farm income

21. Net farm income ratio
    = Net farm income
    / Gross farm income

Includes payments on capital leases

Developed by:
K. Becker,
D. Kauppila,
G. Rogers,
R. Parsons,
D. Nordquist,
and R. Craven

APPENDICES

Appendix F: 2015 Farm Business Management Report Summary

Financial Summary
Southwestern Minnesota Farm Business Management Association
(Farms Sorted By Gross Farm Income)

	Avg. Of All Farms	100,001 - 250,000	250,001 - 500,000	500,001 - 1,000,000	1,000,001- 2,000,000	Over 2,000,000
Number of farms	103	9	29	37	18	7
Income Statement						
Gross cash farm income	997,581	182,457	381,345	694,546	1,237,081	5,983,695
Total cash farm expense	798,226	115,863	271,898	537,458	901,714	5,297,713
Net cash farm income	199,355	66,593	109,446	157,088	335,367	685,983
Inventory change	-68,430	-15,764	2,822	-25,482	-154,161	-459,898
Depreciation	-73,028	-24,836	-43,124	-65,484	-109,640	-232,906
Net farm income from operations	57,898	25,994	69,145	66,122	71,566	-6,821
Gain or loss on capital sales	1,944	214	5,102	385	758	3,201
Average net farm income	59,841	26,208	74,247	66,507	72,324	-3,620
Median net farm income	56,456	25,037	78,581	56,456	72,817	9,396
Profitability (cost)						
Rate of return on assets	1.2 %	1.2 %	3.7 %	1.5 %	1.2 %	-0.9 %
Rate of return on equity	0.0 %	0.8 %	3.5 %	0.7 %	0.1 %	-3.8 %
Operating profit margin	3.8 %	5.6 %	12.8 %	5.2 %	4.1 %	-2.3 %
Asset turnover rate	30.7 %	21.8 %	28.7 %	28.7 %	28.5 %	38.3 %
Liquidity & Repayment (end of year)						
Current assets	842,214	236,093	406,878	854,508	1,086,563	3,074,117
Current liabilities	386,374	84,240	170,557	274,314	587,011	1,901,216
Current ratio	2.18	2.80	2.39	3.12	1.85	1.62
Working capital	455,840	151,853	236,321	580,195	499,552	1,172,901
Working capital to gross inc	48.5 %	89.1 %	60.2 %	84.3 %	45.6 %	21.3 %
Term debt coverage ratio	0.89	1.74	1.15	0.94	0.92	0.45
Replacement coverage ratio	0.61	1.07	0.81	0.57	0.65	0.36
Term debt to EBITDA	2.59	1.73	2.18	2.05	2.53	4.67
Solvency (end of year at market)						
Number of farms	103	9	29	37	18	7
Total assets	3,982,242	1,846,184	2,697,140	4,080,458	4,964,992	10,505,709
Total liabilities	1,402,216	410,416	875,297	1,289,424	1,893,676	4,704,816
Net worth	2,580,027	1,435,768	1,821,843	2,791,033	3,071,316	5,800,894
Total net worth change	46,041	47,689	22,502	17,986	131,790	76,608
Farm debt to asset ratio	37 %	25 %	35 %	34 %	41 %	45 %
Total debt to asset ratio	35 %	22 %	32 %	32 %	38 %	45 %
Change in total net worth %	2 %	3 %	1 %	1 %	4 %	1 %
Nonfarm Information						
Net nonfarm income	36,083	32,236	40,356	39,791	30,499	1,731
Farms reporting living expenses	32	3	10	9	6	1
Total family living expense	64,621	-	57,265	79,869	65,284	-
Total living, invest, cap. purch	158,913	-	127,226	205,503	173,064	-
Crop Acres						
Total crop acres	940	204	541	902	1,218	3,421
Total crop acres owned	226	70	203	229	289	439
Total crop acres cash rented	661	134	281	617	864	2,900
Total crop acres share rented	53	-	56	56	66	82
Machinery value per crop acre	520	712	536	563	640	328

Appendix F: Farm Report...continued

Financial Summary
Southwestern Minnesota Farm Business Management Association
(Farms Sorted By Farm Type)

	Avg. Of All Farms	Crop	Hog	Crop and Hog	Crop and Beef	Other
Number of farms	103	64	5	5	5	19
Income Statement						
Gross cash farm income	997,581	845,947	4,117,015	787,788	764,520	502,972
Total cash farm expense	798,226	662,728	3,728,644	629,557	624,939	369,101
Net cash farm income	199,355	183,219	388,372	158,230	139,581	133,872
Inventory change	-68,430	-33,099	-517,165	-111,099	-54,079	-11,049
Depreciation	-73,028	-73,748	-147,465	-69,388	-70,556	-43,554
Net farm income from operations	57,898	76,372	-276,258	-22,257	14,946	79,268
Gain or loss on capital sales	1,944	2,257	3,504	84	2,577	1,452
Average net farm income	59,841	78,629	-272,755	-22,173	17,524	80,720
Median net farm income	56,456	63,425	-332,361	15,030	-3,070	77,416
Profitability (cost)						
Rate of return on assets	1.2 %	1.8 %	-5.9 %	-0.6 %	-0.5 %	4.7 %
Rate of return on equity	0.0 %	1.0 %	-11.1 %	-4.2 %	-2.4 %	5.3 %
Operating profit margin	3.8 %	5.3 %	-23.8 %	-3.6 %	-2.4 %	16.1 %
Asset turnover rate	30.7 %	34.5 %	25.0 %	16.7 %	22.9 %	29.1 %
Liquidity & Repayment (end of year)						
Current assets	842,214	870,382	2,105,295	773,654	860,339	425,504
Current liabilities	386,374	359,642	1,132,415	524,955	381,272	288,675
Current ratio	2.18	2.42	1.86	1.47	2.26	1.47
Working capital	455,840	510,740	972,880	248,699	479,067	136,828
Working capital to gross inc	48.5 %	62.4 %	26.1 %	34.9 %	62.6 %	28.0 %
Term debt coverage ratio	0.89	1.23	-0.93	0.23	0.28	0.97
Replacement coverage ratio	0.61	0.78	-0.70	0.23	0.17	0.78
Term debt to EBITDA	2.59	2.11	-10.11	6.20	4.90	2.43
Solvency (end of year at market)						
Number of farms	103	64	5	5	5	19
Total assets	3,982,242	3,870,052	7,296,911	4,573,766	4,216,253	2,655,903
Total liabilities	1,402,216	1,330,507	3,112,684	2,028,649	1,523,071	1,027,750
Net worth	2,580,027	2,539,545	4,184,228	2,545,116	2,693,182	1,628,153
Total net worth change	46,041	44,475	-98,709	18,213	-171,584	102,668
Farm debt to asset ratio	37 %	36 %	44 %	48 %	38 %	44 %
Total debt to asset ratio	35 %	34 %	43 %	44 %	36 %	39 %
Change in total net worth %	2 %	2 %	-2 %	1 %	-6 %	7 %
Nonfarm Information						
Net nonfarm income	36,083	39,446	2,483	54,055	20,177	31,579
Farms reporting living expenses	32	18	1	1	3	8
Total family living expense	64,621	59,535	-	-	-	75,376
Total living, invest, cap. purch	158,913	168,341	-	-	-	115,676
Crop Acres						
Total crop acres	940	1,132	1,168	728	996	393
Total crop acres owned	226	242	302	417	292	87
Total crop acres cash rented	661	827	836	312	552	297
Total crop acres share rented	53	63	30	-	152	9
Machinery value per crop acre	520	478	646	634	531	651

2015 Annual Report   RankEm © University of Minnesota

APPENDICES

Appendix G: Net Present Value (NPV) Table

Net Present Value: Present Value of $1.00 to be Paid in the Future

This table shows how much $1.00, to be paid at the end of the various periods in the future, is currently worth, with interest at different rates, compounded annually.

To use this table, find the vertical column under your interest rate (or cost of capital). Then find the horizontal row corresponding to the number of years it will take to receive the payment. The point at which the column and the row intersect is your present value of $1.00. You can multiply this value by the number of dollars you expect to receive in order to find the present value of the total amount you expect. Reference: U.S. Chamber of Commerce.

Years	3.0%	3.5%	4.0%	4.5%
1	$0.970874	$0.966184	$0.961538	$0.956938
2	$0.942596	$0.933511	$0.924556	$0.915730
3	$0.915142	$0.901943	$0.888996	$0.876297
4	$0.888487	$0.871442	$0.854804	$0.838561
5	$0.862609	$0.841973	$0.821927	$0.802451
6	$0.837484	$0.813501	$0.790315	$0.767896
7	$0.813092	$0.785991	$0.759918	$0.734828
8	$0.789409	$0.759412	$0.730690	$0.703185
9	$0.766417	$0.733731	$0.702587	$0.672904
10	$0.744094	$0.708919	$0.675564	$0.643928
11	$0.722421	$0.684946	$0.649581	$0.616199
12	$0.701380	$0.661783	$0.624597	$0.589664
13	$0.680951	$0.639404	$0.600574	$0.564272
14	$0.661118	$0.617782	$0.577475	$0.539973
15	$0.641862	$0.596891	$0.555265	$0.516720
16	$0.623167	$0.576706	$0.533908	$0.494469
17	$0.605016	$0.557204	$0.513373	$0.473176
18	$0.587395	$0.538361	$0.493628	$0.452800
19	$0.570286	$0.520156	$0.474642	$0.433302
20	$0.553676	$0.502566	$0.456387	$0.414643
21	$0.537549	$0.485571	$0.438834	$0.396787
22	$0.521893	$0.469151	$0.421955	$0.379701
23	$0.506692	$0.453286	$0.405726	$0.363350
24	$0.491934	$0.437957	$0.390121	$0.347703
25	$0.477606	$0.423147	$0.375117	$0.332731

Years	5.0%	5.5%	6.0%	6.5%
1	$0.952381	$0.947867	$0.943396	$0.938967
2	$0.907029	$0.898452	$0.889996	$0.881659
3	$0.863838	$0.851614	$0.839619	$0.827849
4	$0.822702	$0.807217	$0.792094	$0.777323
5	$0.783526	$0.765134	$0.747258	$0.729881
6	$0.746215	$0.725246	$0.704961	$0.685334
7	$0.710681	$0.687437	$0.665057	$0.643506
8	$0.676839	$0.651599	$0.627412	$0.604231
9	$0.644609	$0.617629	$0.591898	$0.567353
10	$0.613913	$0.585431	$0.558395	$0.532726
11	$0.584679	$0.554911	$0.526788	$0.500212
12	$0.556837	$0.525982	$0.496969	$0.469683
13	$0.530321	$0.498561	$0.468839	$0.441017
14	$0.505068	$0.472569	$0.442301	$0.414100
15	$0.481017	$0.447933	$0.417265	$0.388827
16	$0.458112	$0.424581	$0.393646	$0.365095
17	$0.436297	$0.402447	$0.371364	$0.342813
18	$0.415521	$0.381466	$0.350344	$0.321890
19	$0.395734	$0.361579	$0.330513	$0.302244
20	$0.376889	$0.342729	$0.311805	$0.283797
21	$0.358942	$0.324862	$0.294155	$0.266476
22	$0.341850	$0.307926	$0.277505	$0.250212
23	$0.325571	$0.291873	$0.261797	$0.234941
24	$0.310068	$0.276657	$0.246979	$0.220602
25	$0.295303	$0.262234	$0.232999	$0.207138

Appendix G: NPV Table...continued

Years	7.0%	7.5%	8.0%	8.5%
1	$0.934579	$0.930233	$0.925926	$0.921659
2	$0.873439	$0.865333	$0.857339	$0.849455
3	$0.816298	$0.804961	$0.793832	$0.782908
4	$0.762895	$0.748801	$0.735030	$0.721574
5	$0.712986	$0.696559	$0.680583	$0.665045
6	$0.666342	$0.647962	$0.630170	$0.612945
7	$0.622750	$0.602755	$0.583490	$0.564926
8	$0.582009	$0.560702	$0.540269	$0.520669
9	$0.543934	$0.521583	$0.500249	$0.479880
10	$0.508349	$0.485194	$0.463193	$0.442285
11	$0.475093	$0.451343	$0.428883	$0.407636
12	$0.444012	$0.419854	$0.397114	$0.375702
13	$0.414964	$0.390562	$0.367698	$0.346269
14	$0.387817	$0.363313	$0.340461	$0.319142
15	$0.362446	$0.337966	$0.315242	$0.294140
16	$0.338735	$0.314387	$0.291890	$0.271097
17	$0.316574	$0.292453	$0.270269	$0.249859
18	$0.295864	$0.272049	$0.250249	$0.230285
19	$0.276508	$0.253069	$0.231712	$0.212244
20	$0.258419	$0.235413	$0.214548	$0.195616
21	$0.241513	$0.218989	$0.198656	$0.180292
22	$0.225713	$0.203711	$0.183941	$0.166167
23	$0.210947	$0.189498	$0.170315	$0.153150
24	$0.197147	$0.176277	$0.157699	$0.141152
25	$0.184249	$0.163979	$0.146018	$0.130094

Years	9.0%	9.5%	10.0%	10.5%
1	$0.917431	$0.913242	$0.909091	$0.904977
2	$0.841680	$0.834011	$0.826446	$0.818984
3	$0.772183	$0.761654	$0.751315	$0.741162
4	$0.708425	$0.695574	$0.683013	$0.670735
5	$0.649931	$0.635228	$0.620921	$0.607000
6	$0.596267	$0.580117	$0.564474	$0.549321
7	$0.547034	$0.529787	$0.513158	$0.497123
8	$0.501866	$0.483824	$0.466507	$0.449885
9	$0.460428	$0.441848	$0.424098	$0.407136
10	$0.422411	$0.403514	$0.385543	$0.368449
11	$0.387533	$0.368506	$0.350494	$0.333438
12	$0.355535	$0.336535	$0.318631	$0.301754
13	$0.326179	$0.307338	$0.289664	$0.273080
14	$0.299246	$0.280674	$0.263331	$0.247132
15	$0.274538	$0.256323	$0.239392	$0.223648
16	$0.251870	$0.234085	$0.217629	$0.202397
17	$0.231073	$0.213777	$0.197845	$0.183164
18	$0.211994	$0.195230	$0.179859	$0.165760
19	$0.194490	$0.178292	$0.163508	$0.150009
20	$0.178431	$0.162824	$0.148644	$0.135755
21	$0.163698	$0.148697	$0.135131	$0.122855
22	$0.150182	$0.135797	$0.122846	$0.111181
23	$0.137781	$0.124015	$0.111678	$0.100616
24	$0.126405	$0.113256	$0.101526	$0.091055
25	$0.115968	$0.103430	$0.092296	$0.082403

Years	11.0%	11.5%	12.0%	12.5%
1	$0.900901	$0.896861	$0.892857	$0.888889
2	$0.811622	$0.804360	$0.797194	$0.790123
3	$0.731191	$0.721399	$0.711780	$0.702332
4	$0.658731	$0.646994	$0.635518	$0.624295
5	$0.593451	$0.580264	$0.567427	$0.554929
6	$0.534641	$0.520416	$0.506631	$0.493270
7	$0.481658	$0.466741	$0.452349	$0.438462
8	$0.433926	$0.418602	$0.403883	$0.389744
9	$0.390925	$0.375428	$0.360610	$0.346439
10	$0.352184	$0.336706	$0.321973	$0.307946
11	$0.317283	$0.301979	$0.287476	$0.273730
12	$0.285841	$0.270833	$0.256675	$0.243315
13	$0.257514	$0.242900	$0.229174	$0.216280
14	$0.231995	$0.217847	$0.204620	$0.192249
15	$0.209004	$0.195379	$0.182696	$0.170888
16	$0.188292	$0.175227	$0.163122	$0.151901
17	$0.169633	$0.157155	$0.145644	$0.135023
18	$0.152822	$0.140946	$0.130040	$0.120020
19	$0.137678	$0.126409	$0.116107	$0.106685
20	$0.124034	$0.113371	$0.103667	$0.094831
21	$0.111742	$0.101678	$0.092560	$0.084294
22	$0.100669	$0.091191	$0.082643	$0.074928
23	$0.090693	$0.081786	$0.073788	$0.066603
24	$0.081705	$0.073351	$0.065882	$0.059202
25	$0.073608	$0.065785	$0.058823	$0.052624

Years	13.0%	13.5%	14.0%	14.5%
1	$0.884956	$0.881057	$0.877193	$0.873362
2	$0.783147	$0.776262	$0.769468	$0.762762
3	$0.693050	$0.683931	$0.674972	$0.666168
4	$0.613319	$0.602583	$0.592080	$0.581806
5	$0.542760	$0.530910	$0.519369	$0.508127
6	$0.480319	$0.467762	$0.455587	$0.443779
7	$0.425061	$0.412125	$0.399637	$0.387580
8	$0.376160	$0.363106	$0.350559	$0.338498
9	$0.332885	$0.319917	$0.307508	$0.295631
10	$0.294588	$0.281865	$0.269744	$0.258193
11	$0.260698	$0.248339	$0.236617	$0.225496
12	$0.230706	$0.218801	$0.207559	$0.196940
13	$0.204165	$0.192776	$0.182069	$0.172000
14	$0.180677	$0.169847	$0.159710	$0.150218
15	$0.159891	$0.149645	$0.140096	$0.131195
16	$0.141496	$0.131846	$0.122892	$0.114581
17	$0.125218	$0.116164	$0.107800	$0.100071
18	$0.110812	$0.102347	$0.094561	$0.087398
19	$0.098064	$0.090173	$0.082948	$0.076330
20	$0.086782	$0.079448	$0.072762	$0.066664
21	$0.076798	$0.069998	$0.063826	$0.058222
22	$0.067963	$0.061672	$0.055988	$0.050849
23	$0.060144	$0.054337	$0.049112	$0.044409
24	$0.053225	$0.047874	$0.043081	$0.038785
25	$0.047102	$0.042180	$0.037790	$0.033874

APPENDICES

Appendix H: Sample Livestock Enterprise Budget

Sauk County Livestock Enterprise Budget

EXPECTED REVENUE

Expected market weight: _____ x expected market price/lb: _____ = $_____/head

COSTS

Variable costs per head during the feeding period:

Cost or initial value of animal	$_____/head
Feed costs	
Purchased feed cost	$_____/head
Estimated value of homegrown feeds	$_____/head
Veterinary and medicine costs	$_____/head
Livestock supplies	$_____/head
Marketing costs	$_____/head
Hauling	$_____/head
Death loss ____% x expected revenue/head	$_____/head
Other variable costs	$_____/head
Total Variable Costs	$_____/head
Return above Variable Costs (*Expected Revenue – Total Variable Costs*)	$_____/head

Overhead (Fixed) costs per head during the feeding period:

Housing cost (daily "yardage" charge x # of days on-feed)	$_____/head
Machinery and equipment	$_____/head
Labor cost (Estimated labor hours x reasonable hourly wage)	$_____/head
Total Overhead Costs	$_____/head
TOTAL COST (*Total Variable Costs + Total Overhead Costs*)	$_____/head

BREAKEVEN MARKET PRICE TO COVER VARIABLE COSTS $_____/pound
(*Total Variable Cost divided by Expected Market Weight*)

BREAKEVEN MARKET PRICE TO COVER ALL COSTS $_____/pound
(*Total Cost divided by Expected Market Weight*)

NET RETURN   (*Expected Revenue – Total Cost*) $_____/head

Appendix H: Livestock Budget...continued

Explanations for Sauk County Livestock Enterprise Budget

Expected Revenue – We need to come up with an estimate of what you expect your animal will be worth at the time it goes to market. To do that, we need to estimate what the animal will weigh when finished then multiply that weight by the price you could expect to receive in the commercial market for a finished animal. Market prices can be found on the market news pages of any of the Wisconsin agricultural newspapers or on the web at: http://www2.communitybankers.org/WKLYSUM.txt

Costs

Variable costs – Costs that are directly related to production and change as production changes. In a livestock enterprise, these are costs that you would not have if you were not raising livestock. The cost of feeder animals, feed costs, animal health expenses, supplies, and livestock hauling are all examples of variable costs.

Cost or initial value of animal – We need to assign an estimate of the value of the animal at the beginning of the feeding period. To determine a value for the animal, we take the actual weight multiplied by the market price for feeder animals of a similar weight. Market prices can be found on the market news pages of any of the Wisconsin ag newspapers or on the web at: http://www2.communitybankers.org/

Feed Costs

Purchased feed cost – The actual cost of any feed purchased during the feeding period allocated on a per-head basis.

Estimated value of homegrown feeds – Keep track of how much homegrown feed is being used in the livestock enterprise each day and estimate the fair market value of that feed. If livestock are on pasture, a value should be placed on that forage too. An example: if you are feeding each steer seven pounds of corn per day (or .125 bushel) and the current market price of corn is $2.10 per bushel, we know that the steer is eating $.26 worth of corn per day. ($2.10 x .125 bu = $.26). If the steer is also getting 12 pounds of dry matter per day from pasture and that forage is worth $.02/lb., we need to add another $.24 to the value of homegrown feed. Total up the value of all of the homegrown feed consumed in the livestock enterprise during the feeding period.

Veterinary and medicine costs – Include vet bills, vaccinations, dewormer, implants, antibiotics, etc.

Livestock supplies – Include ear tags, other supplies, cost or value of bedding used for animal, etc.

Hauling – Include an actual or estimated charge for hauling the animal to market.

Overhead (Fixed) Costs – These are costs that are not directly related to production and do not change as production changes. For example, if you own a livestock building you will have all of the costs associated with the building such as real estate taxes, insurance, depreciation, and interest on the mortgage payment whether you have livestock in the building or not.

Housing cost – Rather than trying to figure out the actual costs of housing, it may be simpler to use a daily rental rate known as "yardage" to estimate housing cost. For beef cattle, the yardage charge is typically $.20-.35/head/day. For swine finishing facilities, the charge is typically $.04-.10/head/day.

Machinery and equipment – Include the actual cost or a reasonable charge for the use of any equipment such as a skid steer, manure spreader, or feed mixer used in the livestock enterprise.

APPENDICES

Appendix I: Using the QuickBooks Budget Function

QuickBooks has a budgeting feature that is quite handy. It will automatically list all your accounts, and allow you to budget by month and also by either class or job. An advantage of using the budget program is that the math and formulas will be trouble-free, and you can expect all of the totals to be correct. This can circumvent the invariable formula errors that can be hard to avoid when using a spreadsheet program. The QuickBooks budget feature is limited in that it will not account for loan activity, or capital purchases and sales. It also is very clumsy in viewing the entire budget as you build it. It will only show your column totals (month or class) in the report views, and not as you are entering the data.

To set up your budget in QuickBooks, click on the Company> Planning and Budgeting>Set Up Budgets tab. When the screen opens follow the prompts to set up the year and other details. Select a Profit and Loss budget. We recommend that you choose Create Budget From Scratch rather than Use Auto-fill From Previous Data. This allows you to make new decisions about each budget item, which rarely stay exactly the same from year to year.

The empty budget screen will show up with your chart of accounts on the side and months across the top. You have the option of entering a number in the first month column and having the number auto-fill across all the months (use this for incomes or expenses that are the same for each period, such as mortgage payment or phone bills, etc.). If you don't want to auto-fill, you will put numbers into each month and they will automatically add together to create the first column, Annual Total.

If you would like to budget using either class or jobs, you must choose those options as you set the budget up. When using either, in the budget template a drop down window allows you to select a class or job. You budget for each account for each month for each class or job. It is easiest to budget by class or job using an Excel spreadsheet rather than the QuickBooks budget function if you are doing a first time budget, or are not too sure of your numbers.

QuickBooks will not allow you to view your entire budget by class or job while you are building it. You can only see this detail as a report. This will be tedious if you want to modify or play with a variety of numbers. Those budgeting for the whole farm by month will be able to see the entire budget in one screen in the budgeting function, but will not see column totals.

If you prefer to only do an annual or quarterly budget, fill in your budget numbers for the first month of each longer period. For example, for an annual budget fill in annual numbers for each account in the January column. This way, when you run a report for the budget compared to the actual income and expenses for the year, the budget numbers will show up throughout the year. For quarterly budgets, enter the quarterly numbers in each of January, April, July, and October. In viewing these budgets using more than a monthly period, you will have to modify the report once it is generated to get rid of the blank columns.

To view your budget, go to Reports> Budgets> Budget Overview (or Budget to Actual, once you get into your reporting year). It takes a few minutes to generate the budget report. Click on Modify Report, then Display Columns By and select Year, Total Only, or Quarter, as appropriate. If you have chart of account items that you don't use, to view a clean budget report you will have to click on Advanced in the modify report tab. Here you click on Non-Zero Rows and Non-Zero Columns. This will reduce your budget to only those items that you have entered numbers for.

Once you have set up your budget in QuickBooks, you will want to export the completed budget into Excel so that you can include at the bottom additional cash flows which are described in Chapter Nineteen. The activity relative to these will not be generated in QuickBooks budget to actual reports and will have to be added by hand from your balance sheet.

Appendix J: Financial Skills Trouble Shooting Concepts

Financial Skills Troubleshooting Concepts

Question	Tool	Concept	Skill	Key Proficiency Areas
What have you got?	Balance Sheet	Net Worth	Identify assets and liabilities and their relationship to each other	Balance sheet prepared annually; reflect cost and market valuations ; document financial progress
What are you earning?	Income Statement	Net Income	Basic bookkeeping	Records updated monthly, reconcile bank statements; comparison to budget to see warning signs and make changes early
How much money do you have on hand?	Statement of Cash Flows	Working Capital	Balancing checkbook	Cash Flow Budgets created at beginning of year; monthly comparison actual vs. budget; policy for investment and withdrawal of capital (minimum capital levels and owner's draw)
Are you good at earning money?	Income per Unit or Cost per Unit	Efficiency	Performance comparison	Identify key performance measures and ratios; Farm Financial Standards Council Sweet 16; Benchmarking and comparison to industry standards
Should you buy or rent?	Breakeven Analysis	Return on Investment	Budget Analysis/ Penciling it out	Enterprise profitability; optimizing capital acquisition decisions; partial budget techniques to determine investments and their overall benefit

The Farm Credit Council | 50 F Street, N.W., Suite 900, Washington, DC 20001 | 202-626-8710

RESOURCES

The following resources supplement the information in this book. Those items with web links can be easily accessed from our website at mosesorganic.org, search for Farm Finances.

Benchmarks of Yields and Prices

Iowa State Ag Decision Maker, Online data for benchmarking www.extension.iastate.edu/agdm/index.html

MN Center for Farm Financial Management generates benchmark and summary reports for crop, livestock and dairy. www.cffm.umn.edu

Selected Alternative Agriculture Financial Benchmarks, Iowa State University Extension, 2012 www.extension.iastate.edu/agdm/wholefarm/html/c3-65.html

USDA-Agricultural Marketing Service, bi-weekly updates on current agricultural commodity prices. www.ams.usda.gov/services/market-research

Wis. Center for Dairy Profitability, Benchmarks for dairy farms, both organic and non-organic, including grazing operations. cdp.wisc.edu

Wis. Dairy Ratio Benchmarking Tool (WisDRBT), Allows you to compare your financial ratios to your farm's past performance, and do a comparative analysis with the industry. dairymgt.info/benchmark/index.php

Books

Building a Sustainable Business**, 2003. 280 pp. A free book from SARE with worksheets on goal settings, determining markets, business planning, mapping out strategies to take on new opportunities etc. Download at www.sare.org/Learning-Center/Books/Building-a-Sustainable-Business

Farm to Market Handbook, Janet Hurst, Voyageur Press, 2014, 176 pp. Guides to markets available to small farmers. Also developing a realistic marketing plan, food laws and regulations and insider tips on how to be a successful businessperson.

Farms with a Future: Creating and Growing a Sustainable Farm Business. Rebecca Thistlethwaite, 2013. 304 pp. Chelsea Green Publishing. A discussion of business management for long-term sustainability using numerous farmers' best practices as examples.

The Lean Farm: How to Minimize Waste, Increase Efficiency, and Maximize Value and Profits with Less Work** Ben Hartman, 2015, 256 pp. Chelsea Green Publishing, Practical, systems-based approach for a more sustainable farming operation.

Making Your Small Farm Profitable. Ron Macher. 1999. Storey Publishing. Down-to-earth advice on planning, farming, and marketing to make your farm profitable.

Market Farming Success: The Business of Growing and Selling Local Food, Lynn Byczynski, 2006. Chelsea Green Pub. 275 pp. An insider's guide to market gardening and farming for those in the business of growing and selling food, flowers, herbs, or plants.

The Organic Farmer's Business Handbook: A Complete Guide to Managing Finances, Crops and Staff and Making a Profit** Richard Wiswall, 2009. 254 pp. Chelsea Green Publishing, Companion CD has electronic templates to create enterprise budgets and farm financials.

Record Keeping for Organic Growers, Kristine Swaren & Rowena Hopkins, 2010. 116 pp, Canadina Organic Growers, templates for organic certification record keeping.

Soil Sisters: A Toolkit for Women Farmers**, Lisa Kivirist, 2015, New Society Publishers, 256 pp. Practical considerations from a woman's perspective, covering business planning to tool use and integrating children and family in farm operations.

Starting and Running Your Own Small Farm Business. Sarah Beth Aubrey. 2007. 176 pp. Storey Publishing. From financial plans to advertising budgets, Web design and food service wholesalers.

NOTE: Books with ** may be purchased from MOSES, call 715-778-5775 or visit mosesorganic.org

Business Planning

AgPlan U of MN Center for Farm Financial Management, 2010. Free business planning app agplan.umn.edu

Agricultural Diversification Compass: A Guide to Choosing New Directions for Your Farm, Minn. Department of Agriculture, 2011. 12-page booklet. www.mda.state.mn.us/protecting/sustainable/mfo/mfo-compass.aspx

Resources...continued

Developing Your Business Plan, video series, U of MN Center for Farm Financial Management, 2013, taatrain.cffm.umn.edu/BizPlanAgPlan/Default.aspx?SectionID=234 612-625-1964

Getting Started in Farming: An Introduction to Farm Business Planning, National Center for Appropriate Technology, free, eight-lesson online course for visioning a successful farming business and developing a business plan. northcarolina.ncat.org

HMI (Holistic Management International) Resources, trainings and free downloadable tools for farm planning and management www.holisticmanagement.org 505-842-5252

Enterprise Budgeting Tools

Ag Decision Maker website, Iowa State University. Numerous templates for various enterprise budgets. www.extension.iastate.edu/agdm/index.html

Ag Risk-Farm Management Budget Library, A one-stop searchable database for crop and livestock enterprise budget information, designed to provide online access to current enterprise budget information and software from throughout the U.S. agrisk.umn.edu/Budgets

Enterprise Crop Budgets, UW Center for Dairy Profitability, Excel budgets for corn, soybeans, alfalfa, small grains) cdp.wisc.edu/crop%20enterprise.htm

Fresh Market Vegetable Budgets, UW Extension, Sample and fillable Excel budgets for a wide diversity of fresh market vegetables, from asparagus to winter squash. www.uwex.edu/ces/farmteam/budgets/fresh-market-vegetable.cfm

Small-scale Livestock Enterprise, Purdue University. Publications and online spreadsheets to help assess cattle, sheep, goat and turkey operations. ag.purdue.edu/agecon/Pages/Livestock-Enterprise.aspx

Veggie Compass, UW-CIAS. You enter cost, sales, and labor data, and the Compass spreadsheet will calculate cost of production for each crop and the profitability of each market channel. www.veggiecompass.com/

Farm Transfer

A Legal Guide to the Business of Farming in Vermont. University of VT. Updated Sept 2015, can be downloaded in 9 chapters. www.uvm.edu/farmtransfer/?Page=legal-guide.html

Preparing to Transfer the Farm Business, U. of MN Extension, 2013, 30-page fact sheet series. www.cffm.umn.edu/publications/pubs/farmmgttopics/transferringthefarm-series.pdf

Managing Debt to Prepare for a Farm Transfer, FLAG, 2006, 12-page booklet. www.flaginc.org/wp-content/uploads/2013/03/EstatePlanningBooklet2006.pdf

Financial Statement and Budget Templates

12 Steps to Cash Flow Budgeting, Iowa State University, 2014, www.extension.iastate.edu/agdm/wholefarm/html/c3-15.html

AgPlan Financial Spreadsheet. U of MN Center for Farm Financial Management, 2016. Downloadable Excel spreadsheet to develop a balance sheet, income statements, and cash flows. farmanswers.org/Library/Record/agplan_financial_spreadsheet

Balance Sheet Spreadsheet, downloadable Excel. KSU, 2016. www.agmanager.info/balance-sheet-spreadsheet

Basic Farm Accounting and Record Keeping Templates, National Center for Appropriate Technology (NCAT) 2012, Downloadable Excel spreadsheet with templates for budgets, cash flows, balance sheets and income statements. farmanswers.org/Library/Record/basic_farm_accounting_and_record_keeping_temp

Cash Flow (Budget) Spreadsheet KSU, 2016, downloadable Excel. www.agmanager.info/cash-flow-sheet-spreadsheet

Farm and Ranch Account Book, Oklahoma State University, 82 pp. printable pdf workbook for hand record keeping. agecon.okstate.edu/farmbook

General Financial Management Resources

Farm Finance Scorecard, Univ. of VT, 2014. PDF form listing Farm Financial Standards Council ratio definitions and benchmarks www.cffm.umn.edu/Publications/pubs/FarmMgtTopics/FarmFinanceScorecard.pdf

Growing Farm Profits online course, Southern SAWG. Developed for farmers to improve the profitability of their farms. Videos, worksheets, presentations and documents. Includes financial and non-financial management info and tracking tools. www.ssawg.org/growing-farm-profits/

Interpreting Financial Statements and Measures, U of MN Center for Farm Financial Management. 2009. Resources to help you learn how to interpret your financial statements. ifsam.cffm.umn.edu

Resources...continued

MN Center for Farm Financial Management, U. of MN, provides educational programs and software tools for farms. www.cffm.umn.edu 800-234-1111

MN State Colleges and University Farm Business Management, Farm business management classes and assistance. fbm.mnscu.edu 218-894-5163

Goal Setting and Planning

Agricultural Marketing Resource Center, USDA national website for value-added agriculture, wide diversity of information on idea assessment and feasibility analysis. www.agmrc.org/business-development/starting-a-business

Exploring the Small Farm Dream Course and Workbook, New England Small Farm Institute, 80-page workbook and course, www.smallfarm.org/main/for_service_providers/exploring_the_small_farm_dream

Evaluating a Farming Enterprise, ATTRA, updated 2011, 20-page fact sheet, attra.ncat.org/attra-pub/summaries/summary.php?pub=277, 800-346-9140

Growing Farms: Successful Whole Farm Management Planning Book, Oregon State University Extension. 2011, 44-page workbook. catalog.extension.oregonstate.edu/sites/catalog/files/project/pdf/em9043.pdf

Planning for on-farm Success, Workbook for Montana's Beginning Farmers and Ranchers, Module 1, Strategic Planning. Community Food Agriculture Coalition, 2015. farmlinkmontana.org/wp-content/uploads/2015/12/Module-1_Strategic-Planning.pdf

Planning for Profit in Sustainable Farming, ATTRA, 2011, 20-page fact sheet, attra.ncat.org/attra-pub/summaries/summary.php?pub=382, 800-346-9140

Square One: Build a Farm to Match Your Values, Goals, Skills, and Resources, Cornell Small Farms Program. Online course to set goals, assess available resources, and explore enterprises. www.nebeginningfarmers.org/online-courses/all-courses/bf-101-square-one

Government Programs & Resources

Farm Answers, USD-NIFA, beginning farmer and rancher web clearinghouse, resources to help new and seasoned farmers succeed. Links to 100s of useful resources created for farmers with support from USDA grants. farmanswers.org

Farm Bill Programs and Grants Overview, National Sustainable Agriculture Coalition. Chart of farm and food-related programs and grants, listed by issue and eligibility. sustainableagriculture.net/publications/grassrootsguide/farm-bill-programs-and-grants 202-547-5754

New Farmers, USDA website, tools, stories, links to Government resources, newfarmers.usda.gov

USDA's Farm Service Agency (FSA) FSA offers variety of farm loan programs, including traditional operating loans, beginning farmer and youth programs. www.fsa.usda.gov/programs-and-services/farm-loan-programs/index

Labor and Employment Information

Beyond Basic Compensation, ATTRA, 2016. 20-page fact sheet. attra.ncat.org/attra-pub/summaries/summary.php?pub=330 800-346-9140

Farm Commons, legal resources for sustainable farm businesses. Articles, videos, webinars and tutorials. Info ranges from contracts to employees to business structure and farm law. farmcommons.org/ 608-616-5319

Farm Labor and Human Resource Management website, Michigan State University, publications and fact sheets including employees handbook template and ag employer checklist. msue.anr.msu.edu/topic/farm_management/labor_and_human_resource_management

Farmers Legal Action Group (FLAG), resources and publications including farm labor law publications for Minn. www.flaginc.org/topic/labor-and-employment/

Organic Growers School, Labor Resources, website listing resources useful for farm workers and mentors. organicgrowersschool.org/organicfarming/laborresources/

Positive Practices in Farm Labor Management, ATTRA, 2008. 16-page fact sheet. attra.ncat.org/attra-pub/summaries/summary.php?pub=278 800-346-9140

Willing Workers on Organic Farms, (WWOOF) International exchange program for those interested in helping on organic farms. wwoofinternational.org 415-621-3276

Resources...continued

Loans and Funders

Farm Credit Network, A network of federally chartered borrower-owned lending institutions and related service organizations that specialize in providing credit and related services to farmers. www.farmcreditnetwork.com 202-879-0850

Financing Your Farm: Guidance for Beginning Farmers, ATTRA, 2011. 8-page fact sheet. attra.ncat.org/attra-pub/summaries/summary.php?pub=381 800-346-9140

FSA Farm Loan Application Forms, Farm Service Agency, 2015, www.fsa.usda.gov

Funding Opportunities Database, ATTRA current announcements for grants, loans, scholarships, awards, challenges, and cost-share and research programs. Online only. attra.ncat.org/calendar/funding.php

Guide to Financing the Community Supported Farm, U. of Vermont Extension. 2012. 70-page book with ideas and case studies, www.uvm.edu/newfarmer/?Page=business/community-supported-farm-guide.html&SM=business/sub-menu.html

Minnesota Department of Ag, Farmer loan programs for MN farmers. 800-967-2474 www.mda.state.mn.us/grants/loans.aspx

Small Farm Funding Resources, USDA, 2016, resources collected by the Rural Information Center: starting a farm business, develop business and marketing plans, funding sources, training, technical assistance contacts, www.nal.usda.gov/ric/small-farm-funding-resources 301-504-5755

Marketing

Comparison of Transaction Costs by Marketing Outlet, Iowa State University, downloadable Excel spreadsheet to plug market numbers into, www.extension.iastate.edu/agdm/authors/cchase.html

Exploring Markets and Profits, (BD 102) Cornell University online course. www.nebeginningfarmers.org/online-courses/all-courses/bf-102-markets-profits/

Guide to Working with Food Market Professionals, Wis. Dept. of Ag, Devt. 6-page pdf, datcp.wi.gov/Documents/mk-it-113.pdf

Wisconsin Local Food Marketing Guide, Wis. Dept of Ag, Trade and Consumer Protection, 2014. 109-page book, free online datcp.wi.gov/Documents/DAD/LocalMarketingFoodGuide_1_16.pdf

Miscellaneous

Farm Transitions Workbook, Oklahoma Cooperative Extension, 2015, 122-page workbook that can be downloaded. agecon.okstate.edu/farmtransitions/

How to Determine the Right Farm Rental Rate, Univ of VT Extension, 2017. 31-page booklet useful for farmland, equipment and infrastructure rentals. www.uvm.edu/newfarmer/land/RentalGuide.pdf

Machinery Cost Calculator, Iowa State University Extension, 2015. Downloadable Excel Spreadsheet to use to calculate the cost of owning and operating machinery. farmanswers.org/Library/Record/machinery_cost_calculator

Transferring the Farm Virtual Workshop, Univ of VT Extension, 2015. Virtual workshop. Online course www.uvm.edu/farmtransfer/?Page=ttf.html&SM=ttfsub-menu.html

Valuation of Raised Breeding Livestock, OK State Extension, 201. 4-page fact sheet. pods.dasnr.okstate.edu/docushare/dsweb/Get/Document-1940/F-323web.pdf

Non-Financial Record Keeping

AgSquared, Online diversified vegetable record keeping software $99-$300+ per year. (non-financial) seasonal calendar, help estimating seeds to purchase, scheduling tasks etc. www.agsquared.com

CSA Toolkit, U of CT Cooperative Extension, 2015. 55-page booklet with information to start and operate a CSA farm business. newfarms.extension.uconn.edu/wp-content/uploads/sites/848/2015/11/CSA-Guide_FINAL_0929151.pdf

Recordkeeping Instructions and Templates for Small-Scale Fruit and Vegetable Growers, Farmers Legal Action Group, 2015. Templates for collecting data useful for planning and tracking data on small farms. www.flaginc.org/publication/record-keeping-instructions-and-templates-for-small-scale-fruit-and-vegetable-growers-2 651-223-5400

Siskiyou Sustainable Cooperative (Oregon) CSA App. Open source, customizable content available to any CSA farm. Designed to provide members with CSA-specific information, including recipes and box information. www.siskiyoucoop.com/csa/app.

Resources...continued

Resources for New Farmers

Beginning Farmer Resources, ATTRA, attra.ncat.org/attra-pub/local_food/startup.html https://attra.ncat.org/attra-pub/local_food/startup.html 800-346-9140

Dairy Grazing Apprenticeship, formal apprenticeship program for beginning dairy producers, www.dga-national.org 715-560-0389

Farm Answers, USD-NIFA, beginning farmer and rancher web clearinghouse, providing resources to help new and seasoned farmers succeed. Links to 100s of useful resources created for farmers. farmanswers.org

Farm Beginnings Collaborative, a network of non-profits offering in-person classroom trainings for new farmers over a series of months. farmbeginningscollaborative.org

Farmer Veteran Coalition, National network offering resources and support to mobilize veterans to feed America. www.farmvetco.org, 530-756-1395

New Farmers, USDA website, tools, stories, links to Government resources, newfarmers.usda.gov

Software & Apps

AgSquared, Online diversified vegetable record keeping software $99-$300+ per year. (non-financial) seasonal calendar, help estimating seeds to purchase, scheduling tasks etc. www.agsquared.com

Capterra, Large list of farm management software tools. www.capterra.com/farm-management-software

Decision Support Tools for Agriculture, Montana State University. Extensive collection of free farm software based on excel spreadsheets. www.montana.edu/softwaredownloads

FinPack, University of Minnesota Center for Farm Financial Management Software program. $149/year. www.cffm.umn.edu/FINPACK/producers.aspx.

Introduction to Farm Accounting Using Quickbooks: Users Manual, Univ of Wis Extension, 2008, farmanswers.org/Library/Record/introduction_to_farm_accounting_using_quickbo

Moneydance, financial software. moneydance.com

"Quick Tips" newsletter, Ag Econ Extension at the University of Oklahoma. www.agecon.okstate.edu/quicken

QuickBooks, financial software by Intuit. www.quickbooks.com

Quicken, financial software by Intuit. www.quicken.com

Quicken for Farm/Ranch Records Manual, 2016, Oklahoma State University www.agecon.okstate.edu/quicken/download.asp

Taxes

Rural Tax Education website provides farmers with a source for easy to understand and current agriculturally related income and self-employment tax information. www.ruraltax.org

Tax Managment Tips for Farmers, 2016, Michigan State University. 7 page fact sheet. msu.edu/user/steind/Tax%20Tips%202016%20November.pdf

Understanding Your Federal Farm Income Taxes, Penn State Extension, 8-page fact sheet. 2013. extension.psu.edu/business/ag-alternatives/farm-management/understanding-your-federal-farm-income-taxes/extension_publication_file

Risk Assessment

Managing Risk in Agriculture, Purdue University website. www.farmriskresources.com

Risk Assessment for the Small-Scale Farm, 2015 New England Small Farm Institute, 4-page fact sheet www.smallfarm.org/uploads/uploads/Files/risk.pdf

USDA Risk Management Agency (RMA) Online publications and crop fact sheets. www.rma.usda.gov/pubs/rme/fctsht.html

GLOSSARY

Accounts payable. An accounting entry that represents a businesses' obligation to pay off a short-term debt to its creditors. The accounts payable entry is found on a balance sheet under the heading current liabilities.

Accounts receivable. Money owed by customers (individuals or corporations) to another entity in exchange for goods or services that have been delivered or used, but not yet paid for. Receivables are usually due within a relatively short time period.

Accrual accounting system. An accounting method that recognizes economic events regardless of when cash transactions occur. Economic transactions are recognized by matching revenues to expenses at the time in which the transaction occurs rather than when payment is made (or received). Accrual systems are preferred by accountants, and are useful in that they show a clearer picture of financial obligations and expectations.

Asset turnover ratio. A ratio of a company's net sales to total assets. This is a measure of how efficiently managers are using their assets to produce salable products.

Assets. In accounting, anything of value that a person or business owns. Assets can be physical, such as land or livestock, a claim on debts, such as accounts receivable or liens, or a right, such as a patent.

Balance sheet. A financial statement that summarizes a business' assets, liabilities, and owner's equity at a specific point in time. The balance sheet gives owners an idea of what the farm owns and owes.

Benchmark. A standard against which performance is compared.

Cash basis accounting. A method of accounting in which the receipt and payment of cash are the basis for recording transactions. Here it is not the date on which goods and services are received that matters, as in accrual accounting, but the dates on which the cash changes hands for the transactions.

Contingent liabilities. A liability that is not currently a liability but may become one upon the occurrence of some future event.

Cost basis. A balance sheet in which assets are listed at their original cost minus the amount that the asset has depreciated during the time the business has owned it.

Current assets. A balance sheet account that represents the value of all assets that can reasonably be expected to be converted into cash within one year in the normal course of business. Current assets include cash, accounts receivable, inventory, prepaid expenses, and other liquid assets that can be converted readily to cash.

Current liabilities. Bills that are due to creditors and suppliers within a short time, generally a year or less.

Current ratio. A measure of a business' ability to meet its short-term obligations. The current ratio is calculated by dividing current assets by current liabilities. Both variables are shown on the balance sheet.

Debt to asset ratio. A measure of a business' risk. It is taken by adding its short-term debt to its long-term debt and dividing the quantity by the total value of its assets.

Debt to equity ratio. A comparison of what the bank owns of a business to what the owners own. This is calculated by dividing total liabilities by owner's equity.

Depreciation. The gradual reduction of an asset's value. It is an expense, but because it is non-cash a person or business usually may reduce his/her/its taxable income by the amount of the depreciation on the asset. There are many different ways to account for depreciation.

Enterprise. Production lines or streams of activity that can be identified uniquely within a business.

Enterprise budget. An analysis of incomes and expenses directly related to a specific enterprise. Useful in assessing if a given line of production is making or losing money.

Expense. The notation of any non-capital expenditure in a business; the things that you buy and services you pay for.

Fixed assets. An asset with a long-term useful life that a business uses to make its products or provide its services. Common examples of fixed assets are land and buildings.

Fixed costs/expenses. An expense that does not change with the amount of production generated. Also known as overhead.

Gross margin. The amount of income above the cost of goods that a given item or collection of items brings in. Margin is the amount available to pay for operating and marketing expenses, and any profit.

Continued on next page

GLOSSARY

Glossary...continued

Income statement. A financial statement that measures a business' financial performance relating to income and expenses over a specific period. Other names: profit and loss statement or statement of revenue and expense.

Institutional customer. A term used to refer to large institutions, such as hospitals, schools, or elderly care facilities, that may be prospective customers for farm products.

Intermediate assets. Assets with a useful life of more than one year but less than ten years. This includes machinery, equipment, perennial plants, breeding livestock that you intend to own for more than a year, titled vehicles such as pickup trucks, and can also include items that are not easily converted to cash, such as stock in a cooperative or the cash value of a life insurance policy.

Inventory. A complete list of items such as crops or feed that are saleable or usable products.

Investments. Putting money into something with the hope of profit. More specifically, investment is the commitment of money or capital to the purchase of assets in hopes of profitable returns in the form of interest, income (dividends), or appreciation of value.

Liabilities. All of the dollars the business owes to others, or would have to pay out if the business were to be sold.

Limited Liability Company (LLC). A flexible form of business organizational structure that blends elements of partnership and corporate structures.

Net farm income. The sum of all income and expenses of the farm during the year, whether or not they represent ordinary occurrences. A line in the farm's income statement.

Net worth. The total assets minus total outside liabilities of a business, which is the amount of investment you hold in your operation. The bottom line in your balance sheet. Other names: net assets.

Owner's equity. The owners' interest in the assets of a business. Owners' equity includes the amount invested by the owners plus the profits (or minus the losses) in the enterprise.

Operating profit margin. A measurement of what proportion of a business' revenue is left over after paying for variable costs of production such as wages, inputs, etc. A measure of efficiency.

Partial budget. A method of analysis that allows you to compare two alternatives side-by-side.

Personal assets. Capital items owned by a family that are independent of the farm operation, usually including the family house, personal use car or other vehicles, etc.

Prepaid expenses. An asset on a balance sheet that comes about when a payment is made for a good or service that has not yet been received, but will be in the near future. A common example of a prepaid expense is an insurance policy.

Price mark-up. The amount added to a product's cost to create the selling price. Generally expressed as a percent of the cost.

Product mix. The composition of goods and services produced and/or sold by a farm business.

Profit. The money a business has left after it pays its operating expenses, taxes, and other current bills. Other names: net income or earnings

Profit and loss statement. A financial statement that summarizes the revenues, costs, and expenses incurred during a specific period, usually a fiscal quarter or a year. Other names: statement of profit and loss, an income statement, or an income and expense statement.

Profitability. The ability of a farm to earn a profit. It is a relative measure of success.

Profitable. Generating profit or financial gain.

QuickBooks. A business accounting software developed and marketed by Intuit.

Records. All of the documentation involved in the preparation of financial statements. Accounting records include records of assets and liabilities, monetary transactions, ledgers, journals, and any supporting documents such as checks and invoices.

Revenue. The amount of money a business actually receives over a specific period. It is the "top line" or "gross income" figure from which costs are subtracted to determine net income.

Schedule F. The IRS tax form that is used to report farm income and expenses. A sub schedule of the 1040 form.

Glossary...continued

Sole proprietorship. A business owned by a single person that is not a corporation, a limited liability company, or anything else. The sole proprietor who owns the proprietorship must list all profits and losses on his/her personal tax return and does not file a separate return for the business. Additionally, the proprietor is personally responsible for all losses and debts the business incurs.

Solvency. The state of a business being able to service its debt and meet its other obligations, especially in the long-term. If a business is unable to meet its obligation, it is said to be insolvent and must undergo bankruptcy in order to either liquidate or restructure.

Variable costs/expenses. The costs of production that vary directly in proportion to the number of units produced. Variable costs often include labor expenses and inputs, as these usually must be increased to increase output.

Working capital. The amount of money a business has on hand, or will have, in a given year. Working capital is calculated by subtracting current liabilities from current assets. Other names: operating assets or net current assets.

INDEX

Symbols
501 (c)(3) charitable organizations 218

A
accounting 33, 39, 54, 257, 260
accounts payable 75, 87
accounts receivable 74, 85
accrual 83-88, 261
advisory team 18, 28, 105
amortization 113, 126
anti-corporate farming laws 211
assets
    balance sheet 69-79
    cash flow 92-97, 189, 193
    chart of accounts 40-41, 47
    enterprises and 150, 155, 157
    farm transfer 213-221
    income statement 84-85
    investment analysis 129-135
    lenders and 139, 142
    monitoring 197
    profitability and 123-126
    ratios 101-106, 110-122
Asset Turnover Ratio 104-105, 117, 121, 123-126, 157

B
back up 57, 61-62
balance sheet 70-81
bankruptcy 74, 76, 92, 93, 126, 136, 141, 144
basis 71, 219
beginning farmers 93, 112, 142, 186
benchmark
bills 31-35, 56-58, 90-92, 103-105, 117, 124-128, 144-147, 184-186
break-even price 152-153, 178
break-even yield 152

budgets
    enterprise 149-151, 252-253
    cash flow 187-199
    partial 161-164,
business structure 208-210

C
capacity 24-30, 110-113
capital assets 76, 78, 86-99, 109, 111-113, 120, 130-132, 142, 184
Capital Debt Repayment Capacity 71, 110-112, 120
Capital Debt Repayment Margin 111, 120
capital gains 75, 79, 216-223
capital gains tax 75, 219, 223
cash basis accounting 83
cash flow 15-18, 22-23, 91-100, 102-106,
    investments and 129-136,
    lenders and 140-145
    monitoring 196-200
    planning 183-195
    ratios 110-114, 115, 119-121
Cash flow from financing activities 94
Cash flow from investing activities 94
Cash flow from operations 94
cash flow problems 71, 103, 113
cash rental equivalent 150
C-Corporation 209, 210
Center for Farm Financial Management 69, 114, 256-260
charitable remainder unitrusts 219
charts of accounts 40, 47-52
checkbook ledger 38
child labor laws 205
classes, using 49-57, 62, 186-187
collateral 71, 142-145, 216
commodity 13, 23, 42, 59, 145, 148, 167, 168, 177, 187

compensation rules 203
competition-based pricing 177
conservation easement 219
contractor 204
cost-based pricing 177-178
cost basis balance sheet 71-72, 79, 218
cost of ownership 131-132, 150
cost of production 23, 125, 152, 173, 178
crop insurance 14, 40
crowdfunding 15-16
CSA 42, 137, 154, 157, 167-172, 187, 203
    farmer examples 23, 68, 96, 179, 189
Current assets 73, 78-81
Current liabilities 78-81
Current Ratio 103-105, 117-118
customer-based pricing 177

D
Dairy Grazing Apprenticeship 2, 10, 19-20, 260
data entry 31-34, 40-48, 56-67, 82, 197
debt structure 113
Debt to Asset Ratio 105-107, 117-118
Debt to Equity Ratio 105-107, 117-118
depreciable assets 79, 111-115, 120, 137
depreciation 24, 40, 78-79, 87, 109, 115, 121, 131, 164, 217
Depreciation Expense Ratio 115, 121
double-entry accounting 39

E
EBITDA 109, 110, 119
economies of scale 155
efficiency 66-67, 105, 109, 114-116, 121-122, 164,
efficiency ratios 114-116, 121-122
employee 126, 202-207
Employee Identification Number 205

Index...continued

enterprise budget 148-159, 169, 252-253
equity 70-73, 105-109, 116-119, 127-130, 141-145, 212-215, 220-223
Equity to Asset Ratio 106, 118
estate 213-214, 219-221
estate plan 214, 221
estate tax 220

F
family living expenses 98
Farm Commons 2, 17, 211, 258
farmers' market 59-63, 154, 167-179, 187-188
Farm Finance Scorecard 148, 227, 244, 257
Farm Service Agency 18, 126, 142, 144
farm startup 13-18
farm transition 17, 212-221
federal tax return 18, 72, 79, 94
FICO score 141
file folders 33-35
Financial Efficiency Ratios 121
FINPACK 2, 69, 114, 115, 260
Five Cs of Credit 141
Form 4797 84

G
General Partnership 209
goals 14-15, 21-22, 26-30, 194-196
goal setting 14-30
gross margin 178-179

H
health insurance 22, 24, 98, 107
heirs 213-214, 220-221
Holistic Management 14, 257

IIncome statement 82-89
income tax liability 76-79, 137
institutional market 169-174
Interest Expense Ratio 116, 121
interest rates 121-122, 133
Intermediate assets 73-81
interns 203
Internal Rate of Return 131-134
Internal Revenue Service 36, 39, 78, 79, 84, 204, 209, 210, 216, 218
inventories, 73, 103, 105
inventory 78, 84-87, 94-96, 124-126, 136, 149
investment analysis 129-138
invoice 33, 36, 45, 56-61, 83
IRR 131-138
IRS 1099-misc 36, 204

K
key ratios 102, 117, 225

L
labor, 202-207
   chart of accounts, in 50-51
   costs of 153-157,
   effeciencies 125, 163
   in budgets 171-174
   ratios 110
   tracking 66-68
   valuing 89-90, 132
leasing 17, 24, 130-136, 216-217
lenders 139-145
liabilities 74, 76, 77, 262
Limited Liability Company 209-211, 213
long-term assets 73-8, 106
long-term liabilities 75, 80, 106

M
margin 178-182, 187
   operating profit margin, 109-110, 117, 119, 123-124
marketing 25-28, 123-125, 152-158, 166-182, 188, 203
marketing costs 152, 169
market value balance sheet 71
minimum wage 203, 205, 206
monitoring 196-200
Monitoring Control Worksheet 199

N
narrative 67
Net Cash Farm Income 88-90, 111
Net Farm Income From Operations 88-89
net farm income ratio 116-121
Net Present Value 130-138, 250-251
new farmers 16-18, 176, 222-223, 260
non-cash revenues 82
non-farm income 94, 98, 110-111, 127-128, 141
non-financial records 64-68

O
OK Farm and Ranch Account Book 41-43, 232-239
Operating Expense Ratio 114-115, 117, 121, 148
operating expenses 86, 91-93, 96, 100, 105, 114-117, 121-122, 136, 139-140, 184-189
operating loan 74, 80, 98, 104, 113, 140-141, 185
Operating profit margin 109-110, 117, 119, 123-124
organic certification records 64

Index...continued

Otto B. Organic
   balance sheet 81
   cash flow statement 95
   income statement 85
overhead 18, 25, 50
overtime pay 205
owner draw 41, 57, 191-192
owner's equity 70-73, 105-106, 118

P
paper-based systems 31-43, 232-242
partial budget 160-166
paychecks 168, 205
payroll 45-47, 189, 194, 206
planning
   cash flow 184-196
   estate 212-215
   profitability 124-126, 155
   resources 256-259
   start-up 13-30
prepaid expenses 73, 87, 261
price mark-up 178
pricing 176-182
product mix 156-158
profitability 92-93, 107-110, 119, 122-127
profitability continuum 127
profitability ratios 70, 76, 88-93, 119
profitability tips 124
profit and loss statement 72, 82-84, 94, 197
pro forma cash flow 92, 184-197

Q
QuickBooks 11, 46-63, 83-84, 186-199, 206, 227, 254, 260, 262

R
Rate of Return on Assets (ROROA) 107-110, 119
Rate of Return on Equity (ROROE) 108-110, 119
ratios 102-121
repayment ability 140
Repayment Capacity Ratio 120
Replacement Margin Coverage Ratio 113
reserve funds 193
retail price points 227, 243
retirement 22, 26, 124, 213-214
revocable living trusts 219

S
salary 23, 107, 191-192, 202-203
scale 14, 20-27, 65-68, 116-117, 124, 127, 143-145, 152-156, 163, 168-175, 199, 212
Schedule F 6, 18, 31, 39, 40, 41, 57, 72, 77, 84, 86, 88, 94, 170, 216
S-Corporation 209-211
Section 179 78-79
shrink 123, 178
single-entry accounting 39
social security 86, 92, 110, 206, 207, 214
software 2, 32, 34, 38, 45-48, 69, 77, 114, 186-187, 198-99, 206, 257-260
Sole Proprietorship 209

solvency 105-106, 118
spreadsheets 36-47, 54-69, 77, 84, 102, 135, 165, 186-203, 254, 257, 259
start-up costs 14
sweat equity, 212, 215-217, 220

T
taxpayer's unified credit 217
Term Debt Coverage Ratio 112-113, 120
tickler file 35, 58
total assets 75, 80, 105-107, 142
trusts 219-220

U
USDA 18, 20, 142, 144, 187, 256-260

V
value of growing crops 86
variable costs 122-123, 150-159, 164
volunteer 203

W
W-2 forms 205
wages 20, 24, 107, 206
weak links 123, 137
whole-farm records 124, 170-175
worker's compensation insurance 50
Working Capital Ratio 104, 118

NOTES

ABOUT MOSES

The Midwest Organic and Sustainable Education Service (MOSES) is a nonprofit that provides education, resources, and practical advice to help farmers grow using sustainable, organic practices.

EDUCATION

MOSES ORGANIC FARMING CONFERENCE
The country's largest conference on organic ag is where farmers learn to grow using proven organic and sustainable farming practices.

ORGANIC UNIVERSITY
Ten all-day courses offered prior to the conference give farmers the chance to dig into a topic.

ORGANIC FIELD DAYS
These on-farm events showcase what works, giving other farmers ideas to put in practice on their farms.

NEW FARMER U
Experienced organic farmers and ag experts teach beginners the field and financial aspects of farming.

PROJECTS

FARMER-TO-FARMER MENTORING PROGRAM
This 14-month program pairs experienced and new organic farmers to encourage the growth of organic farming.

NEW ORGANIC STEWARDS
New farmers find support, community, and learning opportunities through this popular program.
Join the New Organic Stewards group on Facebook!

RURAL WOMEN'S PROJECT
This award-winning project connects women involved in farming and food system change.
Join MOSES Rural Women's Project group on Facebook!

PRACTICAL ADVICE

ASK A SPECIALIST
Trained specialists answer questions about organic production and organic certification:

    Organic Answer Line—715-778-5775 or 888-551-4769

    Online—mosesorganic.org/ask

RESOURCES

WEBSITE
Find information about organic farming practices and organic certification. The *Farming by Topic* section (under Farming tab) has how-to articles and related resources.

mosesorganic.org

MOSES BOOKSTORE
At the MOSES Conference, the store features more than 500 titles about organic farming. The online bookstore offers expert-picked titles year-round. See **mosesorganic.net**.

FEARLESS FARM FINANCES
This resource book is packed with instructions, tips and tools for setting up and managing a farm's financial system. We also offer full day trainings and webinars.

Sign up to receive any of the publications below — see mosesorganic.org/sign-up.

GUIDEBOOK FOR ORGANIC CERTIFICATION
This must-have book covers details about organic certification and the rules for organic production.

ORGANIC FACT SHEETS
More than 30 fact sheets offer easy-to-follow explanations about complex certification requirements or provide insights from our Organic Specialists about topics related to organic farming.

ORGANIC RESOURCE DIRECTORY
This online searchable directory lists certification agencies, buyers, suppliers, processors, and other organic-related organizations in Illinois, Iowa, Michigan, Minnesota, North Dakota, South Dakota and Wisconsin.

ORGANIC BROADCASTER NEWSPAPER
This bi-monthly newspaper provides practical articles and news about organic farming to more than 11,000 readers. Feature stories are written by farmers, researchers and others with knowledge and experience to share.

ORGANIC LINK ENEWS
The monthly *Organic Link* provides news about resources, events, research and funding opportunities related to organic and sustainable farming.

NOTES